The Liberation of Dogma

JUAN LUIS SEGUNDO

The Liberation of Dogma

Faith, Revelation, and Dogmatic Teaching Authority

Translated from the Spanish by
Phillip Berryman

ORBIS BOOKS

Maryknoll, New York 10545

The Catholic Foreign Mission Society of America (Maryknoll) recruits and trains people for overseas missionary service. Through Orbis Books, Maryknoll aims to foster the international dialogue that is essential to mission. The books published, however, reflect the opinions of their authors and are not meant to represent the official position of the society.

Published originally by Editorial Sal Terrae, Guevara, 20, 39001 Santander, Spain, © 1989, under the title *El Dogma que libera: Fe, revelación y magisterio dogmático.*

English translation © 1992 by Orbis Books
Published by Orbis Books, Maryknoll, NY 10545. This edition has been slightly edited.

Library of Congress Cataloging-in-Publication Data

Segundo, Juan Luis.
   [Dogma que libera. English]
   The liberation of dogma : faith, revelation, and dogmatic teaching
authority / Juan Luis Segundo ; translated from the Spanish by
Phillip Berryman.
     p. cm.
   Translation of: El dogma que libera.
   Includes bibliographical references and index.
   ISBN 0-88344-804-1
   1. Dogma, Development of. I. Title.
BT21.S39 1992
230'.01 – dc20   92-3654
                                              CIP

To my brothers and sisters and friends,
Latin American theologians by calling or training,
I dedicate this book,
which was conceived and written to serve liberation.

CHAPTER 1

A Foreword That Isn't

Writing posthumous books is a (regrettable) custom more widespread than many realize. It is not so common, however, that authors themselves write forewords to such books—out of a sense of propriety, no doubt. Nevertheless, a foreword is like the kind of safeguard to which any newborn has a right. Obviously, that is because it is unprotected and fragile. And, of all books, if any newborn needs such protection, and very much so, it is precisely the posthumous book . . .

That is especially so, since, I imagine, no editor will dare to publish it without putting in a foreword—even though the only reason might be to explain *why*, since the author did not have it published, someone else is presuming to do so. In most cases someone is asked to do such a foreword, and who will get the job is anyone's guess.

Whether it be proper or not, I prefer to write the foreword myself and to let readers know—and here I am going beyond the line of impropriety—that they will miss a lot if they do not read it. Let it be clear that in all likelihood they will not miss much by not reading the entire book. But they will lose out, if intending to read it, they disregard my advice, and give in to the time-honored custom of skipping forewords.

A Posthumous Book While the Author Is Still Alive?

Some clarifications are in order at the outset. The first consists of a (necessary) paradox: readers should not be surprised if this book reaches their hands while the author is still alive. It will still be just as posthumous. Its posthumous character does not derive from the fact that at best the author might promise to have died before finishing it or before it is published. He is not even promising, as is sometimes said or done out of modesty, to let it be published after his death.

It is indeed quite possible that this book will be published at any moment. The author still has plans in his head for further books he hopes to have time to finish and publish. Nevertheless, I insist that this book is already posthumous, and will be so whatever its publication date.

No doubt the preceding observations will lead many readers to believe that

1

they now have the clue to the explanation: this must be a *last testament*. But it is not that either. Indeed, this book has something in common with a last testament, but that term does not really suit it. A last testament means a legacy. In the case of writings, it is generally a summing up of what has already been achieved, or even of what has already been communicated in order to transmit the core of it to new generations. If the author is more or less prolific, the testament contains what in maturity—or old age—he or she regards as what is most worthy of surviving, or of being identified with the memory of his or her name.

None of that here. I am conscious that I am most certainly writing the least important of my theological works—that I am, if you will, adjusting one last detail.

And now, so as not to leave the readers—if there still are any—in suspense, I will risk going to the heart of the matter. This work is posthumous because it is putting any further works in jeopardy. Or, if you will, because it will constitute a danger for all the rest, especially if this is not the last. One might think that in terms of basic strategy, it would be better to wait until all the rest have blossomed and put down their roots, and strong roots, before subjecting them to the harsh and demanding weather that this one might unleash.

As readers will have perceived by now, I am referring to the "climate" problems affecting theology in the Catholic Church. The top leadership of the church seems to find it increasingly difficult to allow certain problems to be aired out publicly. "What problems?" some naive reader might question in alarm. Happy the person who could answer that question with assurance and act accordingly!

Instinct is a better guide than logic in this area. An example may help. One might think that the issue of whether or not someone can be saved outside the church—a "new issue" recently introduced by some very clear statements by Vatican II—ought to be regarded as theological terrain that is more dangerous for the ecclesiastical structure (which people presumably want to preserve) than the issue of whether and when papal teaching authority is infallible. That is the case at least if we keep in mind that in accordance with Vatican II (*Gaudium et Spes* 22) the good will of a person pursuing truth and love is a pledge of salvation, whether the person accepts that infallible teaching authority or remains outside the church out of a refusal to accept it.

Such logic breaks down, nonetheless, no matter how ironclad it might seem to be. Actually, the ecclesiastical hierarchy will allow any book claiming or denying the salvation of all people of good will, but not one questioning whether the Holy Father was infallible when he decided to declare the Assumption of Mary a dogma.

I have no reason to hide the fact that in the quarter century in which I have been writing about theological questions, I have tried to avoid—until now—what everyday language very accurately calls "sticking your finger in the fan." In other words I have tried to avoid such sensitive points, if at all possible, even though one can draw up a considerable list of them.

In the opinion of some readers, to thus confess that I have deliberately

Contents

avoided these points or issues might be tantamount to a self-confession of hypocrisy or cynicism. Hence such readers have a right to hear me argue my own case and may even find it useful, for those arguments will to some extent provide the overall key to this book—and to any further books as well.

Theology for a Community

Not through any merit of mine but due to circumstances, from the time I began to work in theology, the human context of my effort has made me avoid two reefs that I regard as both tempting and dangerous, the Scylla and Charybdis of much academic and even pastoral theology: either having to teach or lecture on a *part* (or "treatise") of a theological system within a preestablished program likely to be devoid of any connection with the interests and questions of one's listeners or interlocutors; or having to respond with overly hasty formulas to questions that take their inspiration from a simplistic version of the method known as "see, judge, and act."[1]

What I was expected to do was to provide gradual formation in an overall Christian way of thinking that might shed light on a complex situation in which a group made up primarily of lay people had committed its faith.

Thus described, the theological task might look simple and even routine. In fact, however, it was far from being either, as anyone who undertook it could experience. Since my discussion partners and friends were not students in a theoretical theology course nor activists simply trying to draw on aspects of Christianity to justify and energize what they were already doing, the relationship between theory and praxis became very demanding and complex indeed. However, the group also steered away from those concrete theoretical and practical points that are more sensitive and risky, to which I alluded above.

Instead I had to teach—by teaching I understand providing support for a reflection process—how to "think as a Christian." However insubstantial "thinking" and "thinking as a Christian" might be, they had to be *prior* to one or other specific doctrinal or moral point. Preparing to think as a Christian or proceeding to do so cannot be a matter of first providing a list of the "things" one must affirm—such as, for example, that the Holy Father is infallible, that the substances of bread and wine become another substance in the sacrament of eucharist, that women must not be ordained to the priesthood, and so forth—and then going on to say, "beyond this point you can think as you please."

On the other hand, there is no need, it is worth noting, to systematically doubt the things just mentioned in order to learn to think as a Christian. As Vatican II says, there is an order in which the elements of the faith should be presented so that human understanding might assimilate it and thereby be enriched and humanized. As true as pronouncements might be in another order, they do not teach one to think as a Christian—perhaps because they do not teach one to "think" at all.

I think there are two elements that someone undertaking a task such as I am describing here should appreciate and put to good use. The *first* is that in the situation in which I was working and doing theology—a very vital context that was not at all academic—your discussion partner is there voluntarily and is quite free to leave if you do not provide something that seems "interesting."

I have already indicated that in a context of commitment, such "interest" can never be reduced to listening to a brilliant presentation or a judicious reasoning process. It means that the operative criterion is the measure in which the kind of thinking that comes through Christian faith seems capable of enriching, vis-à-vis experience, people's vision of reality, thus enabling them to deepen their commitment to others and making that commitment more effective. The counterpart to this difficulty—if that is what it is considered to be—is something positive: people do not expect such a humanizing enrichment to come from an isolated scriptural text or a handful of theological ideas. They have (or soon acquire) enough patience so that they do not have to rely on handbooks on how to do theology—whether liberation theology or not—and they get to the point where they can authentically judge the results themselves.[2] Success in one case, although it is always a matter of wagering on mystery, plainly deepens the confidence and patience needed for further development.

Even so, a *second element* was required. Giving shape to *Christian* thinking means running up against the "dogmatic" limits of that thinking. Indeed, if it is taken for granted that Christianity comes from a *revelation* by God, what is called "dogma" lays down—in a manner and through a process that we will have to study—the boundaries beyond which things no longer seem to be compatible with what is "revealed." Of course the lay people I am talking about are moderately confident that the elements of judgment used and discussed in their meetings are actually Christian. They know that there are dogmas (which put limits on Christian thinking as such) although they generally would not be able to distinguish such dogmas from the answers they learned as children in catechism class or opinions they have heard in some conference or read in a book of theology. Nevertheless, they generally trust that specialized knowledge of dogmas enables the "theologian" who works with them to know precisely where those limits lie, thus enabling them to save the trouble of a search that for an ordinary lay person would be tedious and expensive (and in most cases almost impossible).

Dogma Makes Its Appearance

Someone might say that this is a way of finessing a huge problem and that the supposedly "Christian thought" that might arise out of all this has a weak foundation—if it has any foundation at all. That might be the case if logic were the teacher or main impulse of thought. Whether for well or ill, however, such is not the case. An example can serve to demonstrate the point more clearly and concretely.

Let us suppose that a theologian reflecting with a group of Christians on their faith has to explain the meaning—for faith—of the formula that Christians will have occasion to hear and repeat a thousand times: God, Father, Son, and Holy Spirit—the "dogma of the trinity," in technical language.

A very strict and abstract logic might perhaps claim that such a reflection should begin by getting to know the dogma before explaining it. In other words, and more concretely, one ought to begin by questioning where such a continually repeated formula comes from, who initiated it, what authority such a person had to impose it, and so forth. Two very serious things stand in the way of such a claim made by logic.

The *first* is that here — as is perhaps the case in any branch of knowledge — we always begin *in medias res*. In other words, certain things that by pure logic would require prior investigation, are always taken for granted — *ad infinitum*. In the present case of a dogma, it would seem fitting and even necessary that people begin by questioning something even more general and fundamental: What is a "dogma"? With what kind of power or criterion is it established? Can I establish dogmas or change those already established? Always? Never?

However, it is hard to answer these questions without committing another error of logic: the anachronism one falls into when one forgets that most of these questions had not been clearly and precisely answered when the dogma of the Trinity was formulated in the early church.

Indeed, such reflection should ponder the fact that this dogma (to which supposedly fundamental questions refer) expressed in a contemporary language, is a message *translated* from a different — and ancient — language. That language happens to be Greek, but not just any kind of Greek. Since any language has its own structure — synchronically or diachronically — translation is no more than an approximation that can always be improved. Moreover, although it is in Greek, this particular dogmatic formula only approximates the formulas the New Testament uses for treating this same topic.

That fact raises, besides the problem of fidelity of thought, yet another linguistic issue: New Testament Greek, although it was being written by writers whose mother tongue apparently was Greek, usually had to translate an original core of ideas that arose around Jesus. Both Jesus and the first disciples in all likelihood shaped their ideas within a mind-set whose linguistic structure was Aramaic (a Semitic dialect whose patterns were quite different from those of Greek).

However, as I was saying before, this is simply an example. A group of Christians today must entrust an endless number of logically prior operations to an enormous group of specialized scholars, of whom the theologian is a humble amateur representative. I also said there was a *second element* — we will see to what extent it is connected to the one just mentioned — whose effect is that normally theology done spontaneously does not follow a purely logical order. The question of what a dogma is does not arise *until after* a great deal of reflection on dogmas has taken place.

Outside academic circles, theology does not have a truly scientific status. Rather than a science, we should agree that it is an art — or at least that it responds to a human design distinct from that which impels people toward knowing reality for its own sake (although such knowing does not really exist anywhere in its pure quintessence either).

Plainly, in such a natural context, theology, knowledge about God, is set within a *pursuit of meaning for human existence*. The dialogue that ensues when a theological issue is raised always inherently bears an element of existential crisis, whether consciously or not. In other words, theology assumes a degree of difficulty in providing a satisfactory meaning for life and involvement in history.

Whether or not theology is "interesting" depends on this connection being perceived, and being perceived—after the effort of reflection—as satisfactory. That is, it must square with the only criterion of verifiability that a theological proposition can have. Or, to return to the concrete, whether or not theologians find a propitious area for their "art" will depend on this point: how to help human beings be more human by speaking to them of God in a significant way.

Hence, when one speaks of the "Word of God" in such a context, for example, the seemingly normal question of why a particular human word has been called "Word of God" almost never comes up. Nor does the question of how a particular book came to be part of what we call the Bible today—that is, the body of "the words of God."

That is why in this basic normal and healthy situation, theologians, if they so desire, can move about for a long time comfortably within the limits set by dogma, without having to explicitly explain how they are doing so.[3]

Does Dogma Constrict Thought?

What does it mean to move around comfortably within dogma? The idea most believers have of dogma is that of a rigid and precise limit that quickly pops up in any theological issue and condemns anyone who is not very careful in his or her way of thinking and expression (orthodoxy).

Many Christians believe that the church usually called orthodox—that is, those Christians who belonged to the eastern Roman Empire in the tenth century—withdrew from the Catholic Church because they refused to admit a single word, *filioque*,[4] into the Credo. Perhaps some who have a better understanding of the history of Christianity know that the church condemned Arianism, one of the most crucial and widespread heresies in its history, by condemning those who said that the Son of God (= God the Son) was *homoiousios* but not *homoousios*—that is, of a *similar*, but not *same* substance as the Father—in Greek the difference was an *i*, just an *i*! Thus a broad general culture provides at least a vague knowledge of some aspects of this history of how once heresies came on the scene, inviolable limits were gradually laid down in order that Christian thinking might continue true to itself.

Scholarly study of theology, however, as distant as it might be from existential problems, provides theologians in these areas a freedom of movement the lay person cannot imagine, and would find surprisingly broad. A noninitiate would marvel at how easily theologians continue to think about many things even after the church seems to say that the limits of what can be thought and said about them have been firmly determined.

Actually, if that were not the case, the ecclesiastical magisterium would not be able to carry out its particular function, which, as its name indicates, consists of "teaching." Twenty centuries of accumulating dogmas would have reduced theology to being a mere repetition of formulas in all fields and disciplines. Obviously that has not happened, thank God.

Such freedom of movement has nothing to do with cynicism or hypocrisy. It is by no means a case of the theologian having learned to evade the—benign—pincers of dogma, of that very dogma in which simple lay people would remain imprisoned.[5] On the contrary, and without intending to slight the attitude of respect that lay people show toward what is vaguely presented to them (or that they recall from catechism) as dogma, we should note that from both a scholarly and a practical standpoint, theologians are even more respectful toward dogma in this stance of apparent freedom that they adopt toward it. This point is worth examining, because it is related to the purpose of this introductory chapter.

Like any other message transmitted by human beings, dogma ought to be well interpreted. That entails not only a correct translation across different languages but all the historical work needed in order to travel from the dead letter of the message to the living significance today of what the dogma was intended to transmit yesterday.

As will be readily understood, a significant endeavor of historic interpretation (= hermeneutics) will be required. Among other things, one will have to discern what problem was being discussed or what crisis people were suffering when the message was elaborated as a response.

Otherwise, we will be barking up the wrong tree. Thus if we run across this expression, "it is as true that the sun revolves around the earth as that the episcopal see of Rome has primacy over all the rest," it is crucially important to know—and it can be determined *only* through historical knowledge of the context—if what is being discussed is the mechanics of the planetary system or Roman primacy. Indeed, it is obvious to anyone that, whether or not dogma is involved, this same sentence uttered in conversation in the thirteenth century would mean the opposite of its meaning today. In the thirteenth century, anyone using the expression would be claiming that such primacy most certainly exists, while anyone using it today would be saying that it did not exist. How can the same formula, with the passage of time, mean two opposite things? Simply because the context comes into play in the comparison and because in this cultural context, people know that the sun does not revolve around the earth.

Therefore the problems entailed in such a research naturally increase proportionately as one moves further into the past. The theologian must ask, for example, what a particular word or expression meant in the particular period in which it was used to declare a dogma. For words and statements have their history, and their content often varies from one (cultural) place to another, or from one period to subsequent periods.

Thus, a lay person will not understand why there was so much discussion before the church came to the dogmatic formula about the being of Jesus: "one person and two natures." He or she will probably be unaware that one of the greatest problems that the most orthodox theologians at that time had in trying to come to agreement on this point was that the word "person" in its present meaning did not yet exist. That is, they were accustomed to use the *same word* for two things that seem different and opposed today: person and nature. The Greek word *hypostasis* was used to designate the subject (= *subiectum* in Latin) or person, and also to designate substance (= *substantia*) or nature. Anyone who knows something of philology can see this in modern Spanish, since it comes from Latin. This kind of thing was the source of countless misunderstandings in that remote age.

Not only then, however, but still today. For if at that time there was no word for the precise modern sense of "person," is it not logical to ask how Jesus, true God and true man, is understood *today* to be "one person"?[6]

Relationship between Dogma, Life, and Crisis of Faith

It might be said, and with some degree of truth, that in all these examples it is hard to see what interest a lay person might have in this "freedom" with which theologians interpret dogma as part of their work. Of course it has already been noted that in this dialogue with Christians who want a better understanding of their faith vis-à-vis their life and their own history, the problem tends to arise more when they feel that some kinds of attitude or behavior apparently demanded by their faith commitment are clashing with certain barriers arising from dogma (or are presented as such).

Thus for example, very sensitive and loving people who want with all their heart to allow their loved ones to die in a peaceful and dignified way, feel (or used to feel) obligated by dogma (grace, church, sin, judgment, hell) to adopt the most inhumane, forced, and cruel attitudes in order to get them to agree to receive the last sacraments "validly" when they are on their deathbed[7] — for the sake of their eternal salvation.

It is here, I believe, that we come to where the true *practical* problem of theology arises today, along with its connection to dogma. In other words, lay people probably become interested in most cases due to a crisis and an expectation. The crisis arises when they realize that their understanding of the Christian message does not mesh with stances that their very Christian commitment has led them to have toward life — that is, toward their life history with its hopes and enthusiasms, as well as its frustrations. Their interest in theology also comes from an expectation that this understanding now creaking with age, as connected to "dogma" as it might seem, represents a poor and inadequate interpretation of its real meaning.

The theologian is there to give a reason for that hope, and for that radical expectation, sometimes expressed with reservation and often silent. In order to do his or her job the theologian needs that healthy freedom toward dogma I was talking about. I will go further: "dogma" itself needs that freedom.

Returning to what was said before about the anguish of many Christians when their relatives or friends were dying without the (last) sacraments, we must add that the whole church had that same attitude toward those who did not belong visibly to it at the moment of death.[8] Indeed, not only did theologians from the early church onward regard the general principle "outside the Church there is no salvation" as a dogma *de fide divina et catholica*; at the Council of Florence the church went to the trouble of "defining" the practical consequences of this principle: any pagan, Jew, heretic, or schismatic who did not enter the Catholic Church before dying was condemned for all eternity (Denzinger 714).

Vatican II, however, after describing the Christian's path of life toward salvation (within the church) adds: "All this holds true not only for Christians, but for all men of good will in whose heart grace works in an unseen manner" (GS 22).[9]

Ordinary Christians reflecting on their faith as related to vital questions will very probably accept the statement of Vatican II as a piece of good news that relieves them of their previous anguish and lifts barriers to more deeply human attitudes in important areas of their lives.

It is likewise very probable that they will view "outside the Church there is no salvation" as a mistaken and ultraconservative formula that they once accepted *because they regarded it as dogma*. If they continue to think, however, they will now raise (this time clearly and consciously) the problem of error. Indeed, is it not true that Catholic "dogma" went from teaching "outside the church there is no salvation" to teaching "outside the church there *is* salvation"?

Moreover, if such Christians are a bit more perceptive or are used to delving more deeply in their community reflection, they will realize something important and significant with regard to dogmas. The Vatican II statement was accepted by an overwhelming majority, who voted, paragraph by paragraph, for everything in it. In order for that to happen many theologians, and the best of them, must have been teaching *already* and for some time that what the Council of Florence seemed to say—or perhaps did say—about those who died without entering the Catholic Church was not true.

As fortunate as the result from such a theological "rebellion" might have been this time, how did those theologians deal with "dogma" before Vatican II? Normally this question comes up late, but it eventually does occur to Christians who are reflecting on their faith.[10]

Are Truth and Error Completely Contradictory?

In my experience the direction theology can (and probably should) take for untying this knot begins, as we have already seen and will see better further on, by "situating" each definition in its own context. In other words, the idea is to avoid expressing the movement from the Council of Florence to Vatican II in terms that are *simply contradictory*: outside the church *there is no* salvation vs. outside the church *there is* salvation.[11]

Again I note that stating things this way might look like cynicism. Nevertheless, upon examination it turns out to be something that is part of all education. It is often said and with a good deal of truth that the problems that disturb us as children are not resolved with the passage of time: they are forgotten, or better, other problems replace them. Indeed in a much wider and more complex context, the way those problems are posed changes until the problem as such is no longer there. Education does not consist in an infinite series of shifts from error to truth, as, for example, moving from "there is a Santa Claus" to "there is no Santa Claus."

Thus one discovers that in the Old Testament people did not find themselves from the beginning confronting two opposing propositions between which they had to choose: "there is a life beyond earth" and "there is no life beyond earth."

Every exegete knows that for at least eight centuries the biblical writers offer unmistakable proof that they see death as the absolute termination of life. It is only in the intertestamental period or in the deuterocanonical books that we find a clear affirmation of belief in a life that goes beyond death (at least for the good).[12]

However, we must return to the question of the relationship between church and salvation. In order to understand the connection between the two formulations, we must begin with the New Testament context. There we will find that salvation, the power to save, is not primarily an attribute of the church, but of Jesus Christ (Acts 4:12). "Inside" and "outside" the church does not yet have a clear soteriological content. Only when the world is divided into (official) Christendom and its adversaries will the polarity stand out in relief and be "thought" of as a polarity affecting salvation.

The fact that Jesus Christ is the only name given to human beings for them to be saved (Acts 4:12) does not yet indicate concretely how human beings stand vis-à-vis that power. One's first impression is that Jesus Christ becomes an alternative of salvation for those who run across him, so to speak.

Thus it is that the urgency of making a decision toward Jesus Christ—a yes or a no—is first of all a matter for those Jews who were his contemporaries. From there that same urgency extends to the Jews of the diaspora insofar as they are the first to be evangelized, as indeed they are meant to be (Acts 13:46; 18:6; 28:28) and finally to the pagans, when evangelization begins to make available to them the good news of the person and message of Jesus.

Naturally to the extent that Christ "runs across" these groups of people, some of them see salvation in him. Around the apostles they form a group, a community, sect, or church. The distinctive affirmation of this community in its relations with Jesus, who is the unique and total power of salvation, is such that it can be said that "the Lord added to their number those who were being saved" (Acts 2:47). We might say that the dogma expressed in this fashion might be formulated, more clearly and exactly as: "inside the church there is salvation" (or "salvation is inside the church").

However, the New Testament and the historical situation of the church in the midst of the paganism of the Roman Empire do not allow people to draw the conclusion that up to this point human beings "outside this church" had been lost for all eternity, nor even that from this point onward they were being lost. In addition to what can be concluded from some of Paul's central texts (in Romans, for example) we have this significant formula in 1 Timothy 4:10: "the living God who is the savior of all men, but especially of those who believe." Indeed, some of the first Christian apologists strove to prove how the Word of God, the Jesus Christ of the Gospels, was always present everywhere offering to pagans of good will his power to do good and attain salvation.

Thus it is not surprising that there was a transition from the formula "inside the church is salvation" (which does not exclude other possibilities for being saved) to the formula coined, it would seem, by Cyprian of Carthage, "outside the church there is no salvation." There had to be a context where it had to be presumed (unless there were proof to the contrary) that to be outside the church meant, by definition, bad will. That was how Cyprian saw the Donatists. This context, where the non-Christian or non-Catholic becomes a case of obstinacy in evil, the enemy who denies and attacks, understandably occurs above all when the church is identified with the Christian world of the West, and all Europe becomes "Christendom."[13]

Nor is it a coincidence that the first council (an ecumenical council as Rome now measures things)—when the church stops thinking of itself as "Christendom" and regards itself as a servant in a world context where Christianity (and Catholicism in particular) is only a minority—is Vatican II. In this world, which is partly secularized and partly made up of a mosaic of religions, denominations, and sects, Vatican II rediscovers (almost naturally, one could say) the universal dimensions of Christ's saving grace acting in the good will of human beings.

Theologians explaining these "dogmatic" changes are not playing with their audiences or deceiving them. Certainly they want to show that a vision that would show the church facing the *same problem* and solving it with a yes and then with a no, in elaborate and contradictory dogmatic formulas is false or superficial—or better yet, false *insofar as* it is superficial.

For that reason theologians prefer not to use formulas that I have called "alternatives" (outside the church there is no salvation vs. outside the church there is salvation). The historical example mentioned above shows that in general, a shift in the context proves not that the earlier version was false, but that it was insufficient, at least for today; that (at least) one of the key concepts of the earlier formula was more complex or ambiguous than appeared at first sight; and that when this became clear, the formula had to be modified in order to preserve and augment its truth.

In order to take into account this increasing complexity, which history makes evident, a *distinction* is employed. For example, a distinction is drawn between what "church" meant for the delegates to the Council of Florence, and what "church" meant to the delegates at Vatican Council II. One who "distinguishes" in this manner thereby acquires the right, or luxury perhaps, to answer yes in one case and no in another to what seems to be the same question only at first glance.

Hence in ordinary discussion of theology, theologians who want to save themselves (and their audiences) the trouble of getting involved in fruitless contradictions, avoid using the language of simple alternatives for dogmatic formulas in order to avoid getting into the awkward situation of having to answer both yes and no to what in a lay person's eyes seems to be the same question.

Of course one can get out of this jam quite logically making the well-known distinction, "Can there be salvation outside the church? It all *depends* . . . " Of course it depends on what is understood by church. However, the situation is messy and what is worse, the lay person often gets the impression that this device can be used at one's discretion to answer yes or no to any question, even when the terms are well-defined.

Hence it is not vanity or intellectual cowardice that leads theologians doing theology in real life with people just as real to try to save themselves and those lay people the trouble of getting involved in futile problems, by introducing, even *before* a clash provokes doubt, the necessary distinction, which generally flows from different historical contexts, as we have already seen.

Thus before asking whether there is salvation outside the church, the theologian tries to bring ordinary Christians who are involved in the discussion to familiarize themselves with the different possible contents of this word whose context and meaning have varied. When I say "familiarize" I mean just that. I am referring to the fact that the ambiguity of the word becomes so obvious that when the question of salvation "outside the church" comes up, the very lay people who are discussing it press for the question to be reformulated: "But what 'church' are we talking about?"

In mentioning this method, one finds that this was the very path that theology took from the Council of Florence to Vatican II (on this particular issue). Those of us who studied theology a decade before Vatican II, observed the preparation, through a variety of tentative approaches, of this necessary distinction between "church" and "church."

One of the first ways proposed of making a distinction was to admit alongside the "visible church" made up of Christians participating in it through the creed, baptism, and communion, an "invisible church"[14] drawn together by grace and the Spirit of Jesus, although the members of this "church" themselves might not be conscious of belonging. The fact that this distinction was no longer used was a result of history—namely, that it had been used at the time of the Reformation to devalue or relativize the "visible" church—that is, the Roman church.

This is certainly not the moment to follow all the twists and turns of attempts to "familiarize" theologians and lay people with terms which were conducive to a similar distinction. It is enough to note that people spoke of the "Mystical Body" (of Christ) as something distinct from (and broader than) the church as a visible institution,[15] of a "People of God" as something distinct from (and broader than) the Mystical Body (which continued to be used as identical to the institutional church)[16] and of "anonymous Christians" as a sociological reality distinct from (and broader than) the body of those who were formally Christians (Catholics?), and so forth.

Again, it should be clear that this was not merely a logical gimmick, nor was it an effort to dodge the dogmatic task presented by the statements of the Council of Florence and other councils. Something new had come on the scene, something obvious to many clear-sighted Christians during those years before Vatican II. People had made a long mental journey—a journey that was political, and hence theological—since the French Revolution. (For obvious reasons, the revolutions in the Americas did not have the same impact in Europe and hence on European centers of theology.) That revolution saw the eruption of all the ideas and attitudes spawned by the Renaissance and the Enlightenment against the church and the medieval world it shaped and defended. Hence the French Revolution splits the European world and puts (almost) the whole (Catholic) Church on the defensive, forcing it to support a past recognizable as its own: *l'ancien régime*.

However, sooner or later the French Revolution inevitably had to arouse a growing fascination among Christians. For the first time, plainly Christian values — freedom, equality, fraternity — appeared not just as abstract and utopian causes but in the form of embodiments in history (partial and debatable, to be sure), carried out by those who acted as, and professed to be, enemies of the church. A half-century later, people who were even more overtly against the church, most of them atheists, unfurled new banners that were also Christian: the poor (or proletarians) as actors in a new model of society based on an equal distribution of the goods and resources of society.

However, the lesson of the second-century apologists, who recognized the seminal presence of the Word of God in the much more questionable and "anonymous" virtues of idolatrous pagans, could not be totally forgotten, especially as it became ever more obvious that by supporting the old order and big business the church had served systems that dehumanized and debased human beings.

The attraction in practice to the new causes often may have been imprudently tolerant, exaggerated, or one-sided. The institutional church tried to halt that attraction with condemnation or excommunication.[17] Those thinking theologically, however, could not but feel challenged, and when they did so sincerely, how could they deny the good will, the presence of grace, and the destiny of salvation, in so many strivings to satisfy the hunger and thirst for justice and solidarity, whether erroneous or not, successful or failed, which often were paid at a great human price?[18] Thus all the concepts used to keep the reality of "church" limited were burst open to something much broader.

Conclusion: Dogma in Pursuit of Truth

The point of everything said thus far is to show how, contrary to what generally happens in an academic class, in the theological-pastoral reflection of a community carried out in the church with lay people who want to understand their faith better in order to provide meaning for their lives and commitments, theology covers a great deal of ground before questions about the essence, conditioning factors, and imperatives of the realm of "dogma" arise and become pressing — even though they may be logically prior.

Some readers might argue that it ultimately does not matter much if the question arises on the first day or after ten years. In the end it has to be answered. Within Christianity, what is dogma? The fact that I have been doing theology for twenty-five years and for whatever reason have avoided searching for a solution to this problem may demonstrate great agility and may have been very useful, if you will, but it is not enough.

In response I have three observations.

1) I agree that it is not enough, and that is why we stand here facing the problem — and seeking an answer that people are correctly demanding. The reason I am posing this question today (not yesterday and not tomorrow) is that finally it has surfaced clearly among the very Christians with whom I have reflected for many years. Previously, this question did not arise nor was it necessary to resolve it in order to resolve even more pressing questions.

2) The fact that I believe that only now has the moment come to answer

it—and this is the moment when the question has been explicitly formulated—does not mean that theological work must inevitably follow the order of consciously formulated questions. Such a procedure runs contrary to the general understanding that has led people to say that a liberating theology proceeds from praxis. The true, deep, and enriching relationship between theory and praxis in theology means ignoring idle questions—and evasions when they can be detected—that rise from mere curiosity, from an abstract logic, or from a refusal to deal with the real problem. Today, however, one cannot go very far along the theological trail, even with lay people, without inquiring in praxis, what the church's "dogmatic" teaching authority is, why it is exercised the way it is, and what stance one should take toward it.

3) The vital context of the reflection group as church is very important with regard to this issue. It is one thing to ask whether dogmatic formulas are *infallible*, because in the church there is a general suspicion that Rome is exaggerating the function, certainty, and irreversibility of what the magisterium has expressed (or because the ideas of famous theologians on this point have been condemned), and it is something else to ask the question after having felt how one's life is enriched by understanding dogma better and putting everything in its proper perspective.

Unfortunately, the supersensitivity of the official church on these questions leads Christians who have not experienced any of the wealth and positive depth of dogma to rush into books that challenge the pretensions—which are also disincarnate—of the ecclesiastical magisterium.

A book unquestionably takes on its own life. If an author has written a number of works, he or she can "suggest" the order in which the works are best understood—and that is what I am doing by calling this book "posthumous." That also suggests, at least in my own case, the sequence of thought followed by many Christians about their faith. More than that I cannot do.

Yet perhaps something else is possible. That something else is what I do not find in a book with which I would like to engage in friendly dialogue here, Hans Küng's *Infallible?* This "something else," in the subject matter itself, is to relate the problem of dogma, its scope and truth, with other presumably liberating contents from earlier works. I think most of what Küng says in that book could have been said of the dogmatic formulas of Ephesus or Chalcedon in the context of a christological reflection (such as I have sought to do in *Jesus of Nazareth Today and Yesterday*) without overdisturbing the faith of those who might read or study it.

However, centering the issue of "infallibility" on the dogmatic "case" of Paul VI's *Humanae Vitae* (on methods of artificial birth control) has two disadvantages, I believe. These disadvantages, I would add, neither add to nor subtract from the inherent value of his argument.

First, it is dealing with a moral prohibition that is quite remote from the core (and the wealth) of the Christian message, and one that is the cause of serious and painful problems, however justified it might be. Worst of all from a pedagogical standpoint, this authoritarian stance was taken against the majority of theologians consulted and against most of the arguments proposed during the discussion.[19] In short it is quite atypical and peripheral to dogmatic questions.

Second, separating the problem of truth in dogmatic formulas from the way the truth gradually unveiled itself throughout the biblical process and in the faith process of the early centuries of the church (which is connected to what is basic in that hierarchy of truths of which Vatican II speaks) gives an unfortunate and erroneous impression of the problem as a whole. Thus what might have contributed to a healthy liberation from the "letter" (in the realm of dogma) with respect to "truth," seems to become an exaggerated relativization of truth itself for an unsuspecting or untrained reader.

In other words, one does not know nor is it said in what sense a believer can think that formulas that the church has found over twenty centuries for expressing that in which it believes would be in some way supported by the help the Lord promised against the darkness of error and sin. As I conceive it, the "biblical" period was certainly not an age of Eden from which we have had to depart forever. Indeed, it is in that process of revelation that we must learn today in the church how to follow the Spirit whose role it is to lead us "to all truth."

It is only after having spent many days journeying along this road, that out of the very truth, riches, and significance drawn out of those days, that the last question arises, one that is largely retrospective. What signs did we follow? What did I use to avoid pitfalls and discern wider horizons? To what extent did I sometimes have to retrace many days of journeying in order to understand better a sign on the roadside or a section of the map?

For that reason—because I bear all this vivid experience and have such memories of it—this is the book of an old man, and even, if you will, posthumous.

Part One

Dogma in the Old Testament?

CHAPTER 2

Myths and History

"Happy the time," many might say—theologians and nontheologians alike—"when there were no creeds, formulas, or dogmatic authorities, and God inspired the biblical authors and revealed to them the truth that was to be made known to human beings! When they wrote it down, what came from their pens was not 'dogmas' but stories, reflections and prayers."

Indeed any believing Jew, like any Christian and to some extent any Muslim, assumes that God traced out a specific path to the truth for a particular body of people chosen to follow it. Or at least God guided them toward that truth in such a way that they felt enriched in that search in which in one way or another the whole human race should engage: How are we to live our lives in a meaningful way?

When a Christian utters the exclamation above, "happy the biblical age," it is because he or she is comparing those past times with the present period of the church, and comparing them with respect to something basic: how human beings presumably are guided by God so they will not stray or get lost in this pursuit and in this approach to that truth which constitutes both meaning and value for life and teaching about God. Such a comparison between the comfortable past and the uncomfortable present is likely to lead such a person to add more precisely, "happy the age of the Bible when 'dogmas' did not yet exists!"

Of course we should not trust too much in superficial resemblances borne by language. It is not until the end of the fourth century C.E. that we find in Greek the word "dogma" used in the sense it has today: a doctrine that is obligatory on all christendom.

However, the fact that use of the word "dogma" in its present meaning dates from the fourth century does not mean that the word in itself, and especially the mental reality to which it points, began at that moment. Certainly, the word was already used in Greek, the language from which it comes. It originally meant "opinion," although it has some nuances that it would be well to specify, since they are important for these considerations.

To begin with, the meaning of the noun "dogma," as related to the Greek verb *dokeo* (to think), is closer to the plural of the Spanish word than to the singular. Indeed, usage has made the plural of "opinion" suggest something more solid than the singular. While the latter signifies a thought that can easily change since it is not based on logical or scientific arguments ("this is just an *opinion* . . ."), the plural serves to indicate the *fundamental ideas* that structure the thinking and thereby guide the action of a person or group (so-and-so's *opinions*).

Second, until around the fourth century c.e., the ideas people hold firmly and steadily and are thus called "dogmas" in Greek, generally have to do more with practical obligations or duties rather than theoretical points. Hence they constitute the "moral or legal opinions" of a person or group.

Third, in ordinary usage the firmness of these convictions or duties, which are called "dogmas" in Greek, are regarded as deriving more from the external authority promulgating them than from any reasoning or conviction proper to the person who feels obligated by them. Many years later these roots of the term were quite obvious to the Enlightenment. Its attack on "dogma," and indeed the modern pejorative sense the adjective "dogmatic" acquires starting in the eighteenth century comes from this external, heteronomous origin of convictions formed in this manner. Dogma is something in which I believe because someone outside me tells me to. This is so plain in the original Greek that "dogma" and "decree" are equivalent words. Luke, the evangelist, who knows Greek perfectly since it is his own language, uses "dogma" for the edict with which Augustus Caesar ordered the census that brings Jesus' parents to register in Bethlehem of Judah (Lk. 2:1). Luke likewise (Acts 16:4) uses the term "dogmas" for the practical decisions (although they were also dogmatic in the modern sense) made by "the apostles and presbyters (meeting) in Jerusalem" with regard to what should be required of pagans who join the church as a result of evangelization by Paul and Barnabas.

The foregoing is not superfluous erudition. It may be the case that looking for dogmas in the Old Testament, as preposterous as it might seem at first glance, may just make sense, provided we do not anachronistically expect to find the same word used in its current meaning before the fourth century. What, however, are we to say of the thing itself that will subsequently be designated with this term? Of course there is no intention here of trying to avoid the limits of language. We are asking whether in the Old Testament there may not be something similar to what we call "dogma" today, even if it does not carry a sign saying so.

If so, what is it that would have to be present to enable us to speak of a "dogmatic" presence—that is, in order to recognize a dogma? I think the only sensible way to answer this question is what comes from our own experience of language: the easiest way to recognize a "dogma" today is to look at the *kinds of language* that immediately give us the sensation that we are confronting a "dogmatic" expression: *creeds* and *anathemas*.

Of course because it is a stereotyped formula the "creed" Christians recite on some occasions has ended up where it does not belong: in the catalogue of "prayers." One knows the Creed just as one knows the Our Father. However, a bit of attention is enough to make us realize that in the creed no one is petitioning and no one is dialoguing with anyone, neither with God nor with the saints. It is a description of what is believed. We are all vaguely aware that we cannot call ourselves Christians if we do not accept these "articles of faith" which are contained in the creed and which we did not create. Furthermore, we have learned that these creeds we recite today were worked out slowly and painfully, and that each element that appears there was worked out over a long time by many theologians, and that we can hardly find a single word in these formulas which is not somehow aimed at an enemy of the faith—that is, at a heterodox opinion (which, in its own time, had dogmatic aspirations).

Perhaps we have heard it said that from the outset, the church made use of such short approved formulas as a criterion for deciding who could or could not become members of (or who should be expelled from) the church community. Hence each neophyte was asked the questions that are put to godparents today: "Do you believe in the Father? Do you believe in the Son? Do you believe in the Holy Spirit?" After each positive response, the neophyte was plunged into the baptismal waters.

Since, apparently at least, we do not use "anathemas" today, we may not associate them so commonly with dogma as we do creeds. Nevertheless, we should be aware that starting with the first ecumenical councils "anathemas" were used to draw the boundary lines authoritatively between truth and error. The purpose of the expression "let him [or her] be anathema" was not so much to curse someone as to indicate that he or she was outside the Christian community—insofar as he or she might persist in the belief connected to the anathema. Moreover, anathemas are especially interesting to theology. The councils generally first explain a controversial question at some length. Then comes the "canon," which is translated as "norm" of faith. This norm is summed up with a conventional formula: the opinion considered erroneous is set between two (sets of) terms: "Let one who should say that . . . be anathema." The ease with which the negative expression hits the nail on the head—more clearly and concisely than a positive statement—has meant that up to our own time Christian dogma has tended to be sought in these conciliar anathemas which have marked church life for fifteen centuries.

Now that these points have been made, we must return to examine the Bible. Although the Old Testament may here and there furnish some examples that more or less approach our "creeds" and "anathemas," as we will have occasion to see, we are especially interested in examining whether there may not be elements that are similar to them *due to the function they perform*—that is, because in some way they constitute "dogmatic formulas" or what could be reduced to such formulas without doing them violence.

One has a suspicion—which will begin to operate in this chapter—that the Old Testament is not an innocent collection of stories and prayers that one can open at random in an idle moment. One suspects that if one knows how to look, it may be possible to find rich dogmatic developments under the form of literary genres, theological processes, and authoritative interventions different from those familiar to Christians today.

A Dogmatic Narrative:
The Universal Flood

A Literary Genre for Dogmas: Creeds and Anathemas?

A good deal of what the Bible contains, and certainly the part most read and repeated, and summed up as "sacred history," is made up of narratives. Some are highly imaginary, while others are tremendously human and realistic. Some are poetic and legendary, while others claim to be historical.

This is the first barrier to be overcome in the search I am proposing. The language modern people are accustomed to recognizing as more "dogmatic" is also more "digital"—that is, the kind of language which most imitates the kind of scientific language applied to things or abstractions. In this literary genre the aim is to use words that can be clearly identified with definitions that exclude elements of imagination and feeling, so that the dogmatic norm may be as exact as possible and disqualify error with the greatest clarity. Of course even on the scientific or scholarly level the further one moves to the limits of what is living and human, the more one is forced to make use of the opposite—"iconic," figurative, suggestive language—in order to be understood. When Christian "dogma," for example, tells us that the Father, the Son, and the Holy Spirit constitute one God in three distinct persons, it might be possible to think such language is highly scientific and "digital." One would be forgetting, however, that the three main terms in the expression—Father, Son, and Holy Spirit— are three "figures of speech" which appeal to imagination and feeling.

The characteristic feature of creeds and anathemas, from a literary stand-point, is their diminished aspiration to become formulas in "digital" language. Indeed people today are so used to identifying what is dogmatic with this par-ticular literary genre that many theologians today believe that the conspicuous absence of "canons" of condemnation, accompanied by anathemas, proves emphatically that Vatican II does not have any *dogmatic* value. By the same token they believe that this council did not propose anything new that is *oblig-atory for the faith* of Roman Catholic Christians.[1]

In doing so they forget that most of what the church itself regards as the deposit of God's revelation—in both Old and New Testaments: the central divine communication from which all dogma proceeds—is made in language that is primarily "iconic": myths, legends, narratives, and history.

Two facts must be taken into account. It has already been noted that the "dogmatic" datum that Hans Küng makes the main element of his discussion of the infallibility or fallibility of dogmatic formulas is Pope Paul VI's encyclical *Humanae Vitae* on the permissibility or impermissibility of regulating birth through artificial means or means regarded as such (such as the birth control pill). Now papal encyclicals, including this one, generally do not have canons or anathemas like those of dogmas defined at ecumenical councils. However, no one would thereby claim that encyclicals such as this one do not constitute "dogmatic" events. Even though nowhere is that fact made specific with a short, clear, and more or less technical formula, any theologian will sum up the practical import of the encyclical in a short formula like this: "It is unlawful to use artificial means of birth control." Or (why not?) as "One who uses artificial means of birth control or claims that they are licit cannot share in eucharistic communion," which is obviously equivalent to an anathema.

The second fact that should be taken into account before making any comparison between seemingly opposed literary genres is that, as we have already noted in passing, everything "dogmatic"—absolutely everything—in Christianity at least, must *somehow come from the Bible*. The magisterium of the church "draws from this one deposit of faith everything *which it presents for belief* as divinely revealed" (*Dei Verbum* 10). If, moreover, we add that the Catholic Church acknowledges that the books of the Old Testament like the New are "inspired" and that God can and must be regarded as the *author* of the whole Bible, we must conclude that when reading the Old Testament we should keep in mind the "dogmatic" aspects that will necessarily emerge.

Since, however, among the literary genres found in the Bible there are no creeds (properly speaking) or canons with theological condemnations similar to those of church councils, we must conclude that in their own way the literary genres used by the Bible are susceptible to being translated dogmatically through some legitimate procedure. Otherwise, nothing the church teaches would derive from the Old Testament.

A Dogma: There Will Be No More Deluge

Specifically, how might this work? I believe it will be better to begin with some significant examples from the Old Testament in relation to dogma.[2] We can begin this examination by looking at the "new beginning" of creation signified by the deluge and its ending in the book of Genesis (chap. 6–9).

That this narrative is legendary—or mythical, in more technical terminology, as some might prefer—is unquestionably clear from a number of solid arguments, both negative and positive. Among the former, geology and paleontology show that there has been no deluge submerging the earth since the appearance of human beings—that is, since the beginning of the quaternary age. Moreover, such a deluge, at least according to one of the stories, would have been caused by forty days of rain. I believe that reading this in Palestine, which is moderately mountainous, any contemporary readers of the story would conclude that they are reading something legendary.

The most interesting negative argument, however, is that the biblical writers *themselves* are aware that they are transmitting a mythical narrative. That fact, however, does not mean that it is devoid of "truth," or "false." A reader, however uninitiated, who pays even a little attention while reading of the deluge in the Bible, will find repetitions all along the way. What is repeated is not exactly the same, however, and indeed the items of information in these repetitions are not always compatible with one another. Hence they are not mere repetitions, but rather different versions of a generic event (deluge) happening to the same individual (Noah).

A deeper and more careful examination reveals that there are *two* narratives and that they differ on almost all the details but are focused on the very same essential core: Noah standing apart from the behavior of all other human beings; the ark and the animals; the worldwide flooding and humankind's new beginning starting with Noah. Those most familiar with how the Bible was written can go further and identify these two narratives, attributing them, verse by verse, to *two* different authors at least five centuries apart. One of them, who by common consent is called the *Yahwist*,[3] is the author of the first story: Gen. 5:1-8; 7:1-5, 7-10, 12, 16b, 17, 22-23; 8:2b-3a, 6-12, 13b, 20-22. The more recent story is that of the other, or *Priestly*,[4] writer: Gen. 6:9-22; 7:6-11, 13-16a, 18-21, 24; 8:1-2a, 3b-5, 13a, 14-49; 9:1-7.

The result is something that is not unique but certainly quite exceptional in the Bible. (We may recall that there is something vaguely similar in the New Testament — namely the fact that there are three *synoptic* Gospels). This situation forces a question. The editors certainly could have combined the two stories into a single continuous coherent narrative. Why, then, were they so interested in showing that they were telling the same thing, but with different elements, things that were, strictly speaking, incompatible and ultimately an either/or choice?

In other words, one would probably have preferred either greater similarity or greater difference, especially in a "historical" matter. What the authors had in mind was therefore something different. Something similar happens when one encounters two versions of "Little Red Riding Hood" side by side. In one of them, the pessimistic version, Grandmother and Red Riding Hood are eaten up, period. In the "happy ending" version, the wolf's stomach is cut open and Grandmother and Little Red Riding Hood are let out (like the legendary Jonah and the whale). What does this mean — if we have to find a meaning to something so simple? That each version adapts those elements that are significant to the "truth" it seeks to communicate. There is no concern for "history," in the sense of getting an exact copy of something that once happened. What is sought is the *meaning* of what happened — or may not have happened but is narrated — and it is there, in that domain, that the "truth" of the story can be assessed. That is what both narrators did and thought they were doing with regard to the deluge, as did the person who put the two stories into Genesis while keeping them separate.

To these should be added the more important positive argument to the effect that this is a legend that bears *its own* truth. Scholars have found many versions of deluge stories, many much more ancient and fantastic. Where they have found them, in cultural terms, explains many things in the biblical story that would otherwise remain obscure. It is unlikely, for example, that the idea of a deluge that could cover the earth would arise in a rough hilly terrain like that of Palestine, which is bordered by the Mediterranean and the desert, and has only one river, the Jordan (which to be sure runs through a plain). Asiatic Mesopotamia, however, would most certainly retain from generation to generation the memory of the rising waters of the Tigris and the Euphrates, which might appear to have covered everything beyond what the eye could see. Indeed, it is there that the deluge is a myth taking on many forms, some of them as elaborate as the epic poem of Gilgamesh, which are more ancient than the biblical story of the Yahwist, the earlier of the two.

The likely ethnic origins of (part of) the Israelite population in Mesopotamia or the trading and cultural contacts of the sedentary population of Canaan with Mesopotamia would explain how such stories were also popular in Israel. But if they were not indigenous, why were they incorporated twice into the traditions, whether legendary or not, of the literature that was authentically Israelite?

One very reasonable answer, among many possibilities, is that of John L. McKenzie in his *Dictionary of the Bible*. He states that all modern critics admit that the similarities between the biblical stories (of the deluge) and older stories of the Mesopotamians prove that the Bible draws on those stories. As to why they are present in Israel's sacred literature, the author says, "the differences between the Mesopotamian and the biblical stories show how the Hebrews took a piece of ancient tradition and retold it in order to make it a vehicle of their own distinctive religious beliefs, in particular their conception of divine justice and providence."⁵ I cannot go into details here about how exegesis works to discover this content. It will suffice to recall that one of the first articles in which Catholic exegesis set forth what the authors of the deluge narratives wanted to say by adopting these Mesopotamian legends was that of Gustave Lambert. The title he suggestively chose to summarize his exegesis was quite similar to a "dogmatic" formula: "There will never be another deluge."⁶

What is going on? As soon as exegesis tries to reconstruct the intention that led to the juxtaposition of these two mythical narrations, one finds oneself facing a *dogmatic* content. Or, to be more precise, a content that can (and, in order to be thoroughly understood, to some extent must) be translated "dogmatically." Of course to reach this result, one must go from one literary genre to another. The distance between the biblical narration itself and the title of Lambert's article is the same as that between an iconic-tending language and a digital-tending language. However, if the author of the article is right, he has not done violence to the content. The article remains faithful to what the authors of the biblical narratives wanted people to understand. Whatever the theological development or the authority that made such a dogma (there will never be another deluge) obligatory in Israel, there can be no doubt that here we have what McKenzie calls the "distinctive belief" of the people of the Bible.

The narrative, or rather the narratives, of the flood as they stood when an unknown editor finished juxtaposing what had been written on the matter by the Yahwist and the Priestly writers became part of the "opinions" that confer a peculiar identity on Israel, differentiating it, for example, from Mesopotamian peoples. Departing from those beliefs is automatically and subconsciously sanctioned with a kind of social ostracism. Therefore, as will be seen even more clearly in another example below, another even more "dogmatic" translation of the same theological summary is appropriate: "Should anyone say that God can send another deluge to the earth (destroying divine creation and the field of human activity) *let that person be anathema*."

Now that I am in the middle of the Bible, let me take the liberty of doing battle (a little) on behalf of anathemas. I am fully aware of the bad use to which they can be put and often have been put. To have a decided "opinion" on something means a specificity, a difference. To know, in addition, where the difference or specificity lies and at what point or boundary it is lost, for well or for ill, is a normal requirement. It is not the only requirement, but it is indispensable—for continuing to think, and for advancing in thought so as to discover and communicate new things. Confusion is not freedom.

Some have defended the idea that secularization, a Western phenomenon that has dominated our cultural horizon since the Renaissance, and especially since the Enlightenment, has biblical roots. So argues Harvey Cox, among others, in his well-known work *The Secular City*. One of these roots—a dogmatic root to be sure—is that the survival of the earth as theater of human activity does not depend on the whim of the divinity, nor on a juridical decision over the religious behavior of humankind. The earth has been entrusted to the care of humans forever. The rainbow stands as a reminder to both humankind and the Divinity.[7]

But what does it mean to say that one has to *believe* in the deluge?

Before answering that question, it is a good idea to recall summarily what has been established thus far. With a vivid biblical example, it has been shown how a narrative, this one obviously mythological, was laden with an undeniable "dogmatic" intention from its very origin in the Bible.

Certainly this term is still taken here in a very broad, if not vague, sense, in which the adjective "dogmatic" does not go much further than what might be conveyed by the term "theological." We can say, without fear of being wrong, that the narration of the deluge was bursting with theology, indeed that it was intentionally theological.

In the following sections, our investigation will approach what could be called "dogmatic" in the strictest sense. For that purpose, and using another example, I will try to study the theological procedure to which a biblical account is subjected. I believe such a procedure will illustrate the path from what is vaguely theological to what is properly "dogmatic."

Another Dogmatic Account:
The Deuteronomic Creed

I Believe That "My Father Was a Wandering Aramean . . ."

Following upon our first example from the Bible, the one we are now going to study is another, and perhaps even more typical case of the narrative theology currently fashionable. In an apparent challenge to the rationalist ideals of the Enlightenment, in theological circles today it is often said that abstract formulas have been misused in theology and that we must go back to theologizing as it was done in ancient biblical times: through narratives (although of course not everything in the Bible is narrative).

In this connection it is often noted that the first "profession" of faith that emerges clearly in the Old Testament—with its own literary genre—is a kind of "creed," one that is, however, "historic." According to Deuteronomy, the

Israelites had to recite this creed when they went to the temple to offer to God the firstfruits of their harvests. Moses gave the order:

> Then you shall declare before the Lord, your God, "My father was a wandering Aramean who went down to Egypt with a small household and lived there as an alien. But there he became a nation great, strong and numerous. When the Egyptians maltreated and oppressed us, imposing hard labor upon us, we cried to the Lord, the God of our fathers, and he heard our cry and saw our affliction, our toil and our oppression. He brought us out of Egypt with his strong hand and outstretched arm, with terrifying power, with signs and wonders; and bringing us into this country, he gave us this land flowing with milk and honey. Therefore, I have now brought you the firstfruits of the products of the soil which you, O Lord, have given me." [Dt. 26:5-10]

Deuteronomy of course does not belong to the oldest strata of the Bible. In all probability it was written shortly before the exile, when the northern kingdom had been — or was about to be — destroyed by the Assyrians. Despite this late composition date, according to the best exegetes, this profession of faith or "creed" contains elements that are believed to be much older.[8] The reader should not forget that the materials appearing in a work are not always created on the spot. Often in a particular period, elements from the past, even the distant past, are used.

Be that as it may, this passage has attracted attention because it is a kind of summation of Israel's religious tradition — its "dogmas." The very cultic solemnity in which the formula appears or is inserted (when it becomes part of the religious reform of Josiah in Jerusalem) makes it serve as a point of group (or national)[9] self-identification based on a historic and religious content.

Understandably, this passage has been called Israel's first "historic creed." Israel stands before Yahweh and begins by identifying itself, and reminds Yahweh how he has identified himself in the past. Von Rad comments that here "a note was struck which henceforward was to remain the predominant one in Israel's religious life. Israel was always better at glorifying and extolling God than at theological reflexion."[10]

Nevertheless, I am not very satisfied with *the terms* von Rad uses in this last contrast, although I think I agree with what he is trying to say, as I understand it. I have the impression I know where the term "theological reflection" as he sees it is aimed — namely, at a particular literary genre, that of a quasidigital exposition of a religious doctrine. To that he opposes the terms "praise and glorification of Yahweh," which likewise must refer to another literary genre: that which Israel uses to exalt, especially through narration, Yahweh's deeds in saving and liberating the people.

However, taking von Rad's terms literally would seem to minimize one of the most illustrious glories of this people, which is so unusual within the history of religion as a whole: precisely its "theological reflection." For there are many ways to reflect theologically and to write down such reflections. Methodically developing theological treaties is only one of those ways.

As I said, I think this is what von Rad had in mind, for three pages later he explains:

> The chief method employed in the *theological unfolding* of the tradition was a different one still: it was much more *indirect*, for it consisted in the way in which separate pieces of material were connected. The layout of the primeval history, the story of Abraham, the relationship of the period of the patriarchs to that of Joshua, etc., is arranged in such a way that *quite definite theological tensions*, which the great collector intended, *arise out of the sequence of the material itself*. This *indirect theological way of speaking* through the medium of the traditional material and its arrangement makes clear once more that remarkable preponderance of the matter-of-fact historical over the theological which is so characteristic of the witness of Israel.[11]

What is then the general aim of biblical stories? To reproduce correctly events that have taken place? Perhaps in some instances that may be the *direct* intention, but according to von Rad, in the very literary structure we can see *indirectly*—which does not mean collaterally or secondarily—another deeper or higher intention. In other words, on another level, what is narrated constitutes a theological development intended by the author.

Thus the contrast is not between "praise of God for his deeds in history" and "theological reflection." That is why I part company with von Rad over his choice of terms to express something with which I in fact wholeheartedly agree: the Old Testament constitutes one of the greatest monuments of theological reflection, but we must correctly understand the literary genre in which the theological thought (and even "dogmatic" thought, as we shall see) is expressed.[12]

With this point established, we may return to what von Rad and many other exegetes call the "historic creed"—that is, the profession of faith in "historic" terms in Deuteronomy (26:5–10). In it we will try to see something more of the mechanism by which a narrative becomes *indirectly* theological, or perhaps better, becomes theology on a logically higher level than that of the material reality of the facts.

How Story Becomes Dogma

To begin with, it is noteworthy that "dogma," which in the case of the deluge took a mythical expression, as we have seen, here takes an expression that exegetes would concur in calling "historic." We have in mind the summary of the origins of the people of Israel. Even though in some aspects of that "history" it is difficult to distinguish between what a modern historian would call properly historical data[13] and a somewhat "mythical" reconstruction of the past,[14] the balance sheet clearly favors the basically historical nature of the "material" content.

Nevertheless, the relationship between this historical material (plus its mythical extensions, if you will) and *what is professed*—that is, what truly constitutes the object of the confession of faith—is not yet made clear. To speak of a historic creed would seem to indicate that what is thereby being affirmed or "believed" is that the events occurred as the formula presents them in its account. Strictly speaking, however, that is not the case.

To assure ourselves on this point, we need only consider that the very events of this "historic creed," precisely because they were largely historical, were just as familiar to the Egyptians at a particular moment. Nevertheless, to the Egyptians these events must have had a *very different meaning*, or no meaning at all—which for the purposes of this book amounts to the same thing. Here one detail of the biblical account of other events is important—namely, those dealing with the origins of the whole monarchical period in Israel. Only after studying how this history becomes theology can we return with further criteria to the question here being left in the air: Must the events referred to in the "dogma" of the deluge or of the Deuteronomic creed have *truly* occurred? Or is that not necessary to the truth of what is "believed" in those events?

It is well-known that in antiquity kings had groups of scribes dedicated to compiling the chronicles of their kingdom. The Yahwist and the Elohist must have belonged to such groups. What we now call the books of Samuel (1 and 2) and Kings (1 and 2) are mostly written by royal scribes (except for some editorial touches that may grow in importance). From the time of Solomon until the end of the monarchy, first in Israel and then in Judah, a standard phrase is used in the Bible to distinguish between what appears in these books and the overall content of the royal chronicles: "The rest of the acts of Solomon [or Jeroboam or Rehoboam and so forth] are recorded in *the book of the chronicles* of Solomon" (1 Kgs. 11:41).

How did it come about that a part, and *only a part*, of all the events in the royal chronicles became part of this special book, later incorporated into the "canon," or the official list of the books of the Bible? No doubt an implicit but significant answer can be found in the words, "This came about *because* the Israelites . . ." (2 Kgs. 17:7).

In other words, what makes the events that took place during the period in question (and no doubt in any other period) different from the rest is not that they are true. However, they clearly do not stand out to the eyes of the biblical writer (here I am committing an anachronism in method, which I will later examine) except to the extent that a (necessary) connection can be established between them, this "because" that links them to one another and constitutes a sequence that will presumably recur when similar circumstances arise. To put it another way, historical material by itself does not take on importance or "meaning" by being what today we would call "historical." All the events described in the royal chronicles would be just as important. Moreover, nonhistorical events which are so outstanding that they deserved to be narrated twice, as is the case with the deluge, would not be that important. We could almost say the opposite: it is in the mythical domain (intervention by the divinity, which entails an irrefutable connection) that we can best see this rich "necessity" that gives the events recounted their "paradigm" character. It is by virtue of the premise of such a past intervention that this "because" which helps structure the "meaning" of the flow of events is established. Only insofar as they are raised to the level of *transcendent data* — that is, epistemological premises — do certain events become sources of meaning and truth.

Thus the exercise of separating the historical elements from mythical additions to them in the Deuteronomic creed may certainly be a useful scholarly exercise. However, if the aim is thereby to reduce the value and function of this "creed" to simply *knowing* or stating what "really" happened, the result is a greater hermeneutical error than what would result from confusing the historical and the mythical. To put it another way, such a procedure misunderstands the literary genre being used and its function in language and human existence. The result is an unpardonably bad interpretation of the biblical text.

That is not all. The reader will be right in asking why I insist on using the term "mythical" when I intend to refer to this higher level where the meaning of (fictitious or real) events referred to on the lower level is structured. Would it not be enough to call it "existential," for example? Let us see.

Dogma: The Human Being Creating Experience

As has already been observed, in order that a succession of events move from being *insignificant* — being mere historic "matter," something that just happened and that is all there is to it — to having a *significance* — that is, becoming normative for subsequent historical interpretations — it must in "fact" become "paradigmatic." It must point to a "because" which *necessarily* unites the series of events. It is this "transcendence" over the material and empirical datum that raises it above other events (the rest of Solomon's deeds, for example).

To go from seeing events as randomly following and combining with one another to perceiving a necessary sequence that is repeated, presupposes a very characteristic and common mental operation: something — or someone — above mere events is guiding them and pointing them toward a meaning. Otherwise, repetition would be due to sheer chance. It is only from an agent endowed with will that history can be expected to present *redundancies*. Hence, the first redundancies noted in life tend to be those imposed on events by the first de facto necessities we recognize (beyond mechanisms which will in turn be explained analogically further on). Those redundancies depend on human wills: those of our parents or of persons taking care of us.

In other words, any premise of meaning, any transcendent datum, ultimately presupposes not only a meaning structure in our mind itself, but also a personified "agent" whose guidance over history can be felt — in other words, a "supernatural" intervention in the broadest sense. Thus we come to the mythical dimension. In its most essential meaning, the mythical does not mean that paradigmatic events are false or imaginary, but that they are seen to be "personal decisions" which organize the chaotic flow of events once and for all. Indeed this is the very way meaning is established amid the flux of everyday events. It is never the effect of chance but rather of someone's intention or purpose.

Personalistic language thus becomes inevitable in any hermeneutic of what

is suprahistoric.[15] In the Deuteronomic creed, for example, Yahweh's intervention, his "strong hand and outstretched arm," is another way to note that all
historic reality bends to this norm, and obeys the value at work in the divine
will, and that out of this norm emerges the meaning of what happens in the
legend, from which it *passes* into history and comes down to me. Hence,
throughout the Bible, the layout of the story "is arranged in such a way that
quite definite theological tensions . . . arise out of the sequence of the material
itself," as von Rad said.

Myths, Legends, and Histories in Which God Is Revealed

Myth and Revelation in the Deluge Accounts

What is then the (even vaguely) "dogmatic" content emerging from this
theological procedure used in narratives, both those that are mythical and those
that claim to be historical? In the examples of both the deluge and the Deuteronomic creed, what is it that a believing reader should feel obliged to
"believe" after reading them?

In the case of the deluge the reasons why the accounts must be regarded as
plainly mythical have already been indicated. That was even true of the writers
who put them into the Old Testament, hence it should be true of any alert
reader. The fact that there are two accounts of the same event with aspects
incompatible with each other, and that they nevertheless enjoy the same
"authority," indicates that they cannot be intended to generate the belief that
things really happened as they are described.

We will note below that we need not exclude the possibility that both
accounts of the flood might have different theological contents. That happens
elsewhere in the Bible, for example, in the two accounts of how the monarchy
was established in Israel. However, there is no logical requirement that material
differences in the account must imply different theologies on the higher level
of meaning.

If we agree with Lambert that the dogmatic "intention" of both deluge
stories taken from the literature of Mesopotamia and reflecting its theological
background was to correct the meaning they already had and to make it clear
that Yahwism provides assurance that the earth will never be destroyed by
Yahweh in the future no matter how serious human sins may be, both accounts
would coincide in the formula: there will be no more (universal) deluge.

How does this (transcendent) datum structure the meaning of human existence? We have already pointed out that meaning is derived from the fact that
some power is at work organizing the incoherent flow of events. This order
must become paradigm or epistemological premise if people are to understand
the meaning of what happens and act accordingly. Such a premise (again always
assuming that the same theological purpose is at work in both deluge accounts),
would respond to a particular human situation. There are moments when evil
mounts up to such a point that people are led to fear something like a "divine
regret" (Gen. 6:6–7), or in other words, that having gone off track, humankind
stands on the brink of destruction.

The "dogma" emerging from both accounts, which are materially incompatible with each other, is that love and compassion for human beings will always
prevail in God's heart. After any increase of evil, the sequence that has become
paradigmatic will always put in place a new beginning, but from the deluge
onward it will not be preceded by destruction. In mythical language, God tasted
destruction as punishment and did not like it. The authors of the account are
not saying that God has given up punishing, but that God will punish in order
to heal, and that punishment will be used to the extent that it heals and does
not destroy human history.

In this fashion, I believe, we can grasp how relevant it is for Israel's own
identity in history that it has "copied" as it were a myth known throughout the
East in order to make it bear a new datum which is destined to radically change
the meaning of existence and human effort in history.

History and Revelation in the Deuteronomic Creed

What are we to say of the other example, the Deuteronomic Creed, to which
I promised to return? Certainly what seventh-century Israelites know of the
history of their people is compressed in this narration which begins, "My father
was a wandering Aramean . . ." "Meaningful" history is never reduced to that
level. Nor is history what we used to call it jokingly behind the teacher's back:
la sucesión de sucesos sucedidos sucesivamente [the sequence of happenings happening sequentially]. It is indeed true that historic time, this sequence of events,
is initially a sentence incomprehensible to human beings, a mass of letters or
phonemes seemingly without punctuation. There are no paragraphs, no com-
mas, no question marks.

If meaning is to be injected into this chaos, if the sequence of events is to
become "history," it must be *punctuated*. That, however, depends partly on the
text that is given and partly on oneself. Thus, with a little attentiveness and a
great deal of good will and imagination, we perceive, or think we perceive, that
the sequence of events is not simply chaotic and that there is a certain "redundancy" in this happening of things one after another. We "recognize" similar
sequences. Possibilities of "becauses" that might link events arise. Soon certain
historic phrases begin to look familiar to us, and therefore seem likely to be
repeated.

We need only think of two very simple examples. On the one hand, we think
we can perceive that whenever an "evil" action takes place, sooner or later an
"evil" event, something negative, follows. By analogy with what happens in
human relations, we then call this sequence of events a "punishment."[16] On
other occasions, observing events more patiently—that is, testing long sequences
as our hypothesis—we come to the conclusion expressed in the sayings: "no
evil lasts a hundred years," or "every evil brings some good."[17] Thus we gradually build up what we call our *experience*. That is, we do so with "historic"
material and epistemological premises, the latter acting as means for "punctuating history."

Let us now see how this punctuation operates in the Deuteronomic creed.
Observing the material (or, if you will, "historic") content of the creed, we can

see that it refers to the events of the three periods of the exodus (up to the occupation of the promised land) and finally the period of the one reciting the formula (not that of Moses but of the practice of Deuteronomy).

The first period opens with the wanderings of the patriarchs in the lands of Canaan, and especially with events around Jacob the wandering Aramean. Under the protection of the "God of our Fathers" (Abraham, Isaac, and Jacob-Israel), this wandering of a few nomad shepherds forces them to go down to Egypt where Israel will become "a nation great, strong and numerous."

The second period shows what happens to this people at the end of their stay in Egypt. As great, strong, and numerous as the infant Israel might be, the Egyptians are a thousand times greater, and they shift from treating Israel well to persecuting it. In that situation, the Israelites decide to call on Yahweh, identified as "the God of our Fathers." Yahweh hears them and "with his strong hand and outstretched arm" he frees them from the power of the Egyptians and leads them through the desert to the land promised to them.

Before going on to the third stage, it is useful to note that the earlier ones show similar or parallel sequences. The "God of our Fathers" watches over the journeying of this wandering Aramean, who is Israel's forefather (Israel is likewise another name given to Jacob) and it is just at the most critical moment—when the nomads go down to the great country, which is well-organized and powerful, and submit to it—that God makes the weak descendants of Jacob a large and powerful people. Yahweh (whom Moses identifies as "the God of our Fathers") protects this people under domination, and also at the most critical moment, marvelously saves it from the power of Egypt and leads it through the desert to the promised land.[18]

As can be seen, there are certain significant parallel details in these sequences: God's accustomed protection seems to end in a kind of weariness or decline (the "descent" to Egypt and falling under its sway is the result of a great drought, according to Genesis; the journey to the promised land is long and discouraging, and only the second generation will see its end). Nevertheless, a religious stirring seems to make God bend down in compassion over his friends, who are under his protection, to set them new goals and to make them new proposals and promises.

How much of a third sequence is there in the Deuteronomic creed? Obviously, the occupation of the country of Canaan—that is, the land which has been promised, and according to the creed, "given" to Israel—signifies the end point, a kind of "new paragraph," for this historic sentence which has already been recognized twice in Israel's history. Is it perhaps not a paradigm destined to be repeated further? The Davidic monarchy did not think this sentence would be repeated, because it would no longer be necessary. However, those more or less happy times have passed, and we now find the Israelite in the distressing context of Deuteronomy. Now if there is a "Deuteronomy"—a "second law" attributed to Moses—it is because in some way it is understood that what has been lived thus far can no longer be regarded as completely fulfilling the original promise.

The thought that as in the past Yahweh is prepared to make history repeat itself in a similar historic sentence, astonishes and beckons to prophetic hearts. Yahweh is going to effect new and mighty deeds on behalf of a smaller Israel under threat, and Yahweh is preparing deeds that will dwarf and almost make forgotten those of the past. The true "promised land," truly "flowing with milk and honey," not the poor parched land of the present, is in the future, not in the past. It is during the last days of the Northern Kingdom that all of this begins to be the surprising thrust of a new prophetic message exhorting Israel to again take on the attitude demanded by that paradigmatic sentence: a people whose entire hope is set on Yahweh and who want to serve Yahweh with all their heart.[19]

For good reasons it is acknowledged that wherever Deuteronomy may have been (initially) composed, it is strongly influenced by this extraordinary prophetic message. Hence its purpose is that Israel should feel the "today" quality of the divine promises. Writes von Rad:

> It is pathetic to see how Israel, just immediately before the catastrophe, is, so to speak, once more given the offer of "life" (Deut. 30:15ff.). The means by which this is done is as follows: Deuteronomy wipes out some seven centuries squandered in disobedience, and places Israel once again in the wilderness, with Moses speaking to her. But it has to be borne in mind that this Israel is in no way comparable to the ancient people of Israel that stood once at Sinai: the conditions in which she lived were utterly different in culture, economy, and politics, and she is a stubborn people (Deut. 9:6, 13; 31:27). None the less, she is offered present salvation on exactly the same terms as before: "today you have become the people of Jahweh your God." Nowhere else does the impassioned endeavour to make the commandments given at Sinai relevant for its own time find such a clear expression as in the endless variations played upon the word "today," which the preacher drums into the ears of his audience.[20]

The reader will thus see that in this light the theological intention of the Deuteronomic creed is not to make a *racconto* of the past. It teaches to the extent that it is "dogmatic," or to the extent that it teaches a norm, a paradigm for *punctuating events* in such a way that the *today* of those times, despite all the dissimilarities, is brought into an already known and experienced sequence: that of the first two historical sentences that appear in the creed. By returning wholeheartedly to Yahweh, Deuteronomy teaches, what remains of Israel will see Yahweh's saving deeds emerging unexpectedly with the same order and the same "fidelity" as in the past, and even more so.

Thus the point was not that Israelites who might be reciting this creed in the seventh century B.C.E. should close their eyes to say that all Israel was oppressed in Egypt or that the land they were tilling with so much sweat was the same promised land flowing with milk and honey. Obviously their "faith" did not depend on such an effort of the will to see what they could not see. The theological function of this creed did not depend on the possibility of knowing for certain whether the exodus was actually surrounded by wonders, nor on statistics on the comparative abundance of milk and honey in their desolate or threatened territory. It should be recalled, moreover, that by allowing two different accounts of the deluge to stand side by side, Genesis was already indicating the same thing about the "historicity" of what was narrated there.

Furthermore, we know this is the case because the way of punctuating events that we find in the Deuteronomic creed is not limited to this passage, nor even to the book itself. The same paradigm is the basis for the way books such as the book of Judges are constructed. Exegetes attribute Judges to the author of Deuteronomy or to his school. The internal evidence for that conclusion is simply that they find there the same theology of history. The way events are punctuated and the way the familiar and significant way of divine action is recognized in the succession of events amounts to the author's signature.

Deuteronomy (along with the work of the Deuteronomist) is a last and desperate attempt in Israel to bring a particular theology up to date. As we will see, this effort was unsuccessful. Certainly it sought to impose that theology without violence; but with its authority it does not hesitate to control experience. For Deuteronomy, the remnant of Israel is made up of those who situate themselves in that "today" vis-à-vis the "second" law of Moses, as his contemporaries set themselves vis-à-vis the "first" law in the desert of Sinai. This identification and boundary is intended to be "dogmatic."

In the period of the Yahwist what made Israel what it was and gave it its identity in a dogmatic sense was that it did not believe in a history punctuated by deluges subject to the whim of the gods, and it made this refusal an "article of faith." In the same fashion it later identified itself with another theology, that of this "creed" marked by a precise way of punctuating history. A people, like a church, is never identified by the exactitude of a physical fact, but by a constitutive "meaning," something that is the object of "belief."

CHAPTER 3

Process and Truth

A reader thinking about the discussion in the last chapter will wonder what the true punctuation must be. What has been uncovered there may indeed represent an advance, but it raises another problem: Are *all* the transcendent data that emerge from the Old Testament accounts, when translated into what we might call "dogmatic" language, equally true?

What must have become clear from our previous discussion is that underneath a narrative literary genre—which as we will see is only one of the many literary genres present in the Bible—lies concealed a theological reflection and intention. It may be added that the theological conclusions of such accounts can be formulated in propositions that are more "digital," expressing in another way the transcendent data that determine the identity of what we could call Yahwist faith, or Israel's faith.

If such is the case, the importance of paradigmatic events does not lie in their "historicity." We have been able to establish that the biblical authors themselves do not hide the legendary origin or components (which they have taken the liberty of correcting in accounts that are actually mythical) of a number of these accounts, which nevertheless have become paradigms of historic interpretation. In the realm of meaning, what is most important is their literary function: that they be clear and eloquent in showing a punctuation framework that enables people to subsequently build an "experience," thus opening the way for them to leap into the dimension of history in a more human fashion.

It is true that the prestige of these accounts that provide paradigmatic sequences, such as that of the deluge and the one found in the creed of Deuteronomy, give an impulse to this apprenticeship in how to interpret one's own history (or group history, since the former is indissolubly linked to the latter).[1] What has been said about the prudence of the editors—that they left parallel accounts of the same events that were factually incompatible with each other—does not mean that average Israelites would not have thought that such series of events had really taken place in the past.[2]

Thus in the form of books with no theologies and no dogmas the biblical collection as a whole and the Old Testament in particular contain *substantially the same thing* as what the church will later formulate under another literary

36

genre: creeds and anathemas. It should be noted, however, that I say "substantially the same thing," since one cannot go from one literary genre to another with impunity. That is especially true when the movement goes between what we could regard as the two poles of this spectrum which extends from what is most iconic to what is most digital in these matters, which have to do with the meaning of human life.

Of the several differences noted in this movement there is one that especially stands out. This difference is important theologically, although there is no reason to exaggerate it and turn difference into opposition. This difference is that a story does not have the effect of dividing (at least that is not its first effect). Two persons can listen to the same story, and even though one of them regards it as false or highly imaginary, he or she will not thereby be aroused to enmity with another person for whom what is related really happened. Moreover, one does not always come to the deeper level—that which makes the account paradigmatic—in a conscious way, at least upon the first hearing. By contrast, the now classic way of expressing what is dogmatic leads one who hears the literary genre that normally goes along with or transmits it, to raise the question: "Is this the *truth*?" Moreover, it should be emphasized that we need not assume that it is only or even primarily those who accept the materially true part of the account who will raise the question and answer it in the deepest way.

I was saying that we need not exaggerate this difference. We are all familiar with stories that repel, make enemies, and create division. After all, the "iconic" likewise has an intimate connection with truth, although it may not be expressed in the same way. Ultimately, it can divide people who listen to the story. In this connection I recall an example in a humorous book (*Los Cuadernos del Mayor Thompson*, by P. Daninos) on the differences between the English and the French. A married couple whose son was being educated for a period in one country and then in the other, complained that in England he was taught that as a shepherd Joan of Arc had heard "voices" (*in quotes*) calling her to liberate France, while in France he was taught that she had heard voices (*no quotation marks!*).

A particular kind of thought and opinion different from (and even opposed to) other kinds can be transmitted through stories. The transmission will be more diffused and slower than what is carried by an "anathema," but it may seep much further down.

Thus after the Babylonian exile when Israel began to formulate the "hypothesis" that perhaps Yahweh's hand need not be regarded as intervening in events in accordance with the morality of those involved, such a hypothesis encounters resistance as "heretical"—or to put it better, as a kind of betrayal of the "opinions" of the national community. To turn it into a thesis would draw down an "excommunication."

This is the experience the author of Psalm 73 undergoes:

> I almost *lost my balance*;
>   my feet all but slipped,
> Because I was envious of the arrogant when I saw them

> prosper though they were wicked.
> ... And they say, "How does God know?"
> And "Is there any knowledge in the Most High?"
> Such, then, are the wicked;
> always carefree, while they increase in wealth.
>   [Ps. 73:2–3, 11–12]

But a "dogmatic" fear restrains him at the edge of the precipice. "Had I thought, 'I will speak as they do,' I had *been false to the fellowship of your children"* (73:15). This is the problem, now explicitly "dogmatic," which demands deep and difficult reflection: "Though I tried to understand this/ it seemed to me too difficult" (73:16).[3]

Indeed, this task is as difficult as that facing theologians a few years ago (before Vatican II) if they wanted to follow the signs of the time, and were moderately aware of developments in (New Testament) biblical theology, and wanted to make those signs compatible with orthodox faith. The problem of reconciling the dogma that only those who specifically and visibly joined the Catholic Church before death (Council of Florence 1438–1445; see D. 714) could be saved with the growing conviction that God offered a share in the paschal mystery of salvation to all people of good will was just one example among so many similar dogmatic anxieties (and acts of courage) in the history of the church.

Thus the study undertaken in the previous chapter leaves us facing a new set of issues, which will be our object in this chapter. It is becoming clear that with various literary genres the Old Testament represents a theological reflection on transcendent data in process, and that these data are marvelously rich and varied so that they could (and should, at least for the sake of Christian theology) be translated into another (theologically more unified) language, without losing their most meaningful elements, and of course without replacing in real life the stories with more general and abstract formulas. Nevertheless, although this discovery is generally acknowledged, we have yet to take advantage of it in practice.[4] As astonishing as it might seem, Christian exegetes have devoted very little — disproportionately little — in-depth study to the specific *content and dogmatic development of the Old Testament.* Why is that so?

Revelation in Process

Old Testament Theology or Theologies?

Certainly there are many hypotheses for explaining this strange and suggestive fact. Some of them seem quite simple and convincing, and indeed complementary. Others, more contrived, give the impression that they are being evasive in the face of the "dogmatic" problems the Old Testament presents, especially in the eyes of the church, which tends to regard "dogma" as something given once and for all, in a single "revelation."

Of course we can find in all modern languages a number of "Old Testament theologies," especially in recent years. That is true, but the plural applies only to them as a whole. As a general rule, to which I know of no exception, no work dares to put that plural in the title: "Old Testament theologies."

I do not want to be unfair, for many of these works make it quite clear that the Old Testament went through a long process, one that was fertile in discoveries and making corrections. Nevertheless, I think the prevailing tendency is to insist on the similarities. The result is that although the process is explicitly acknowledged, these studies fail to see so clearly the complexity and richness of the steps covered over by these similarities.

A single example will suffice to show what I mean. It is acknowledged that at least since the exodus the God whom Israel adores has a single name: Yahweh. But does this *name* guarantee the *unity* of the content? If God means the Absolute, must one assume that each time God's name is pronounced, the speaker is referring to the same values? This question is all the more meaningful for Christians since Vatican II has warned them that they can be generating atheism, when under the very name of God they are showing in words or actions — with positive or negative features — a "face" which is not (and cannot be recognized as) that of God.

God's Self-Definition and Compassion

Here we come up against one of these (questionable) "similarities" I was talking about. We have something of a definition of Yahweh through the *values* Yahweh represents, a definition that begins with the Yahwist, and is then repeated throughout the Bible up to the fourth Gospel, one of the last works. The Yahwist calls Yahweh God "rich in love (mercy) and fidelity" (Ex. 34:6); the hymn that makes up the prologue of the fourth Gospel calls the Word of God "full of grace and truth" (Jn. 1:14). Grace is synonymous with merciful love, as truth is with fidelity. The definition is the same.

Are these actually the same "values"? Is what is true of the words, also true of the attitudes toward which they point? The problem is as deep as the distance separating the Yahwist from the fourth Gospel is long. Indeed, right there in the definition of Exodus 34:6 the text goes on to speak of Yahweh's "mercy," "continuing his kindness for a thousand generations, and forgiving wickedness and crime and sin; yet not declaring the guilty guiltless, but *punishing children and grandchildren to the third and fourth generation for their fathers' wickedness!*" (34:7). This is not exactly what we would call "justice," let alone "mercy."

If we ask to whom this mercy mentioned in the definition extends, we realize that the title "God of Israel" does not mean just a preference. It is likewise a limitation on what Yahweh is by definition: merciful. Indeed, seven centuries after hearing this divine formula, and while referring to a past that was very different, Deuteronomy teaches that the God of Israel is so jealous as to condemn all the nearby Canaanite peoples to extermination. After defeating them Israel is to kill all men, women, children, and animals, "lest they teach you to make any such abominable offerings as they make to their gods" (Dt. 20:15–18).

A lot of water still has to go under the bridge before Paul can argue on the basis of God's mercy *toward the whole of humankind*: "Does God belong to the

Jews alone: Is he not also the God of the Gentiles? Yes, of the Gentiles too" (Rom. 3:29).

That we have here a "process" of revelation is hardly a secret to those who study Old Testament theology. As we will see, once we overcome the notion long held in the church that God is the author of both Testaments because God "has dictated them," thus preventing them from sliding into any error, it is relatively easy to understand that Old and New Testament revelation looks more like a process of education. As the reader will have occasion to see more clearly, the church acknowledges that we have here a "divine pedagogy" rather than a process of dictation. Moreover, it must be acknowledged that there are imperfect and transitory things in this pedagogy, such as, for example, the notion that life is completely ended in death. That notion appears here and there throughout the Old Testament, until gradually the way is opened to a life in which justice survives beyond death, especially in the deuterocanonical books (Wisdom 1:15).

Let us return, however, to the theme of "mercy" as an intrinsic identifying and constitutive feature of Yahweh. Is it the same God being talked about when at one point God is presented as ordering the faithful not to have mercy on their idolatrous neighbors and at another point as having mercy, as the creator of all, of the whole of humankind that God is? One who regards God's revelation as a process will discover a strange and almost pleasant coincidence. Yahweh, the God who in the exodus is both merciful (toward Israel) and relentlessly jealous of any worship of other gods, shifts, one might say to looking upon those gods with irony. The gods are idols—that is, works of human beings—who after making them foolishly set about adoring them, fully aware of their emptiness.

How did this movement from relentless destruction to mercy take place? What the exegete discovers here is that this shift took place *in tandem with* an emphasis on the conception of God as unique creator of the whole universe (Gen. 1, work of the Priestly writer). This insistence on Yahweh's uniqueness and transcendence (Is. 40, work of Second Isaiah) was in response to the religious crisis that was occasioned by exile in a foreign land, which lived under the protection of other gods whom it adored and who seemed to have defeated Yahweh.

In other words, in this educational process, God's universal generosity is seen to be a corollary of the strictest monotheism. However (and the best exegetes have said this perhaps without daring to draw the appropriate theological consequences) Israel was not strictly monotheistic until the exile. Until the sixth century B.C.E., the great Yahwist writings are *monolatrous* rather than monotheistic. Israel adores Yahweh alone—and does so unswervingly. However, while it acknowledges other rival divine powers—thus explaining the "jealousy" it puts in its notion of Yahweh—it entrusts its fate to the hands of the only God who has chosen Israel as his own and has mercy on it *alone*.

This means that in the first stages of this "divine pedagogy"—more than half of the Old Testament—there is, as it were, a polytheistic backdrop against which Yahweh and the exclusive covenant with Israel are projected. Indeed, the Jerusalem Bible assumes that this is a very well-established conclusion of exegesis. There is an unusual prophecy in First Isaiah: "That day, Israel, making the third with Egypt and Assyria, will be blessed in the center of the world. Yahweh Sabaoth will give his blessing in the words, 'Blessed be my people Egypt, Assyria my creation, and Israel my heritage' " (Is. 19:24–25). The ordinarily very prudent Jerusalem Bible here unhesitatingly says in a note, "A passage much later than the foregoing. It dates perhaps from the time when Jewish settlers began to establish themselves in the Delta." If one asks why it is regarded as not being the work of First Isaiah where it now sits, the obvious answer is that its universality, rising from strict monotheism, does not fit with the conception of Yahweh before the exile.

"Why not make an enriching and humanizing theology out of this whole process?" one may wonder. I think the difficulty lies in the fact that at least Catholic exegesis, in psychological terms, has still not freed itself from the notion of God's dictating the scripture. Scripture is regarded as God's self-revelation. So how can we conceive that this self-revelation might begin with the acceptance, more or less tacit but quite obvious, of polytheism? It can also be said that the existence of a life beyond this world was also unknown for centuries, but in this case there is a tendency to play with words. "Was unknown" does not mean that any error was made, but simply that a truth was unknown. So why not say the same thing and draw the obvious conclusion that God's uniqueness is a truth that was likewise unknown and that God gradually suggested it as an answer to the problems connected with God's mercy toward the whole of humankind? There are so many misunderstandings here that it is very hard to untangle everything.

It is assumed that in the Bible God speaks primarily of himself and that God could not even begin his self-revelation leaving human beings ignorant of that which was the central element in divine knowledge: God's uniqueness.

It is assumed, it is assumed . . . The Bible itself tells us something else — and it would be better to listen to it. But someone doing biblical theology knows that people's ears are not yet accustomed to hearing certain things and accepting them, even though the process of learning to learn, the process of a pedagogy that does not pile up items of information, but helps human beings go deeper into their problems and to resolve them through an experience evermore measured and complex is much more human, and therefore *more worthy of God* than the function of dictating.

Nevertheless, what I have just said is simply a raising of the issue in an overgeneral fashion. In what follows, I will try to come closer to the mental mechanism employed by this "revelation" which becomes "dogma" in the church.

The Second Level:
The History of the Composition of the Bible

Apparent Structure and Real Structure of the Bible

The reader will recall that the previous chapter spoke of *two levels* of content in the stories and other literary genres of the Bible in general, and of the Old

Testament in particular. One of these could be called the "material" level—that is, the content narrated or expressed *directly*, whether it be mythical or historical (to encompass the full range of possibilities). The other level was made up of what I called the transcendent "data" borne by the material contents. Thus, whatever the truthfulness of what was related, the value of the account did not stop there: on a higher level the narration was teaching how to punctuate events, how to discover a meaning in their seemingly chaotic sequence and to act accordingly.

It would be good to pause a moment to see the difference between the Old and New Testaments *from the standpoint of the material content.* As is well-known, the Bible is a collection of writings moving forward in time. The chronology is that of the events to which the works refer, not the time of their composition. In other words, today a person standing in front of this collection—*Bible* [Spanish, *biblia*] in Greek means "books"—may not notice that the various materials are placed there not in the order in which they came out or were written, but in accordance with the "time" to which their contents refer. We have already seen, for example, that Deuteronomy is placed among the first five books of the Bible (the Pentateuch) because it deals with Moses as legislator, while prophecies such as those of Hosea, Amos, or Isaiah come much later in the collection because they refer to events contemporaneous with these prophets. Nevertheless, it is well-known that Deuteronomy was composed somewhat later than the preaching of these prophets, since it is influenced by them.

An even more well-known example is that of the first two chapters of Genesis. Since in some fashion these two chapters contain two accounts of Yahweh's work of creation, they have been placed at the very beginning of the Bible. Nevertheless, the Priestly author, writing what we call chapter 1 with its account of creation in seven days, is at least five centuries later than the Yahwist account of creation in chapter 2. I think the reader will see how important a history of the composition of the Bible is for being able to follow the true history of the transcendent "theological" data in this process of revelation by which God guides Israel.

Moreover, this way of organizing biblical "material" enables us to see immediately a very important difference between the Old and New Testaments. The former "refers" to a vast period stretching from the creation of the world until the coming of Jesus Christ. The latter goes from Jesus Christ up to what it was thought should be the end of the world during the first Christian generation.

Of course we do not have to think that the biblical authors actually had even an approximate idea of the enormous span of time between them and the origins of the universe. They did not have the scientific data on this matter that we have today. In accordance with the chronologies present in the Bible, it could be said that they placed the beginning of the world at some four thousand years before their own time. Even so, however, they were aware that in dealing with the first members of humankind they were talking about very "primitive" beings. The Yahwist's references to the development of herding, musical instruments, and metal working (Gen. 4:20–22) are a convincing indication. That they were also "primitive" in their customs and, what is of more concern here, in their religion and morality, is even clearer and is attested by accounts and the witness of earlier (Mosaic) legislation. Even heroes and "models" of religious life, friends of God like Abraham, certainly would not have passed an examination in these same qualities as they were conceived in subsequent ages and were written down in the Bible.

The Second Level and Catholic Exegesis

However, we must take another step and move to another level. One cannot understand the biblical writings without noting, as von Rad was saying in a passage already quoted, the tensions the authors intentionally introduce into the world of their accounts in order to structure the meaning-world of human existence. Consequently we must move from the history *related* to the history of *how it is related* — that is, to the history of the composition of the Bible and the history of its composers.

In 1943 Pope Pius XII revolutionized Catholic biblical exegesis as it then existed with *Divino Afflante Spiritu*, an encyclical on correct biblical interpretation. Vatican II confirmed this hermeneutical direction as follows:

Since God speaks in sacred Scripture *through men* in human fashion, the interpreter of sacred Scripture, in order to see clearly what *God* wanted to communicate to us, should carefully investigate what meaning the sacred writers *really intended*, and what God wanted to manifest *by means of their words*.

Those who search out the intention of the sacred writers must, among other things, have regard for "literary forms" ... the interpreter must investigate what meaning the sacred writer *intended to express and actually expressed* in particular circumstances as he used contemporary literary forms *in accordance with the situation of his own time and culture*.

If we keep in mind this new level, the history of the composition of the Bible, the time span of the Old Testament material is certainly shortened. If the content of the Old Testament extends from the origin of the world until Christ, and if that of the New Testament goes from Christ until the (supposedly imminent) end of the world, the "history of composition" of all this material is much shorter. In the Old Testament it extends from ten centuries before Christ (kingdom of David or Solomon) to Christ; and in the New Testament it scarcely occupies fifty years. The first writers of significant parts of the Bible, the Yahwist and the Elohist, probably lived shortly after the monarchy was established in Israel (that is, a little after the year 1000 B.C.E.). With regard to the New Testament, it is generally accepted that the first writings, Paul's letters to the Thessalonians, date from 47 or 50 C.E., while the final ones, the Johannine writings, are to be dated at around the year 100.

Thus, the "primitivism" of the first biblical writers and therefore of the theological meaning they intended to put in their stories (and in the other literary genres they also used) is considerably reduced. Even so, however, there are ten centuries between the two extremes (compared to the half-century covered by the New Testament).

Thus we encounter a theological problem that is by no means inconsiderable. There is no way to hide the fact that there is no single meaning in the Old Testament; there are many meanings throughout these ten centuries. We have not only a history of events; there is also—and this is what is most relevant dogmatically—a history of histories, or rather, a history of interpretations which strive to take meaning by storm and (why not?) sometimes amount to *different* interpretations of the *same* events. That is why it is so difficult to write an "Old Testament theology." I suppose I now run into a reader's logical question: Which of these successive meanings should be regarded as correct and true?

Nevertheless, it would be a good idea to pause to consider briefly the difference between both Testaments in this respect. Anyone can see that the New Testament likewise presents different "significances" of Jesus. Since all of them are (almost) contemporaneous, however, it is relatively easy (or tempting) to assume that they are all compatible and that we need only add them to one another. Countless works of contemporary theology combine a quote from John with one from Paul, for the obvious reason that they both refer to the same Jesus. On the other hand, it is almost impossible not to see that in the case of the Old Testament the interpretations cannot be combined, since they follow one another. The difference between periods and contexts makes them incompatible in the sense that one cannot "add" for example, the *jealousy* Yahweh has about worship of other gods with the divine *irony* that follows on the discovery that these supposed gods are only images (= *idols*) made by human beings and then adored out of human stupidity.

A Recent Example of Historical Exegesis

I believe that an example closer at hand will be enough to keep the reader from getting lost in this matter of the division of logical levels between the material and direct content of the narratives and their indirect theological content and also perceive just where the theological difficulty to which I am pointing lies. The history of any Latin American country or that of the whole continent can provide this example. For more than a century, Latin American students have had history texts from which they study the events experienced by their ancestors before the Spanish and Portuguese conquest, during colonial times, during the period of Independence, and then from that time until the present.

Each text of national or Latin American history bears the author's particular way of punctuating events in order to present them with meaning to those students who will use those texts. As everyone knows, this punctuation largely comes from our identity as Latin Americans or as belonging to a particular nation on this continent.[5]

Due to a series of factors that we need not detail at this point, today any serious and intelligent historian must by way of preamble draw up *the history of the history* of his or her own country or of the continent. It is not by chance that very different historical punctuations of the same events have come following upon one another. Thus, for example, in some countries, a history that punctuates national events in accordance with the "epistemological premises" most meaningful to those small groups who gained political power in the new nations once they were independent have been prepared and published. However, sooner or later it becomes clear that in these countries most of the population was made up of slaves or of "second-class citizens" and that the events that seemed decisive for those political groups to whom I was referring (and which punctuated history for them) were not the most decisive for that majority population and their interests, nor did the events mean the same thing to them.

Old Testament Theology

Thus we move, as is readily apparent, from the lower level of history to the logically higher level of a *history of history*, or, if one prefers, to the level of *metahistory*. This step, however, entails new kinds of problems. For the lower level, "truth" demands investigating into the "material" accuracy of events recounted as history (to the extent that such objective accuracy is humanly possible). For the higher level, "truth" demands that one possess a (hermeneutic) premise for choosing one standpoint over another, and for determining which historic premise will better serve to open up the meaning of events.[6] From a theological viewpoint, taking our example this time from the New Testament instead of the Old, we have three questions, one following another: (1) to what extent, how often, and with what inclinations has the gospel of Jesus Christ been read by Christians? (2) From what angle, or with whose group interests in mind, has it been interpreted? And (3) what is the basis for making an *option for the poor* in this respect and what is the hermeneutic result of such an option?

However, it is not easy to get down into this labyrinth of interpretations following one upon another. In addition, we observe another difficulty here, one that derives particularly from theology—namely, the claim to possess a truth that is unchangeable and protected from any subjective factor that might make it change over the course of time—that is, that it has a guarantee of permanence and even of immutability. It would appear that the certitude to which "dogma" very naturally aspires does not mesh with a metahistory in which different punctuations follow one another leading to their own respective results.

This difficulty is especially observable in the way Catholic theology (not alone to be sure) has evolved in its notions of the Old Testament. The reader will perhaps recall that not long ago it was still common to speak of the Old Testament as a *sacred history*. The order in which biblical material was presented indeed suggested such a "history," and the adjective "sacred" assumed that these extraordinary events had to be attributed to the divine omnipotence. Thus people were quite confident that the newly developing field of archeology in the Near and Middle East would show that "the Bible was right" (that all humans had come down from a single couple; that there had been a deluge; that all Israel had been in Egypt, and that their growth had led to fears for the security of the country; and that their pursuers had been miraculously destroyed in the passage through the Red Sea, and so forth).

A second step was taken after the encyclical *Divino Afflante Spiritu*, one that was related to the discovery of a second level in this flow of events—that is, with the "history" of that "sacred history." In other words, this was the level represented by the intention of the narrators, and more specifically with the study of "literary genres"—except that this step was, more than anything else, reductive. The aim was to establish what was then called "salvation history." Here it is appropriate to stress the "history" part, since the reduction focused on seeking "true" events with which God had gradually guided Israel's journey toward the truth of Jesus Christ. Without ceding very much to the mythical, the assumption was that God had been aiding Israel, always augmenting—by addition, one could say—what the people had to understand so it would gradually be prepared for the revelation par excellence: the one God would make of himself and by himself.

However, exegetes were not content with this second step of "salvation history"—nor could they be. A further, third, step was necessary. Beyond "the" history of salvation it was necessary to establish a *meta*history, since it happened that instead of providing "a" history of salvation, the Bible kept returning over and over to the same events, interpreting them differently in each age in accordance with Israel's needs, which likewise varied. The "truth" had to be found among these "histories."[7]

Some biblical examples, which stand out in their eloquence and clarity, can help us visualize concretely this problem that Old Testament theology can no longer escape, that of its "dogmatic" development. One of these places in the Bible that stands out, a place where there are two or more different punctuations *in a single work*, seeking to comprehend the flow of events with meaning, is the collection of the Psalms.

Different Punctuations in the Book of the Psalms

We have already referred to Psalm 73, wherein there arises the question of whether favorable actions from God are compatible with impious (or unjust) behavior on the part of human beings. If any questions are crucial, this one certainly is. There the psalmist (by hindsight since the collection of Psalms was written over a period of years by many different authors) was describing his "temptation" to admit that possibility. It was his "dogmatic" fear of being left out of the people chosen by Yahweh and faithful to him that saved him from that possibility.

Since the psalms are a work of theological piety from different periods and situations, it should not be surprising that several of them examine the same problem. In other words, to someone reading the collection, which was probably put together after the exile, it is clear that there were different hypotheses for punctuating events *in relation to the moral conduct of the human being* (as individual or group). Besides that fact, it is worth noting that the compiler of this collection of prayers (and theological assumptions) is very aware that he is including prayers that implicitly or explicitly respond to this problem differently and even in an opposite manner. Thus, I am justified here in taking the psalms as a whole, precisely to better raise the issue of truth and error.

The first part of the book of Psalms, generally regarded as the most ancient (probably pre-exile) begins with a psalm that is particularly meaningful from a theological standpoint: "Happy the man who . . . delights in the law of the Lord . . . Whatever he does prospers. Not so the wicked, not so; they are like chaff which the wind drives away" (Ps. 1).

Throughout the Old Testament the notion that whatever one who keeps Yahweh's law undertakes will prosper is not an individual promise. Rather it is connected to the notion of a collective covenant between Yahweh and the people. In a period when no other award is seen as possible except one received in this life, the significant events are not so much those that happen to the individual but those that happen to one's clan and descendants. Hence, in accordance with Psalm 1 already quoted, the psalmist declares, "Neither in my youth, nor now that I am old, have I seen a just man forsaken nor his descendants begging bread" (Ps. 37:25). In accordance with this punctuation, what is observed and experienced is the series of evils befalling one who shows injustice or wickedness: "The just man shall be glad when he sees vengeance; he shall bathe his feet in the blood of the wicked. And men shall say, 'Truly there is a reward for the just; truly there is a God who is judge on earth!'" (Ps. 58:11–12).

This last phrase is theologically relevant since it shows that the attitude of those called "wicked" is not made up only of evil, but that it is based on *another* punctuation—that is, on a different hypothesis on the relationship between good fortune and human morality. It is a different "wager," or, in language to which the reader will now be accustomed, a different "transcendent datum." Naturally, the psalmist, who recognizes this different theology or epistemological premise, disagrees: "The *fool* says in his heart: 'There is no God'" (Psalm 14:1). As the previously cited psalm made abundantly clear, this is not an affirmation of atheism. The "wicked" in the psalms are simply expressing their opinion—their "dogma"—that God is not present in the flow of events, arranging them in accordance with the human being's conduct. Thus the wicked set up their punctuation on the premise of the divine absence:

> For the wicked man glories in his greed . . .
>   [and] sets the Lord at nought.
> The wicked man boasts, "He will not avenge it";
> "There is no God," sums up his thoughts.
> His ways are secure at all times . . .
>   his eyes spy upon the unfortunate . . .
> He stoops and lies prone
>   till by his violence fall the unfortunate.
> He says in his heart, "God has forgotten;
>   he hides his face, he never sees." [Ps. 10:3–11]

Let the reader note that what we have here is not a narrative literary genre, as in the cases examined in the previous chapter in order to show that the fact that something is narrated does not prevent works from containing a deep theological reflection and its corresponding "dogmatic" impact. The psalms belong to another literary genre, that of prayer, whose theological translation, even though it is not direct, is even clearer: *lex orandi, lex credendi*. Here the events to be punctuated so as to find a meaning in them are not narrated, but are simply mentioned in passing.

Two Dogmatic Frameworks in Conflict?

Thus, in what might be called *dogmatic framework 1* the events mentioned in the psalms we have looked at are clear and unmistakable. On one side stand efforts that "prosper" and on the other are opposite events, summed up under the formula "not so." This negative characterization is made explicit with a figure of speech: that of the chaff that the wind drives from the face of the earth, clearly a reference to the fact that what is planned is not accomplished or does not last. These efforts are said to "end badly." The sentence "for one who takes delight in the law of Yahweh everything undertaken turns out well, and for one who shows contempt for that law everything turns out badly" is thus a dogma. There are many examples of it in that same psalm, as well as in others: the just man will never be abandoned, his descendants will never beg for bread, he will joyfully see the ruin of his wicked enemies, and so forth.

This *dogmatic framework 1* is, as I was saying, a way of "punctuating" the flow of events, and of discovering a significant "redundancy" in them. The two sequences that repeat in accordance with this pattern are: pleasure in the law—observing the law—success, and on the other side, contempt for the law—nonobservance of the law—failure or ruin. This way of punctuating ought to enable a person to know on the basis of an event witnessed, the nature of the preceding event (Job), and how the next event will be—all the way to the end of the paragraph where the sequence stops. At that point, the (personified) redundancy who controls the flow of events will repeat the same sequence.

Readers may be puzzled. Let me assure them that I also agree—unless I am very much mistaken about their reaction—that such a way of punctuating events is *false*. To be sure, simply calling it false is also tricky, and may be guilty of a similar oversimplification.

Indeed, it is not easy to recognize similar or parallel sequences within a flux of countless events or, if you will, within a flux of events of countless different types. It is something that must be learned—and it is learned with great effort and with the help of others. One of the ways often taken in teaching this necessary punctuation consists of creating *artificial* sequences, which have the advantage of being simpler than the confusion and variegated quality of reality, just as a novel (or artificial life) as fiction leaves aside an infinite number of details that would make a narration striving to be "completely realistic" tedious and obscure. The very details of everyday life often do not allow one to see the skeleton of events that the novel presents to us in the form of a "plot."

Any learning, at least among human beings, begins with the recognition of sequences that our teachers have prepared "in the laboratory": if we manage to recognize the sequence and do what we are told, we are given a reward. Such a piece of candy, a reward, is called a "reinforcement" in the jargon of specialists in psychology or education, and in other terminology it could be called the appropriate response to a redundancy in events. Thus, reality as somewhat arranged and simplified, to be sure, provides us with the kind of sequences discovered in the psalms we were examining.

We can thereby understand something as ordinary as the fact that the first steps of human education are characterized by the decisive importance of "stories" or narratives—and the equally important fact that these paradigmatic sequences are extremely simple, and by the same token, present a kind of series that ends in reward or punishment.

That is why I said that it was perhaps too much to claim that the "dogma" to which I was referring (that everything turns up well for one who fulfills the law and vice versa) was utterly *false*. Indeed, when it is set up as an irreplaceable step in an educational process, its very simplicity meant that the "truth" was going through a necessary basic phase in this learning process. To what extent can something that is part of a necessary learning process and will lead to a deeper and more mature "truth" be called "false"?

Before answering, however, we must return to the situation described in the psalms we have examined. There it is clear that a subsequent careful and repeated observation of the "facts" should sooner or later correct what was simplistic or "false" about the punctuations inserted in them. Revelation performs its task with the support of a degree of experimental verification which inserts a crisis in the previously assumed "certainty." "Events," however, are never right there, unclothed, for one to see and be disabused of previous error.[8]

For example, the psalmist has said that in his long life—he is now old—he has never seen the descendants of the just man begging for bread—that is, "punished" with poverty or similar things. One vehemently suspects that "reality" must have shown him the contrary, at least once. However, we must assume that even if that happened, there are probably two mechanisms at work, now leading him to say *he did not see it*. One is more indirect: laziness or fear of moving away from what one has accepted dogmatically, losing group identity and falling under the sanctions that punish such desertion in many ways (and indeed fear leads one to see apparitions or not see things that are real). There is another more direct mechanism: a reasoning process, whose starting point is one's epistemological premise. If X's descendants are begging for bread, it must prove that despite appearances, X did not keep the law nor was he the just man he seemed to be.

Nevertheless, these mechanisms are not omnipotent. As Gregory Bateson says, epistemological premises are *almost* self-validating. With such circular reasoning they would justify themselves entirely, whatever the facts, if the latter did not have "some" independent strength. Despite justifying mechanisms, the facts at least bring in the "temptation" to change dogmas and to test other hypotheses, as can be observed in the psalms.

It is obvious that the "dogma" opposed to the one we have been studying, the one of those called "wicked," is contained in this formula of faith—or nonfaith—attributed to the fool: "There is no God" (Ps. 14:1). As we have seen, this is not an atheistic dogma, but rather a denial that God acts by creating this redundancy of happenings expressing the divine will within them. God exists of course as God's law exists; but keeping or not keeping the law does not seem to have influence in any observable sequence.

Hence, as it will be recalled, the opposite affirmation is not about the existence of God considered abstractly and directly, but about the decisiveness of God's intervention to arrange events in accordance with the fulfillment or non-fulfillment of God's law: "Truly there is a reward for the just; truly *there is a God who is judge on earth!*" (Ps. 58:12).

It is not unusual, then, that observing certain facts that seem to refute this conviction constitutes a clash which forces one at least to think and question somewhat further. It puts an important question mark after the generalization that has just been proclaimed as "dogma." For example, if a person can claim to have seen many of the just (especially if they were close through friendship or family ties) "abandoned" and many descendants of the just "begging for bread," he or she will at least have to conclude with the psalmist, "Though I tried to understand this/ *it seemed to me too difficult*" (Ps. 73:16).

Out of this theological effort another approach to a solution will sooner or later arise, and indeed that happens. Significantly and illustratively, the psalms to some extent continue to retain the first sequence (or, if you will, the two opposing sequences, reward and punishment) but they make it *more complex.* "Something" of God's absence will be accepted, but God's generic presence as judge over the earth acting in events taking place one after another is not thereby invalidated.

The reader will recall that the wicked man proclaimed God's absence, likewise in a generic way, "God has forgotten; he hides his face" (Ps. 10:11). As much as it disturbs him, the just man has to accept this "datum," but he regards it as a brief interval between human actions and Yahweh's intervention which brings justice. Moreover, prayer can shorten the interval. Hence, without an unbroken solution the psalmist cries out, "Rise, O Lord! ... *Forget* not the afflicted! Why should the wicked man despise God, saying in his heart, 'He will not avenge it'?" (Ps. 10:12–13).

Thus, something of a momentary forgetfulness or falling asleep on the part of Yahweh—who is as it were "in bed"—is postulated by this temporary interval which experience suggests or teaches must be brought into the series, so that the theological punctuation can really fit reality—that is, so it can be "truer."

What is the result of this arduous effort to understand on the part of one who sees how "the wicked ... always carefree ... increase in wealth" (Ps. 73:12)? It is simply that after experiencing temptation to heresy or sin as we have been discussing, the temptation is overcome: "until the day I pierced the *mystery* and saw the end in store for them: they are on a slippery slope, you put them there,/ you urge them on to ruin ... When you wake, Lord, you shrug them off, *like the phantoms of a morning dream*" (Ps. 73:17–20).

The very same device is applied to the group history of all Israel in Psalm 44, although probably in a previous period. In the midst of a religious renovation, probably that of Josiah or that of Deuteronomy, the psalmist runs up against the harshness of events: "All this has come upon us, though we have not forgotten you, nor have we been disloyal to your covenant" (18). Nevertheless, Israel is going from one defeat to another (vv. 12ff.). And so the psalmist prays to Yahweh, "Awake! Why are you asleep, O Lord? . . . Why do you hide your face, forgetting our woe and our oppression? . . . Arise, help us!" (24–27).

Thus there is another piece in the sentence that punctuates events. The series has become more complex, better able to deal with reality, "truer": esteem for the law—fulfillment of the law (keeping the covenant)—often unfavorable fortuitous events (that is, God's being distracted)—God's reaction and the final victory of the just. Of course there is the opposite series: disregard of the law—nonfulfillment of the law—sometimes favorable fortuitous events (while God apparently forgets to judge)—God's reaction, and final ruin. This is what can and should be called *dogmatic framework 2*, in relation to the previous one.

Thus, as we compare these two patterns or ways of punctuating the seemingly chaotic flow of events—of changing them into a paradigmatic phrase or sequence—which one of them is *true*?

The Imperfect and the Transitory in Truth

Warning on Anthropomorphisms

Before beginning to respond to this central question, it would be well to dispel a possible misunderstanding. In the last two punctuations—belonging to *dogmatic framework 2* in the previous example—there is an intermediary period or interval characterized by Yahweh's inactivity in controlling earthly events, at least insofar as Yahweh does not use them to render a judgment on human beings and their behavior. The way that the Bible refers to this interval in such a plainly anthropomorphic way may shock some readers: Yahweh is in bed, Yahweh is sleeping, Yahweh's face is covered, Yahweh raises his head. Such readers may wonder whether it makes any sense to speak of "truth" in connection with such obvious anthropomorphisms. Or indeed, can expressions assuming God's acting in this manner be compared from the standpoint of their possible "truth"?

I think that these obvious anthropomorphisms should not stand in the way of a serious comparative evaluation—just as a certain kind of (almost necessarily) "animistic" language used with very small children does not stand in the way of discussing whether what is being presented with such language is a good or bad education for this being whose "knowledge" and attitudes are rapidly changing. In this case there are two reasons why such anthropomorphisms used for speaking about God should not prevent a serious comparative evaluation of the two frameworks.

First, such anthropomorphisms are not limited to the last two punctuations we have been examining. We may recall that the first two are as anthropomorphic as the last. The difference is that their anthropomorphic character does not come through so clearly as long as they are dealing with Yahweh's "activity." It stands out when one has to speak of a temporary suspension of such activity.[9]

Secondly, from the angle that interests us here and sidestepping the question of whether it would be possible to use nonanthropomorphic language to narrate or list the works—or nonworks—of God, it seems obvious to me that we must understand this language as *metaphorical*. I hasten to add that I believe that is very probably what the psalmist himself did. I believe that this is enough, especially keeping in mind that in the previous section we have given a "dogmatic" version of these frameworks for punctuation events in terms that are much more abstract and less anthropomorphic. It should also be kept in mind that in matters of "meaning," no "digital language" can be coherent all the way to the end. In order to speak about what God thinks, decides, or does, it will always be necessary to utilize a large measure of "iconic" language, the very kind of language we use to refer to the human beings around us. Of course we must occasionally make sure that we add signs pointing to the formality proper to the divine—that is, that it lacks those limits that go along with the attitudes and activities of persons whose nature is human.

Now that these observations have been made, we can return to the issue left hanging in the previous section—namely, the comparison of *dogmatic frameworks 1* and *2* in terms of their supposed "truth."

Does the Disjunction Error-Inerrancy Work in Education?

The first thing that strikes us here is that a dogmatic datum affirmed (positively and negatively) in the first framework seems to be clearly denied in the second. All things go well for the just, and vice versa, says the first framework. All things do not go well for the just, and vice versa, says the second. Assuming that the road to the truth leads from one proposition to the other, must we conclude that the first data *were* (and are) "false" and that the second *are* "true"? Is that not the logical conclusion once it has been established that they are contradictory? Furthermore, can we imagine that the same God has *revealed*, even in succession, *both* things?

I think this will make it easier to understand the hypothesis I set forth at the beginning of this chapter about how little the church uses the Old Testament "dogmatically," even though it has acknowledged that as a whole it is as "revealed" as the New. My hypothesis was that the progress of exegesis has led to the discovery that over the long period encompassing the composition of the Old Testament, a vast number of (transcendent) data emerge from it, which, translated "dogmatically," do not simply follow one after another: they amount to a disjunction, since they are truly contradictory.

Furthermore, these disjunctive meanings are not only about secondary matters. They have to do with problems that are decisively important for the meaning of human life and at the same time for the conception human beings have of God and of their relations with God. Thus the question of life after death (which deals with the problem of making justice and providence in Yahweh mesh together) is first answered with a no[10] and later with a yes, although this latter response is found almost exclusively in the so-called deuterocanonical books or in the theology of the Pharisees as reflected in the New Testament.

Moving to another point, the problem outlined in the first section of this chapter now reappears. A moderately alert exegete knows that the "orthodox"

Jewish people were not always truly monotheistic in the strict sense—unless of course monotheism (holding that there is only one God) is confused with monolatry (adoring only one God even while assuming that there are others). Thus in reply to the question of whether believing in and adoring only Yahweh assumes a strict monotheism in the books in the Bible, we must respond first (that is, referring to the earliest books) with a no, and only after the exile with a firm yes. Thus von Rad can write: "The very frequent and completely frank references to the existence of other gods continue down to the period of the monarchy (cf. Gen. 31:53; Judg. 11:24; 1 Sam. 26:19; 2 Kgs. 3:27)."[11] The Yahwist himself attributes the sign that the exiled Cain must wear to Yahweh's inability to see and protect him, once he is gone from the sight or "face" of Yahweh in territories that lie under their own gods (Gen. 4:14–16). We have also noted that Yahweh's "jealousy" presupposed a polytheistic background.[12] In other words, the Old Testament answers the question of whether there are other gods besides Yahweh first with a yes and then with a no.

Now these issues, matters such as the future life or monotheism—or whether human morality is rewarded in this life or another—are not trivial in a way that God's supposed revelation should give contradictory "dogmatic" responses, even one after another. What then is *the* theology of the Old Testament? And does it still make sense to claim that the Bible is without "error," even in its core subject matter: relations between God and humankind?

It is good that this question should arise since it is especially relevant after what we have just studied. There is no point in trying to hush it up with authority. However, I think we are still not ready to answer it fully. Does the reader know why? I presume that the modern reader, and especially the Catholic reader, is almost certainly the victim of a misunderstanding—or, if one prefers, of an anachronism very much connected to the "dogmatic" authority that exists or is exercised in the church today. It is very difficult not to project onto the distant Old Testament past the image we now have of the author—or authority—laying down dogma. Let us see.

When we ask whether the Bible can err or not, we are asking specifically whether the "biblical author" can fall into error. The misunderstanding, the anachronism, lies in the fact that in those times what we today call the "biblical author" did not exist. The author, in his own eyes and those of others, was *simply* an author. If he was *already* inspired by God, that could not be known by any criterion except the internal quality of his writings. The Bible, this external reality, which assures us even before we get to the contents of its writings that it is "God's word" and hence cannot contain any error, did not yet exist.

On the other hand, the image any Catholic has spontaneously and unthinkingly of the "dogmatic" magisterium in the church is that of an author (or various authors) writing *already aware* that what they write cannot contain any error. Such confidence is the exact opposite of the anguish of one who writes without any external guarantee of infallibility. Even if one were to claim to have such assurance in divine inspiration (how would it be recognized?), certainly that would not constitute any sign that could be recognized externally. Therefore anguish over possible error would have to carry over at least to the reader.

The writer would have an equally painful feeling of being unable to assert his or her authority except through the quality of the writings and arguments themselves (which could be verified in some rational manner). In other words, the relationship with error in the Old Testament, as in normal human life, has an unmistakable character of *seeking*, risk, and wager, the sense of which seems to have been either surpassed or conjured away in the history of the church, at least in modern times.

What connection is there between this very clear difference and the shift from one dogma to another, such as occurs in the Old Testament, as we have now seen through several examples?

Error as Generating Crises and Adjustments

Role of Crises in the Process of Learning to Learn

Thus far in our study of the development of Old Testament dogma, we find a strange feature. What from the viewpoint of a pure logic seemed to be two contradictory dogmas—"for the just all things go well" and "for the just all things do not go well"—when set within an educational process—that is, in a process of learning to learn—did not become a denial or subtraction of incorrect information but rather an affirmation or multiplication of knowledge—a further step toward truth.

The reader will recall that our interest in "dogma" did not lie in penetrating into a rarefied realm of theology open only to a specific group of mortals, but rather in punctuating the flow of events in a way that allowed its "meaning" to be perceived. Similar sequences perceived as a result of this learning process left in an active memory—that memory which organizes the items of knowledge we call "experience" in an existential, nonscientific way—enable human beings to foresee events in terms of the significance and values they seek to put into them.

As could be seen in the various examples studied, such an experience sometimes entered into crisis. We could see that the sequence leading to the dogmatic expression "for the just all things go well" did not take into account *everything* present in the repeated sequences. An important element had been overlooked. In particular, it was necessary to allow for periods of chance occurrence, as it were, unexpected events, in which one was forced to admit something of a divine "absence," periods in which things happened "as if" God did not exist, and hence did not judge through events the moral behavior of human beings, individually and in groups.

Even though this (second) broadened paradigmatic sequence would also enter into crisis for obvious reasons,[13] and would thereby lead to much deeper and more critical theological reflection, as in, for example, the book of Job (the sinner suffers beyond what his sins should entail) and even to the theological reflection of the New Testament confronting the death of the innocent Jesus Christ on the cross, the result would not be a mere rejection of what went before. It does not mean beginning from scratch the task of punctuating historical sequences that were too elusive, no matter how much that might make that seem to be the case according to simple, but dead, logic.

Critical Experiences and Discovery of New Factors

Quite the contrary, what has happened in this crisis is the discovery of a *new factor* — rather than a mere adding of information — in sequences incorporated into experience. Hence if the two seemingly opposed "dogmatic" contents are put into formulas, the important thing for truth will not be the choice of one over the other, but rather the succession that leads from the first to the second (and not vice versa).

Thus, the order in which "dogmas" appears takes on decisive importance. That the idea of life beyond earth should arise *after* the belief that life comes to an absolute end at death is quite different from matters proceeding *the other way around*. That is especially so because what we are dealing with is a process of learning to learn, wherein the main truth learned is not simply the most recent (which in turn will be further modified and enriched) but rather how to overcome crises and how to go deeper into those things that lead to crises and continue to do so.

In this manner, establishing that no period in history can simply be regarded as bringing a divine judgment on the moral conduct of individuals, groups, or peoples, becomes not so much the definitive truth about the existence of a life beyond earth, as the truth that reveals a path leading toward a deeper and fuller truth.

The same can be said — and is indeed quite obvious — of the path followed in more recent times between the two propositions which set forth as alternatives would read: "outside the church there is no salvation," and "outside the church there is salvation." We do not possess the truth as fully as possible when we simply go to the magisterium in order to be able to *opt* and decide which of the two is "true."

The reader will recall that in chapter 1 I pointed out that although Vatican II seemed to replace the formula that had formerly been universally accepted, "outside the church there is no salvation" with the positive statement that "outside the church there is salvation," it was *more appropriate* not to present the dogmatic development that took place between the Council of Florence and Vatican II as a shift from a denial to an affirmation of the same point. What happened here, as in the examples taken from the Old Testament, was the *deepening* of a crisis which generated the creativity needed to overcome it. A superficial, quantitative, and external concept of the church went into a crisis, and when people sought a deeper and richer concept of this reality in relation to the rest of humankind, they likewise discovered that the limits of human salvation were being extended to the far reaches of the horizon.

This was thus a step forward on the road to truth. The formulas which instead of being disjunctions, evidenced this development and deepening were not simply more "diplomatic." Above all, they were more faithful to the learning process God was carrying out in what Christians today call "revelation."

Recent Example of Confusion between Crisis and Error

I believe it is extremely enlightening to apply these same observations to the path leading to Pope Paul VI's taking the decision he took in *Humanae Vitae* against the opinion of the majority of the commission of theologians he himself had appointed to study the problem of artificial birth control. As I understand it, Hans Küng is right when he sums up this journey:

> We can see now the real reason why the progressive majority of the commission were not able to convince the Pope. To judge from their own progressive report and the progressive official reaction of the commission, they had plainly not grasped sufficiently the full weight of the argument of the conservative group: the moral inadmissibility of contraception has been taught as a matter of course, and even emphatically by all bishops everywhere in the world, in moral unity, unanimously, for centuries and then — against opposition — in the present century up to the Council (and the confusion which arose in this connection), as Catholic moral teaching to be observed on pain of eternal damnation: it is therefore to be understood in the light of the ordinary magisterium of pope and bishops as a factually *infallible* truth of morals, even though it has not been *defined* as such. This was the argument which finally convinced the Pope (for the theory of development plainly broke down here).[14] He could not be expected — so he must rightly have said to himself in the light of this conclusion — to abandon as an error a moral truth constantly and unanimously taught by the ordinary magisterium and therefore in fact infallible.[15]

As I said, I agree with this "explanation" of the facts and the argument Küng accordingly develops with regard to what seems to be a conservative decision made out of scrupulous fear. Like him, I think that in this case which here stands as an example of many similar ones (whether or not a "definition" is involved), those who defended more progressive positions often minimized the main argument brought forward by their opponents: when there were two *contradictory* formulas, to declare one true after having declared it false for a long time seemed to be tantamount to declaring that the magisterium had been mistaken and destroying its credibility.

However, unless I am mistaken about Hans Küng's moral conclusions, he is attacking the decision precisely for not having had the humility needed to make such a confession. In other words, Küng does not seem to be aware of any other way out of the disjunction. If there is no way out, the only remedy is that the ordinary magisterium recognize that it has made errors, even if in some of its statements it proposes what is called technically a truth "of the Catholic faith." Moreover, it should say so to the faithful even though in the past it has solemnly stated that if they did not accept such a truth, their very eternal destiny was at stake.[16]

If what I have said thus far seems plausible, the true solution to the problem consists in not getting involved in it — that is, in not presenting what was taught *before* and *after* as a disjunction between error and truth. I think the reader who has followed the whole preceding development does not need to be told that this procedure is not an escape move (in which any disjunction would disappear) but a recognition of the highly pedagogical character of the process followed. Otherwise, let it be recalled how in the case of the psalms *dogmatic framework 2* should not for internal reasons be presented as simply a case of truth vs. error vis-à-vis *dogmatic framework 1*.

The Decisive Importance of Historical Sequence

We now come to the last important point to be made in this chapter. If, as the verse goes, "you make your path by traveling," it is extremely important in these cases to identify steps *in the order in which they were taken*. In other words, it is not enough that *frameworks 1* and *2* not be presented as a matter of truth over error or even as childishness vs. maturity or routine vs. creativity. They must likewise always and ever more be identified as 1 and 2, and *not the other way around*. This is the condition for understanding and assessing the road that has been traveled. This procedure is not reversible, for truth is pulling from a single pole.

In this connection, the fact that Israel went from monolatrous polytheism to strict monotheism is not equivalent to going from monotheism to polytheism, had that been the case. Israel's recognition that the very justice of Yahweh required that there be a life beyond earth so that justice might have the last word *after* it knew from experience that justice did not make itself felt enough during the span of earthly life, is not the same as the opposite possibility of deciding to accept with resignation such justice as might be obtained during the short and capricious span of earthly life, out of a concern that justice beyond earth might become the "opium of the people."

Example of Clear Sequence: Frameworks 1 and 2

With these considerations in mind, we are now in a position to return to the Old Testament. We have already seen here how many biblical writers explicitly stated that certain "dogmatic" pronouncements (formulated in different literary genres) were insufficient and proposed solutions to the problems raised by such data. Will the effort to find in these works some trace of what these authors might think about these antinomies and how to resolve them practically turn out to be some kind of mission impossible? Were they somehow aware that they were "forging the path," that they were part of a single process toward truth, that they were part of something like a mosaic in process, that would acquire the meaning being pursued only when seen in its entirety?

Let us leave for the next chapter the fact that the biblical authors were not aware that they were writing "the Bible," nor that they constituted a single "magisterium" whose "inerrancy" it was their responsibility to uphold. If the prophets, for example, think that God is inspiring them to say one thing or another, the same is true of false prophets (see Jer. 28). That is, in order that they be declared "inspired," there had to be *another* criterion besides their own particular aims.

In this chapter we have been examining the case of "dogmatic" change or development which occurs in several of the psalms. The fact that the Psalter is not a single piece of literature but a collection of units belonging to different

ages and authors demands a degree of caution in stating that the author of one
might feel that he was in dialogue with the author of another, and that they
might have felt that what they were writing were connected. The problem does
not go away, however, but it has to be transferred from the authors to the
editor. Is he aware, for example, that in the same collection there are psalms
which from a dogmatic viewpoint can be reduced to antithetical formulations,
to a disjunction of truth and error? I think it will be hard to deny such an
awareness, at least to the minimal extent needed to perceive that one psalm
undoubtedly corrects the assessment of experience pronounced by another:
Does everything the just man undertakes really prosper or not? And so forth.[17]

Nor does it seem that there can be any doubt that the author of the collection
knows which opinion is corrected and how it is corrected—in other words, which
is *framework 1* and which is *framework 2*. Indeed, it could be said that in the
very way he compiles, he is somehow indicating to the reader the overall direction taken in this search for truth.

Less Clear Sequence: The Profane and the Sacred

Less clear cases can nonetheless be found. I am referring particularly to
those in which different writers in the same work describe a (historical or
mythical) event differently in accordance with their distinctive theological view-
points.[18] Two examples will be brought forward for comparison here. I hope
they will help shed more light on this matter.

The first example is that of the two different versions given of the deluge,
which are, as we have seen, those of the Yahwist and the Priestly writer. Here
I will be referring only to the *cause* that one or the other indicates for explaining
the reason for this divine "punishment."

For the Yahwist, the story of Noah—and obviously what leads up to the
deluge and the subsequent salvation and covenant[19]—begins with the narration
of a mythical sin: sexual relations divine beings have with human women (Gen.
6:1–5).[20] The author immediately speaks of the increasing wickedness of human
beings, without specifying in what it consists, and of God's regretting having
created human beings of both sexes. That regret leads to the deluge as punishment and anticreation.

The Priestly writer who follows the Yahwist narration step by step, although
with variations, ignores the sin of the "angels" (a theological euphemism for
those divine beings who have relations with women) and attributes the deluge
to the punishment God sends human beings as a whole ("all flesh"), accusing
them of "lawlessness" and "depraved conduct" (Gen. 6:11–12).

My argument here does not depend in strict logic on a recognition in the
Yahwist narration of the sin of the angels as the cause (total or partial) of the
deluge. It is enough that as a result of this mythical sin, God should decide to
shorten the original life of human beings, even without relating it to the story
of Noah, the deluge, and the ark. It is interesting that the Priestly writer ignores
this important factor in the proliferation of human sins prior to the deluge. In
any case, for exegetes who acknowledge any kind of cause-effect between the
sin of the angels and the deluge the following argument is even clearer: the

Yahwist and the Priestly writer would thus be attributing different theological causes to the same event, the deluge.

In that case we would have a case which in broad outlines is very similar to that of the psalmist. The difference is that here the editor is undoubtedly more conscious that he is juxtaposing different theologies of the same case and the same topic, and is also aware of which follows which. The point is worth examining more closely.

According to the Yahwist, the sin that the divine beings and the women commit in their sexual relations is a *profanation*. As von Rad writes, "now the boundary between man and the heavenly beings was thrown down" (see Ex. 19:12, 21–24; 20:19).[21]

At the Yahwist's stage of theological reflection, "profanation"—that is, a person's or thing's crossing the line that separates the profane from the sacred—has a fatal, quasiphysical effect, something like coming into contact with a high-voltage line. In other words, and for calculating the result, *the one on the receiving end is always to blame*. The result is as blind to the morality of the act as in the case of electricity. Good intentions do not count. Only the "lower" being suffers as a result. Hence, it is not surprising that the "active" sinner (that is how the Yahwist clearly paints the *bene Elohim*) goes unpunished and it is the human beings who are punished (whether with the deluge or with their days on earth shortened).

When the Priestly writer deals with the same case several centuries later in the context of the exile, the conception of sin has changed. It has deepened and become more precise, it has been purified of its quasiphysical aspects and mechanisms, and of its poor aim, as it were, with regard to culpability. What the Yahwist allowed is no longer allowed. "Only the one who sins shall die," exclaims the prophet Ezekiel, the Priestly writer's contemporary (Ez. 18:4, 20). Hence, the latter sees the deluge as due to an overall misconduct by human beings. Since Noah is "a good man and blameless in that age" (Gen. 6:9), there is no deluge for him.

Nevertheless, despite his own different "dogmatic" conviction, the Priestly writer does not change or leave out the Yahwist text, even if he does so elsewhere, as would be logical if he wanted to stress his disagreement with that primitive theology. He juxtaposes two different versions and lets the reader choose (or a later editor does so—in any case it little affects the argument here). Or rather the reader is encouraged to learn how people have gone from one conception to another, one that is deeper and richer. He appeals to their "experience."

Indeed readers in those times, as little alert as they might be, had an important key for recognizing the direction in which these two "steps" were going. It would not take much effort to see which of them was a more primitive and imperfect conception, and which was more "advanced." We should not forget that when the narratives were juxtaposed, the readers were also in the same period as the Priestly writer, and those reading later were even closer to us (and further away from the primitive stage of the Yahwist).

Moreover, any reader who has a "biblical" memory has many other elements for checking this crucial item about the direction that the search for truth has taken in this case. For this problem of guilt in the case of such quasiphysical transgressions of the sacred domain was very much discussed even in the times of the Yahwist and the Elohist. Biblical figures as above suspicion as David did not look favorably on a theology that would entail seeing guilt in such "sins."

In 2 Samuel there is an account of how David, when he established his royal capital in Jerusalem, had the ark of God transferred on an ox cart, under the guidance and protection of two men who had the right and privilege of approaching Yahweh in worship, Uzzah and Ahio. "When they came to the threshing floor of Nacon, Uzzah stretched his hand out to the ark of God and steadied it, as the oxen were making it tilt. Then the anger of Yahweh blazed out against Uzzah, and for this *crime* God struck him down on the spot, and he died there beside the ark of God. *David was displeased that Yahweh had broken out against Uzzah* . . . David went in fear of Yahweh, that day. 'How can the ark of Yahweh come to me?' he said" (2 Sam. 6:6–9).

This displeasure makes David prudently hold back from transferring the ark of God, with the danger it bears, to Jerusalem. Modern readers might find it hard to understand wherein lay the danger, but it was not a mystery in those times: *without intending to*, Uzzah had committed a profanation. He had dared to treat the sacred ark with a profane, everyday gesture, like propping up something that was about to fall. He had brought this gesture that was too human—profane—into a domain where only sacred gestures prescribed for worship and ritual belonged. For not even the priests were exempt from the moral division between the sacred and the profane (Num. 4:15; Ex. 25:13–15, both of which are by the Priestly writer).

Coming back, then, to the story of the deluge, if both the Yahwist and the Priestly writer acknowledge similar rules on the proper separation between the profane and the sacred, and the deadly consequences of presuming to cross this barrier against the divine will, what is the source of the "dogmatic" divergence between them? It is that the displeasure attributed to David had gained ground.[22] The separation between sacred and profane was not yet erased, but a "sin" and its consequences could no longer be conceived in such an external way and so independently of interior morality.

Readers could tell that the movement was going in this direction and not the other way around when they read the line from Ezekiel already quoted, "Only the one who sins shall die." The context of this sentence is an allusion to the previous theological framework, which is being replaced by the one present in a stock phrase, "What is the meaning of this proverb that you recite in the land of Israel: 'Fathers have eaten green grapes, thus their children's teeth are on edge'? As I live, says the Lord God: I swear that there shall no longer be anyone among you who will repeat this proverb in Israel . . . only the one who sins shall die" (Ez. 18:2–4).

Although the problem was no longer that of a too "physical" conception of how a human being might be profaned, it was something quite similar: the "biological" connection, which meant that children had to bear the sins committed by their parents. Over time in both cases people discover that Yahweh's justice is compatible *only* when sin is weighed against one who committed it from within his moral consciousness. Thus *framework 1* and *framework 2* show very clearly the order of sequence.

An Even Less Clear Sequence: The Monarchy in Israel

The second example I now intend to present is, by contrast, much more complex. Raising the issue will to some extent take us beyond the limits of this chapter.

The royal chronicler in the time of David or Solomon regarded the monarchical system that had recently become a part of Israel as something normal that reflected the will of Yahweh for his people. That much can be seen in 1 Samuel 9:15–16 and 10:1, which is dated quite close to the events themselves. When this same story is related some centuries later in the Deuteronomist's Haggadah, the fact that Israel is being governed by kings instead of judges or prophets (inspired and guided by Yahweh) is presented as a great sin, an apostasy by Israel, which is committing idolatry by accepting a custom from the surrounding peoples. Yahweh will make Israel pay dearly for this infidelity.

The first item of interest here is that this last and antimonarchical version does not appear in some other historical moment nor in another history of the monarchy (such as that of Chronicles) but is *juxtaposed* to the version that is favorable to the monarchy and in the very account of its inauguration, in a way that makes the inconsistency quite plain: 1 Samuel 8:10–18; 12:1–5.

The second item, which is even more interesting for the problem we are studying is that the second (antimonarchical) version is an application to the present (at that time) of what is known or thought about God and about the relations Israel ought to have with God. As we have just said, this present is the time of Deuteronomy—that is, that of the final crisis of a crumbling monarchy—shortly before the exile. As long as this "present" lasted, it was easy for the reader to distinguish one version from another and place them in temporal sequence. The second one was seen more clearly to be a kind of correction that well-known public events had made it necessary to introduce into the promonarchical version, which had been prepared in times of prosperity and triumph.

Time went on, however. The exile occurred and the monarchy disappeared. Centuries later it must have been difficult to assess what was positive and negative about the monarchy—both in God's eyes and with respect to the signs of the times. The monarchy was no longer an issue. Perhaps there was not even a clear perception that the two versions standing side by side were in conflict.

With regard to our specific problem (What did the person who juxtaposed the two versions think, what did he have in mind?) much depends on the time in which this strange composition took place. If it was done by the Deuteronomist editor himself, the problem practically comes down to the previous case. The writer assumes that readers will recognize the order in which the evaluations are presented, since they are aware of the context. Naturally in this case there is no anticipation that in the future it may be much more complicated to do the same thing.

However, it is quite possible that both versions were separated until an editor put them side by side after the exile, knowing that this way of doing it would make it difficult for the reader to know which was the "final" theological assessment of the monarchy.

Certainly there is no question whatsoever of minimizing the antagonisms between the two assessments. The Deuteronomist regards Israel's request to have an earthly king as nothing less than the greatest collective sin it could commit: abandoning Yahweh in order to be like any other pagan people (1 Sam. 8:7b–8; 10:18–19a). Nevertheless, Samuel the prophet receives from God the order to obey the people's desire and institute the monarchy, and so the earlier promonarchical version is preserved.[23]

Hence it is significant that even though he was aware that at that moment Israel was confronting its destiny as Yahweh's people, the person who juxtaposed the accounts, whoever it was, did not want to suppress (as erroneous) the promonarchical version or did not dare to do so. As the reader will have realized, the reason was not that he regarded the old version as sacred or even "biblical." That notion and the absolutization that went along with it did not exist at the time when the editor was dealing with the materials in the text that has come down to us.

Naturally, we should be aware of the fact that there was a great deal of respect for ancient writings in general and that this respect played a role in the preservation of older notions that were later surpassed. That does not explain everything, however. Respect for what is old is not so great as to prevent placing alongside it things that to some extent correct it as erroneous or stand against it for the sake of a deeper truth.

This procedure does show that those postexile editors — and here they are not an exception in the Bible — had a vision of truth that was much more closely linked to the creative process of a tradition, and much further away from any timeless absolutization of a "dogmatic" formula. It was, if you will, a more "ecological" notion of the mind in its journey toward truth, than what is the norm today in this realm of dogma.

All of this, however, must have been already quite clear in the previous examples. The point being considered very briefly at the close of this chapter, which is already long, is a somewhat more specific issue within this problem. If the editor is juxtaposing these two conceptions of the origin of the monarchy some time after the exile, it would be appropriate to ask him: What did you think would happen in the heads of your readers? Would they know how to get their bearings and recognize the creative sequence in which the two ideas had arisen? Was he not concerned that they might go off in the wrong direction?

It is hard to answer these questions. For one thing, it is logical to assume that the very fact that he put these two conceptions side by side means that he did not regard which one the reader would choose as a matter of life and death. It is as though one might say: the best answer to the problem is forcing the student to think. Indeed, if we are to judge this question by the result, Israel as a whole did not make a choice. Actually, the Old Testament shows that *both lines* of thought on the theological assessment of the monarchy underwent considerable further development.

On the one hand, works written or put together after the exile gather a very valuable kind of material we could call "monarchical" in its origin or thrust: the Psalter, Proverbs (at least in their older parts), and the history of the Maccabees.

On the other hand, the wisdom literature, which is perhaps the most characteristic of the postexile period, takes on an apolitical and even ahistorical character in which the (religious) ideals of the monarchy have been replaced by the individual search for wisdom or by apocalyptic expectation: Job, Ecclesiastes, Wisdom, Daniel, and so forth.

The long-range result confirms moreover that the Israel that emerges in the New Testament has not opted on one side or another with regard to that theological opposition, monarchy vs. antimonarchy. Or it has opted for one side or the other without "dogmatic" inhibitions, without splitting apart. Tradition has followed both lines in parallel (and has even added others). A more popular current yearns for the glorious restoration of the Davidic dynasty as a central element in the hope of Israel. In Jesus' time that line is represented by zealot guerrillas. Other currents seeking guidance more directly from Yahweh leave aside any interest in transformation within history and devote themselves to worship and pragmatic wisdom (Sadducees) or strict observance of the law (Pharisees).

How these (final?) results are evaluated can vary, but the Old Testament books that led to them, and the literary procedures used, as we have been able to see in these examples, constitute, in the eyes of the church which is going to write the New Testament with its own message, an educational process which is "inspired" by God. Hence it cannot be revised. As Vatican II will say, this "true divine pedagogy" (DV 5) still has much to say and teach. There is a "magisterium" at work within it, although where it lies may not be very clear. The next two chapters will be devoted to this question.

CHAPTER 4

Inspiration and Inerrancy

In the previous chapters, especially the last one, the reader may have perceived that a degree of violence has been done to the overall content of the Old Testament. There would be nothing strange about that, since such has been its fate almost since the beginnings of Christianity. It has been forced to serve as an introduction to Jesus of Nazareth. I believe, nevertheless, that despite whatever reservations should be made, in the two previous chapters I have made a certain sincere effort to respect it for its own sake.

Obviously, the very title of this "part" of the Bible forces it to serve as an introduction to the "part" that comes afterwards. What is past is always the introduction to a present. In the Bible the Old Testament was forced, as it were, to point toward what happened in Israel with Jesus Christ—that is why it is called "old." That amounted to forcing this collection, which already had a limited meaning, onto a Procrustean bed: to be reduced to acting as a prolegomenon that might make the contents of the "New" Testament possible, understandable, and plausible.

Today the most perceptive Catholic exegetes have become aware—after having sinned a great deal in the past—that if the Old Testament goes beyond the bounds of the "official" exegesis of Judaism, it is also richer and more open than its interpretation and usage at the hands of "official" Christianity.[1]

It is all the more important to reflect on this situation insofar as the church's usage of the Old Testament will furnish the ingenuous reader with a good measure of surprise. If ordinary Christians with an average knowledge of the Bible are asked what they "believe" in the Old Testament with the same religious faith with which they accept a Christian dogma or an article of the creed, their answer will almost certainly come in one of two strange forms: "everything" or "almost nothing." There is no reason to doubt the sincerity of such answers, but they are clearly evasive. They also attest to the violence or force used against what comes before Jesus Christ in the Bible.

When the answer is an emphatic "everything," it generally means an *empty everything*. That is, such ordinary Christians would have a hard time detailing the parts or specific elements making up this "everything." Their response is really the same as what was learned in the old catechisms about "Catholic

64

dogma": I believe everything holy mother the church believes and teaches.

The answer "almost nothing" reveals more thought and a greater theological culture. It goes along with the way the Old Testament was *used* for centuries until very recently in Christian preaching, liturgy, and catechesis. In practice the Old Testament served as a pastoral tool in two ways: properly expurgated, it provided a series of edifying stories (aimed more at moral behavior than at faith in the strict sense); and it was a privileged place for Christian apologetics, which drew on a few very well-known texts, which seemed to offer very clear and quasimiraculous prophecies of the coming of Jesus the messiah.

Apparently centuries before Jesus came into the world, the prophets saw him with wonderful detail, even though he was far off in the distance. For example, "A virgin will conceive a son and will name him Emmanuel" (= God-with-us); or the songs of the Suffering Servant of Yahweh, with their frightening and very exact details: "I gave my back to those who beat me, my cheeks to those who plucked my beard; my face I did not shield from buffets and spit-ting."[2]

People thus had the impression that the fact that the Old Testament flowed in this fashion into the New was something of a magnificent and persuasive miracle—or that it was at least a moral education by means of which God led a resistant and uncultured people (described that way by the Bible itself on almost every page) to the entrance way into the sublime demands of the gospel, remaining there and pointing respectfully toward that entrance. That was why the moralizing "epistle" occupied such an obviously secondary place (especially when it came from the Old Testament) vis-à-vis the theologically definitive and supposedly clear teaching of the "gospel" in the liturgical cycle of the Mass.[3]

In the Roman Catholic Church the decisive theoretical shift in exegesis, which was (unintentionally) destined to enhance appreciation of the Old Testament, was the result of Pius XII's 1943 encyclical *Divino Afflante Spiritu*. Although it took time for the magnitude of the change to be noted and to have dogmatic influence, it was decisively important in subsequent decades and up to the present day. In 1965 the Vatican II document *Dei Verbum* marked an important stage in this journey by both confirming this change in practice and deepening it theoretically.

Neither of these documents actually constituted a radical innovation in scholarly exegesis. They were, however, an innovation insofar as Catholic exegesis had the bad habit of putting interpretation at the service of previously established "dogma." What these documents did was to get Catholic exegesis to move along the same line in terms of scholarly rigor as that which was common among Protestants—except for fundamentalists, of course. Proper autonomy had to be allowed to the interpretation of the Bible, to what the Bible "intended to say," or if one prefers, to what the human authors really meant in what they wrote.

This pursuit of what was called, perhaps unfortunately, the "literal meaning" (in place of striving for forced meanings intended to provide support for theological opinions) was made official in the following passage of *Dei Verbum*:

Since God speaks in sacred Scripture *through men* in human fashion, the interpreter of sacred Scripture, in order to see clearly what *God* wanted to communicate to us, should carefully investigate what meaning the sacred writers *really intended*, and what God wanted to manifest *by means of their words*.

Those who search out the intention of the sacred writers must, among other things, have regard for "literary forms" ... The interpreter must investigate what meaning the sacred writer *intended to express and actually expressed* in particular circumstances *as he used contemporary literary forms in accordance with the situation of his own time and culture*. [*Dei Verbum* 12][4]

Readers will correctly say that the previous chapters, especially the first two, have amply justified the accent placed on literary genres. That will not be the source of the uneasy feeling that Old Testament exegesis is somehow being pushed too hard.

The fact is that in the previous chapter the center of interest shifted from the problem of finding the appropriate literary genres to that of inquiring about the *truthfulness* of what was being communicated through them. This question takes for granted another of the elements pointed out in the *Dei Verbum* text just quoted—namely, that God wanted to communicate something to us, which is tantamount to saying that this "something" must *necessarily be true*.

In other words, in the previous chapter the problem of the Bible's "inerrancy" precisely because it is "God's word" began to come to the fore. Although *Dei Verbum* does not seem to be aware of it, this problem introduces a possibly dangerous anachronism into Old Testament interpretation, putting pressure on it to the extent that it is being asked about something that its writers do not intend to, or even cannot, answer.

They cannot answer because when they are writing it does not occur to them that their writings are part of the "Bible," or collection of God's words. Since they have no such awareness, they do not perceive that they have any relationship to a divine support for which they also bear responsibility. The possibility that they might fall into error and have to correct it or be corrected by others later on does not weigh more heavily on them than on any other writer. Hence it is doing violence to them to raise questions to them that they had not the slightest intention of answering, or at least did not intend to do so with such clear-cut intentions.

How, when, and why were they granted this seal of "inerrancy" by the inclusion of their writings—some of them—into the "sacred scriptures," while other similar writings were not included? In this chapter I will try to examine the *theological* answer that has been offered to these questions, and in the next chapter I will deal with the corresponding *historical* answer.

Thus this chapter and the next will discuss the drawbacks of an exegesis based on the hermeneutical *assumption* that the biblical writers were divinely inspired. I am not doing so out of a lack of belief in such inspiration, it should be noted, but because an exegesis already sure of what such inspiration (and its consequent inerrancy) is about, before it examines the history of how it came to be acknowledged, does double violence to the texts against the express and perhaps still naive intention of *Dei Verbum*.

Divine Inspiration of the Old Testament?

Questioning the Continuity between the Two Testaments

The first Christians were adherents of the Jewish religion. While Paul is devoted to the gentiles as an apostle, he still regards himself as belonging to the religion of his ancestors, even though he recognizes that "orthodox" Judaism relegates him to the category of "sectarian" or "heretic." What are presently two religions remained one for some time, even after tensions had arisen within this common trunk. The process of separation is observable in the synoptics in the different ways Luke and Matthew recall Jesus' words on *the reason* for not putting a new patch on an old garment (Lk. 5:36 and Mt. 9:16). Even though the separation has taken place in many places and even though Christians are not regarded as "orthodox" adherents of Judaism, Matthew sees Jesus as a "culmination" of Jewish religion (Mt. 5:17–18). It is the other side that is "heterodox," the generation that is "adulterous"—that is, unfaithful to Yahweh—in accordance with the classic metaphorical use of that adjective in the Bible (Mt. 12:39; 16:4).

A common trait both before and after the split is that theological matters are not autonomous. Theology is an effort to raise to intellectual comprehension—so it can then become intelligent and humanizing practice—what is transmitted in those sacred "scriptures" that we (Christians) now call the *Old* Testament.

This was first a *fact*—something imposed by events. Jesus appears within the Jewish religion and refers to the Jewish "scriptures" as something representing the word of his God. Later when Christians go back to reading these scriptures for the first time without Jesus, they find that Jesus of Nazareth is prefigured and announced in them. They can attribute this miracle or "sign" only to God. Hence, Christian "theology" reaffirms that the sacred Jewish scriptures are indeed inspired by God (2 Tim. 3:16).

This *fact* lasts only a moment, however. As soon as the Christian message becomes sure of itself and independent, its theological view of the Old Testament becomes quite critical. Granting that "some things" in that Testament can be regarded as prophecies of Jesus' life and message, what is to be said of the remainder, about everything charged to God in the Jewish scriptures—that is, attributed to God as God's word?

If the memory of the early Christians and the evangelists is accurate, Jesus himself begins that critical process. Recall, for example, the six parallel expressions which Jesus is said to have used, proclaiming so radical a change between yesterday and today that it is now no longer clear who was speaking yesterday: "It was said to you . . . But I tell you. . ." (Mt. 5:21). In these six cases, what comes after the "it was said to you" (or some other equivalent expression) is the *biblical* quotation of a word or commandment attributed to Yahweh.

Hence it is not surprising that a more intelligent or more alert reader of the

Christian gospel would end up raising the issue: How logical was it to continue to profess that the Jewish scriptures were God's word, when one accepted the faith proposed by Jesus? Indeed it was only about one hundred years after Jesus' death that Marcion declared that the *entire* Old Testament was not inspired by God.

Or at least—in order to come a little closer to this thinking that called into question the very source of "Christian" theology—the Old Testament was not presented as inspired by *the same God* as the New. In other words, the objection seemed to destroy the very argument that we have been making thus far: that the Old Testament represented a process in which each crisis made it necessary to take one more step toward the truth. That idea was now being challenged.

There were certainly arguments that could be put forward. Did not the claim that this whole pursuit had always been heading in the direction of the same "merciful and faithful" God (as in section 1 of the previous chapter), toward the Father of whom Jesus talked, run up against proofs to the contrary? One need only read passages such as those I am about to cite.

The reader will recall what was said about Deuteronomy. In 20:10–17, Yahweh's will and explicit command is presented in this way: "When you march to attack a city, first offer it terms of peace ... But if it refuses to make peace with you ... lay siege to it, and when the Lord, your God, delivers it into your hand, put every male in it to the sword; but the women and children and livestock and all else in it that is worth plundering you may take as your booty ... This is how you shall deal with *any city at a considerable distance from you* ... But in the cities of *those nations* of Canaan which the Lord, your God, is giving you as your heritage, *you shall not leave a single soul alive*. You must doom them all ... *as the Lord, your God, has commanded you*" (2:34; 3:6; 7:2).

The psalmist representing with tacit approbation the feelings Yahweh inspires in those who have been deported to Babylonia, writes: "O daughter of Babylon, you destroyer, happy the man who shall repay you the evil you have done us! Happy the man who shall seize and smash your little ones against the rock!" (Ps. 137:8–9).

It was when confronting texts like these that Marcion wondered whether the God who seemed to be supporting them was the same as the one of whom Jesus talked. For are these thoughts or attitudes, which the Old Testament attributes to Yahweh, pre-Christian so that one could say that in some fashion Jesus is their goal or culmination? Or on the contrary, are they simply non-Christian and even anti-Christian?

Of course Marcion was condemned. However, the proof that his objections could not be easily dismissed lies in the fact we mentioned at the beginning of this chapter: how little the present church draws on the Old Testament, especially for dogmatic purposes. Was he partly correct, then?

The New Testament's Apologetic Use of the Old

Why did the church not begin with a fresh slate instead and thus save itself the trouble of having to make both Testaments compatible? The reason is very likely the one already given: Christianity presented itself—and its credentials—

mounted, as it were, on the shoulders of the Jewish religion. It was the sacred Jewish writings (the Bible), that were generally used (even by Paul, the apostle of the gentiles) to "prove" that centuries before in "the Law and the Prophets" of the Jewish people, God had promised Israel a messiah who would likewise be the savior of all humankind (Acts 18:28; 17:3, 11, etc.).

Thus the fact that the Hebrew people, who did not acknowledge Jesus' messiahship, regarded those books as inspired by God which served the Christians as the foundation for more radical claims, outweighed the profound dissimilarities that might lie in the "dogmatic" content of both religious conceptions. Furthermore, despite what we have seen in previous chapters, Israel had been losing the idea that the different things assumed to be divine suggestions or commandments in the Jewish Testament were actually a *process*, in which the (Jewish) human being was moving toward the truth in steps that were always both human and limited (Mt. 19:8).

That being the case, it is not surprising that while Marcion claimed that the overall *content* of the Old Testament was not Christian—precisely because it was old, erroneous, and surpassed—the nascent church, looking at its *formal aspect* as a prophecy of Jesus Christ, declared that this same Old Testament was (Christian) sacred scripture. In other words, it was condemning Marcion in order to be able to attribute to this same "word of God" its claims of Jesus' messiahship.[5]

Hence the paradox: Marcion sought to do away with the quality of "sacred scripture" in the Old Testament—and even in some works of the New Testament—because of their resemblance to the Old.[6] What he brought about, dialectically, was the opposite: the establishment of the list of Christian "sacred scripture" as "New" Testament. As John McKenzie says, Marcion "hastened the definition of an orthodox canon, which first appeared in the Muratorian Fragment, written about 200."[7] That is, the list or "canon" of the "new" Christian scriptures, the complementary compilation of the word of God called the *New* Testament.

However, although Marcion's unintended influence prompted the determination of the canon of the New Testament faster than might be expected (or desirable), it also influenced the somewhat "extrinsic" way that Christian theology made the Old Testament to some degree its own. From that time onward, it became a well-established custom of the church to precede the list of sacred Christian scriptures with the Old Testament canon whether in the form of the Alexandrine canon (or list of books featured in the translation of the Hebrew Bible into Greek, known as the Septuagint, from the third or second century B.C.E.) or of the properly Hebrew canon (also called the "Masoretic" canon, which was fixed in Christian times).[8]

The Old Testament in Itself

In other words Christianity projects *backward* an idea of what this Testament was, but we can say that it is very difficult for Christianity to see what this Testament was *in itself*, as a progressive journey toward truth. It is the Old, and the New is assumed to be sufficient unto itself. Looked at from the New, the

Old works primarily as apologetics: it is a prophecy insofar as it seems to contain true predictions about the Messiah Jesus. It is prophecy also in the sense that many of the things and figures in it are interpreted as allegories of the *reality* that becomes fully evident only in the New.

Here we encounter something very important which brings back the problem posed in an overall way in these chapters. In view of what has been said, it is not surprising that the Vatican II document *Dei Verbum* says that "the principal purpose to which the plan of the Old Covenant was directed was to prepare for the coming . . . of Christ" (15). That is indeed the case for the Christian. However, how complete that statement is depends on how it is interpreted. For one thing, it is significant that twenty years after *Divino Afflante Spiritu* Catholic exegesis had to introduce a qualification—that is, that such is its "principal" purpose. For now, thanks to the search for the "literal" meaning required by that encyclical by Pius XII, we are fully aware that the human authors of the Hebrew Bible were not only striving to "prepare for the coming of Jesus Christ." They took their own crises and issues very seriously and they directed their efforts toward solutions in which they believed, at least at that time. The notion that God was preparing the definitive revelation in Jesus constitutes what theologians call a christology "from above." The point is not that such a theology is false, but certainly such a *theological* explanation should not be confused with *historical* explanation.

There is more to be said, however. Scholarly exegesis—that which respects the meaning the human authors intended to impart to what they were writing—gradually uncovered what might be called the proper consistency of the Old Testament. From a historical standpoint, it was organized primarily around its own contents. Seen within their literary genre and their historic context, the formal prophecies about Jesus Christ were no more than (foreseeable) events very close to the biblical authors, when they were not simply prophecies *ex eventu*, with their own literary genre and what it permitted. The net of allegories that Christianity cast back over the complex and rich reality that Israel had experienced could not constitute the "true" meaning of those ancient writings.

Not surprisingly, between *Divino Afflante Spiritu* and *Dei Verbum* those Catholic theologians who were concerned with biblical exegesis showed signs of alarm. Hence it became fashionable to acknowledge above and beyond the "literal" (or natural, not to be confused with literalistic) sense, intended by the human authors, a "fuller" sense—*sensus plenior*—placed in these writings by God without the writers being aware. This sense either referred prophetically to Jesus Christ or was an allegory of Christian realities to come.

Although there is no longer talk of such a fuller sense put into Old Testament works from on high, what has been said thus far raises again the issue of what "authority" is guiding the steps taken by "dogma" toward truth in what we now call the Old Testament, and what Christianity thinks about this guarantee of truth as it looks toward its own past in the Bible.

The Old Testament as Revelation of Yahweh

Why Is the Bible, among All Books, God's Word?

The previous section could give readers a misleading impression or draw their attention away from the question this chapter seeks to clarify. Such would be the case if the "inspired" character of the Jewish sacred scriptures were attributed to a Christian theological decision—namely, the one set in motion by the controversy with Marcion.

That is certainly not the case. The (Old) Testament was regarded as sacred scripture, inspired by God and hence free from error, long before Jesus Christ and the development of Christianity. At most this can only have made more urgent or hastened the establishment of the list of such sacred books *for Christians*, as we saw in the previous section.

Why, then, is so much importance given to the "Christian" conception of the scriptures, to their "inspiration" and to their presumed inerrancy? For the simple reason that Christian exegetical blind spots with regard to the Old Testament come from *Christian* theology, which not only inherited those scriptures, but more importantly turned them into something *different*.

With regard to Judaism we can observe that as the period of the New Testament draws near, its biblical seeking is centered in the Law, what it means and how it is applied. With respect to the scriptures that transmit this Law, there occurs something similar or parallel to what in Christianity leads to talk of inspiration (in the theological and technical sense of the word), canon (of sacred books), and a certain inerrancy (which appeals to faith in its truth).

Independently of whether the Gospels judge them fairly or not, in the New Testament the Jews of Jesus' time are seen to have as their starting point for thinking a certitude that everything normative in the scriptures comes from Yahweh. In other words, at least at that moment Jewish religion was no more critical than the Christian religion in accepting, for example, that Deuteronomy should attribute to Moses a "Law" promulgated six hundred years after the lifetime of Israel's great legislator. Apparently there is no realization that the "today" that resounds throughout this book is not the today of those who supposedly stood before him on Sinai or the shores of the Jordan, but rather a device prepared through the effort of people who, facing the threat of exile or simply disappearing, want to avoid such evils through a deep religions reform, and hence they *make Moses contemporary*.

The commentator on the law during the intertestamental period no longer knows what the editor of Deuteronomy (and probably most of his contemporaries with a degree of culture) knew. In their overall sacralization of scripture, both Jews and early Christians have lost sight of the character of process toward truth that the Old Testament unmistakably possesses. How and with what criteria the list of books and works constituting the Bible was drawn up seems to have been forgotten. Jesus alludes indirectly to this theological conventional assumption—which, like all conventional assumptions, is uncritical. It no longer has means such as those that were needed to determine this canon: knowing *when* God's revealing presence can be verified in something said or done. This had to be done, moreover, in the absence of signs from heaven.

However, our concern here and now is not with the issue of Jewish theology, but rather with how Christian theology came to regard these books of Jewish tradition—these and not others—as inspired, divinely dictated, and preserved from all error. That is why it was important to examine in the previous section how this was not due to any intrinsic assessment of the (possible dogmatic) content of the Old Testament by Christianity. The decision to include them was made within a particular category of relationship to truth and through a different theological mechanism—that is, unrelated to this slow journeying and "making the way" toward truth. To some extent, the more this feature linking truth and history is passed over, the more unquestionable and vertical will seem the divine authorship of works which, leaping over time, speak of Jesus of Nazareth from ages immemorial.

Thus we come to the crux of the matter from a theological perspective. Jesus is the center of revelation, since he is Truth itself (which can neither diminish nor grow), and the Old Testament, even while unaware, testifies to it with a vast and wondrous prophecy. Only God could be the author of this miracle. Such a procedure did not tend to diminish the Old Testament. Indeed the miracle was all the greater insofar as this prophecy broke into a work seemingly aimed at celebrating other deeds and dealing with other issues. *Therefore*, if God is the true author, the human beings writing the works of the Old Testament were God's instruments,[9] inspired by God. *Therefore*, since this divine inspiration cannot teach or suggest any error, from any source whatsoever, there must necessarily be no error in those (and only those) books on the list or canon of the Old Testament and (even more obviously) the New Testament.

Authorship, Inspiration, Inerrancy: Theological Deduction

Thus *divine authorship*, *divine inspiration*, and *divine inerrancy* constitute the three steps of a perfect theological "deduction." If anyone asks how these books are in the Bible, the theologian can answer with any one of these three reasons—or claim that such is the case because they have these three characteristics by definition. The argument is the one we use so offhandedly: if they are in the Bible, it is because they are "God's Word."

It is very important that the reader pay attention to the epistemological quality of this reasoning: it is tautological precisely because it is strictly deductive. That is, a few lines above where the argument is reduced to its purest expression, each sentence beginning with a *therefore* actually repeats the previous sentence in another way. It is just as valid as the previous sentence.

I am not claiming here that there is any deceit in such reasons or even that the fact that it is tautological means it is superfluous to go over these steps. The path to knowledge is largely a matter of making explicit what we already know. Forcing ourselves to go through the effort clarifies and organizes things.

As useful as it might be, what tautology cannot do is describe the historic route by which people go from one thing they know to another. Although it is carried out in time and takes time, tautology is not "historic" in its logic. Contrary to history which is irreversible, tautological explanation can move from proposition A to B or from B to A. I believe that one of the most common tautological errors in the area we are studying here is to believe that authorship, inspiration, and inerrancy explain the history of how what was "God's Word" came to be distinguished from what was not.

Thus with regard specifically to the Old Testament, throughout the centuries of Christianity what it means to declare that all these works are constitutive of the "Word of God" has gradually been refined and become more exact. The Council of Trent says that "God is the *only* author of both Testaments" (D. 783). Vatican I spells out that such authorship consists in the fact that all their books are "inspired by the Holy Spirit" (D. 1787), to which Leo XIII in his 1898 encyclical *Providentissimus* adds that this inspiration by the Holy Spirit means that such books have been "dictated" by him (D. 1951).[10] Consequently they contain "*without error* the revelation" that God makes to human beings for if there were any error, it would have to be attributed to the principal (or, according to Trent, only) author, who in his dictation would have transmitted it as true, and that has to be regarded as impossible (D. 1787, 1951, and DV 11).

I have already indicated that, rightly used, tautology has its own justified function in knowledge. The function is that of *explaining*, precisely in the etymological sense of the word, unfolding or unrolling what is already present in a statement but in a way that is still not clear. The danger of tautology lies in the same place as does its usefulness, especially in theological matters.

Why is that particularly so in these matters? To a degree we have dealt with this when we talked about anthropomorphisms. Certainly God does not have any special language for communicating items of knowledge to human beings — and not even items related to that region of being we call "the divine." The only language the human being understands is that arising from human experience. Despite all efforts to eliminate from such language anything that touches on the limited, the imperfect, and the contingent, each term used bears the trademark of the experience out of which it arises. God *always* reveals "himself" by referring to human realities.

Now let us consider the question at issue. Among human beings, what does it mean to be a writer? That one write or dictate the formulas bearing the message oneself. In such a case being the *only* author assumes that one alone is responsible for the truth or falsity of what is communicated. Thus it seems obvious that if that is to be the case, anyone else collaborating with such an "author" must be as little independent as possible. Thus arises the notion of "dictation" in a civilization unfamiliar with more exact ways of reproducing messages such as records, tape recorders, and so forth. Finally, since it is claimed that God is the only author of a "book" (or of this collection of books called "the Bible") and that this book reveals God's very self, the concept of truth or error is applied to "everything the book communicates" — that is, to *all* the information it contains.

It took the Catholic Church a long time to escape from these facile tautologies. I have already indicated that the shift took place unexpectedly during a period otherwise characterized by extreme theological repression. The innovating authoritative element was Pius XII's 1943 encyclical *Divino Afflante Spiritu*. Within Protestantism free examination of the scripture heralded by the Reformation had the virtue of accelerating this process a good deal, despite the resulting fragmentation and fundamentalist reactions. It may have had the opposite effect of halting that process for a long time in the Catholic Church (and in the Orthodox Church as well). Be that as it may, *Divino Afflante Spiritu* began a process of correction that went by way of Vatican II's *Dei Verbum* and continues today.

Human Authorship

What was involved in that process? Basically it was a matter of giving due importance to the *literal meaning* of scripture for the sake of determining the "word of God." Paradoxically, however, what seemed to be obligating one to listen more directly to that divine word also led to discovering how important the human author was. Indeed, "interpreters must be extremely careful in aiming to see and determine what is the meaning of the biblical words which is called the *literal* meaning" (D. 2293), as opposed to any, even spiritualizing, manipulation of the Bible which would have recourse to "other transferred meanings."

This led to an emphasis on all those conditioning factors within the divine word that come from the "intention" of the human being who actually wrote the biblical texts. "Let the interpreter strive to investigate the character and living conditions of the sacred writer (= hagiographer), what age he lived in, what sources he used (whether written or oral), and what forms of expression he employed. For thus he will be able to know more fully *who the hagiographer was and what he intended when he wrote*. For it is obvious to everyone that the highest norm of interpretation is that which investigates and clarifies what *the writer intended to say*" (D. 2294).

As the reader can quite easily recognize, although it does not use the word "author," this text clearly speaks of the "sacred" writer as the person who had previously been regarded merely as a secretary taking "dictation" from God. Now, however, he is endowed with intention, he decides what literary genre he is going to use, and he has a story that we must decipher if we are to understand *the word of God* itself. Of course, there is still talk about the "immunity from all error" proper to this word which remains divine (ibid.). Nevertheless, the logical connection between *God's unique authorship* and the notion of inerrancy is no longer a mere tautology, while the human being is assumed to be an inert instrument. Hence, it now becomes necessary to explain concretely how God acts in order to "inspire" a human being who remains free, creative, and limited to the knowledge and means of his own period in such a way that the result of this double and unequal authorship remains free from any error.

Let it be noted, moreover, that the problem to be treated in the next chapter is now accentuated and clarified: "revelation" is useless unless there is a sign enabling it to stand out from other kinds of knowledge. Now when we examine the works that emerge from the creative activity of those we call "hagiographers" today and when we perceived that these men were limited and conditioned, how does one "recognize" this most special kind of author amid all the rest whose vocation and achievements seem to be identical? In other words, what made it possible to isolate them and put them on the list of those communicating a truth that cannot fail since it comes from God?

Inerrancy of the Author or Divine Pedagogy?

We must not get ahead of ourselves, however. Earlier in this same section, I was saying that the destruction of the tautological argument (as a historical explanation) continues in Vatican II, particularly in the document on divine revelation, *Dei Verbum*. That document clearly says that the men who wrote the Bible are its "true authors" (DV 11), without intending to say, however, that God ceases to be the author. Speaking even more clearly than Pius XII's encyclical, this document states that "since God speaks in sacred Scripture through men in human fashion, the interpreter of sacred Scripture, in order to see clearly what God wanted to communicate to us, should carefully investigate what meaning the sacred writers really intended, and what God wanted to manifest by means of their words" (DV 12).

That is not all, however. The autonomy, relative as it might be, of these true human *authors* of the Bible is thus affirmed even to the point of being compared with what the Incarnation means for the Son of God: "just as of old the Word of the eternal Father, when he took to himself *the weak flesh of humanity*, became like other men" (DV 13).[11]

What does this "weak flesh of humanity" mean? With regard to the Word of God, it means being alike in everything *except sin*. That is what the New Testament says—without adding "and also without error." Nevertheless, *Dei Verbum* does add that point in connection with what the inspired authors put in writing. Hence it says that with God "acting in them and through them, they as *true authors*, consigned to writing *everything* and *only those things* which He wanted," and it follows logically that the books of sacred scripture teach "firmly, faithfully, and *without error* that truth which God wanted put into the sacred writings" (DV 11).

A very brief examination of these last statements makes it obvious, I think, that under such conditions what God wants to communicate cannot but be "truth." What is not so clear is wherein lies the "weak flesh" of human authors who when they write cannot depart from their task of saying "everything and only those things" that God wants. It is true that properly speaking the expression "without error" refers in context to the act of communicating, not to what is communicated (and the point of reference is what God intends). Logic leads immediately to the conclusion that given complete fidelity, there will be no error in the content. In other words, the human author does not err by getting in the way of what God wants to communicate through him, nor does he err in putting it into writing. The writing still contains the "truth" God wanted to communicate—all that and only that. Once more we would seem to be facing a tautological argument.

Nevertheless, there is a point to continuing to ask about the weakness of the human author, a weakness that the Word of God thus takes on. The church document we are studying replies in one specific case: that of the Old Testament. Astonishingly for anyone who has read this far, it says that "the books of the Old Testament, in accordance with the state of mankind before the time of salvation established by Christ . . . though they *contain some things which are incomplete and temporary*, nevertheless show us a *true divine pedagogy*" (DV 15; emphasis mine).

Truth-error, inerrancy-pedagogy: How do they fit together and combine with the imperfect and the transitory? We now have the precise question which we must address.

The Infallibility of the Divine Pedagogy

Infallibility of Everything the Bible Says?

We must still take the last, and most important, step. In the job of disman-
tling these conventional notions associated with the tautological argument we
find ourselves facing the most radical consequence that can be drawn from the
assumption that God is the author of the Old Testament. That is, we find
ourselves confronted with the problem of determining what relationship these
books have to *truth*. Or in other words, to what extent am I obliged to believe —
dogma — in what is in all these books? Furthermore does such "believing" mean
that there is no error in them?

Let me introduce this issue with a significant testimony, that of Xavier Léon-
Dufour, who was an advisor to the Pontifical Biblical Commission for a long
time. In one of his books, *Les Evangiles et l'Histoire de Jésus* (Paris: Seuil, 1963,
p. 25n.) he makes this brief observation on *Dei Verbum:* "Remarkably, the
Vatican II document on divine revelation avoids the term 'inerrancy.' "

With all due respect, as I understand things, this is not so remarkable — in
the sense that the remarkable aspect is not really where Léon-Dufour situates
it. The term *inerrancy* is too academic, and as such is not found in the major
documents of the magisterium. They prefer to use formulas that are more plain,
direct, and conventional, such as "without error" (D. 1787), "without any
underlying error ... in such a way ... that any error is excluded" (D. 1951);
"the books of Scripture must be acknowledged as teaching firmly, faithfully and
without error" (DV 11). Thus, as displeasing as it might be to Léon-Dufour,
Vatican II does not "avoid" but rather affirms biblical inerrancy (without using
the term).[12]

I think that there is no such remarkable fact. Naturally Léon-Dufour could
have written, and more accurately, that it is remarkable that, coming back to
tautology once more, Vatican II omits the verb to "dictate" to characterize the
way divine authorship is exercised in the Bible. Such dictation no longer fits
with the council's conception of the human author as a "true" *author* (although
subordinated to God).

What is most remarkable here, however, as I understand it is that an advisor
to the Pontifical Biblical Commission should show such obvious interest and
even undisguised satisfaction over the (assumed) disappearance of the term
"inerrancy" with regard to scripture. We are entitled to ask — or to ask him —
whence this annoyance over the term *inerrancy*, or over its equivalents, for as
we have seen, such terms appear in *Dei Verbum* and in similar documents to
which no doubt someone like Léon-Dufour is reacting.[13]

The hypothesis now to be set forth is that *Dei Verbum* implicitly points toward
a replacement of "divine (literary) authorship" by the key term "divine pedagogy." That is, God is not so much the author of one or several books as the
author of an *educational process* whose stages make up the content of those
books. Thus it is understandable that, the education itself can be *infallible* and
yet the books that narrate this process or any formula proper to a *moment*

within that process, can contain things that in themselves are "incomplete and temporary" (DV 15). This hypothesis, I believe, deserves to be spelled out more fully for the sake of the reader.

Revelation Is Not Dictation of Assured Information

If God were the "author" in the sense of *dictating* something as information and making the human author say "everything and only those things which He wanted," it would not be comprehensible how the result could contain "incomplete and temporary" things, as Vatican II says so plainly, even though the formulation itself is timid in referring to such things. When it is a matter of propositions and statements about "faith and customs," the incomplete and temporary looks a lot more like the erroneous. In fact, to state it right away, it looks a lot like an "erroneous dogma" which in the future will be discovered to be so. Even if that were not the case, it is very hard to see where the imperfection and transitoriness can come from if the human agent is reduced to taking dictation from God, the Absolute Truth. Even a somewhat deprecating allusion to "the state of mankind before the time of salvation established by Christ" is of little help.

If, however, the incomplete and the temporary are due to the fact that this "divine pedagogy" utilizes the relative autonomy of the human authors (as it could not do otherwise), the consequence is even more important for theology. Bearing in mind that this feature does not change *with the New Testament* since it is also not a dictation, the incomplete and temporary qualities cannot be explained by the fact that the Old Testament stands "before the time of salvation established by Christ." The same cause is thus at work there and even *afterward*. However, we must not jump ahead to what will be discussed in chapters to come.

Léon-Dufour could have said, and more accurately, that the remarkable thing is that Vatican II should leave aside the verb "to dictate," which obviously points to a situation in which information is simply given and one need only decide whether it is true or false. Such dictated information, however, would not fit with the conciliar conception of the human author as a true *author*, albeit one subordinated to a divine "pedagogical" plan.

Now what happens when a human author is drawn into this mission with all his or her "weak human nature"? Obviously, such weakness derives from his or her own intellectual capacity,[14] to which are added the limitations and conditions (ignorances) deriving from society and culture.

From my student days I recall that when the question of how, according to the third Gospel, Jesus "grew in wisdom" (Lk. 2:52) came up, we had to go through a whole balancing act. It had to be shown that not knowing certain things at a particular age need not lead to any error (especially in someone who since he was also God with his infinite knowledge had to possess a mastery of all reality). Things went so far that we were told that if Jesus as a child only knew how to add, he would not thereby make mistakes whenever there was a need to subtract or divide. That was because—no doubt in order to prevent the problem from coming up—he did not do subtraction or division (until the exact moment when he could do so without making mistakes)!

Similarly, *ignorance* of the fact that there was another life (extending practically throughout the Hebrew testament) did not entail error, as long as no
one could be caught writing the fateful words that might result from such
ignorance, an outright denial that there is another life. Through a very handy
sort of miracle it seemed that God had prevented error in the scriptures by
preventing people from making statements about what they believed about life
after death. Naturally, here even more tricky balancing acts were required, since
there were very eloquent biblical passages on the question. Even leaving aside
those texts, however, was not the kind of life led in such ignorance already an
"error" and indeed a grave error? As a result of not knowing this truth, are
not people forced to punctuate the events they perceive in a way that is contrary
to what they would have been forced to do, had they been aware of this key
datum?

It may be that ignorance, and the "temporary" nature of "incomplete"
knowledge, may not *formally* constitute error with regard to particular circumscribed items of information (as in the example of arithmetical operations).
However, the ignorance of certain decisive aspects of life manifested by certain
cultures is not a mere "not knowing," and it is certainly the source of criteria,
attitudes, and actions that are erroneous and often tragic. Yet, as we have seen
through numerous examples in previous chapters, it is just the experience of
these "errors" that can lead to a crisis in the previous "incomplete and temporary" knowledge, and rather than replacing it passively, can lead human
beings to create hypotheses from which they may find answers that are more
complete, although not more *stable*. The reason is that the divine plan does not
consist in distributing correct information once and for all, but in furthering an
educational process in which people learn to learn. Hence the Council says that
the Old Testament, which because of the long time span of its writing makes
apparent (more so than the New) how incomplete and transitory certain "pos-
sessions" of the truth are, shows us "true divine pedagogy" (DV 15). This
pedagogy may be made up of provisional statements, but it is not *itself* provisional—thank God.

I believe what has been said will show how deeply correct Léon-Dufour
was—more than it seemed—when he congratulated himself (for he undoubtedly
was taking credit for it) that Vatican II did not use the term "inerrancy."

From Error "toward" a More Human Truth

Let it not be thought that this idea of the "true divine pedagogy" in relation
to error is valid only for this strange and wonderful thing, the Bible, or that it
was first expressed at Vatican II. It is very familiar in the sciences that deal
with education. Since it is new in the field of theology, however, I think it may
be useful to recall another instance. The case came up in another area of
theology a decade before the Council, but nevertheless it points to the same
idea of how real human beings move toward truth.

On December 20, 1953, Pius XII was speaking to Italian Catholic jurists on
a question very close to, and in fact almost an application of, the one we have

been dealing with: what should those who have *power* in society do about "truth"? Pius XII's answer was disconcerting to some because it was new in the teaching (let alone the practice) of the church. "The statement that religious and moral deviation must always be prevented when possible, because tolerating it is in itself immoral, cannot be regarded unconditionally as an absolute value ... It must be subordinated to *higher and more general norms*, which in some circumstances allow, and indeed may make it *better not to prevent error* in order to promote a *greater good*." Pius XII offered no further explanation. However, with regard to our topic here we can ask whether God might have used the same principle with the human authors of the Old Testament or those of the New Testament. If the principle is valid for human processes, "revelation" is one of them. The fact that God is guiding it does not make it less human in its conditioning factors.

Matters did not end with Pius XII's statement. Some years later, in 1958, Cardinal Lercaro, explicitly referring to that papal address, took up again the "new" issue of tolerance, now with greater depth and more explicitly. In the magazine *Sacra Doctrina* he wrote:

> What is this greater good that justifies and even demands tolerance? In general the virtue that justifies tolerance is prudence insofar as it is right judgment about what is to be done. However, should prudence in this case be regarded as clearsighted practicality due to a historical situation which no longer permits burning heretics, or on the contrary is it for the sake of *higher principles*, such as *respect for truth*? ... We say it is respect for truth and for the *human way of arriving at it*, more than respect for freedom.[15]

The reader may think that this explanation leaves what was to be explained even more obscure. Why should tolerance for error be based on nothing less than respect for, and the primacy of, truth, and not as we usually hear, on respect for the human freedom and dignity of those who err? The answer lies in what Lercaro adds to the word "truth": *the human way of arriving at it*. Error forms part of this "human" manner and distinguishes it from a material truth, the poor "truth" a parrot or tape recorder may "contain" when they transmit a correct bit of information.

An objective "truth" only becomes subjective *as well*—that is, it only becomes part of oneself and internally prompts new truths—when it is able to confront crises. For it is in crises that new formulations of issues and new hypotheses begin to be prepared, and the human being sets out on the journey and forges the path. Let it be clear, however, that these dynamic crises derive from the discovery of what is "not true" in one's own knowledge—or perhaps, more accurately, of what is not *completely* true, or is not sufficiently true, of what is partially true. Reality pushes the human being toward ever greater truth through a procedure of what is called in epistemology trial-and-error. Hence the error that is tested, detected and corrected becomes a component of every process of internalizing truth. In other words, it is part of all "pedagogy," and obviously of the divine pedagogy.

Perhaps the reader will call me inconsistent. From the outset of this book I have been pointing out that precisely because dogma has to do with a journey toward a truth that is ever beyond our effort, it was not a good idea to present each step as facing alternatives of a yes or a no. For that was a way of establishing a complete disjunction between error and truth. Now in this section I would seem to be returning to the terminology of the disjunction, error vs. truth. An attentive reading of what we have been studying in this chapter will nonetheless show that I am returning to the terminology of error vs. truth *because that is the conception that underlies the ordinary notion of inerrancy.* Thus it was necessary to take on this terminology to demonstrate its radical insufficiency.

To conclude this chapter, it should be clear that a "true pedagogy" that is "without error" does not mean that the learner is reduced to adding up objectively accurate items of information.

Thus, when we say we have "faith" in the ("dogmatic") content of the Old Testament—and in all of it—we mean that we are completely confident that by following the path laid out and posted there with incomplete and temporary things, as is the case in all education, we will always find ourselves confronting an ever greater truth, and a deeper wealth of meaning for our human existence. Such faith becomes more "rational" or, if you will, "reasonable" to the extent we do not feel bombarded with isolated "true" statements, but as in any pedagogical process, pushed toward crises that lead to discoveries. The Absolute whom we follow does not impose on us blind obedience to unintelligible mysteries, but rather guides us as free and creative beings, toward a truth that is ever-deeper and more enriching.

CHAPTER 5

Recognizing Revelation

It is too easy to assume that there is no obstacle to recognizing what God wanted to reveal to humankind. Do we not know what is in the Bible, which is God's divine word, both in the Old and in the New Testament?

In the previous chapter we referred to this strict *deduction* whose starting point was the fact that God is the author of all the sacred scriptures. With that established, the features of these writings and of the human writers who had taken part in their composition were spelled out—by means of clarifying tautologies. One of these features, spelled out in the last section, was that the product of this "action" by God could not contain any error.

And yet we have also shown how particularly since 1943 the habit of inquiring into what the "true" authors of the Bible wanted to say little by little led Catholic exegesis to understand that it was dealing with an educational process and not mere information. That in turn led the church to realize that the former classical deduction *assumed*—or presupposed—things that were open to discussion. Among these the last point was that whether any education, including one that God was leading forward through the experience of human beings, could avoid moving by way of trial and error.

The upshot is that biblical theology here finds itself facing a problem which has a very close analogy with what happens or has happened in other areas of theology. Vatican II explicitly points to the main analogy. The "Word of God" in the scriptures poses *the same set of issues* as the "Word" of God incarnate: from what point are we to recognize it and hear it as it should be heard and thus understood?

If it is agreed that christology occupies the central place and is the hermeneutical principle for all of theology—that is, for all speaking of God and the things of God—then in the theology "of revelation" we will find the same two tendencies as those for interpreting Jesus Christ, the Word of God incarnate: that which leads to christologies "from above" and that which leads to christologies "from below." Thus, we can begin to hear the Word of God from above or from below.

The first line of argument, mentioned a moment ago, by beginning its deduction from the fact that God is the author of the scripture, and moving from there to the features of the supposed biblical "authors"—their divine inspiration—is completely analogous to a christology "from above." In such a christology the starting point is that Jesus is God incarnate and that we already know what God is, and from that known concept it is a matter of deducing the characteristics that a God must of necessity have when God becomes flesh and dwells among us. The very same thing happened with the Bible.

In the case of the scripture the opposite route is, as we have seen, the one exegesis has followed from *Divino Afflante Spiritu* to *Dei Verbum* and down to the present. The starting point is what can be perceived—certainly things that are "incomplete and temporary" in the Old Testament—with the hypothesis that a "true divine pedagogy" is at work there, and that it does not seem to be deceived nor to deceive. In other words, this is just what is done in so-called christologies from below. In such christologies, the starting point is the limited, controversial, human story of Jesus of Nazareth, with the hypothesis that God is not outside this story but in it, and wants to be known and understood there. Indeed, it is assumed that when we think we see some incompatibility between our ideas of what God "ought to be" and what we observe in Jesus, the correct route is to "correct" not the story of Jesus but rather our idea of divinity (Jn. 1:18). We are to do so, moreover, not out of love for historical accuracy but out of obedience to the God revealed in Jesus.

As I have had occasion to say in another work on Jesus Christ, the two christological ways are not exclusive.[1] Hence they need not be so in (dogmatic) interpretation of the Bible. The two ways ought to travel the same route although in opposite directions. Nevertheless, it would be better to speak of two levels that are neither separated nor contradictory, nor are they confused or mixed; that much is a basic requirement for speaking properly about the divinity of Jesus, according to the Council of Chalcedon.[2]

With the scripture one is also—or rather is for the first time—facing something happening on two levels, one divine and the other human. It is the revelation of God which will culminate in the "christological" or personal revelation of God. Here also, it is certainly permissible to start from the divine, provided it does not entail denying what is perceived on the human level (or reducing it, in a Docetist way, to being a useful appearance) as is the case when the biblical author is turned into a kind of tape recorder, as accurate as one might want, but with no spontaneity, no life, and no errors of its own.

Posing the Problem

A Word of God among the Words of Human Beings
An example will make this clearer. The reader will recall that the "inspired" authors posed one last basic question, which the previous chapter (about Old Testament dogmas) left pending for this one: How were such ("inspired") authors recognized *among so many others?* What were the criteria for choosing the books or works that were to be catalogued as "Word of God," and thus became part of the Bible and particularly of the Old Testament? We seem to be facing a clear disjunction: either they are in the Bible because they were

written by authors who were inspired by God, or they are known to be written by authors inspired by God because they are in the Bible.

Vatican Council I seems to choose *one* of the terms of this disjunction: "The church regards them [the biblical books and at least those making up the Old Testament] as sacred and canonical not, because after they were composed *by human effort alone*, the church *then* approved them with its authority; nor to the extent that they contain revelation without error; but because, written by the inspiration of the Holy Spirit, they have God as their author" (D. 1787, emphasis mine).

In this formula, the Council, which is following a "top down" formula, does not err. It is obvious that if the biblical authors were inspired, they were so *from the beginning*—for that is all the Council says. Inspiration is not a quality that exists only *after* the fact of being put on the canon or list of the sacred scriptures. The formula does not take up the question of determining *when it is perceived* or how. As the statement stands, however, it could lead believers into error if they did not realize that there are in fact two sets of issues located on different levels of logic): the *historical* problem of knowing how certain books which, hypothetically are not known yet to be inspired (or better, whether they have been inspired from the outset), *at a particular moment, which is not that of their inspiration*, became part of that collection of books defined as "Word of God," and the *theological* problem of knowing whether it was only at that point that they were considered inspired, accidently, as it were, because they were helpful for clarifying the divine revelation in Jesus Christ.

To take the theological answer as a solution to the historical problem of the formation of the canon, would be exceptionally stupid since it would be guilty of begging the question: in order to become part of the collection of sacred scripture the human author would have to give indications that he was not conceiving what he wrote by his own effort, but rather was taking dictation from what another—and not just any other—was suggesting. Such proof cannot be proffered, however, except by arguing that it had to be that way, because the author is included in the canon of sacred scripture.

A Biblical Example: True and False Prophets

In this connection, what happens in the Bible when two prophets claim to be equally "inspired" in their opposing prophetic messages is instructive. A specific example is that of the clash between Hananiah and Jeremiah (Jer. 28). Obviously neither could produce prior verifiable proof of his "divine inspiration." Yet in accordance with the Vatican I formula quoted above, one of them was *already* an inspired author and *therefore* worthy of entering the canon and becoming part of the collection of sacred scripture—and the other was not.

But how can that be determined in real history—that is, at the time when both are prophesying? According to the Bible, both prophets point to the facts so they can "show" which of them can claim to represent genuine "divine revelation." If the facts should fit the predictions of a prophet it would indicate—but only for cases of prophecy—that *another* was speaking through him, opening up a future that it would otherwise be impossible to guess. That position has serious disadvantages, however. If one doubts, consider the following.

To begin with, as has been suggested, only "prophecies" inasmuch as they have a statement about the future (and that is not their essential value) would show signs of divine inspiration before being declared to be part of the canon or list of scripture and placed there. Although, as we have seen, the church has been somewhat tempted along these lines with regard to the Old Testament— to reduce it to a prophecy "fulfilled" in Jesus Christ—the result is a loss of the revelatory meaning of the bulk of the biblical writings which are not just predictions of the future, but stories, legends, prayers, proverbs, or simply prophecies about the present (how God views what is being done or taking place in Israel). There would be no possibility of verifying any possible "inspiration" of the authors, and people would no longer perceive this whole wonderful process of "divine pedagogy" represented in the Old Testament despite—or perhaps because of—its incompleteness and temporary character, mentioned by *Dei Verbum*.

Secondly, moreover, such an approach empties the prophetic message of what is deepest in it. Any exegete knows that "predicting the future" is not the core of biblical prophecy. What makes the prophet a "seer" is not so much knowing now what is going to happen in the future, but representing the way God looks at—assesses—the present, and sometimes the past. To say, for example, that Second Isaiah is valuable because he predicts the coming of a suffering messiah in a distant future (in his poems about the "Servant of Yahweh") amounts to bypassing the norms of exegesis, which, as we have seen in the previous chapter, mean that we must inquire what the biblical author intended to say when he was writing about Cyrus the Great, whose liberal decrees gave Israel reason to hope for a new and glorious exodus.

Third, and closely connected with the foregoing, "prediction" is hardly helpful for recognizing divine inspiration. That is especially true of course when the prediction stands confronting an opposite one. It would only truly be proof in a negative sense, when its nonfulfillment would serve to prove that no inspiration from God was at work there. When prophecy is backed up by events, it is either remote, and is then open to figurative verification, or it is recent, and then it can be attributed to the human insight of the person making it.

This can all be seen better, I believe, by returning to the example we were examining: in fact neither Hananiah nor Jeremiah was right in his predictions of the future—although Jeremiah's margin of error was less. Moreover, the great prophets of Israel were wrong countless times in their visions of the future (when they were not giving oracles *ex eventu*). Nevertheless, they were chosen to be included in the list of "inspired" works which today constitute the Bible.[3] If we acknowledge that they were *already* inspired when they issued their prophecies, we must resolve the *historical* problem of how and with what criteria Israel drew up the list of the inspired books which then went on to the Christian church as the "Old Testament." That is the aim of the present chapter.

Does that mean that the inquiry carried out in the previous chapter has been of no use and that we now find ourselves just as ignorant as before about the origin of the list or canon of sacred books of the Old Testament, including their dogmatic content? Despite appearances, I do not think that is the case. To reduce the number of working hypotheses, clarify the field, and put aside explanations which in themselves may be legitimate but refer to a logically different level and thus serve more to confuse than to help, all this represents progress.

Thus, what we have seen in the previous chapter enables us to inquire with more meaning and precision: How did the Old Testament canon actually take shape? After that, and in theological terms, it will be appropriate to raise the question reserved for the second part of this work: *Today* what does it mean to be magisterium—that is, God's instrument for teaching and leading the understanding of our faith toward all truth? After Jesus how are we to continue the "divine pedagogy" of the past?

Judaism: Religion of a Book

A Religion without Worship—the Synagogue

I will try to untangle things beginning with the historical angle. Let us see whether by following this path more light might be shed, theologically, on how this wonderful pedagogy, by which God guided the steps of his own self-revelation in the Old Testament, took place.

Very few certain data are available on the formation of the canon of the Hebrew Testament. Historians work primarily with hypotheses and conjecture, up to the third and second centuries B.C.E. when an implicit canon has already taken shape. That one is assumed to underlie the Greek version (almost entirely translated from the Hebrew) of the Hebrew *sacred books (Bible)*. The list of books edited there in itself constitutes a canon.[4] The fact that these books are not simply traditional, but are properly sacred and revelatory is plain in the (admittedly subsequent) legend that the translators, as well as the authors, had been aided by divine "inspiration."

However, as I was saying, one is reduced to conjectures in trying to determine with certainty how this list of sacred books began to be formed. The cyclical ceremonies of Jewish worship do not seem to have included *readings* that might have gradually acquired thereby the distinctive character of the sacred, which might then have overflowed into the idea of inspiration by God. The bold hypothesis that Deuteronomy reflected the structure of a religious feast in which the covenant was renewed and its main parts were read,[5] was subsequently abandoned by most exegetes.

In fact, it would seem that at least in Jewish religion, the existence of sacred (= inspired by God) books is inversely proportional to the importance of worship. In this sense Israel is an almost unique people. For a number of reasons, worship did not play a very important role within it—comparatively speaking, of course. This significant fact becomes even more obvious during the last six centuries of the Old Testament.

Israel and the Yahwist religion indeed had many temples and an intense and significant worship, but only from the conquest of the land until the waning days of the monarchy.[6] Nevertheless, it is well-known that this situation changed with (the consequences of) the reform of King Josiah, who in the Kingdom of

Judah, between 640 and 609 B.C.E., unified all worship in a single shrine, the temple in Jerusalem. (The Kingdom of Israel, with its ambiguous worship, had fallen to the Assyrians a century before.)

Thus, and without even taking into account the extinction of worship during the critical but creative period of exile in Babylonia, the cult element is significantly reduced, especially for the masses. The liturgical ceremonies are socially and economically limited to those who live in or near Jerusalem or who have the means to be able to go there for one or more of the major annual feasts. This situation remains unchanged until the destruction of Jerusalem and its second temple by Titus and the Roman armies in 70 C.E. and the subsequent definitive abolition of worship.

Being deeply religious, Israel had to find a substitute for a worship it could no longer practice, at least regularly. Thus it was that first during the Babylonian exile and later with the beginning of the Jewish diaspora in the Greco-Roman empire, a new form of religious life was to develop. It was to survive the destruction of the temple and its worship, and to come down to our own days. The religious tradition was to live in "meetings" which were to take place around something divine: the sacred books of Israel — that is, in the *synagogue* (= meeting). The parallelism — which is primarily architectural — that makes us compare Jewish synagogues to Christian churches (whether they are faithful or not to the Christian tradition of worship) is deceiving, at least with regard to the original conception of the synagogue. It was not a temple, there were no priests (or clerical celebrants) nor was any cultic liturgy, properly speaking, celebrated. From the outset its center was reading and commentary on the books of the Jewish Yahwist tradition.

In practice the first Christian communities, until the Christian "religion" is made official for the Roman Empire under the Emperor Constantine, follow a model very similar to that of the Jewish synagogue.[7] They do so for reasons that are partly pragmatic and partly theological, among which is the conviction that the worship of the old covenant has ended with the arrival of this "priest" and this "sacrifice," who *is* at the same time Jesus Christ.[8] What is certainly common to both types of "meetings," Jewish and (early) Christian, is reading of, and commentary on, the sacred books of the Jewish tradition, to which the Christian communities soon add reading of, and commentary on, their own books, which recall and interpret Jesus of Nazareth and his message.

Indeed, such an interpretive convergence or competition between Jews and Christians around (almost) the same scriptures, puts pressure particularly on the former to definitively clarify the list of their sacred books — that is, the canon of sacred Jewish scripture. As has often been claimed, this very probably took place at the synod of Jamnia between 90 and 100 C.E. From that point onward, this list has been set forth in what is called the Masoretic Canon, which up to the present fixes the twenty-four books which for the Jewish religion contain the entire divine religion and must therefore be regarded as inspired by God.

These are then the facts, which with a greater or lesser certainty, make up, as it were, the skeleton history of the formation of the Old Testament canon, or the sacred scriptures of Judaism that we can trace today.

The value of the observations and conjectures we can add in the next few pages will depend on the reasons we can provide to sustain them. I believe, nonetheless, that two observations, which go beyond the facts laid out, are plausible and relevant to what was said in the previous chapter and thus far in this one.

The Synagogue, a Lay Phenomenon

My first observation is, if you will, negative. I have in mind the extraordinary lack of centralized organization with which the synagogue system functioned. Yet that did not translate into anarchy or a proliferation of sects. To begin with, the system was *lay*. Not only was the president of the synagogue lay, but so also were the people normally responsible for explaining the sacred scriptures that were read. The fact that a priest was occasionally present did not change this order. A degree of control, typically "traditional," was exercised, of course, but it was also by lay people: the "elders." The college of *presbyters* (= elders) who likewise exercise this function in the early Christian communities is not an invention of Christianity but one of the elements borrowed from the synagogue.

There is no indication that this whole system (which extended as far as villages in Palestine such as Nazareth) was especially dependent on a kind of "clergy" gathered together in Jerusalem around the Temple and made up of priests and scribes. This kind of organization, seemingly so flexible and so little centralized, makes it all the more remarkable that certain books were chosen for reading and commentary, that such a similar choice made everywhere continued as new works or writings appeared, and that finally, after certain vicissitudes but no break, a definitive list was made.

Naturally an initial core of this collection was fixed very early, a long time before the birth of the synagogue system during (or after) the exile. This is what is called "the Law" and later "the Law and the Prophets" in Hebrew. However, the fact that the collection continued to grow rather homogeneously with new "writings" and without any imposition by a central authority, all bespeaks a strongly collective choice — although we must beware of exaggeration. In the synagogue and its readings, and (usually) confronted with a different religion and culture, Jews found united two things that constituted their collective identity. John McKenzie expressed it in a sentence in which I take the liberty of underlining these two elements: "More than any other single factor the synagogue was responsible for the survival of *Judaism as a religion* and of *the Jews as a distinct people* against the powerful assimilative forces of Hellenism."[9] If these books were a safeguard for both things, both things were also part of the criterion, which had to have had a decisive influence on the definitive choice.

Historically speaking, therefore, it is not that "inspired" books are sought and found so they can be separated from the rest and be made into a collection for reading and for commentary in the synagogue. When they are already separated because they have become part of the faith and destiny of a people or community, they are "canonized." In other words, people discover in them — with the eyes of faith and destiny — God inspiring them (from the moment they were written).

Note well that this statement is not the same as that earlier theological statement, according to which these books would have been written *without divine inspiration* simply with human effort, and their *being* inspired would derive solely from their being placed on the list or canon of the scriptures. What is being stated is a historical sequence: the books were selected without any initial recognition that they were inspired. They were chosen from among others because they better represented the religious and national identity of a people which had made a covenant with Yahweh. Later when their eyes opened to the fact that the wonderful journey they had taken could not be due merely to human effort, they made the discovery that from the beginning these books had been God's work, without thereby ceasing to have been written by authors who were profoundly human.

Sacred Books about Human Issues

The second consideration arising from the human authors themselves is positive, in the sense that it forces open the area of *divine* inspiration to all the areas covered by these authors in the works selected. The result is a powerful modification of the idea of "inspiration."

The reader will recall that following the direction of the "theological" issue outlined in the previous chapter, here I have spoken almost continually of "inspired" books in connection with Israel's *religion*—as though divine inspiration and religious subject matter were correlative. However, when we study the works that have been chosen historically for the lists to be read in the synagogue as sacred, we encounter a surprise. If we study what the human author of the Bible *intended* to say and in fact said, we find that there are not only paragraphs but chapters and even whole works that do not deal with God specifically, but rather with intense human—sometimes too human—problems. Moreover, if we ask by what criteria such "lay" writings were collectively privileged and "canonized" for the synagogue, we can easily conclude that they were chosen because the humanity they described was vital or substantial for Israel. This reality, which throughout the Old Testament seems to have so little to do with religion, cannot be separated from what is inspired thus giving it secondary status, or simply leaving it free from error.

The Living Human Being, "Object" of Divine Inspiration

If this is the case, what are the "dogmatic" consequences? The aim of the two observations at the end of the previous paragraph is to show how much the classical idea held by Christian theology for a long time on the *object* of divine inspiration in the works making up the Old Testament has to change once our starting point is a "realistic" history of the composition of the Bible and the formation of its canon. In the last section of this chapter we will try to formulate these necessary changes in a concise way.

For the moment, however, I think it will be more interesting to the reader to develop the concrete content of these observations with some examples at hand. We may begin by noting that as long as the search for figurative and "transferred" meanings outweighed concern for the "literal" meaning—that is, before *Divino Afflante Spiritu* (D. 2293)—people did not really see how strange many of the things in the Old Testament were from a theological standpoint. Why not? Because this kind of interpretation left aside what the human author wanted to express and sought a "fuller" meaning in what was written (obtained by transferring what had been lived as process but formulated as "dogma") in the subsequent realities of Jesus Christ and his church.

In this respect, the reader will recall the legendary story of Jonah, the rebellious and frustrated prophet, who begins by fleeing God's call, setting off toward the west, when God is telling him to go east, with an admittedly difficult message. He is supposed to announce to the inhabitants of the great city of Niniveh the imminent destruction about to fall on them. Jonah finds this task so irksome that he flees, but his flight is halted by a storm so great that he is thrown into the sea and swallowed by a whale or a huge fish. *After three days*, the fish leaves him alive back on the shore from which he had set out. At that point Jonah finally decides to obey and to assume his mission as a prophet of disaster, and so he sets out toward the east.

Now the Christian evangelists (at least Matthew and Luke) recall that Jesus spoke of Jonah. However, they indicate clearly that Jesus was referring not to Jonah's fleeing, but to the next part of the legend—that is, to his preaching in Niniveh, whose inhabitants were converted even though Jonah did not show any wonder or "sign" from heaven in support of his infuriating prediction (Mt. 12:39, 41; Lk. 11:30, 32). Jesus simply draws a conclusion from the literal meaning of the book of Jonah: the historic sensitivity of the Ninevites leads them to see in Jonah's preaching a valid sign of the times. Matthew, however, thinking of Jonah, cannot resist a temptation that gets the better of him, although strictly speaking at that time it was not a temptation. He sees there a transferred, "fuller," sense, by means of which Jesus, *contradicting what he is teaching* in that passage, would have taken the figure of Jonah as a prophetic sign of that other, higher sign, that heaven would send to earth when God was to resurrect his Son from death on the third day: "Just as Jonah spent three days and three nights in the belly of the whale, so will the Son of Man spend three days and three nights in the bowels of the earth" (Mt. 12:40).

Nonetheless, in this case the change now demanded of Catholic exegesis has no other disadvantages than that of returning to the obvious theological meaning of the allusion to Jonah in the Gospel passage according to its original source (probably Q).

Examples

1) *The succession of Solomon to the throne of David.* However, the shift in exegesis from the transferred to the literal sense has much more radical consequences in other cases. One of them is that of the history of the succession of Solomon to the throne of David. As the reader will recall from an earlier reference, this history is a long story whose main character is David. Since he is one of the most classical prefigurations of Christ in the Old Testament (according to classical exegesis) and with the Psalms (traditionally attributed to him), the story of David from 2 Samuel 7 to 1 Kings 2 provides a wide open field for exegesis using possible transferred senses.

One finds something else, however, when, in keeping with the kind of hermeneutics that values what the human author wanted to express, one sets out
in pursuit of the meaning of this long history, one of the literary gems of the
Bible. What is surprising here is the—relative—absence of God and God's
direct intervention in these events which are so human. It is a commonplace
that the Bible contains the "Word of God." Naturally that is first of all because
it proceeds from God, who is speaking in it. However, it is also, and secondly,
Word *of God* in the sense that it contains the divine self-revelation, or the
revelation that God makes "of himself." It is a word about God. Now in this
long, complex, and emotional story of the succession of David, which occupies
twenty-one chapters, there are only three references to God as involved in the
events unfolding where so many powerful human passions come into play. Von
Rad understandably observes, "What the alert theologian finds most striking
here is the astonishingly profane quality of the account."[10]

Here are the three places where God is mentioned. With regard to David's
marriage to Bathsheba (after David had her husband Uriah killed) we read
that "the Lord was displeased with what David had done" (2 Sam. 11:27). After
stating that Bathsheba gave birth to Solomon, the narrator notes very briefly
"the Lord loved him" (2 Sam. 12:24). Of the events revolving around the rebellion of Absalom against David and the different tactics adopted by David's
enemies, we read, "for the Lord had decided to undo Ahithophel's good counsel, in order thus to bring Absalom to ruin" (2 Sam. 17:14).

Yahweh is so immediately involved in guiding the exodus or the Israelites'
occupation of the promised land that these "deeds" actually serve to reveal
him. They manifest the values that God impresses on things, the human attitudes most appropriate to God's plans in history, and more generally the transcendent data that frame and condition those events. But "almost" none of
that happens here. God does not see fit to explain through the inspired author
why he loves Solomon, the child of adultery (although not immediately), in
contrast with what happens to the first child of David and Bathsheba. The fact
that Yahweh does not approve the murder of Uriah which follows and crowns
David's adultery reveals "almost" nothing about God, since besides God's
"striking" the innocent child (2 Sam. 12:15), everything else indicates, if anything, the divine predilection for the marriage deriving from that sin. It is a
good thing that Uriah died, one might say, since his death enables Israel to
have the most famous of its kings, the one most beloved of Yahweh, the only
one who will be promised an eternal dynasty—the one, that is, who came in
through murder.

Why, then, and how is all of this work inspired, God's word, the revelation
of what Yahweh does and is? We may now stand on the threshold of an important theological discovery. But perhaps in order to make it we must move away
from a conventional idea from which von Rad himself is probably not entirely
free. For it is obvious that he points to these three passages as the only ones
on which the specifically biblical revelatory character of the Bible could be
based, with regard to this long narration of the succession of David.

Nevertheless, from the exegetical standpoint, it very much poses the problem that the human author *intends* to create a work of *historiography* with this narration. That is "scientific" history to the extent that a literary genre would then allow:

> In the Old Testament these chapters represent the oldest form of historiography . . . The narrative we are studying really does deserve that rather formal term, which as is well known can rarely be said of the literature of ancient peoples. "Genuine historiography, which rises out of a period, always and everywhere grows out of political life, whatever its nature and shape may be" (E. Schwartz) . . . Historiography is one of the most delicate fruits of human cultural activity. In order to grow and mature it needs a wide foundation in a citizenry and a highly politicized environment."[11]

We may then appropriately wonder whether this foundation for citizenship, this politics, and the complex interaction of human interests and passions, *are not therefore somehow God's word*, revelation of God? Would they not necessarily enter into this educational process in which God is revealed at the same time as human beings are exploring the possibilities of meaning in their life and gradually discovering under God's guidance transcendent data that would not be such (nor would they have "dogmatic" value) were they isolated from these deeply human experiences? Finally, although it might seem strange, are not a certain distance from religion and a certain secularity not presuppositions for hearing and understanding more fully what God *is?*

Otherwise, why would the church's magisterium want scholars to go tracing what the human author *intends to say* if what he really wants to say is how Solomon comes to occupy the throne of David in history? And now that we are on the point, Why is this same magisterium afraid of finding what it asked scholars to pursue?[12] Is it possible that as a result of this officially encouraged search, these twenty-one chapters would no longer be part of the "word" or "revelation of God," since as von Rad says, they are deeply and richly political? Are they a parenthesis with no dogmatic value?

2) *The Song of Songs.* A second example will make it clear how the questions just formulated are not some strange madness. In the Bible there is a book called the Song of Songs—that is, in accordance with language usage of the time, what today would be called the Song par excellence. "Of all the Old Testament books," says the Jerusalem Bible very frankly in its introduction, "this has been the most variously interpreted."[13] Why? For the reason indicated above for doubting whether the chapters that narrate David's succession deserve to be part of the Bible. Indeed in the same introduction, the Jerusalem Bible says that people "have found it surprising that a book that makes no mention of God and whose vocabulary is so passionate should figure in the sacred canon." This time we are not dealing with few references to the divine— there are none at all.

If the reader is curious to see how people finessed this tricky situation, the answer is that since ancient times, when scholarly exegesis did not yet exist, allegorical interpretation was utilized. For (once again) if this book was in the Bible, *it had* to speak of God. If it did not seem to be doing so, it had to be deciphered in order to draw out its hidden meaning. The main character of this passionate love, seemingly so human, actually had to be God. And the beloved had to be Israel (for Jewish exegetes) or the church (for Christian exegetes).

With respect to specifically Catholic exegesis, this procedure could work until Pius XII's 1943 encyclical on biblical interpretation. Even then, as a result of the singular difficulty of fitting into the Bible a book of this tenor, the Jerusalem Bible observes that the "allegorical interpretation is accepted, under various forms, by the majority of Catholic commentators today." But not all are prepared to follow this approach which, as the "introduction" concedes, is not "the natural sense of the text," the one that *Divino Afflante Spiritu* said should be investigated first. Hence, others pay attention to this natural meaning and "for them the Song is a collection of hymns to true love sanctified by union. The topic *is not merely profane*; it is also religious *since God has given his blessing to marriage*." I have taken the liberty of underlining the two logical steps involved in elaborating this unique solution the Jerusalem Bible finds for the problem. The first involves showing that the topic is not merely profane, but is also religious. The second involves showing why it is *also* religious: because God has blessed matrimony.

These two steps of the argument bear the unmistakable traces of the old notion of biblical inspiration, unaware of the profound correction demanded by the conciliar vision of *Dei Verbum* about revelation as a process of education. Such an education encompasses all of human existence and not simply the realm of the "religious." It is a matter of leading human beings as a whole to go deeper into the meaning of their own existence in such a way that the transcendent data offered by God penetrate into the corresponding questions that arise within the whole of human experience. When things take place in this manner, there is no dividing line between what is human and what is "inspired" — just as, in accordance with the Council of Chalcedon, the human cannot be separated from the divine in Jesus. That is not because both must enter into some sort of mixture, but because the incarnation takes on the human (with all its weaknesses, says *Dei Verbum*) as the only complete revelation of the divine. We do not have here a theology class or a treatise on the specific things that God has blessed, but a pedagogy by which God leads the whole human being to be more authentically human, since if this takes place, the result will be "knowledge of God" (Jer. 22:16).

Due to an impoverished concept of what "revealed truth" is, the separation of human development from dogmatic development has thus led the ecclesiastical *magisterium* in modern Christianity to claim a function that is both frightfully reductive and unduly absolutized.

I think this will be made even more clear in a third example from the Bible that will demand a somewhat more extensive exegetical treatment.

3) *Wisdom and Its Transformations in Israel.* Pursuing the issue along these same lines, I would now like to take up the question that arises from two strange Old Testament books, Ecclesiastes and Proverbs.

It is no coincidence that the same introduction in which the Jerusalem Bible dealt with the profane character of the Song of Songs, added that a similar question is raised about two biblical books of wisdom, Proverbs and Ecclesiastes. I would go so far as to say that the problem of the profane character comes up even more seriously in Proverbs, and especially in Ecclesiastes (or the book of Qoheleth).

It is not as though the word "God" were notably absent as is the case of the Song. It is certainly present, but the serious thing is that in both books one sees a kind of *positively* profane character — that is, something like an intentional segregation of religious topics, or perhaps better, the religious inclination. It is as though getting this distance seemed necessary in order to provide the profane with its full meaning. It calls to mind Job's surprising cry to Yahweh: "Let me alone, that I may recover a little Before I go whence I shall not return" (Job 10:20–21) or "Let me alone, for my days are but a breath . . . How long will it be before you look away from me, and let me alone long enough to swallow my spittle?" (Job 7:16, 19).

In Ecclesiastes and Proverbs this cry of the "impatient" Job is a mature, extended, and reasoned (although not always clearly explicit) reflection. Due to recent biblical studies even Catholic exegesis, which is generally more prudent than that of Protestants, has come to recognize this surprisingly profane and anthropocentric character not only of Qoheleth's conclusions, but especially of (the oldest part of) the collection of Proverbs, despite the fact that they frequently mention God. Among these studies those of Walther Zimmerli have been very important.[14] Here I will summarize for readers some of the most reliable results of this exegesis and those most relevant to our topic.

At least until the period of the exile, it was normal for the Hebrew mind-set, schooled in the conception of this historic covenant with Yahweh, to divide people into "just" and "impious." This clumsy terminology — logically it should have been just/unjust or pious/impious — can be understood if we keep in mind that according to the covenant one had to prove that one was pious by observing the law — that is, being "just." We should likewise keep in mind that one who was not practicing justice was, in the context of the covenant, not only failing to keep the law, but sinning against the One behind the law, the God of Israel. That is what made one impious.

After the exile another division of human beings into "wise" and "foolish" became more common. No doubt we should seek the primary explanation for this semantic change in the fact that with exile in Babylon, Israel for practical purposes ceases to be an independent nation. It no longer has its own history. Its religion, which has been linked to history through the notion of covenant, is replaced by another more individual and internal religion. Hence issues of "justice" are increasingly absorbed by those of "wisdom."

While that is certainly true, it does not explain everything. The rise of the wisdom theme is not due merely to the loss of a sense of history. Actually, the topic of "wisdom" is not proper to Israel nor did it belong there. The two great nearby cultures of Mesopotamia and Egypt trained and honored "wise men," especially in their courts. Here as in the case of the deluge we encounter an assimilation. Wisdom passages in the Bible have been found to be traceable to parallel texts of Egyptian wisdom from which they were taken. However, in this case the assimilation was similarly creative and not a mere copy, as will be demonstrated below.

We should note, however, that the word "wise" [Spanish *sabio*, which also means "learned"] is ambiguous and that the term "wisdom" is clearer. Today the adjective is used a great deal for people who would otherwise be called scientists or scholars, while the noun "wisdom" continues to refer rather to the art of knowing how to live. Proverbs, whether maxims or sayings, are short formulas condensing the "wise" experience of generations on this difficult and elusive art.

As we have previously said, education is to mere instruction as wisdom is to scholarship or science. More specifically, however, biblical wisdom is what was acquired in the education in or for the royal court. The proverbs recalled often bear signs of their birthplace. Thus we encounter the question of when the wisdom material we now have in Proverbs was created. Its attribution to Solomon (Prov. 1:1 and 1 Kgs. 5:12) is an extremely common procedure in antiquity and has no historic value (as in the parallel case of Ecclesiastes). In the case of Proverbs, nonetheless, and taking into account that it is a collection of such sayings, the problem of when it was created becomes more difficult to resolve.

Exegetes generally agree that the oldest material is that in Proverbs 10:1–22:16. The next oldest is the material in chapters 25–29, and the most recent, along with other additions, is said to be what today constitutes the Prologue, Proverbs 1–9. In this view, the oldest part might come down by memory from the final period of the monarchy in Israel. More recent proverbs are to be dated in the period of the exile and postexile (and bear more traces of Israel's fluctuating political fortunes amid the surrounding empires). Ecclesiastes, with its strange underlay of cynical pessimism, would come last (a little before what is called the "intertestamental" period).

The Wisdom Question: Ecclesiastes. Zimmerli insists, correctly I believe, that in order to understand biblical literature on wisdom, we must understand the existential question people are asking and to which wisdom is the response. It so happens that paradoxically, due to the radicality and pessimism of Qoheleth, the *question* is best expressed in the last of these works, Ecclesiastes, while the possible *answer* appears most clearly in a less pessimistic period, in which the older proverbs are more prominent. The gradual destruction of this optimism (with its implicit question) makes it imperative to make the question more explicit and go deeper into it. However, this question is not (as the reader might imagine) "What does God want human existence to be?" or "What meaning has Yahweh set for human life?" The question is astonishingly less "religious."

What question do the "wise" ask as they confront life? The question is continually present throughout the short work of Ecclesiastes: "What profit has man from all the labor which he toils at under the sun?" (Eccl. 1:3). "For what profit comes to a man from all the toil and anxiety of heart with which he has labored under the sun?" (2:22). "What advantage has the worker from his toil?"

(3:9). "What then does it profit him to toil for wind?" (5:16). "For who knows what is good for a man in life, the limited days of his vain life (which God has made like a shadow)?" (6:12). These are simply examples.

We are perhaps too accustomed to such questions to perceive how radically new they are, and how strange is the direction they take within the overall movement of biblical literature. Hence one should make a certain effort to recover a proper sense of surprise in the face of such a human-centered approach where Yahweh is unquestionably the main character. We should do so, moreover, independently of whether the question is answered positively or negatively. By simply raising this question, says Zimmerli correctly, the "wise" man is putting himself in a context in which it is no longer central to belong to a chosen people which has made a covenant with Yahweh, in which the crucial element is to observe the law God has laid down and to do so "with all one's heart." Indeed, after the exile the central religious idea gradually shifts from the notion of "covenant" to that of the essential relations between creatures and the creator, between the contingent and the transcendent (Second Isaiah, Is. 40, as well as Ezekiel and the Priestly Code). Neither the limits set by the law nor the creaturely condition is being denied. Ecclesiastes recognizes them as limits that reality imposes on human beings. They are the context of his question—but not the answer. They provide realism, but not meaning.

The Answer: Proverbs. Now if we go back in time, we will run into the answer the wise person finds to this existential search for meaning. What human beings can "get out of their toil under the sun" is the positive task about which the book of Proverbs offers instruction. As was pointed out, this reversal of question and answer over time is not at all strange: it is a crisis in the answer that makes it necessary to formulate the question more explicitly and more radically.

As the very name of the book indicates, the wisdom teachings are expressed in the form of *proverbs.* These brief formulas range from *maxims* (moral or simply practical), warnings or advice, to *refrains*, which point to certain constants observable in events, which the wise person must bear in mind in order to act with good sense.

This terminological difference between maxims and refrains, which I bring in for reasons that will soon be made clear, does not obscure the fact that the proverbs generally reflect the same anthropocentric character found in Ecclesiastes' anguished question. To get the most profit out of life entails acting wisely, with good sense, and that begins to happen when human beings in their activity do not allow themselves to be carried away by unreflective impulses. The wise man has a law (a *torah*), but that law is not purely and simply the law that God dictated through Moses, as it was up to this point in the Bible. Wisdom warns the candidate about being a "wise man": "Hear, my son, your father's instruction, and reject not your mother's teaching" (Prov. 1:8). Again, replacing the voices of father and mother with those of wisdom: "My son, forget not my teaching, keep in mind my commands; For many days, and years of life, and peace, will they bring you" (3:1–2). These three verses can set the appropriate search in motion.

In Israel the *torah* has been the term traditionally used to designate the teaching about how to orient human actions toward absolute value. The use of this consecrated term to designate the wisdom teaching does therefore indicate a shift in this absolute value, if this is not the *torah* in the traditional sense, as it certainly seems we must conclude.

At the time when Proverbs was composed, the law of Moses was already written down and was interpreted authoritatively. It would not seem easy or plausible, then, to simply identify it with what was transmitted through education from one's father and even less with what one learned from one's mother (given the condition of women in Israel at that time). The law already means a book in Israel — or a number of books. What *authority* then gives the precepts of this wise "law" their value?

An initial characteristic will help us determine it. It is found in the first word of the first proverb quoted above, and the word runs through the whole book as a key: *listen*. Instead of responding spontaneously and individually, the future wise man must turn and listen to an authority that could be regarded as "social."

Society educates the young person in wisdom, and the methods used for that purpose indicate that this is not information on the commandments that must be observed. One who doubts can read the following: "Like a golden earring, or a necklace of fine gold, is a wise reprover to an obedient ear" (25:12). "A wise man by hearing them will advance in learning, an intelligent man will gain sound guidance" (1:5). To achieve that purpose it will be helpful for the young person to learn the difference between unreflective actions and those proven to be advantageous through punishment, an artificial punishment brought about by education: "Folly is close to the heart of a child, but the rod of discipline will drive it far from him" (22:15). "The rod of correction gives wisdom, but a boy left to his whims disgraces his mother" (29:15).

I think the reader is becoming increasingly aware that we are facing something different from the teaching of purely moral commandments contained in a divine law or drawn directly from it. This feature becomes even more clear when we note a second characteristic: the moral commandment is categorical, while the "advice" of wisdom is *debatable*, in the sense that it can be the object of reflection and independent decision. Hence it is said that "the way of the fool seems right in his own eyes, but he who listens to advice is wise" (12:15). Hence the obedience demanded is not that unconditional obedience which a Hosea or a Jeremiah demanded with regard to the law. What is here required is a willingness to weigh what is heard and how it should enter into the elaboration of one's plans. Mere obedience thus becomes prudence, and even astuteness, and so we move away from what is purely moral or legal. We also understand better what that instruction (or *torah*) which one's father and mother provided was all about: "Plans made after advice succeed; so with wise guidance wage your war ... If one curses his father or mother, his lamp will go out at the coming of darkness" (20:18, 20). The aim of teaching wisdom is "that resourcefulness [translated as "astuteness" in the Vulgate] may be imparted to the simple, to the young man knowledge and discretion" (1:4).

A third feature of the two classes of proverbs, maxims, and refrains is relevant here for understanding what constitutes this "astute prudence" which results from education in Wisdom. Backing up his argument with statistical evidence, Zimmerli shows how the refrains (observation of certain constants in the way events follow one another) prevail in the older parts of the book of Proverbs. By contrast, the more recent part—namely, the Prologue—is made up almost entirely of maxims—that is, of advice and warnings. Obviously the astute prudence characterizing the wise man is more a matter of internalizing the refrains than of accepting mere advice, but this is simply an overall appearance.

Actually most of the pieces of advice can be turned into refrains. They should in fact be understood as such and not as pieces of advice that are absolutely valid. Thus, for example, "Entrust your works to the Lord, and your plans will succeed" (16:3) cannot be understood merely as advice to trust in Yahweh, period. Rather it is a refrain laying down a sequence of events and could be reworded as "the plans of those who entrust their works to the Lord will succeed." Similarly "love not sleep, lest you be reduced to poverty" (20:13) means "one who loves sleep becomes poor." As can be seen the advice or warning does not refer to a moral obligation, but is rather the result of a "prudent" and utilitarian observation of the consequences that follow from particular actions. Here again we find the same feature already pointed out: neither Yahweh's intervention in the course of events nor the law is forgotten, but they form part of a broader context in which human beings seek to get the most out of their lives. In contrast to Ecclesiastes, they think they can actually do so. In this respect—which is so decisive—one of the most typical proverbs may be, "my son, fear *Yahweh and the king*, do not rise up against *either of them*, for the destruction they (Yahweh or the king) send rises instantaneously and who knows how much both can punish?" (24:21–22, text restored following the Greek).

Furthermore, and this is the fourth feature, the anthropocentrism of wisdom in its response to the challenge of existence can be seen in the way it relativizes advice. As distinguished from a judgment that follows from a moral norm, the judgment of wisdom-guided prudence weighs circumstances to such an extent that it leaves its criterion in the air, so to speak. Potential wise persons must consider which of these contradictory—and juxtaposed!—counsels to follow: "Answer not the fool according to his folly, lest you too become like him. Answer the fool according to his folly, lest he become wise in his own eyes" (26:4–5).

One here imagines God present and smiling, perhaps with a bit of irony, but oasically good natured and approving, observing this almost preposterous attempt, this incredible striving of human beings to get the most out of their lives and to guide their actions on the basis of this socially and prudently acquired store of experiences, where divine and human causes are submitted to the same measuring stick of an age-old wisdom.[15]

Conclusion on Inspiration in Profane Matters

Who would dare to regard as "inspired" by God such a book if he or she did not already know that the work was part of the biblical canon (which would be an anachronism or begging the question)? Thus we have proof that when people do not study how this canon was formed historically (as is frequently the case in *theology*) and the criteria actually used for determining it, fundamental aspects of Old Testament "dogma" are ignored. The tautological argument indicating that if a book was in the Bible it should be regarded as inspired was not so innocent after all. By stating something so obvious, the question of how God had actually carried out the divine pedagogy was left in the shade. Further ignored was whether God could have done alone what demands a "recognition" that only the dialogue partner can give, as is now obvious. For lack of attention to this point, the consequences of which I have been trying to indicate in this section, whole areas of the Bible were reduced to insignificance, because, despite all statements to the contrary, it was not clear how God could be revealed there.

The final section of this chapter allows me to return to the theological problem of divine inspiration and revelation, with the aid of the examples studied in the two middle sections.

Criteria for Recognizing Divine Revelation

False Solution: Sacred vs. Profane Zones

Readers will recall that the idea of "inerrancy"—although it was correct insofar as it presumed that something inspired by God should have a privileged relation to truth—was nevertheless still very superficially linked to gathering information. The idea that God was the "only" author of the scripture had contributed to such a conception. The result was to reduce the significance and importance of the human authors along with their intentions, searchings, and contexts. God had "dictated" something and logically this something ought to come down to correct information about the divine mystery and thus be timelessly true.

With this notion people were projecting back onto the Old Testament past the idea they had of a dogma and of the function of the dogmatic magisterium based on the present. The echoes of the Galileo case, his condemnation and very recent rehabilitation, may be deceptive. It was not so much with science that the church clashed as a result of this over-simplistic and superficial view of divine inerrancy and dictation. That case, however, may have been the first (public) siren of alarm since it showed that certain concessions simply had to be made.

For centuries (until 1965 at Vatican II) a "reductively theological" (in the sense of being ahistorical) conception of how the canon was formed hindered the recognition of anything "incomplete and transitory" in the Bible and the Old Testament in particular. Starting from the idea that a list of "inspired" books whose only author was God had been drawn up, the expectation was that the works on the list would have no possibility of error.

Of course the "scientific" errors in the Bible, such as the famous example of Joshua, who had stopped the sun's rotation in order to aid or extend Israel's victory, began to draw attention to the fact that this conception of the Bible and its inspiration was untenable.

However, given the church's attachment to that concept, the answer found was, theologically speaking, worse than the formulation of the issue, or as the saying goes, the cure was worse than the disease. If the biblical canon contained "dictation" it was necessary to cordon off zones, *areas of subject matter* that went beyond the dictation. "Dictation" seemed to belong to the idea of inspiration, and it assumed inerrancy. Obvious errors of prescientific times made it necessary to reduce this divine procedure to parts of the Bible where God seemed to be "interested" in communicating something—or better, communicating the divine self—to human beings. Inspiration was reduced to what was regarded as "religious" or "theological" in the Bible. Elsewhere the human authors were recovering their initiative and were making mistakes like other mortals.

In this distinction between zones of inerrancy and errancy, the church saw a danger of subjectivism and free examination. The "canon" must not encompass anything but revealed, certain, and entirely infallible truth. That position led to one of the things the Catholic Church condemned in the doctrine of those Catholics called Modernists early in this century. In biblical interpretation, the Modernists stood half-way between liberal Protestant and traditional Catholic exegesis. In his encyclical *Pascendi* Pius X condemned them, offering this description of their position:

[The sacred books] do not deal with science or history but only with religion and morality. In those books science and history are wrappings covering religious and moral experiences, so that they might be more easily spread among the masses. [D. 2102]

In 1920 Benedict XV expressed their position in a more nuanced way in his encyclical *Spiritus Paraclitus,* but still condemned them. In this view the biblical material was said to be totally inspired but "inerrancy" was limited to the "religious" element. Thus it was possible to exclude from the religious element that "which belongs to the profane disciplines and only serves revealed doctrine as a kind of outer vestment for the divine truth." According to the Modernists, God merely "allows this and leaves it to the weakness of the writer" (D. 2186; along the same lines, see *Divino Afflante Spiritu,* D. 2315).

Why was there an insistence on this condemnation, even after the Modernist crisis was over and when in fact the doors of Catholic exegesis were opening to scholarly methods? Because these methods, by taking the human authors as true authors, and by acknowledging the differences between literary genres proper to different ages, cultures (or lack of cultures) and levels of scholarly knowledge (or ignorance) were paving the way for the recognition of "incomplete and temporary" things, as Vatican II puts it in *Dei Verbum.* That was another way of saying "errors." Since they did not yet grasp how these errors could "demonstrate the divine pedagogy," Catholic theologians without admitting it had introduced into the practice of biblical exegesis the well-known

distinction between historical and scientific statements on one side and dogmatic statements on the other. They went on to put all the "errors" (especially
in the Old Testament) in the first column, leaving the second column infallible:

> A religious group of people, Christians, under the spell of Jesus ... had
> recognized its own group identity in particular inspiring writings, as the
> expression of the faith experiences of fellow Christians within a devel-
> oping tradition of Christian experience and an already existing *regula fidei*
> or norm of faith.... Furthermore, they had already arrived at their Chris-
> tian identity through the liturgical reading of these writings. For them the
> authority of this literature was existential, and derived from its content;
> in it they found an expression of their own understanding of themselves
> as Christians. For this reason, in the end they were able with justification
> to formulate this existential authority in the language of faith and say,
> "These writings are inspired by God" ... .[16]

If this is true of the New Testament, everything said here shows that it is
even more obvious in the Old Testament. Indeed, when we uncover the seemingly human motivations and experiences that led Israel to choose the works
in which were set forth both its identity over the course of a long experiential
maturing process, and the result of a divine guidance leading the whole process
toward that end (which is revelatory of the very being of God), there emerges
the "reasonable" faith that this *whole* journey with its vicissitudes, crises, errors,
and discoveries rested on the truth and fidelity of the one who had made Israel
his people.

If at some time the human cultures now populating the earth had to go forth
and choose new and different dwelling places in outer space; if on this journey
of no return they could take only those works of literature that had made up
the backbone of each culture in order to preserve their identity and their human
values, the peoples of Hispanic roots would no doubt include *Don Quixote* in
this tiny and crucial bit of baggage. No doubt during the long journey they
would often have long passionate discussions on it. No doubt they would vaguely
remember the context of that golden age and would regard it as ever more part
of their being and as unsurpassable. No doubt with each passing day they would
regard this work as being as "providential" as the spaceship carrying them and
the map of the stars guiding them. No doubt, as little as it speaks of God, or
the Absolute, or the transcendent Reality journeying with them, they would
sacralize and canonize this book, even though they were quite aware of the
poor human genius who had written it.

Indeed some day, this book, which began by challenging the logic of what
was then regarded as constituting fame, would turn out to be "inspired" by
God (from the beginning) for errant space travelers. I know—I will be said to
be stating the very opposite of what Vatican I says in defining that the books
of the Bible are not inspired because they are in the canon, but rather that
they are there because they were in fact inspired. I am not saying the opposite,
however. I am only saying that these people "will discover" that *Don Quixote*

had been inspired *from the beginning,* not from the moment it was included in the list of books that the spaceship was to carry. Inspired, certainly with all the human weakness and all the temporary and incomplete things it contains.

I hope that this science fiction example helps the reader reflect on this last step taken here in order to understand what "dogma" the Old Testament contains, and how and with what kind of magisterium God obtained this result: God's self-revelation to human beings. The first chapter of part 2 will review the steps taken up to this point and will open the door I believe, for the reader to question how this same God continued revealing his being to human beings in, and based on, Jesus Christ.

Part Two

Dogma in the Christian Church

otic multitude of examples offered in previous chapters may have the effect of not leading the reader to perceive that this process toward truth — which according to Christian faith is guided by God — does not look very much like the way a Christian today enters into the realm of the "dogmatic." Nor does it look like the way the ecclesial authority of the magisterium is exercised in this area today. Only when it is projected against this backdrop of what is today regarded as a dogma, does the summary that is to be made here stand out in relief and indeed surprisingly so. The benefit will be all the greater to the extent that this backdrop by its difference, makes more obvious the features studied in that dogmatic process of the past.

Conciliar and Papal Definitions

It is for that reason, and not out of any taste for demolition, that I decided to make this summary vis-à-vis the idea or conception most common among Christians about what a dogma is. One does not need many sociological surveys to verify that if Christians have to point to an example of what they understand a dogma to be, the dogma *par excellence* that will come to their minds will be a "definition *ex cathedra* made by the Roman Pontiff." Since they are scarcely familiar with the procedure and scope of (ecumenical) councils it is not very likely that they can cite a specific example of a conciliar dogma. They are vaguely familiar with, and sometimes especially recall, the second papal definition of a "dogma," and know that (according to Vatican I, D. 1832–40),[2] such a definition must be regarded, and believed, as infallible.

Why does the quintessence of Christian dogma seem to be concentrated in these definitions? Undoubtedly, it is partly because that was how the last dogma, the Assumption of Mary into heaven, was defined in 1950, not so far removed from our own time. However, I believe there is another and deeper reason — namely, that no other aspect of dogma more captures our attention for it has a relationship with the truth that is so elemental, simple, complete, definitive, and, I would say, miraculous. Anyone who doubts need only examine the matter and keep in mind especially that I am speaking of the *common* notion of what a dogma is — common among Christians and even theologians. Actually a *conciliar* definition, anathema, or canon likewise enjoys this same character of infallibility that Vatican I attributed to *papal* dogmatic definitions (for the first time in an explicit and extraordinary manner).

Whence arises this astonishing prestige, as unusual as it is recent (in its official recognition) of papal *ex cathedra* definitions? As time went on, the most classical theology kept adding conditions limiting the infallibility of the dogmatic definitions that had arisen out of the general councils of the whole church. Such conditioning factors, while perhaps not difficult to fulfill, are at least difficult to measure. Thus the common opinion is that in order for a conciliar definition to be regarded as infallible, the council producing it must be ecumenical (that is, bring together the universal church) and in addition be convoked and approved by the pope. One may therefore ask: Are the councils that have been convoked after the division of the church of Christ — brought about by the Eastern schism (separation of the Orthodox church) or the Reformation (separation of the "evangelical" or Protestant churches) — "ecumenical" (= universal)? If the answer is yes, as is customary among Catholics, how is ecumenism to be carried out, if at the same time it is admitted that the existence of millions and hundreds of millions of "separated brothers and sisters" does not render "incomplete" — incapable of promulgating infallible truths — a council where only Roman Catholics have voice and vote?

In addition to all this complicated historical conditioning, councils decisive for Christian dogma seem to have been convoked by emperors and not by the supreme pontiffs of the period. Finally, in order that this very special relationship between defined formula and infallible truth be valid, it must be sifted through a consultation with the pastors of the whole church, and in the end it depends on an ultimate guarantee: papal approval. Would it not be "reasonable" to believe that formulas worked out after such a long and difficult process, even without much faith in special help from God, cannot lead the church off track?

By contrast, an irreformable pontifical definition is incomparably more efficient. In itself it does not require any of this. The only requirement is the pope's express intention to exercise his supreme authority in matters of faith and morals in order that the formula thereby emerging be completely bound up with truth forever. In other words, the statement formulated becomes "irreformable," in view of its infallibility.

Thus, it is not surprising that these formulas be seen as reflecting a kind of miraculous mechanism attributed to the Holy Spirit. This is indeed a "miracle" seemingly always at the disposition of the Roman pontiff, for neither its exercise nor its infallibility depends on approval from any other power in the church — not even on a prior consultation with the church. Almost more surprising than the possession of such unheard of power is that it has not been used more often for the sake of the church community, in the dispelling of doubts and elimination of conflicts. This power, privilege, or responsibility has been used only twice and for matters in which what is essential to the Christian message did not seem to be in danger: in connection with the Immaculate Conception of Mary and her Assumption in body and soul to heaven, in 1854 and 1950 respectively.

Here we have the second term of comparison to be used in the following summary as the background against which the dogmatic characteristics uncovered in the Old Testament will stand out in relief. I believe that the reader will thus understand that choosing what we might regard as two poles of the spectrum "of the dogmatic" is not due at all (and could not be due) to a premature (hasty?) disregard for the second term, but rather to that wise and ancient procedure used unendingly in the *Summa* of Thomas Aquinas — to make each statement understood through a comparison with its opposite: *videtur quod non*.

Iconic vs. Digital Literary Genre

A first characteristic of "dogma" in the Old Testament was that it appeared under unexpected literary forms, and especially *iconic* forms.

I have just written "unexpected." Obviously, that should refer to a degree of surprise experienced today when one sees dogma surface where least expected — that is, in expressions which are today not associated with it. Indeed, the language used for the expression of dogma, and perhaps worse, for its transmission, today displays a clear tendency to be as "digital" as possible, or to resemble a scientific formula to the extent its content permits. Moreover, the approach to dogma in order to interpret it, fix its exact content, and transmit it as completely as possible, is "digital," if the adjective may be used in this manner. Hence any imaginative or emotional excrescence is purged from it. Indeed it is reduced to what could be called the main statement, or expressed in more technical terms, to what is stated in the formula *in recto*, directly.

We have said that the dogmatic content of the two deluge stories (in Genesis) could be summed up in the formula "there will be no more deluge." However, it is immediately apparent that this very formulation would imply that *there was* a deluge, a flood covering the whole earth. In order to avoid this pseudohistorical supposition, the "more" alluding to a first time, and the "deluge," alluding to an event which actually did not take place, would have to be omitted.

A more "scientific," or if you will, more "digital" language would have to be used. The following negation would do the job: God will never regret having made human beings and having entrusted the earth to them. The omission of the "more" after "never" avoids the mythical element of a first divine "regret" (Gen. 6:6–7). The result is a timelessness much closer to the formula of a digital or scientific expression.[3]

Independently of the fact that *another* mythical element has been introduced (this time the "divine regret"), what has been lost in this new formulation with its attempt — never complete — at assimilating the iconic into the digital? Several very important things. I believe we can observe the loss of two elements, and they will be even more obvious if we compare the two expressions related to the deluge (both the account itself or its iconic expression and its shortened digital expression) with a recent dogmatic formula such as the declaration of Mary's Immaculate Conception.

The first thing that disappears (largely if not entirely) in a digital formulation of dogma is the connection between the formulation of this "truth" and the existential predicament of the human being. In its very expression of the response the iconic points unmistakably to the question. Thus the deluge account forces to the heart and lips the decisive (for primitive humankind) question to which the answer is "there will be no more deluge." The knowledge that Yahweh will never again regret having created the human being may be quite correct, but it ignores what that human being is asking and why. Similarly, the dogmatic formula on the Immaculate Conception of Mary makes no reference to the human predicament generating it, or that should be generating it, in order for the question to acquire meaning. This is different from showing God first regretting having created the human being and then, having followed the vicissitudes of the lone survivor, regretting (for all time) the earlier regret. I have already indicated that the point is not to "demythify" the mythical account, but to recover the emotion that prompted it, by interpreting it as the author himself wanted it to be interpreted. It would be useless to say that something similar should take place, but does not, with regard to the dogmatic formula affirming the Immaculate Conception of Mary (even when there is no talk of myth in this case).

Secondly, story (like other literary genres of an iconic nature preferred by the Old Testament) makes dogma "believable." By pointing toward the attitudes behind events (and of which the events are signs) they make one "see" the admittedly very special rationality of this way of punctuating events—that is, of the transcendent datum that the dogma bears. When that datum becomes digital, faith almost inevitably suffers the temptation of becoming *fideism*; in other words, of believing such and such because I am being told that I have to do so, even though I do not very much know why. Thus we have the typical "doubt of faith," sociologically speaking a recent phenomenon, which indicates not that faith is declining but rather that its expression was never rooted in the very reasons for which one lives. In the Old Testament, faith is as vital as the very orientation structuring all of existence. By contrast, in a typical dogmatic statement, such as that of the Immaculate Conception, doubts can arise and multiply insofar as what is commanded does not seem to be connected to any of these essential alternatives that function as "premises" of human activity on all levels of life, either providing meaning for what is done, or emptying it of meaning.[4]

Educational Process vs. Information about the Divine

A second feature discovered in Old Testament dogma was that it was a *process*—that is, a gradual movement toward truth—or, if one prefers the negative expression, that it does not constitute information that is valid forever. Each and every step toward the truth thus contains continuity and discontinuity *alike*. In other words, they are "incomplete and temporary" in the terminology of *Dei Verbum*. This became quite plain when we saw that faced with a similar problem the biblical authors (if the anachronism may be excused since they were not "biblical" when they wrote down their ideas or combined various existing documents) preferred not to reduce the various answers given to a single one, but to offer them, different as they were, for their readers to think about. It should be added that such different and even incompatible versions were not in the eyes of the editors or authors of the biblical canon any hindrance to declaring these discordant writers, ideas, or passages "inspired by God."

This characteristic led our reflection here to some important conclusions.

The first is that reading the Bible—which follows the order of a "sacred history" or "salvation history"—gives clear indications that such an order ought to be transcended. From learning what happened the reader should go up another step and get onto the idea of a "learning to learn." To put it another way, the story of events, some of them mythical and some historic, all of them literary, should prompt a "metahistorical" reading. It should lead to the understanding that the deeper truth transmitted in the texts is not the kind that would consist in gathering exact information about each event and its interpretation in isolation, but rather the kind acquired in an educational process.

For education, like culture or tradition, is not brought about by adding "truths" and subtracting "errors," but by multiplying *the factors* that must be kept in mind in order to act with meaning and attain values which have been previously determined. Hence each new factor discovered multiplies information: it changes everything else. It does not turn it into an error to be abandoned or thrown out, but into an insufficient understanding that must be surpassed. In traveling along this road lies what is *irreversible* about truth.

It is true that Vatican II perhaps for the first time (at least in many centuries) reminds theologians that "there is an order or 'hierarchy' of truths, since they vary in their relationship to the foundation of the Christian faith" (Decree on Ecumenism, 11). Nevertheless this fruitful observation appears in one of the Council's *decrees* rather than in one of its basic *constitutions*. It is not surprising that it is only in ecumenical dialogue that what was written there has been taken into account — although not in actions — and that the internal arrangement of Catholic theology seems to continue to ignore it.

Nevertheless, what is more important is that this "order" of truths points to a hierarchical arrangement of beliefs in accordance with their proximity to, or distance from, what is central to the faith. Yet this order is still somewhat remote from the procedural order of an education in which everything is or should be equally central but not equally mature and developed. Finally, the practice of the church as it tries to make infallible dogmatic definitions out of topics such as the Immaculate Conception of Mary (with the division it naturally generates in the ecumenical domain) indicates that this principle has not penetrated deeply enough so as to bring about a reformulation of theology.

Furthermore, when a formula is regarded as "infallible" or "irreformable," it is thereby disconnected from a process toward truth, but is linked to truth itself. Returning to the terminology of levels of logic, truth — with its most absolute character — is thereby placed on the lower level (that of proto-learning) rather than on the higher level (that of deutero-learning = learning to learn). Hence an ignorance that leads to committing errors, and an erroneous formula itself, are regarded as diametrically opposed to "truth," thus ignoring the task that the church's magisterium itself in its moments of greater lucidity or depth has attributed to the process that consists in testing error and thus learning to detect and correct it. Dogma and experience are thus separated, as are also faith and life, in what Vatican II regards as one of the greatest evils of our age.

The resulting impoverishment of the concept of "truth" and the indifference that goes along with it thus seem to be, on this lower level, like the continual Manichaean-like confrontation between error and truth; the great *epistemological* truth of the parable of the weeds is ignored. Hence the danger of a *premature* (first level) infallibility lies in withdrawing from reflection, dialogue, and experience (through condemnation) everything regarded as error or as "incomplete and temporary" ideas.

This experience of imperfect truth, which is essential for moving beyond it in the depths of the human being, does not arise from speculative dissatisfaction or from an academic exigency. Since faith prompts the emergence of transcendent data that make it possible to punctuate with meaning the flow of existence, it is there that what is imperfect appeals for judgment, for discernment. We have seen how all the transcendent data of the Old Testament arise out of existential crises and therefore refer intrinsically to them. Hence we may conclude that a formula declared infallible without being connected to any crisis, as seems to be the case of the dogmatic definition of the Immaculate Conception, cannot be seen as set in a real process of education or magisterium—that is of steering toward the truth. It is a kind of meteorite truth, which tends, as we have seen, to fall under the impoverishing disjunction: fideism or doubt.

Subject-People vs. Object-People

The third conclusion flows from the theological interpretation of how in the course of history the books in the Bible became what they are today, books or works included in this canon or list of the sacred scriptures. In other words, the way they came to represent (first for Jews and then for Christians) the "deposit" of the *Word of God* is a problem which has both a theological and a historical aspect.

The most common answer touches (only) the theological aspect and works in a purely logical way—that is, by deduction: If they make up part of the canon of sacred books, vehicles of "God's word," it is because God inspired them—in other words, because God wanted to make use of these writers in order to transmit to us in human language what God wanted to communicate to us of the divine mystery.

That means that we are not dealing with books that *began to be inspired* the moment when they slowly began to be placed on the canon of sacred scripture. They were inspired from the moment they came from the pen of the human authors and God's higher authorship. At least in appearance, this is as simple as recognizing an infallible dogma when a human being, the supreme pontiff, defines *ex cathedra* a truth as belonging to Christian faith.

However, the argument takes for granted something that *in historical terms* remains to be discovered. What remains to be discovered in the Old Testament, in contrast to the case of papal definitions, is how these books were recognized—little by little and from among many other books with similar features and claims—as radically *other*, charged with a word that was divine and not merely human. For indeed the historical data we have show quite clearly that their divine authorship did not constitute any visible feature or "sign from heaven" making it imperative to incorporate them into the biblical canon but rather that certain human beings had to act with the incredible audacity of judging the merits of their content.

Furthermore, we can see that in drawing up this list, especially through reading and commenting on it in the synagogues, motivations of an obviously human tenor had a very decisive influence, rather similar to what can be traced in the history of the early ecumenical councils where the trinitarian and christological dogmas were set. In the case at hand, a decisive factor is undoubtedly the fact that a people, now suffering under subjection after a magnificent previous history, identified itself culturally with such books, which were religious to a greater or lesser extent, and attributed them to God, absolute Truth.

From this point we find some surprising features of dogma in the Old Testament.

The first such feature, and one that is extremely important, is that of fixing the canon or list of works that are to make up the Bible. This is a constitutive part of God's revealing plan—not because it makes "inspired" what was not previously so, but because it enables that inspiration to be recognized and to establish the tradition which brings it down to the present. In this fixing the *people* of Israel play a role almost as important as the authors themselves. There would be no point in their being "inspired" had the discernment and choosing of these from among a thousand similar works not been similarly "inspired," and indeed by the divine author. That is so, because, as we have seen, "inspiration" is not an "extrinsic" feature discernible by simply looking, but the object of a discernment in view of the value of these (presumably) inspired works. This discernment can be done only by a faith that restlessly sinks its roots in the reasons for living and acting that human beings can collectively recognize.

Hence biblical dogma has as it were two kinds of authors at the opposite poles of literary work: on one side those who are properly called authors, those who under divine inspiration are the creators of the documents in which God's revelation or word is deposited. On the other side there are those who are the receivers and who out of faith in the one guiding the process fix (in a way that is certainly more passive but not less decisive) where this process is to be found.

Thus it comes as a surprise, and as something foreign to the customary divine attitude of involving the human being in Yahweh's plans, when dogma, with the infallibility that the divine guidance confers on it, fails to involve, as though it were a trouble-making element, the community of faith in the process of Yahweh's self-revelation. The recognition of Yahweh's word thus is reduced to a single authoritarian agency that can act without even consulting this community or consulting it only "formally"—that is, consulting it directly on the dogma but not on its problems, hopes, and crises in relation to this particular dogma. This case would seem to apply to, among others, the definition of the Immaculate Conception of Mary (and the consultation which it is claimed was made with the church about it).

The second surprising feature is that from the dogmatic standpoint in God's very self-revelation in the Old Testament there does not appear to be any dividing line separating the religious from the profane. What I mean is that the criterion with which Israel recognized the divine inspiration of certain books in the Bible *did not take into account such a dividing line*. The God that Israel recognizes and to which it attributes the inspiration of these books is actually the God whose glory is "the living human being," as Irenaeus was to put it in a famous phrase.

Hence the revelation of the Old Testament extends to the whole Bible and not to those areas regarded as "religious" (in subject matter). The transcendent data the Jewish people learned to recognize as God's revelation are the same that it recognized as humanizing and liberating in its historic human existence. For as Irenaeus also says, "what is on earth—including what the Bible, which is also on earth, says—*is reducible to* the plan of the salvation of the human being."

We have also observed that in the Old Testament these transcendent data do not appear in abstract or clinical formulas, but rather are incarnated in stories, prayers, or figures of a real or mythical history. Thus one of the most decisive or suspenseful moments in the whole history recounted of Israel is not explicitly determined by an attitude toward God. The king to whom God has entrusted the never-ending monarchy of Israel wrestles with his own fate when he listens to the words of Nathan, the prophet. The one listening is an adulterer and a murderer. He is not told, nonetheless, that he has sinned against God or God's law. Nathan tells him how a rich man stole from a poor man his only sheep in order to lay out a feast for a friend. This human *injustice* stirs up David's heart and draws from it a death sentence against one who has thus shown contempt for what is deeply human. When he is told that it is *he* who has done it, he has enough "humanity" (critical consciousness and sincerity) to apply his own verdict to himself. This represents growth in humanity, but as was said at Medellín, "We cannot but feel the passing of the God who saves when ... human beings move from less human to more human conditions" (Introduction, no. 6).

It is the significance of being human that thrills us when we read passages about the utterly free cleverness of Abraham the wayfarer or the powerful love scenes in the Song of Songs where God is not mentioned, but where Israel feels God's presence and revealing power. By contrast, without long and complex "translations" to reality, we Christians today have difficulty understanding what sort of human liberation is "pending" in the content of dogmatic formulas seemingly only related to the level of the "religious," such as that of Mary's Immaculate Conception, especially when theologians try to "reduce" them to their infallible core.

Third and last, historical study of the fixing of the Old Testament canon not only shows that the "religious" is meaningless to God when isolated from what is humanizing. It also shows something incredibly more unexpected: that the very process of God's revelation teaches humankind to put the proper distance between God and the religious. Naturally this is incredible only for those who have forgotten or skipped over whole pages of the Gospels and of other New Testament works, and indeed, whole chapters in the Pauline letters. It is true, however, that in recent centuries dogma has been *reduced* to what we might call the specifically religious. Not only does it not include experiences that are in themselves humanly enriching and humanizing, that do not come from the faith community itself, but it seems to regard as even more shocking that the limits to their ambiguous religiosity be pointed out to the faithful. This last point is treated, if at all, through administrative rather than dogmatic procedures.

Establishing where sound religiosity, with its erroneous as well as its successful venturings begins and ends, is something inherent in old Testament dogma, because in order to understand God human beings need the earth and time — they need history with its complex causalities. The fact that this dimension is not ultimately autonomous does not mean that it has no autonomy or worth of its own (GS 36). When human beings want to become reductively theocentric,[5] they not only destroy themselves, but they destroy the image that God has revealed.

The myth of the deluge, the conception of the covenant, one of the versions of the origins of the monarchy, the search for wisdom are all instances of a balance that is difficult and unstable but "inspired" by the same God. However, this seems to have disappeared from dogma today. Dogma speaks of the Immaculate Conception of Mary, but not, for example of the risk that certain religious attitudes connected with Marian worship and theology can be deformations of the human being and of the revealed God alike. Finally, cannot atheists contribute to Christian "dogma"? Is it merely courtesy that commits the church to examining "these questions . . . seriously and more profoundly"? (GS 21).

Punctuations with a View to What Is to Come

As I come to the end of this obligatory summary, I think there is something I must punctuate, even if only so as not to sacrifice what I regard as deeply true in this investigation.

The constant comparison of what has resulted from the search for dogmatic elements and methods in the Old Testament to an extreme *example* that I have also constantly used as a background—Pius IX's declaration of the Immaculate Conception of Mary as a dogma—may irritate and block thought instead of moving it along. Therefore in order to move to a more balanced vision of things and to prepare for what is to follow here in part 2, I think it necessary to punctuate something of what has been said thus far.

First, the features that I have regarded as positive in the Old Testament no doubt really are so. However, they were not sufficiently so to prevent in the end a degree of dogmatic petrification within Judaism, paralleling if not exceeding the one being examined here. The description in the New Testament of the main theological tendencies in the time of Jesus (Pharisees, Sadducees, and— although their positions are not clearly laid out—Essenes and Zealots), as partisan and somewhat deformed as they may be, offer witness as do other documents from Judaism during the same period.

Second, when a dogmatic definition is taken out of its context, even though it be to use it as an artificial background accentuating certain differences, the result is a loss of certain elements which can rescue, if not the precise example in question, at least the overall development of dogma in the Christian community. What is said here should not be taken as a judgment for or against the Immaculate Conception. However, it should be taken as an example of a reductive and impoverishing conception of how a dogma, even one that may be true in itself, comes to be established.

Third, readers will not be mistaken if they conclude from what has been said in this summary that the author does not agree with the way the ecclesiastical magisterium has proceeded, at least in recent times (to which the comparison refers directly) in fixing dogmatic truth in the Catholic Church. Does this mean that the aim is to go back to that truth resulting from the process of pedagogical searching as recorded in the Old Testament? And if that is not the case, as indeed it is not, what sound proposal can result from the comparison—which I myself have regarded as forced, although not meaningless—that has just been made? These questions, which may be premature but I believe are on the mark, make it necessary to punctuate even now some things which are somehow implicit in the treatment of the topic thus far.

As has been said, the comparison made thus far in this summary chapter seeks to a degree to startle readers and make them pay attention. The point is not to convince them that the Old Testament process is "better" than the one that has taken place in the New Testament and in the church. For one thing, in making this comparison we are not unaware, as we just said, that what could be called the dogmatic process of the Old Testament—if it is represented by the most fervent and (supposedly) most orthodox group in the period to which it leads, that of the Pharisees—shows signs of lacking the sensitivity to perceive Yahweh's revealing presence in the life and prophetic message of Jesus of Nazareth. Does that not invalidate all the good discovered in the way in which the divine pedagogy gradually led the people of Israel toward the truth? And does it not therefore likewise invalidate the effect of the comparison that the material thus far has sought to draw?

However, if we look carefully, we will see that the question itself assumes something unproven: that we stand before *two* processes. What would be the case, however, if we assume—as Christian faith in the truth of *both* Testaments seems to oblige us to do—that these are phases in the same process? In that case, to regard Judaism as a process would seem to be an error in pedagogical perspective. The theology Jesus attacked did not represent Yahwism in its highest and most developed expression. Rather it was showing signs of being in another of its crises, to which Jesus' life and message represented the appropriate solution, although it in turn would not resolve all problems once and for all. If that is the case, the comparison made in this chapter shows only that the method used for seeking truth changed a great deal from one Testament to the next, at least with the passage of time and under different sets of historical conditions which influenced the institutionalization of the church. For one thing, the pedagogical method could no longer be the same when the subject of this divine pedagogy went from being a physical unity, a particular people in history, to a universalism which had to base its unity on a *particular* faith.

Of course not everything that has happened from Jesus Christ until now is thereby justified. Only some—indeed, much—of that development is thus explained. That much should be complemented by the history of the variations that the concept of dogma itself has undergone since its *new* origins—that is, as Christianity itself, up to our own time. It is certainly the proposal of this work to offer reasons for thinking, like the author, that these variations constitute a certain impoverishment, especially on the institutional level, which is ever more visible as time goes on. Hence the last chapter of part 2 seeks to show that it was not and is not necessary, and that conditions now exist for returning, or better for taking a step ahead, toward an idea that is richer and more faithful to the sources of what the Christian pursuit of the "complete truth" must be.

The aim will be to show that as history has unfolded this pursuit of truth in the realms of depth and creativity has never stopped. What religious sociology and even official theological formulations show is not always a faithful portrait of Christian reality. Hence the aim here is not to say something "new" in the sense that it has not existed until now. This impoverishing way of coming to dogma to which I have referred especially in this chapter, is fortunately not the only one present in the reality of history, nor does it operate in the pure state. There is in fact a whole labor of theology and pastoral activity which rebuilds the bridges that dogma thus understood seems to destroy between truth and the committed, critical, and creative life of the church community.

Moreover, as we will see in part 2, even prior to Vatican II and especially within it, there have been official proposals of perspectives which, when understood and put into practice, are intended to correct the imbalance of dogmatic endeavors which turn away from life. Collegiality of bishops; the role of lay people and the fact that they are central to the church; the unity of biblical revelation and biblical tradition; the hierarchy of the truths of the faith; the positive value which even the church's enemies and persecutors and good-willed atheists have not only for real life but for correcting dogma — all this shows that the backdrop utilized here to clarify and highlight what we have discovered in the Old Testament, does not represent anything but the Christian conception of dogma. We thus have a road on which to travel and have already begun to move along it. Indeed, somehow and to some extent that road has always been traveled.

CHAPTER 7

Encounter with Absolute Truth

In the previous chapter I placed the dogmatic development we have examined in the Old Testament at one end of the "spectrum" and I confronted it on the other with a dogmatic *fact* of the Christian present: a papal definition *ex cathedra*. Even then I indicated that I was doing so fully aware that generally speaking reality was not located on the extreme ends of the spectrum but in areas that could be called intermediate. In other words, as I was doing so I was aware that I was not doing justice to either kind of "dogma." The first type was not so rich in ideas of how the human being, with God's help, journeys toward truth, nor was the second so poor. This was a didactic device — with a real basis to be sure — and as such I would now like to erase it from the reader's memory and study more closely and more precisely the phenomenon of how the way "dogma" was understood developed within Christianity.

For *with the New Testament* we are going to enter a domain where reality is more complex and where dogmatic poverty and wealth again clash in a battle to decide who is to prevail.

I would dare to say that the complexity condenses around the singular and seemingly exorbitant Christian claim that with Jesus we have come to the immediate and personal revelation of Truth. In capitals. If *Jesus is God*, what can there be of the new or open ended that would continue to justify "search[ing] for truth" (GS 16) and to still be on the road leading to it?

Viewed in broad outlines, the history of this question for the past twenty centuries would seem to be the parallel development of two opposite responses. One of them is that there is nothing to seek and that the "new" task is a matter of conserving and spreading the truth already possessed. The other is that nothing has been interrupted by the "fact" of God's incarnation and appearance on our earth, and that the process toward truth continues and will continue as long as human beings inhabit the earth.

Someone might say that this last answer cannot be sustained for a very long time and that the human being's stance toward truth cannot be the same before and after such a "communication" on the part of God, and indeed would be almost a contradiction in terms. God has "finished" revealing himself to us and *dogma* cannot ignore this "finish." If it has any further mission it cannot be that of moving through crises and questions toward transcendent data as yet unknown. The only thing appropriate might be something very different and supplementary: to explain better, to define more carefully and thoroughly, to apply to new contextual situations the datum finally known, and to convince slothful and resistant minds of it.

As we arrive at this point readers will not be surprised if I tell them that this problem, as important as it might seem, is only the application to a particular topic—the development of dogma as search for truth and its result in a "tradition"—of a central overall problem that the Incarnation of the Son of God poses for human beings. What is left of all our own history after God pitched his tent among us and then went on to fold it up with his death, leaving us, like the apostles after the Ascension, looking up toward that heaven where Jesus had disappeared for good (or at least *until* a second coming that would put an end to the universe and to history)?

It is not unusual that here also—or here first—the two parallel and opposite answers mentioned with regard to the pursuit of truth have been offered. The discovery of an urgent eschatology in the preaching attributed to the historic Jesus, and certainly present in the first Christian communities, has led many theologians to a certain conception of the Incarnation as the culmination and real end of history. Indeed at the end of the New Testament, the urgent eschatology of the synoptics gives way particularly in the Johannine theology so that one can speak more properly of an *already realized* eschatology. As an example of the latter, I will take one of its most recognized exponents in recent Catholic theology, Cardinal Jean Daniélou. For him, "first, history is not conceived as an indefinite progress, but as finite in scope; it is a determinate circumscribed design ... Secondly, Christianity is *itself the term of development*: Christ professedly comes 'late in time', and inaugurates the *stage that will not pass away*."[1]

This definitive character imparts very precise features to various realms in which theology and reality cross paths: collective eschatology, soteriological ecclesiology, theory of development of dogma (by unfolding), and so forth. These notes may perhaps be summarized in the concept of *ahistoricity*. For as Daniélou says, after Jesus judgment has already begun[2] and profane history is no longer heading toward anything of great importance: it is merely in suspense.[3]

Nevertheless, the observations in the previous chapter about the (somewhat forced) comparison between the two forms of "dogma" brought face to face there should serve to sound the alarm. Could it be possible that the "wealth" of the final and highest divine self-communication should lie in our ceasing to think or in our thought giving up its creative venturing toward the truth and be limited to acknowledging and spreading it in the short amount of time still remaining? Is not "truth" part of that "freedom" proper to the age of adulthood, which Paul places as a determining criterion for having entered into—not having left—our condition as children and heirs of God? For our endeavors toward freedom, what meaning would there be in being heirs, if there is nothing to build and the reality of history is already finished?

I believe the answer to this question cannot be too simple. We must carefully examine the data we have pointing in either direction. For the same reason, in this introductory chapter on dogma in the New Testament, I would like to indicate in a very brief and panoramic way, the explanatory foundations for this shift, if not between the two extremes of the spectrum already mentioned, then certainly from a complex and rich development of dogma in the Christian era toward recent formulations and notions that impoverish it within the Catholic Church.

This panorama will not be, nor could it be, either an impartial vision, much less a complete vision, although it certainly strives to be as objective and truthful as possible. For objectivity is not a matter of leaving behind values and proceeding as though they did not exist. The earlier part of the work has pointed to a great human wealth in the dogmatic development of the Old Testament. By contrast, the last chapter has indicated the poverty of certain recent forms of a different approach to dogma which can be recognized in some unquestionably regrettable aspects of the modern life of the church. The hypothesis presented here is that this poverty need not be so, and that this is not the authentic Christian conception of access to truth, much less to divine truth. However, my intention is not limited to a mere critique of this way of exercising the dogmatic teaching authority, or if you will, of formulating dogma without exercising a true teaching authority. I believe not much is gained, and much can be lost, by limiting oneself to discrediting this teaching authority by showing its actual errors and letting matters stand there.

What can be helpful is trying to show, as I will attempt to do in subsequent chapters, how from the New Testament itself down to the present a different conception has always been present and alive, even though dogma has suffered from historical mechanisms reflecting the circumstances through which the church has traveled. I furthermore believe that today the church is objectively ready to travel this new and old road as soon as it draws the appropriate consequences from its own principles and becomes aware of where and why it largely departed from those principles—although it never did so entirely, since it was being taught by the Spirit for the tasks awaiting it today.

Incarnate Truth—"He Did Not Want to Hold Us Back, but to Go on"

Does Truth Go Away or Remain?

In the New Testament, and especially in one of its last embodiments, Johannine theology, there is a surprising statement about the incarnate Word of God. I do not think I am being unfair when I assume that if it did not have this statement right there in the Bible the magisterium, as it is now, would be inclined to condemn it as heretical if it did not have it right there in the Bible. The statement actually speaks of a process toward truth continuing after Jesus toward a more complete truth and for the sake of which *it is better that Jesus cease being physically present in our history*. The words are placed on the lips of Jesus himself, but they are undoubtedly a statement by that great New Testament theologian John (or his school): "It is much better for you that I go. If I fail to go, the Paraclete [or Holy Spirit] will never come to you, whereas if I go, I will send him to you ... I have much more to tell you, but you cannot bear it now. When he comes, however, being the Spirit of truth he will guide you to *all truth* [= to the complete truth]" (Jn. 16:7, 12–13).

Johannine theology also alludes to this process toward truth, which encompasses the truth incarnate and continues after its manifestation in history with that declaration of happiness (= beatitude) likewise put on Jesus' lips, which gives greater credit to those who believed without being present at that manifestation than to those who "saw" it (Jn. 20:29).

Moreover, Paul, although he is not so explicit on this matter as John, had also insisted on this same "transitory" character of Jesus. In 2 Corinthians 5:16 he presents himself as someone who "did once know Christ in the flesh" — that is, as one of those supposedly privileged ones who were present for the visible and audible manifestation of God's truth. But he adds, *"that* is not how we know him now."* He obviously thereby wants to give pride of place to this present knowledge. Paul's example, however, is even more eloquent that his words and (epistemologically) more daring than Johannine theology: even though in his case we only have letters, everything we know of Jesus through him is "creation." He neither quotes Jesus' words nor narrates what he did during his life. We could say he meets Jesus and keeps moving ahead.

Thus St. Augustine is able to pick up the expression we have quoted from Paul on the two ways of knowing Christ and draw this remarkable epistemological assertion toward its ultimate consequences in one of the most radical phrases written about the human conditioning that God-truth assumed in becoming incarnate: "The Lord himself insofar as he deigned to become our *way* did not want to hold us back, but to *move on*."[4] In order that we might walk, he had to disappear from sight.

In the chapters devoted to constructing the process and authority of dogma, I will take up more extensively these and other basic data which point toward this educational process in which Jesus, even considered as eternal Word of God, is involved and passes on. He is — why not say it with the same elegance as the New Testament and patristic texts? — *surpassed* (= it is better for you that I go) within an educational function that is guided by the very Spirit of Jesus, who is also the Spirit of Truth.

At this moment, however, in accordance with the plan already laid out, we should look at the contrary tendency, that which makes Jesus the end point of the communication of, and search for, truth. I would say there is nothing mysterious about the rise of this tendency. It is much more obvious than the former and its historic causes stand out clearly. Nevertheless, that does not make it any less necessary that we recognize this development. We should recognize it in the sense of carrying out a reconnaissance or search to know what happened (in case it might be necessary to retrace our steps) and also recognize it as a means of *metanoia* — that is, as repentant knowledge (when we see the human, too human, factors that have played a role in this particular tendency, from the past until today).

Different Identity of the Christian "People"

Thus we come to the *first element* which necessarily had to produce an important change between the role played by dogma in the Old Testament and that which it plays and will play even more as time goes on in the Christian community. In this section we will be speaking about the *apostolic* Christian community—that is, that which lasts for perhaps half of the New Testament period, when Christians are living alongside most of the apostolic college. I am leaving for the next section the changes observable in the New Testament when this apostolic community is followed by another which can no longer find support in eyewitnesses to the life and message of Jesus.

In the Old Testament the dogmatic, if we can use the phrase, is one activity among others, albeit the highest, within a people that has already taken shape on the basis of a bond that is both ethnic and cultural. Even the Jew who is stoned for not following the religious obligations in force in Israel is "taken from the midst of his people," as the biblical condemnation reads, but only in a literal and physical sense—by dying. He does not go on to be something else, however. He dies a Jew. Especially after the unity gained by the monarchy and further fortified by the "ghetto" situation, nationality is a stronger identity than religious orthodoxy (or orthopraxy).

So much is this the case that down to our own day Judaism as a religion is a living paradox. It is regarded as one of the great *universal* religions. It is so, largely as a result of its heterodox branch: Christianity. In itself it is (only) the religion of a race, a people, and a particular nation. This case is unique in the realm of universal religions: anyone who does not belong physically to Israel cannot but remain on the fringe of the religion of Yahweh, as a sympathetic foreigner, or as a proselyte or follower.[5]

The only point being made here is that the function of "dogma" inevitably had to change and in a radical way, when Christianity went from being a heterodox Jewish sect to a "universal religion." Of course to say this is to consciously commit an anachronism. The early Christian community is not striving to be a "religion." However, the very fact that it goes from being a Jewish sect to a community with a universal "membership," let us say, is what will later allow it (perhaps through a misunderstanding) to exhibit the features of a universal religion. In any case, the misunderstanding will affect the noun "religion," not the adjective "universal." This shift toward "universality," nonetheless, has nothing to do with numerical growth. It is already implicit the first time a non-Jew is accepted into the Christian community as a first-class member—that is, ranking equal to Christians who have come from Judaism. Paul may not be the very first to begin this new phenomenon, but he is certainly the one who spreads it and its "founder" (in the sense of having provided the precise theological foundation for such membership—and not a simply de facto basis as did Peter).

Now if the bond of union can no longer be provided by nationality, if "there are no more [distinctions between] Jew and Greek," because both "are one in Christ Jesus" (Gal. 3:28), now it is *dogma* which must safeguard the unity that previously sank its deepest and most immediate roots in race and nationality. The "nationality" of Christians is their baptism, along with the creed in whose name they receive it (Gal: 3:27); and baptism itself points to the "dogma" contained in the good news of Jesus Christ.

That is how Paul expresses it in a memorable text, very similar to the historic creed of Deuteronomy, which we discussed in part 1 of this work:

> Brothers, I want to remind you of the gospel I preached to you ... I handed on to you first of all what I myself received, that Christ died for our sins in accordance with the Scriptures; ... that he was seen by Cephas, then by the Twelve. After that he was seen by five hundred brothers at once, most of whom are still alive, although some have fallen asleep. Next he was seen by James; then by all the apostles. Last of all he was seen by me ... the least of the apostles ... In any case, whether it be I or they, *this is what we preach and this is what you believed*. [1 Cor. 15:1–9, 11]

Like the Israelites reciting the Deuteronomic creed, those reading this formula or creed in the Christian community are certainly reminded of a past that gives them identity, and indeed an identity backed up by God. There is a fundamental difference, however. In the case of the Israelites, this past is biological and ethnically *constitutive* of their identity, but there is no ethnic or biological basis grounding Christian identity. It is based on the Pauline creed, and that is all. Here dogma must replace that tangible foundation and become the principle of community identity as well as the limit or border beyond which that identity is lost.

As the exegetes, including Cullmann, point out, this "new" constitutive function of dogma is especially noticeable in connection with baptism—that is, in the incorporation of a new member into the Christian community, although not only there. Cullmann believes the story of the baptism of the eunuch of the Queen of Ethiopia by the deacon Philip in chapter 8 of Acts has paradigmatic features in this regard. The first obvious question that had to be resolved in each baptism was whether or not there was any impediment to the acceptance of the new member. Hence the question, not natural but legal, "What is to keep me from being baptized?" as well as Philip's response, which is also stereotyped (according to a very ancient gloss in the Western text), "If you believe with all your heart, it is possible." Continuing with the early baptismal liturgy, if anyone wants to know what this dogmatic identity required, the gloss thus furnishes us with the eunuch's response, *"I believe that Jesus Christ is the son of God"* (Acts 8:36–38).[6]

We could find numerous examples of such short formulas of faith, always used with the same function in the early Christian community, such as the identity that had to be reaffirmed in the face of martyrdom. In my view, however, it might be far more instructive to ask why from the outset "dogmatic" formulas employed for this new and necessary function were not taken from the very words with which, according to the synoptics, Jesus summed up his own message or mission, which were more iconic and more likely to evoke emotion and commitment. Why, for example, were not the words which, according to Luke, Jesus himself had formulated as the center of his prophetic message: I believe the poor are going to be happy for theirs is the Kingdom of

God? Was not this in fact the core "gospel" of Jesus, as is also indicated by the very place it occupies in the Gospels of Matthew and Luke?

Post-Easter Shift

We now find ourselves facing the *second element* our search offers us. If we ask why the constitutive dogma of the early Christian community was not the same transcendent datum that "constituted" the community of Jesus himself, the answer to this question which will shed light on the difference in style between early Christian formulas of faith, must take into account the change brought about by the paschal events between Jesus' preaching and the (post-paschal) preaching of the early church, as Luke presents it. I believe the accent undeniably shifts from the reign to the person of Jesus himself. It shifts from history to imminent eschatology (without history or with that "history in suspense" of which Daniélou spoke). Within a religious message it shifts from the predominance of (anthropological) faith to the predominance of ideology (religion as instrument of salvation).[7]

Dogma consequently acquires an unquestionably pragmatic tint: in view of the imminence of the parousia, the accent is on reaching the community of the "savior." Jesus is the messiah, the son of God, but above all the (only) one who can save! According to Luke, one of the earliest instances of Peter's preaching makes this clear: "in the name of Jesus Christ ... there is no other name in the whole world given to men by which we are *to be saved*" (Acts 4:10, 12). Hence, the question "What must I do to be saved?" is not answered with Matthew 25:31ff., for example, but by mentioning entrance into the community, the constitutive element of which is simply faith in Jesus: "Believe in the Lord Jesus and *you will be saved and your whole household*" (Acts 16:31; cf. 2:37, 41, 46). Even Paul does not express himself differently, though in him the historic dimension becomes crucially important once more (after the two letters to the Thessalonians): "we have our citizenship in heaven; it is from there that we eagerly await the coming of our savior, the Lord Jesus Christ" (Phil. 3:20).

In comparison to the function of dogma in the Old Testament supporting the search for meaning in human life, who cannot perceive a kind of "short circuit" here? As rich as its intrinsic truth might be, when it is somehow reduced to short, digital, static, identifying formulas, dogma is endowed, as it were, with an instrumental saving power. It is as though, even though human problems remained unresolved, dogma were resolving them all at once, by placing human beings almost magically in a different existence where all questions of meaning have suddenly vanished.

Such a whisking away of the problem of history should not be surprising, however, for the post-Easter early church not only goes from Jesus the preacher to Jesus preached, but also from awaiting the reign to awaiting the imminent parousia or second coming of Jesus in order to put an end to the world and to history. The short circuit is already present in the first New Testament document we have when Paul speaks of the result of his preaching to the Thessalonians—namely, that they had turned "to God from idols" and were now awaiting "from heaven the Son he raised from the dead—Jesus who *delivers* us from the wrath to come" (1 Thes. 1:9–10). Here "dogma" seemingly has no other importance than that of "placing" the Christian in the community of salvation. Naturally, it may be that this line of meaning of the faith and another one are complementary, and that will indeed occur and deepen later on. However, the accent placed here is very different from the function dogma has within Israel. It might be said that only when history once more occupies a central place in the Christian community (if indeed that happens) will it be possible for a liberating process of seeking truth to recover its authentic meaning and humanizing potential.

The Church—Between the Synagogue and the Mystery Religions

A *third element* connected to dogma in the apostolic age—that is, in the church contemporaneous with the first part of the New Testament—deserves mention.

In this disappearance of the theme of the reign of God—as constitutive of the church community—and its replacement by the theme of Jesus the savior, exegetes perceive a power shift within the church: the Judeo-Christian church (that of James, for example) soon cedes hegemony even in Jerusalem, to a Judeo-Hellenistic church (that of Stephen, or particularly of Paul—that is, Jews who come from, and belong to, the Jewish diaspora in the Mediterranean and consequently are marked by Greek culture). Certainly a part of this power shift would be the increasing entrance of uncircumcised (= pagans or "Greeks" like Barnabas) converts whose literary ability, as in the case of Luke, was to lead the Christian message to become acclimated in the Mediterranean world of Hellenic culture.

According to Bultmann and others, this is related to the shift in accent toward Jesus as savior. "Of course," writes Bultmann, "other influences are also at work in the use of the title 'Savior.' They are: first, the Old Testament tradition, in which God is called Savior ... and second, the Hellenistic usage in which both mystery and salvation deities and divinely worshiped rulers bear the title [of 'Savior']."[8]

Among these three factors which may be enhanced by literary erudition, I believe only one is particularly significant from the sociological standpoint— that is, as a mold for "institutionalizing" the new community united around the Christian message (and hence for separating it from the "synagogue" model): the mystery religions or religions or salvation.[9]

As has already been indicated, the early Christian community has features that are deeply its own, especially from the time it splits from the main trunk of the Hebrew religion. From the moment the first pagan is admitted into the new community as a fully fledged member, it has to stop using as its institutional pattern the synagogue, with which in addition to a common past it had many similar sociological elements inspired by the story of Jesus, as we saw in the chapters on the Old Testament. On the pagan side, however, the "religious" was institutionalized in the rather degenerate forms of religious worship of the emperor and the amorphous mass of gods and cults that the Roman Empire had been piling up in an uncritical and disorderly way in its successive conquests. In this context, how was this community to move from being a spontaneous group to being an effective and significant institution in society? Neither the Jewish nor the Roman religion provided an institutionalizing structure in tune with its own temperament.

The accusation—subsequent, to be sure—made against Christians that they were an "atheistic" community shows that this problem was raised in a serious way and that the option could not be completed until much later. Indeed, it shows that this was an attempt to create something that had never been done before and was incomprehensible within the usual patterns of religious sociology. Reading Paul (and the deutero-Pauline letters) between the lines, as we will do further on, we can perceive this attempt to create a new kind of institutionalization for the Christian community, one that was original, not very feasible, perhaps, and in any case, incomprehensible due to its nonsacral character. At the same time, however, the (super-religious, or ideologico-religious, to use the vocabulary I defined in volume 1 of my work *Jesus of Nazareth Yesterday and Today*) reactions Paul encounters in his community at Corinth (1 Cor. 1–3) show to what extent the pressures toward the only remaining kind of religious institutionalization, that of the mystery religious, to which Bultmann was referring, were indeed "natural" and strong.

Generally speaking the mystery religions steered their initiates away from both ethnic particularities and conflicts, and the base polytheistic syncretism of the official religion (although in most cases their adherents continued to practice it externally). They were higher and purer forms of charismatic religion, based on secret participation in a "mystery"—belief or worship—capable of providing initiates with peace, forgiveness for sins, purification, contemplation, salvation. Although we should not exaggerate the degree of universalization, the contrast between the mystery-and-initiation or secret-and-revelation along with the consequent saving effect, tended to have the effect that the belief favored by belonging to this kind of religion would end up in the "short circuit" I have mentioned, in which a useful truth already absolutized once and for all is entrusted to some extent "ready-made" to the person who comes in to share in the secret and sacred dogma. We can glimpse what is so important here sociologically by reflecting that if this is how dogma becomes constitutive of the new kind of religious society it has to present itself as somehow attractive, and the way to do so is precisely this close and quasimagical connection to a total salvation.

Here it is interesting to reflect that Paul in his letter to the Romans claims that with Jesus Christ humankind has entered into a third stage in which, after the privilege entailed in the revelation of the law, God was returning to *not giving religious advantages* to anyone (Rom. 2:6–11; 3:23–29, and passim). Nevertheless, less than two centuries later Origen tells us that the great objection against the church by pagans like Celsus lay precisely in the obvious inconsistency between the fact that it had been founded recently yet claimed to possess the *secret* of salvation.

Whether the church liked it or not, this had to have a serious impact on dogma. Indeed it seems that unlike the Old Testament, no mystery religion had spent centuries following the vicissitudes and crises of a human group seeking enough meaning through experience in order to live human existence in history in an ever-richer and more complex way. Moreover, to do so did not lie in the *nature* of a mystery religion. Its kind of dogma, connected to supernatural efficacy and received from the possessors of a secret, was not open to being somehow confronted and checked by the "reality" of facts, as was the Old Testament process.

Nevertheless, had it not become common to view Christianity through this mystery religion prism, it would have been difficult to conceive of this shift that the church was to make in the Roman world—namely, arriving at the point when it was used politically as the empire's official religion. That shift was to leave its mark on the church institutionally for many long centuries.

From the Apostolic to the Post-Apostolic Church

A New Structure for the Post-Apostolic Church

Before getting to that point, however, the New Testament already presents us with a panorama different from what we have just seen. That happens when the church of the apostles of Jesus, and most particularly the Twelve, gives way to the *post-apostolic* church.

It is true that the supposed authorship of the New Testament books does not allow for such a temporal distinction. Indeed the titles of most New Testament works claim to indicate that they were written while the apostles were still on the scene. The only *names* of authors clearly outside the apostolic college which accompanied Jesus from his baptism to the resurrection—and leaving aside the single case of Paul who was regarded as an "apostle" by extension— would be those of the evangelists Mark and Luke. They, however, offered particular guarantees of style and documentation (Lk. 1:2–3) assuring that their works were written during the lifetime of eyewitnesses and with their assistance.

Nevertheless, matters are not so simple, as any New Testament specialist knows. Even in the first centuries of the church there is an awareness that biblical authors had employed the procedure, very common in the ancient world, of attaching a famous name to works to enhance their value. This happened in the Old Testament with the legislative writings (Moses), the psalms (David), and the wisdom books (Solomon). The attribution of letters to Peter or Paul continues along this same path. In other cases, it is difficult to know with certainty, what influence, direct or indirect, central or marginal, the eyewitness to whom a work is attributed, such as Matthew or John, may have had.

What is clear is that within a period of some fifty years in which the New Testament is composed, elements of a necessary shift from the apostolic to the post-apostolic church gradually appear. The eyewitnesses have undoubtedly first scattered in a world with few means of communication. Then they die (1 Cor. 15:6; Acts 12:2), leaving the scene for good, and taking with them the direct recollection of what Jesus said and did. The church goes on without them, something that is easy to imagine after centuries of succession and continuity, but which was not easy to do when the spontaneous still far outweighed the institutional.

It is far from my intention to retrace here the history of that important change and the even more important changes issuing from it. Edward Schillebeeckx's historical and theological study on the evolution of ministries in the early Christian communities—leaving aside some incidental discussions it has prompted—comes to very clear conclusions on certain points that are crucial here.

"Apostolicity" in Dogma

The first of these conclusions is that with the end of the apostolic church, the post-apostolic church opens with a question or, if you will, with a concern, that of assuring its "apostolicity." Schillebeeckx says, "Of course, logically and also historically, apostolicity became an explicit theme only after the death of the apostles, in particular in the New Testament post-apostolic period, in which ecclesiology, the doctrine of the church and its ministry, was worked out more clearly."[10]

The author shows that at this beginning of the church, apostolicity was not a feature of each particular church, in a legal sense, because it had been directly founded by an apostle or because its bishop stood in a direct line from a designation made by one of the twelve. It was a note of the universal church, and this note referred to dogma. The church was conscious that it was living the trustworthy message of Jesus, as it had been transmitted by the faithful testimony of the apostles.[11] As long as the latter were alive, the great creative activity of the nascent church is manifested in a parallel proliferation of ministries, among other things. These are all apostolic for, as we have seen, this was a universal feature of the church. It is important to add that several of these "apostolic" functions had a connection to dogma: apostles (besides the Twelve), prophets, and doctors (for example, 1 Cor. 12:28).

Apostolicity and College of Presbyters

One indication that dogmatic "apostolicity" is perhaps becoming a problem is the fact that:

> From Jerusalem, and somewhat later, from Rome, presbyteral church order replaced the undifferentiated church order of the first period throughout early Christianity [see note], also and even above all in the Pauline communities. I Peter is typical of the disappearance of the undifferentiated, charismatic type of church in which "prophets and teachers" were the most prominent figures, in favour of the institution of a presbyteral leadership of the church."[12]

It is well known that it is very difficult to distinguish between the episcopal and presbyteral functions in the early Christian community. According to Luke, on his way to Jerusalem, Paul gathers the "presbyters" of Ephesus and addressing them, calls them *episcopoi*—that is, bishops or inspectors. In other words, he does not distinguish between the functions of the two groups. Nor do we find a clear separation between the two functions in other New Testament passages. Nevertheless, there are some anticipations of what is to come. The "presbyters" seem to act together or collegially. On the other hand, and even bearing in mind the exception just indicated, it would seem more coherent with the meaning of the word that the *episcopos* or inspector be the "pastor," or administrator, of the Christian community. Indeed that seems to have occurred more and more.

Be that as it may, the dogmatic concern to accentuate more and more "presbyteral" authority (perhaps in a kind of "council of elders," like that maintained by the synagogue tradition) is that of an apostolicity made to rest on a *temporal* community (the oldest = *presbiteroi*) rather than on a charism for transmitting Jesus' message to new contexts. It would seem as though the apostles themselves, confident that they had control over fidelity to Jesus, dared to encourage dogmatic creativity to a very great extent. Indeed it is difficult to imagine today how a Paul, in the face of strong criticism, could formulate a theological vision of Jesus' message and significance that was so personal and creative. By contrast presbyteral control felt perhaps less secure with regard to such dogmatic creativity. It no doubt trusted more in criteria based on numbers and age—that is, on the foundations of the "memory." In any case the criterion for measuring what might be a creative fidelity became more difficult simply with the passage of time.

I do not want to exaggerate this danger and its influence on the hardening of initial church authority, among other reasons because even the post-apostolic era in the New Testament provides examples of undeniable richness and creativity. The other great New Testament theologian besides Paul is the creator of the great Johannine theology (whether it was in its origins the apostle John or more likely John the Presbyter; see 2 Jn. 1) which comes from this period. We would also have to add the author (somewhat ignored today, but decisive in his own time) of the letter to the Hebrews, which was mistakenly attributed to Paul for a long time.

Moreover, it could be said that the college of "presbyters" did not hinder a rich dogmatic evolution where it was first at work—namely, in the synagogue. That is nonetheless no more than a debatable opinion. What is of interest here is that presbyteral authority in the synagogue was largely balanced out by the very antiquity and the weight of the fame of the books consecrated as scripture (at least of the earliest, the law and the prophets). By contrast, if only a century and a half after Christ there is already a "canon" or list of Christian scriptures (later in the time of Origen called "*New* Testament") the only authority that could have made that selection is that exercised by the presbyters in the church. Somehow here there is missing the settling out process—which we could almost call "popular"—present in the Old Testament, as we have seen. The New—a slight anachronism, to be sure—is "judged" almost immediately, without the crises, mediations, and testing that made the Old so fluid during centuries of long effort. That having been said, we should not ignore the fact that in the case of certain works and authors the canon of Christian scriptures was debated for three or four centuries. However, these seem to have been mainly technical debates over authorship, and do not give evidence of the same concern for coming to a judgment on the content itself.

The End of the "Deposit of Revelation"

At this point finally there appears an element whose importance will only be perceived much later, but which is germinally present in the preceding. Against Pauline and Johannine theology (at least in certain aspects of the latter) people to some extent begin to think that with Jesus divine revelation has come to its end, in both meanings of the term: culmination and finality. What follows is now regarded more as a problem of fidelity and continuity than of creation and newness—that is, of being faithful to a message rather than of struggling fiercely with what is real in order to find in it, with the support of what tradition has gathered, a deeper and richer meaning.

Of course it took many centuries for this notion to attain publicly the status of dogma. Only at the beginning of this century in the decree *Lamentabili* of the Holy Office under Pius X was the opinion condemned as erroneous that "revelation, constituting the object of Catholic Faith, was not complete with the apostles" (D. 2021). In any case, the idea that the deposit of revelation ends with the last of the apostles is not, as we have seen, a modern theological opinion. It is to some extent already clearly present at the bottom of the doctrine of the "two sources" of revelation indicated by Trent. The Council begins by saying that "the Gospel . . . which Our Lord Jesus Christ the son of God first promulgated with His own mouth, and then commanded 'to be preached' by his apostles 'to every creature' " is "the source of every saving truth and of instruction in morals." Then going directly to the topic we are discussing, it adds that "this truth and instruction are contained in the written books *and in the unwritten traditions*, which transmitted as it were from hand to hand, have come down to us *from the apostles*" (D. 783).[13]

Further on we will examine the vicissitudes through which this theory of the "two sources" undergoes. What is interesting to observe here is that in effect this notion means that at a particular moment in history the flow of a body of information which God was assumed to be pouring first over the chosen people and later over the church came to a halt. That moment is clearly located: it is Jesus of Nazareth—except that the information coming to us from him is not direct (since he did not leave anything written personally) but is borne by a very clearly defined group of reliable witnesses: those who went along with him in his preaching and to whom Jesus, according to Mark's witness, "explained everything privately" (Mk. 4:34).

Obviously this Tridentine conception cannot be simply projected back into the post-apostolic period of the New Testament. Only the seed is there, but certain similar or, if you will, anticipating, elements can be discerned. In the very fact that the "canon" of the Christians is fixed so early there is something like a judgment over the time it took God to carry out the educational process contained in the five centuries it took to compose the Old Testament, in comparison with the half-century in which the process comes to its end in the New.

The Christian scriptures, undoubtedly more connected to the office of presbyter than to the choice of their readers, would thus seem to be seen as a perhaps unconscious effort to *bring to a conclusion* something which is not called "word of God" without a reason. From that point it is too easy to move to the conclusion that God does not say or reveal anything more. The supreme message coming from Jesus is regarded as definitively imprinted in two kinds of files: those crystalizing the apostle's "memoirs" about Jesus or gospels, and those crystalizing either other teachings Jesus imparted, or the understanding each of the apostles had of what he had witnessed about Jesus' message. Thus to say that divine revelation ends in Jesus *in practice* means that it ends in his apostles. When they die, it is closed.

That this is an important part of the truth about the post-apostolic period (even when it is not the whole truth) is made plain in the doubts about the New Testament canon which in some cases lasts until the fifth and sixth centuries. The works questioned are Hebrews, James, 2 Peter, 2 and 3 John, Jude, and Revelation. John McKenzie points to four reasons for these doubts: (1) the authorship of letters, which are presented as being by an apostle but evidences a style very different from words by the same author (Heb. and the rest of the Pauline letters; 2 Pet. in comparison to 1 Pet.); (2) doctrinal difficulties, among which those emphasized by Marcion doubtless have to be included— namely, being more in tune with the Old than with the New Testament (James and Jude); (3) the trivial nature of the subject matter (2 and 3 Jn.); and (4) obscurity and strange style (Rev.).[14] It is quite easy to see that what is being questioned in most cases, especially in the more important, is whether the writing is really of "apostolic" authorship and comes from "apostolic" times. Linked to this concern is the consequent effort to exclude from the "canon" whatever is beyond the boundary marking the end of the apostles' witness.

Summing up this section, we can see the problems human beings seem to experience almost inevitably in connecting the absolute revelatory value of Jesus and his message with anything besides "information," and more importantly with definitive, "finished" information. Although, as will be observed, the church has had other perspectives, or if you will, other richer ways of conceiving this difficult relationship, the tendency here uncovered in the shift from the apostolic to the post-apostolic church will leave a long and important mark on the future understanding of what function dogma should have within Christianity.

Revelation and Apologetics in the Greek World

The Gospel of John and Apologetics

After finishing the previous paragraph, it is too tempting to examine the atypical case of the fourth Gospel. That is the case for two reasons, one of them related to the previous section, and the other connected to the topic I will treat in the next chapter which deals with the patristic age, and in it, the apologetic effort of the Christian church in the midst of the Hellenistic world.

With regard to the first reason, there is good reason to ask why a work that was so clearly post-apostolic was not questioned, or rather, why its inclusion in the New Testament canon took place without great problems, when some other New Testament works met such harsh resistance, as we saw in the previous section. Anyone looking askance at the attribution of the letter to the Hebrews should have done so even more at the attribution of the most sophisticated work in the New Testament to a country fisherman from Galilee. In more general terms, it would seem logical to assume that the obvious discrepancies between the "memoirs" of Jesus presented by the three synoptics and the profound theologomena John presents in narrative form, would make people think that it was impossible to attribute this semiphilosophical work to the son of Zebedee. Those who were capable of distinguishing the style of 1 Peter from that of 2 Peter would not be deceived about whether John was or was not of the same time period, and whether he belonged to the group of the apostles who had been direct witnesses to the teachings of Jesus of Nazareth.

Be that as it may—and here we have my second reason—the fourth Gospel had the merit of occupying a more prominent place in the history of Christian literature—namely, leading the parade of the literary genre that is to flourish right after the New Testament—namely, the genre of the apologists. We will deal with them in the next chapter. Here suffice it to say that in a church, which especially after the apostles undertake the enormous task of converting the surrounding pagan world, dialogue with the central or higher core of this culture becomes both an imperative and a creative stimulus. What has been said of Justin, the great apologist of the second century, that "he is the first to look outside and to raise the issue of relations between Christianity and the world,"[15] could be said even more fittingly of the fourth Gospel.

Paul, it will be said, began this dialogue—and how he did so!—he who was at the same time a Pharisee and a Roman citizen. Nevertheless, his case is quite different from that of John, or of whoever it was who deserves to be regarded as the main author of the fourth Gospel. Paul is normally understandable to a pagan, because his thought, entirely Jewish, is turned out in concepts that are understandable to an ordinary person with a basic education, except for rare exceptions, such as when he repeatedly hesitates between the (biblical) usage of "flesh" and the (not entirely Greek) equivalent of "body" to designate something like the "human condition" or the "creaturely condition." However, his thinking is continually subordinated to biblical ideas and categories, well or poorly translated into Greek, and it is from them that he argues. He is certainly obscure in his style of argumentation, but this negative characteristic is not due to the possession of a degree of culture inaccessible to the majority.

Audience for the Fourth Gospel

The case of John is different, no matter who it was who used that name. Culturally speaking, his work is so peculiar within the New Testament that modern exegesis, with all its arsenal of erudition, does not know how to establish its, let us say, "genealogy." Jewish, Essene, Judeo-Hellenistic, Platonic, gnostic, hermetic thought?—these are some of the hypotheses contending in the hermeneutic field with regard to the fourth Gospel.

By no means is the aim here to untangle such a complicated situation. However, it is not impossible to shed a bit of light on this problem by examining the very arguments put forth. Moreover, the specific literary genre of John's Gospel will help us make our way around the various pitfalls in this controversy. Even leaving aside the Prologue (Jn. 1:1–18) because it is probably a preexisting hymn, the (true) conclusion to the Gospel (Jn. 20:28–31) shows us that the point of the work is an apology for the faith: " 'Happy are those who have not seen and yet believe' . . . These [signs] are recorded *so that you might believe* . . . " However, the faith being talked about here has an extremely specific cognitive content. Of course the Gospel is talking about Jesus, the "messiah and Son of God," but the "sign" preceding this conclusion ends with Thomas's solemn words to Jesus, which are unique in the whole New Testament: "My Lord and *my God!*" Thus it is not enough to believe that Jesus is the messiah of Israel and therefore "son of God." *Son of God* here is more than a metaphor (alluding to messiahship). It designates the very "only-begotten of (God) the Father" (Jn. 1:14); the only-begotten who is within the (invisible) Father (Jn. 1:18); he who can, like the Father, say of himself without any predicate "I am" (Jn. 8:24, 27, 58; 13:19).

Without going into all the rest of the fourth Gospel, these brief indications show that we are confronted with a literary task that is *new* within the New Testament writings: defense of faith in the divinity of Jesus. Now to believe that the words John puts on Jesus' lips—"The Father and I are one" (Jn. 10:30)—are the truth about him could strictly speaking be a matter intended to be debated exclusively among Jews. The fact that it is *also*, and even primarily, a discussion among Jews would be enough to explain all the arguments that some exegetes produce in their effort to show that this work is typically Hebrew and deeply rooted in the Jewish scriptures. It is not contradictory, however, to claim that this defense is *likewise* aimed at the highly cultured Greek world, and that it is by that very fact the most explicitly Greek of all the works in the New Testament. It is not without reason that the first great Christian apologist, still within the New Testament, clearly raises the issue of relations between Christianity and the Greek cultural world.

Hence one cannot but agree with the overall conclusion with which one of the best exegetes of our age, C. H. Dodd, ends the first chapter of his book on the fourth Gospel:

It seems therefore that we are to think of the work as addressed to a wide public consisting primarily of devout and thoughtful persons (for the thoughtless and religious indifferent would never trouble to open such a book as this) in the varied and cosmopolitan society of a great Hellenistic city such as Ephesus under the Roman Empire.[16]

The Literary Genre of the Fourth Gospel

If this be the case, as it undoubtedly is, unprepared readers of John's Gospel suddenly find themselves facing a nothing less than completely unexpected panorama opening up before their eyes. Ordinary Christians are familiar with the fourth Gospel primarily through the way it has been used in the liturgy for centuries. There this Gospel, whose use in Sunday readings is only slightly exceeded by the more moralistic Gospel of Matthew, looks like one more "synoptic" Gospel. Readers believe they are in the present of a fourth "memoir" of Jesus' (historic) deeds and sayings,[17] when they are actually in the present of a philosophical and theological work where every event and every word points toward an (apologetic) argument whose aim is to show a pagan of Greek culture the plausibility of the "divinity" of Jesus (without thereby ceasing to be a Jew).

Doubtless the reader notices that Jesus' discourses in this strange Gospel are quite mysterious. Thus the procedure for reading (and preaching) is likely to be a matter of ignoring what one does not understand, and sticking with the moral content that comes out of what happens in the story. However, even in what people think they understand they turn to simplistic procedures. Thus, for example, when Jesus says, "I am the true vine," the understanding is that this must be a comparison that is a little exaggerated. People think they know that the *true* vine is the "real" vine, the one everyone is familiar with and that Jesus must mean, therefore that he is "like" this (real) vine, except that he is more important than it is. The Johannine text certainly becomes readable today in this fashion, but the price is too high, a failure to understand something central in the fourth Gospel: nothing short of one of the arguments or expressions of the divinity of Jesus. For the Platonism at work in the higher expressions of Greek culture, the world of reality was split into two: an eternal unchanging world where all ideas, such as that of a "vine" had their ideal model, and the perceptible and perishable world of appearance, where vines "copied from the model" were like deceptive contingent shadows. In this cultural context, the fact that Jesus is the "true vine" is an accurate expression, not a comparison or figure of speech. It means that all the good and truth existing in a visible vine are present in the reality of Jesus in their pure, eternal, and divine state.

Likewise when one hears that he is the "Word" of God, the word "word" is ignored, because there does not seem to be any relationship between the noun, which designates one of the grammatical elements in any sentence, and Jesus. The only thing left of the word used by John is an empty concept which is filled with what we know from the rest of the Johannine prologue: that Jesus is God, God incarnate. The universal function that the term *logos* has in Greek culture and especially in Stoic philosophy (as well as the personification of Divine Wisdom in Jewish wisdom literature) thus remains in darkness—even though that is the most important point. In this manner, people are reading a Gospel which may have as rich a transferred sense as one likes, but it is not the work that John wrote and his contemporaries read.

It should be noted that this is as true of Jesus' "deeds" as it is of his sayings in the fourth Gospel. For John purifying the temple of Jerusalem of the buying and selling going on there is not, as it was for Jesus himself, an active preaching on the kind of detachment and purity that ought to prevail in God's house. For Johannine theology, the implausible placement of this purification at the *beginning* of the preaching of a still unknown Jesus is explained by the theological intention of presenting him as the "true" temple, the only "real," eternal, spiritual temple. That is done in a part of the Gospel where there is talk of "the new beginnings" (Jn. 2:18–21, and parallels; 4:17–24).

The "Incomplete and Temporary" in the Gospel of John

Our concern here, however, is not the surprise of a reader of John seeking to follow the guidelines of *Divino Afflante Spiritu* or *Dei Verbum* in exegesis of the fourth Gospel, but rather a strange paradox. When we approach this dialogue between incipient Christianity and the Greek cultural world, we sense two very different, and somewhat opposed, things. On the one hand we discover a "new" fourth Gospel and a theology that is brilliant, provided we keep in mind the elements the author had at his disposal for demonstrating what Jesus was and signified for the highest and purest Greek world. However, we also feel the discouragement of encountering a book that is "surpassed." Of the books of the New Testament this is perhaps the one that has aged the most. To that extent what *Dei Verbum* says about the principle of the incarnation in biblical hermeneutics is true here as it is of the New Testament itself: "For the words of God, expressed in human language, have been made like human discourse, just as of old the Word of the eternal Father, when he took to himself the *weak flesh* of humanity, became like other men" (DV 13). He who according to Augustine, "did not want to hold us back but to move on" really moved on in that Greek culture which today, despite its proximity to us in some respects, looks so obsolete to us, so incapable of reflecting our problems.

What is theologically surprising is that this "weak flesh" and its consequence—things that are "incomplete and temporary"—are not only said to characterize the Old Testament "before the time of salvation established by Christ" (DV 15), but continue with the very message of Christian salvation, after God has deigned to reveal himself in the Son. But in this ongoing pursuit of truth, even after it has visited the land of human beings, is not the imperfect and the transitory the very mark of what is serious and deeply liberating and humanizing about the incarnation of truth in time? The very Gospel of John, who dealt with this issue for the first time, and with incredible boldness, is also faithful to the very "divine pedagogy" to which the Old Testament bore witness.

Indeed when I spoke of the fourth Gospel as "surpassed" I did not thereby mean that it had become useless or that a different and better truth had subsequently been found. What certainly must be said is that the complex of issues to which its author tried to respond—and really did respond—has been surpassed. The upshot is that the process of learning to learn goes on—not through any shortcoming of the truth manifested there, but just the opposite: because of its overabundance of meaning—that is, because of its ability to continue to humanize humankind in its advance through new contexts into deeper and richer problems. The dialogue of early Christianity with Greek philosophical culture did not take place in vain. Even today it has a great deal to offer and teach, provided, however, that it is interpreted within its limits and that we surpass them in moving toward the present (insofar as it offers problems that are more crucial, especially because they are *ours*).

Thus our intention here has been to show within the short time span of the

New Testament some elements of what constituted the difficult problem of reconciling, in a humanizing and liberating way, the certitude of being in the presence of the personal revelation of God's absolute truth, and of nevertheless continuing a process of learning to learn that had not thereby come to a halt. From this point on, the situation is going to undergo notable change, and the conception of what dogma is, and how to establish and teach it, is going to change as well.

CHAPTER 8

Power and Truth in the Patristic Age

A process several centuries long now obliges us to take a great leap forward and to change style and technique. Certainly the few centuries remaining to the (Western) Roman Empire after the culmination represented by the New Testament do not occupy much space, especially when compared with the one thousand years we have had to analyze in the space of a few chapters when studying the development of what we have here called "dogma" in the Old Testament. These centuries inevitably look large, however, just after we have devoted a whole chapter to that short space of time, no more than fifty years, spanning the composition of the New Testament.

Nevertheless, as we move toward the present, documents become more and more numerous. If we had to apply the same detailed method of searching with regard to all the factors which must have influenced the notion of dogmatic truth in Christianity during the last nineteen centuries, dozens of volumes would not be enough.

Naturally that is not the aim of this work nor would its author have the necessary qualifications. So what are we trying to do in the sections to come? We are not concerned with the unfolding of Christian dogmas, but of two opposed tendencies in the overall idea of dogma. Let the reader not be deceived: this book is not a history of dogma. Its intention is simply to be a reflection on the general understanding of what dogma is in the Catholic Church and on the factors that have probably had an influence in making it what it is today.

Since this work attempts to trace the reason for a particular way the conception of revelation and dogma has developed in this same church, it will necessarily have to restrict its search to those elements of history which, in accordance with all probability and *logic*, must have been most influential in that development.

For that purpose, from the New Testament onward, three periods will be sketched out: the *patristic* age, which in the West by and large parallels the remaining life of the Roman Empire — that is, until the fifth century (and which includes a crucial important factor, the turning of the Christian community into the official religion of that empire); *christendom*, or the medieval period, in

136

which the ecclesiastical structure linked to feudalism becomes increasingly built up, centralized, and sacralized; and the *modern age*. From the viewpoint raised in this work, the modern age presents two aspects of a single reality: the attacks against the "Christian" order created during the Middle Ages, attacks led most prominently by the Reformation, the Enlightenment, and Modernism, and the milestones in the defense of that same order waged by the church at the Councils of Trent and Vatican I, until Vatican II, when the climate changes.

Two observations are required here, I believe, for the sake of understanding and assessing what is to come. The *first* has to do with the procedure I will follow with regard to the three stages just mentioned. As already indicated, passing over centuries (a thousand years for the Middle Ages, five hundred years for the modern age), can easily lead to extremely vague generalizations. As an example, one that will provide particular material for reflection in this work, we may take the familiar term "Constantinian" era, which refers to the profound change the church underwent when Christianity became the official religion of the Roman Empire. It thus acquired a social and political power in the West which has not yet been completely undone.

More careful reexaminations of this final stage of the Roman Empire will deem it unjust to attribute such a change to Constantine. For one thing he never made Christianity the official religion of the empire. Moreover, the church's true political power resulted from the imperial power vacuum in the territories occupied by the new peoples, called "barbarians," who converted rapidly and en masse to a lower form of the Christian religion.[1]

The truth probably should lie more or less between these two extremes. What is of interest here is that inquiry into what happens to dogma in the Christian world cannot ignore these milestones, which constitute clichés in history, and as such are wearisome, sometimes superficial, and in some cases treacherous. The only thing that can redeem this obligatory passage through such clichés is the target at which we are aiming here: to bring together the elements that explain the present situation of dogma in the Catholic Church and which point toward a change that may, and perhaps ought, to take place.

As I said, this intention depends more on the internal *logic* than on how exact an item of historical information may be. Thus the notion is not that the day the church became the official religion of the empire under Constantine or any of his successors, it simply went from being a prophetic minority in the catacombs to being comfortably established in the embrace of political power. The logic is more complex and jagged and not so linear—but the logic is there. Sooner or later, a church that plays a particular political role *will relate* dogma to it. I am not saying that it will disfigure or betray it. However, it is inconceivable that one can pass close to the fire without getting singed.

The second observation may serve as somewhat of a counterweight to the first. Care is required so as not to bring into play a logic based on anachronistic comparisons. In other words, as was already noted in previous chapters, we must be careful not to impose on concepts from the past the content those same concepts have today.

This observation is all the more necessary here insofar as we are dealing

with dogma. As it has developed, for reasons that will have to be studied, dogma has tended to accent disproportionately — in order to highlight its truth and even its infallibility — what is assumed to be a perfect or visible continuity of things and *concepts* (especially the latter).[2] There has been an effort, for example, to make people think that the "Peter," of whom the synoptics talk and to whom Jesus spoke, equals an authority Jesus already regarded as his "vicar"; that the latter in turn equals "bishop of Rome"; and finally that "bishop of Rome" in the second century equals "supreme pontiff" in the twentieth century.

Nevertheless, historical criticism cannot but work against such radically fallacious anachronisms, and theology actually comes out the better — especially with regard to dogma. That is the case, not because there is an urge to undermine the authority of the supreme pontiff, but in order to give him the authority that is due, and for the just reasons that actually support that authority. Hence the point is not to ruthlessly dissociate such apparently similar concepts, but rather to investigate when and why they came to be presented as interconnected to the point that they became theological synonyms.

Keeping in mind these cautionary remarks, it is now time to move into the period stretching from the end of the New Testament (around the end of the first century) to the fall of Rome and the practical end of the Roman Empire in the West (beginning of the fifth century). The disadvantage of such a procedure is that we are flying over centuries, and indeed centuries in which situations vary significantly. One of these variations, which will be extremely relevant for the purposes of this work, is that which brings the church to shift from a situation of being in a minority and frequently persecuted, during most of the period here studied, to that of being the only religion allowed (and even sometimes itself indirectly doing the persecuting) during the final decades of the period.

Nevertheless, within these complex variations in history I will try to introduce something of a connecting thread, bearing in mind three elements linked to the dogmatic function here being studied.

The Internal Structure of the Patristic Church

Change in the Relationship between Bishop and Presbyters

The first such element is the change observed during this period in the very structure of Christian communities or churches. Obviously it is not easy to follow the twists and turns of that evolution, but a comparison between the beginning and end of the period in this regard will be quite illustrative for my purposes.

From the previous chapter it should be clear that with the end of the apostolic age properly speaking the dogmatic need to safeguard the "apostolicity" (or, if you will, the "orthodoxy" or fidelity to the message that the apostolic witnesses transmitted) comes to the fore. The authority specifically charged with discerning this essential quality from within the charismatic is *in practice* the group or college of *presbyters* or elders in each church.

The situation of the church as described in the pastoral letters toward the end of the New Testament period also indicates another authority, that of the *episcopos* or inspector. To the extent they can be differentiated—and that is questionable—the pastoral letters seem to attribute to the latter a function that is less "dogmatic" and more administrative. Perhaps it would be more accurate to say that the presbyteral college on the one side and the *episcopos* (who also has the office of "teaching" and who gradually replaces the "teachers and doctors" of the apostolic age) on the other side, carry out different and complementary dogmatic functions: a more active and creative office, that of bishop, and an office of vigilance, that of the presbyteral college.

There seems to be, furthermore, a corresponding tendency to exercise presbyteral authority in a collegial way, while episcopal authority apparently belongs to a single person. It becomes common to refer to the bishop (singular) and the presbyters (plural). In any case what is most interesting is to observe that both authorities function parallel to each other. One does not seem to depend on the other. A comparison from today that might shed some light would be the separation of powers between the executive and the legislative branches in modern democracies. The presbyters lay hands on the *episcopos* or bishop, which is a way of saying that in some fashion they thus designate him for his function. One of the episcopal duties is in turn that of "establishing presbyters." The fact that the two powers have as their object the same fidelity to "dogmatic" truth also comes out in the fact that one of the main functions of the bishop is that of "teaching." In other words, with regard to dogma, the presbyteral college and episcopal authority seem to be complementary without duplication. Both seem to stand on the same level. Their functions are quite interconnected, although over time they tend to become more specific. Or at least that would be the direction in which things move in the Pauline churches (see 1 Tim. 3:1f.; 4:13–14; 5:17f.; Tit. 1:5; 2:1).

By the time the period in question has ended, this situation has changed almost completely. Most importantly for subsequent theology, is that this change of situation in no way seems to be linked to any "divine right." It emerges from the reality itself. It is not that Jesus—or the apostles—had foreseen to what kind of authority he or they would entrust the task of translating the Christian message into the pursuit of meaning for human existence. It is true, however, that causes that are sociologically detectible have made it evermore preferable or necessary that there be a monarchical or single-person authority within each church or Christian community.

Returning to what can be observed at the end of the period (fifth century), the picture is quite clear. The churches are governed by bishops. They in turn have presbyters as helpers to whom they entrust the *same* task as their own, except that it is on a smaller territorial scale. Committing a (didactic?) anachronism, we could say that something like a twofold hierarchical scale has been set up: the high and low clergy. Each presbyter has become a subbishop to whom is entrusted a territory or a defined group of persons within a broader Christian community. They are the first anticipations of what appears to be today, even in the wake of Vatican II, the "eternal" structure of the church. According to *Lumen Gentium*:

Priests, prudent *cooperators with the episcopal order*, as well as its aids and *instruments*, are called to serve the People of God. They constitute one priesthood with their bishop, although that priesthood is comprised of different functions. Associated with their bishop in a spirit of trust and generosity, priests *make him present* in a certain sense in the individual local congregations of the faithful, and take upon themselves, *a share* in his duties and concerns, discharging them with daily care. [LG 28, emphasis mine]

However, we should keep in mind that things were not always thus. As proof that this *was known*, we may cite the prohibition that the famous Council of Chalcedon raises in opposition to an existing practice which assumed this familiar conception of the presbyterate as a mere "instrument" and inferior analogate of the episcopal order: "No one may be 'ordained' priest or deacon in an absolute manner . . . unless a local community is clearly assigned to him." If nevertheless this is done, "the holy council resolves that their *cheirotonia* (*ordinatio* or appointment) is null and void."[3]

The "Crystalization" of the Episcopal Function

Between the two extremes of this period and from a very early moment onward, one can observe a line or tendency which we might call, following Ratzinger's study, the "crystalization of the episcopal function."[4] If I am not mistaken, it is connected to two rather clear sociological factors.

The first is related to the internal life of each Christian community. There is a certain fear of the potential anarchy of charism, and of course that fear is not entirely baseless. Thus it seems increasingly clear that having just one authority is an effective way of dealing with such anarchy. Even though Ratzinger does not expressly say so—generally speaking, he does not like to bring sociological factors into theological discourse—he hints at it when he notes:

Taken as a whole the church is a spontaneous community, but within it the community itself cannot be chosen; that it is one *as a whole* is manifested concretely in that it is one *in each locality* . . . The category around which the church lives and thinks is not the "circle"—it is the "people of God." The unity of leadership in the local church (which initially may have been collegial, but which even then had but *one* leadership) expresses this indivisibility and this relatively "obligatory" character of the community which one accepts when one accepts the church. This is the point from which the solid theology of the bishop must be understood, both in Ignatius of Antioch and in Cyprian of Carthage. The demand that there be "only one bishop per community" derives from this way of understanding the church as a public and indivisible community, and it militates against the tendency to turn the church into tiny private chapels.[5]

However, in the same indirect manner, Ratzinger shows the influence of another factor, this one beyond each local church. In the period under study, the church is developing rapidly throughout the Roman Empire. Doctrinal or "dogmatic" differences now affect not only the unity of each local church. They increasingly require a discernment going beyond particular communities. We need only call to mind the theological schools being established in cultural capitals like Antioch or Alexandria, and the trinitarian and christological controversies being debated everywhere at this time.

Taking into account the fact that the world did not then have the means of transportation and communication common today, we will see that the presbyteral colleges were inherently cumbersome means for resolving problems that required dialogue and responses between churches. In this regard it is logical to think that the pyramid style of imperial administration had to exercise a degree of pressure, at least as a model. Actually even before Christianity became the only religion allowable in the empire, still in the third century, the church had to appeal to Roman civil power in connection with the use of its own goods in the conflict between orthodox bishops around Antioch, and the excommunicated bishop of Antioch, Paul of Samosata who had possession of them. The solution of the Emperor Aurelian shows that, "in the eyes of the pagan emperor, there existed not only local churches but a catholic church whose unity was safeguarded by the communion of the bishops."[6] Moreover, it is not difficult to imagine that this imperial conception, endowed with a power to which the church itself had to appeal, must have been at work shaping both the very notion the bishops had of their function and likewise the way their authority should be exercised.

As is only logical, this tendency would be accentuated in the shift from a pagan to a Christian emperor like Constantine. Since, however, that is a second aspect to be studied, it would be better to pause here and reiterate specifically the observation made at the beginning of this chapter with regard to the risk of falling into anachronisms when the concepts of the present are translated too quickly and readily into situations in the past.

In Ratzinger's expression, some have spoken of a "crystalization of the episcopal function." However, during the patristic age this crystalization little resembles—I would say *very* little—what we observe today. That is the case for two reasons, which will be understood without much difficulty and which can be summed up with the observation that despite all appearances of similarity, the bishops of the patristic age look more like the fathers of the church (the vast majority of whom were bishops) than the modern image of a bishop.

Election of Bishops and the Local Community

The first difference characterizing them is that such "crystalization" was considerably less when the *episcopos* was *elected* and not designated from a distant, centralized, bureaucratic power. Of course it is very difficult to know exactly what procedure was followed—if indeed there was just one and not many different procedures—for designating a local bishop. However, two factors in the decision stand out clearly: the local community was decisively involved; furthermore the bishops of the surrounding region who consecrated the new bishop had to agree. It is worth noting that although these neighboring bishops did not belong to the particular community in question, through their own community and frequent contacts they were nevertheless responding to the pressure of their own faithful.

With regard to how decisive in elections the faithful and local presbyters were, we have clear testimonies, which are eloquent for today. In the middle of the third century, St. Cyprian, standing up to Pope Stephen himself, writes (*Epist.* 4, 5) that "no bishop is to be imposed on the people whom they do not want." And that is not an isolated and heterodox opinion. At the beginning of the period here studied, Pope Leo the Great (*Ad Anast.*: *PL*, 54, 634) formulates the principle: "He who must preside over all must be chosen by all."[7]

Freedom and Creativity in Patristic Theology

The second feature making it necessary to differentiate what being a "bishop" meant then from the current notion of the episcopal function is very important for the very topic of "dogma": those *episcopoi* have left an enormous theological literature that is both of great value and bears their characteristic personal stamp. A good number of them were theologians, not armchair theologians or professional theologians, but certainly doctors of their own flocks. Although among the fathers of the church, some theologians are lay (like Justin) and some are deacons or priests (like Jerome), most of them are local bishops, and consequently their works are largely sermons or catechesis in which one can sense the concerns, problems, and what has been called the feedback of the community. Even when adjusted to the more or less intellectual disposition of its authors, patristic dogma is never far removed from the people, as is to be the case in subsequent periods.

Finally, it is worth adding something that apparently constitutes another difference between the Christian community of that time and our own, but which must also indirectly have influenced the latter. In general terms we could say that the "massification" of the church—as it is known today—only becomes general with the Constantinian shift, when being a Christian becomes an aspect of moving up in society or adjusting socially. What nevertheless remains even clearer is that from its origins to the fall of the Roman Empire in the West, the Christian church experiences a period of creativity and expansion.

Within a highly civilized world endowed with a magnificent intellectual culture, Christianity moves ahead—perhaps only in minority terms, but with a surprising power. These are not Christians of the ghetto. They go out to the world, and are fully part of its culture (even though they reject certain idolatrous acts, or in varying degrees, certain occupations, such as the military), and they use its categories in order to express their own doctrine. The fathers of the church, often bishops in this kind of Christian community, participate actively in this work on the frontlines. Today the church as it confronts secularization is a church on the defensive. Perhaps on the basis of the church today, it is difficult to imagine how episcopal authority was exercised.

Christianity as Official Religion of the Empire

Conversion of Constantine

In this process of internal transformation of the structure of the Christian church—a structure perhaps affecting dogma more than it does today—a *second* element must be given a special place. We have already spoken of it several times with a somewhat misleading expression: during the first half of the fourth century Christianity becomes the official religion of the Roman Empire, and despite certain vicissitudes remains so until the fall of Rome under the pressure of invasions by the barbarian peoples. It is a historical cliché to say that from this moment onward, the church enters into the so-called Constantinian era, which does not seem to have completely ended even with Vatican II (depending of course on one's concept of that era).

From having emerged in the Roman Empire, incipient Christianity went through successive periods of freedom (or tolerance) and persecution. The last, and one of the longest and most violent, the persecution of Diocletian, extends into the early years of the fourth century. However, in 324, when Constantine defeats Licinius, and in practice becomes emperor of East and West, it becomes historic fact (whether foreseeable or not) that the new emperor is now "Christian." How Constantine evolved personally and how much his conversion was a matter of conviction and conscience is still a matter of mystery or controversy. In any case it is quite real for the effects of any census, and politically it means that absolute power in the Roman Empire now lies in the hands of someone who openly practices the new religion (although paradoxically he is not yet baptized).

I referred to a misleading impression because Constantine never actually declared Christianity the official religion of the empire. The fact that this change does take place under Constantine, or under one of his immediate successors, and to an ever-greater extent, is due to something that is sadly more complex: after a short and uneven period of general religious tolerance, the Christian church gradually fills all the spaces of freedom. When in 391 under Theodosius all pagan worship is prohibited, it can be said that broadly speaking Christianity has indeed become the de facto "official" religion of the empire, and of an empire which in the West is already fatally wounded.

However, that misleading impression had a sad meaning in history. A situation of general tolerance in which the Christian religion could have continued to convert the most influential groups in the empire without any obstacles, or an imperial declaration in which it was granted the title of official religion, but without being exclusive, might have been a more natural change. Actually, however, Christianity becomes official to the extent that the persecution of which it was previously the object is now unleashed against paganism, and violently wipes it off the map. Political power uses force to impose "the truth."

According to reliable historical research, while he was a Christian but not baptized (that took place only on his deathbed in 337) Constantine was striving for something different, religious tolerance:

> That was all he did in 324 when after having defeated Licinius, who had also become a persecutor, and seeking to *restore security to pagans* in the east, he said "Let each one follow the opinion each prefers." Nevertheless, such declarations could not prevent the breakup of a balance it was no longer possible to maintain, since the man and the emperor were one and the same.[8]

In fact under Constantine certain kinds of pagan worship are prohibited, and (the Christian) Sunday becomes the legal day of rest, when "no official act can take place ... except the freeing of slaves."[9] It is also under Constantine that the bishops obtain a separate law code for the members of the clergy. "Its arbitration was recognized without appeal to civil processes among lay people, even if only one of the parties had requested it."[10]

Already in Constantine's time, the imperial measures just mentioned—which under Theodosius reach the point of prohibiting the practice of pagan worship under pain of death—go beyond the framework of the emperor's personal convictions.

> They can only be explained by the desire to make the church an official body, and to associate it with the life and functioning of the state and reinforce the latter through the influence of the ecclesiastical hierarchy over the faithful. Thus through an extraordinary but almost fatal reversal of the situation, Christianity, which on the eve was still a prohibited religion, on the morrow began to be a state religion.[11]

Imperial Politics and Christian Dogma

All these developments and many others, some of which are yet to be mentioned, demonstrate something of unquestionable relevance for this thing I have called *dogma*. Dogma is basically nothing but the pursuit, systematized by tradition, of a truth that can give a deeper and richer meaning to human existence. This "system" is simply a tradition in which a divine pedagogy is believed to be discernible. When the use of political power to "facilitate" the acceptance of this truth and the suppression of error is allowed, it is inevitable that a high price will have to be paid. That price is paid in the depth with which truth gets through to human beings for their humanization.

Certainly here we should not fall into an easy anachronism. At this stage of human development the use of the *raison d'état* in religious matters was rather like slavery: it was not challenged. It seemed to be part of the very nature of things. Moreover, Israel's Yahwism also went through this same subjection to *raison d'état* during the five centuries of the monarchy, as attested from 1 Samuel (the story of Saul) to Jeremiah. Christianity is to be subject to it for much longer: from Constantine until far into the modern period. During the Reformation, in matters of religion the solution to the breakup of the Holy (Roman-Germanic) Empire into different nationalities could only get as far as the principle of the right of each prince to determine the religion of his subjects: *cuius regio eius religio*.

When considering dogma in the ancient period here in question, we must moreover keep in mind the pressure placed on the very conception of truth by the imperial aim of hooking up Christian theology to the carriage of the state. To begin with, it was predictable that controversy and its concomitant pluralism (as well as the corresponding creative work in theology), would be sacrificed to religious unity and security, since the latter was in turn a pledge and guarantee of the unity and security of the state.

In the case of Constantine it is extraordinarily interesting that when the church is divided over christological and trinitarian matters, and specifically in the controversy between Arians and Athanasians, it is the emperor, not the bishop of Rome, who convokes the first ecumenical council at Nicea.[12] His goal is to end division at any cost and restore unity. It is also he who makes the dogmatic resolutions of the council effective in the ecclesiastical domain (although later he goes in the opposite direction when he exiles Athanasius). Furthermore—and from the standpoint of our inquiry this is probably what is most decisive—he sets up the council of Nicea in such a way that the bishops who come together there from all over the empire become fully aware of their new function at the service of the state, whose civil servants they have become. Anyone wanting to check this need only examine the lists of princely provisions which were to go along with episcopal vehicles. Thus it is not surprising that in this period and in the councils, where on the surface it is matters of high theology that are being discussed, one hears acclamations to the emperor as though they were arguments.

To the extent that the Christian church becomes the state religion during the last century of the Western Roman Empire, the episcopal function is not simply accentuated by becoming politicized. A decisive point is reached during this period: by its end the episcopal function has also been *centralized*. That centralization is not around the bishop of the see where Christianity began, but where the imperial capital is located, namely Rome.

Centralization of Authority in the Bishop of Rome

Qualitative Leap of the Pontificate during This Period

With this third section of the chapter we enter into another issue which will likewise be decisively important for Christian dogma: its further growing dependence on a central dogmatic authority, one that is personal and is destined to be regarded as infallible—namely, the Roman pontificate. Since this section began with the focus on the impact on the episcopal function of Christianity's shift from being a minority persecuted religion to being the official imperial religion, one naturally might think that here we are establishing or will seek to establish a simple, direct causal connection between this shift and the institution of that pontificate. Clearly, however, that is not the case.

We may note at the outset that there was no way of foreseeing this final development at the close of the New Testament period and the beginning of the period we are examining. At that point it would not have occurred to anyone to call a bishop of Rome, as the bishops of Macedonia were to call him in the year 422, "pontiff" of the "first" church (D. 109c). This first church in turn precedes the second, that of Alexandria, and the third, that of Antioch, in a list of preeminences. This forgets, undoubtedly for pragmatic reasons, that according to the New Testament, Peter's "primatial" function began and was exercised in what was really the "first" Christian church, that of Jerusalem. Who would find in the New Testament itself the Christian titles for the capital of Roman paganism?

Furthermore, the use of the word "pontiff," which was rejected by the early church, along with other terms deriving from the realm of the sacred and cultic, such as "priest," "liturgy," and so forth, indicates how far the conversion of Christianity into the imperial "religion" must have had an influence on completing the process by which it became identified as one more religion. It was undeniably very logical that the new function it had to fulfill required it to rethink and reshape its local meetings, structures, and authorities. Moreover, for obvious pragmatic reasons, what the new Christian emperor expects of Christianity squares with no pattern that is not somehow copied from the centralizing model of the empire.

But rather than determine the distance separating the beginning of the period from the end on this specific point, our aim is to study the steps leading in this direction.

Reasons for Appealing to the Bishop of Rome

The first is indicated by the most ancient existing testimonies about the beginnings of the practice of appealing to the apostolic see—that is, the bishop of Rome—in order to resolve problems that the regional churches had not managed to resolve to the satisfaction of the contending sides. This kind of supreme tribunal *"was not founded* initially on the fact that the bishop of Rome was the successor of Peter because he had assumed Peter's prerogatives as (presumably) described in Mt. 16:17f."[13]

This is not meant to deny, we should note, that *starting in the New Testament* Peter enjoyed an unquestioned authority within the apostolic college, an authority that he did not assume on his own but that was present in Jesus' activity and words.

In any case, in the year 341, we observe St. Julius I writing to the Antiochenes, "a judicial investigation ought to have been made according to the ecclesiastical canon . . . Or do you not know that it is the *custom* to write to us first" (D. 57a). Under this same Julius I, at the provincial council of Sardica, the bishops explain such a "custom": "If perchance in any province some bishop has a dispute with a brother bishop, let no one of these summon the bishops from another province. But if any bishop has been judged in some case, and he thinks he has a good case, so that a new trial may be given, if it seems good to you, *let us honor the memory of the most holy Apostle, PETER* . . . Is this agreeable to all? The synod replied: It is agreeable" (D. 57b).

What is being talked about is obviously a "custom." No one mentions any law or obligation, but rather a consensus in honoring the memory of St. Peter, who, in accordance with an ancient tradition is believed to have been martyred in Rome, although this cannot be proven with scientific certitude. Moreover, there is no indication at all that this is about having recourse to his "successor." Indeed, there are even fewer scholarly data to indicate that Peter exercised the episcopacy in Rome, even if his stay or his martyrdom there were to be proven.

That we should not take this higher level of judicial appeal as a disposition of "divine right" is also indicated by the powerful and decisive pragmatic reasons implicit in these or similar decisions. Whatever remains of the church in

Jerusalem, it is, for plainly practical reasons, no longer regarded as the see to be honored on account of the primacy Peter exercised after Easter in accordance with the will of Jesus. Although Jerusalem still has a small Christian church, it is not even an archdiocese, but a mere diocese, suffragan to that of Caesarea. The importance of what appear as the leading three churches — Rome, followed by Alexandria and Antioch — in all probability derives from the fact that these cities are centers in the cultural realm, the latter two constituting something of vice-capitals in relation to Rome. The proof is the subsequent claim of the church of Constantinople, once it has become capital of the Eastern Empire (New Rome), and has a similar ecclesiastical authority, to be parallel or equal to that of Rome, even though it has no possible link to Peter.

Rome, Apostolic See: Peter and Paul

Ratzinger in particular has highlighted a second aspect with regard to the duty felt by local churches to appeal to Rome in order to settle their conflicts. Ecclesiastically speaking, Rome is the *apostolic see* (cf. D. 100, 109, 110, etc.).[14] It is associated not only with the "memory" of Peter, but also with that of Paul, thus covering the full range of Christian ministry, since as Paul himself proclaimed, he had been "entrusted with the gospel for the uncircumcised just as Peter was for the circumcised" (Gal. 2:7). As we can see, although they are fully aware of both Petrine and Pauline influences in building the definitive church of Christ, church writers do not mention a divine authority conceded by Christ specifically for the successors of Peter in an episcopal see determined by geography.

From a dogmatic standpoint, the two elements noted here are very relevant for the future. They are so to the extent that they show in a very clear way that, within the growing authority conceded by custom to the Roman see, the church at this period does not think of interpreting biblical revelation as the basis for a primacy of jurisdiction of Peter's successors — in Rome — over the rest of the Christian churches.[15]

Toward a Biblical Foundation

A third fact, at the end of the period, proves that it is only then that there takes place the step which seems not to have occurred to anyone at the beginning. There begins an attempt to find in the words of Jesus to Peter in the Gospels the foundation of a jurisdictional authority proper to the Roman see over the whole church. To be sure this takes place gradually, and the nuances are sometimes eloquent. Thus, for example, in the letter of St. Zosimus to the bishops of Africa in 418 we read:

> Although *the tradition of the Fathers* has attributed such great authority to the Apostolic See that no one would dare to disagree wholly with its judgment, and it has always preserved this [judgment] by canons and rules, and current ecclesiastical discipline up to this time by its laws pays the *reverence* which is due to the *name of PETER* . . . since therefore PETER the head is of such great authority and *he has confirmed the subsequent*

endeavors of all our ancestors, so that the Roman church is fortified ...
by human as well as by divine laws. ... [D. 109]

It is striking how clearly this passage evidences the "human" support behind
reverence for Rome, and only hints at how historically fitting it is that such
authority has come to be accepted, whether because of the benefits it has
brought the church or because of the new "political" situation, to which the
church must inevitably accustom itself as state religion.

As readers will have noticed, however, what is new here on top of everything
else is the mention of "divine laws." St. Boniface, who in this same year 418
rises to the pontifical throne, four years later writes a letter to the bishops of
Macedonia in which we find the (today very) familiar divine justification for
the Roman see on the basis of Jesus' words to Peter according to the Gospel
(Mt. 16:18–19).

In short, there is no denying the growing centralization of the episcopal
function around someone who begins to call himself "bishop of the most holy
Catholic Church" (Letter of St. Cornelius I to St. Cyprian, in the year 252; D.
44). However, from the standpoint of dogma the important thing is not so much
the centralization, but the existence of two tendencies for explaining and justifying it.[16] The more recent of these, although it does not exclude human
historical factors leading to its justification, ends up using for that purpose a
transferred interpretation of New Testament scripture. The other tendency,
which is tacit but very clear, especially the further back in the sources one goes,
gives hints that it has a clear consciousness of the historical fittingness that led
the church to gradually set up this authority. In terms of dogma, perhaps it
would be more accurate to say that the second is not more "secular" than the
first. When it ends up attributing to Christ himself the centralization of authority in the bishop of Rome, it understands that this attribution must be understood in the sense in which he who entrusts his Spirit to the church to continue
his work demands that the church develop its creativity in history for that
purpose, and aids it when it does so.

The Inculturation of Christianity in Hellenism

Pros and Cons of a Necessary Symbiosis

The development of the dogmatic function in this period, however, makes
it necessary to look at yet a third factor, without which the foregoing cannot
be understood correctly. Already several times in this chapter it has been
observed that the similarity between terms used yesterday and today may easily
lead to anachronisms, and the danger is ever-greater the further back in time
one goes.

Previous sections have been dealing with a "crystalization," a "politicization," and a "centralization" of episcopal and finally papal authority. These
tendencies become increasingly clear as we move toward the end of the period.
No doubt these three features, precisely as associated with episcopal authority,
could give the impression that even then people were experiencing something

that is today quite obvious and is of concern to the most serious theologians today. Such theologians fear that the limitless expansion of these features will neutralize the church's efforts to pursue the truth by taking a more creative direction and one more honestly in line with its origins.

If I were to commit such an anachronism, I would not be doing justice to one of the things that is most remarkable about this period. We have already noted one very important element for explaining how such crystalization, politicization, and (Roman) centralization of episcopal authority did not at that time lead to the theological sterility or narrowness today associated with those tendencies. We must indeed bear in mind that until the end of the period in question, Christianity was moving forward, that the Christian communities were not made up of passive masses that had to be administered, and that an episcopacy elected by these very communities (within prudent limits) was much more likely to represent that same overall creativity.

Perhaps the most decisive aspect of this creative activity is that people still do not live in a Christian world. Dialogue with one of the richest cultures—namely, Hellenism—which in its origins is completely foreign to Christianity, forces the church to deal every day with questions that have the realistic quality that characterizes everything rooted in a great cultural tradition.

Of course not everything in this dialogue is positive and the theology of our own era has repeatedly pointed out in a more or less balanced way the negative aspects of the inculturation of Christian theology in the categories of Greek thought. Indeed we must admit that everything was far from perfect or even positive in that Hellenic world with which the church engaged in dialogue during the patristic period. If we are more conscious of this fact today, it is because of what was to happen when the period studied in this chapter came to an end: due to the cultural vacuum produced by the fall of the Roman Empire under the barbarians, for many centuries the Greek mental world was going to prevail among the intellectuals within Christendom, thereby dominating their notion of dogma, and hence of what kind of authority should be in charge of preserving and teaching it. Even in the midst of the modern age, the desire to protect Christendom or the Christian world was to lead the church to remain fiercely attached to ways of thinking which, while they may no longer be fully Greek, are still increasingly incapable of dealing with the expanding set of issues of the culture of the last five hundred years.

G. Ruggieri is right when he speaks of the three pitfalls that the church's conception of divine revelation, and therefore of the dogma defining the beliefs of the church, have had to maneuver around, from New Testament times to the present. For now leaving aside the latter two (the "Gregorian shift" during the Middle Ages, and the Enlightenment) the author describes the first as follows:

Three developments have left a negative mark on the awareness of revelation over the course of church history in a way that has been decisive for everything that followed. We are not saying this here in the sense of a mistaken reading of church history, such as an accelerating decline away from its origins, but in the sense of three dangers that had to be overcome in studying the nature of Christian revelation. The first of these developments is present already in the patristic period and it is connected to *the acculturation of Christianity within Hellenism.*[17]

Ambiguity of Greek Categories for Dogma

Ruggieri goes on to show that this first dialogue of the church with the rest of the world inevitably entailed ambiguity. I am quite aware that to say "first" might look like erroneous history. Was not the church's first dialogue the one it had to hold with the Jewish world from which its own message came? What justifies my speaking here of a first dialogue with Hellenism is that when the early church addressed the Jewish world (as hostile as the overall reception of its message might have been) it was not truly "dialoguing": it was speaking the same cultural language and was expressing its message by making use of its own tradition.

I assert that this ambiguity was unavoidable, for the passage from Ruggieri points to something obvious—namely, how necessary it was that the church assume this risk of inculturation within Hellenism. The point is not that Hellenism was uniquely dangerous in this respect. Something of the sort would have happened with any dialogue between cultures. Ruggieri continues:

> In itself the utilization of expressions foreign to the Jewish view of the world manifests the universal dimension of Christian revelation as it took shape in Jesus Christ. Therefore, the Hellenization of Christianity is not something foreign to Christian revelation initiating a process of decline in awareness of the gospel (A. von Harnack). Indeed within the New Testament itself there is a movement from Jewish to non-Jewish conceptions. Hence the Platonism of the church fathers is continuing a process already begun in the New Testament with the opening to pagans. However, this movement entailed the risk of conceptualizing the Christian mystery *from within* the universal categories of Hellenism ... That very fact demonstrates the need for risk. If faith wants to be responsible to human beings, it cannot but enter into real dialogue with these human beings and with the specific shape they assume in history. However, it must then continue to be aware of the continually lurking danger of understanding revelation on the basis of preestablished ontological categories.[18]

At this point I find a tiny scruple that may ultimately separate me from Ruggieri. He seems to hint that Christianity had to be inculturated into the world of Greek thought because the Jewish world was too particular, whereas the Greek world, having arrived at fully ontological categories, could provide what Christianity needed in order to attain its universality. If that is the case, I must say that as I see things, Greek "ontological" thought was as particular as the categories employed by Hebrew thought. The need to aim toward universality had to lead a message bearing the imprint of its initial Jewish form, toward whatever other kinds of culture there might be, beginning with that which was closest because it was the one in which the church was dwelling.

Be that as it may, this unavoidable ambiguity, this danger inherent in any inculturation, had to be taken on. We should keep that fact in mind when considering the familiar variations in historical scholarship, both secular and theological, when they attempt to evaluate this period that we have called "patristic."

"Daring Capacity for Error"

González Faus is more on the mark when he writes of this radical initial acculturation of the church (on the basis of the apologetics with which the church addresses the Greek world): "Today the (church) fathers are accused of having effected a Hellenization of Christianity, wrapping it up tight in reifying, static, and Platonistic categories, lacking the personal dimension and the historical dimension, and steeped in a dualism toward which we now feel somewhat allergic."

That is the case. However, as the author is well aware, that is only one side of the coin:

We are not going to deny those accusations. They may have their reverse side, however. Is not the lack of synthesis of patristic theology the result of its enormous creative capacity? Today when there is so much talk of theological pluralism and the freedom of the theologian, we ought to recall that theology has never been so free as it was during the patristic period. Perhaps that is why it has never been so alive, never closer to the people, and never more in dialogue with the surrounding culture ... If we try to mingle our lives with those of the fathers some of their "daring capacity for error" may rub off on us. That is also important, because God did not overcome error by removing it from our presence for our own ease, but by turning it into material for a future truth.[19]

I think this last sentence will assure the reader that by including the last quote which attempts to give a favorable accent to the dogmatic period in question, I am not abandoning my basic concern. With the expression, "God changed error into material for a future truth," he is unmistakably hinting, albeit with other terminology than that used here, at what I have called several times in this work "second-level learning," or learning to learn, in contrast to a comfortable process consisting in simply adding items of information to others equally true. This is the only process of knowledge or "pedagogy" that can be part of a revelation of God that continues to develop after God's historic and personal presence among us. It is also the only one in which the method of trial and error cannot be seen as simply a vestige of "incomplete and temporary" things which one would almost say are attributed to the Old Testament out of pity. It was, and continues to be, the divine pedagogy itself that requires that things be so. As Lercaro says in a remarkable text already quoted, it is in this way, and only in this way, that the human way of approaching truth and making it really one's *own* is respected.

If there are three qualifications I would like to make to the passage from González Faus, it is not out of a desire to stake out my own thinking apart from his. It may indeed be due to the fact that the specific topic of the present work is not the same as what prompted his statement. I furthermore believe that these three qualifications are in some fashion implicit in that passage, or that at least they would not grate against the author's overall thinking. In any case, readers should understand that they are not qualifications to the judgment González Faus makes there but to the facts to which he refers and which he is evaluating. The first has to do with the term of comparison used to measure this favorable assessment or shading of patristic theology. The second has to do with the concept of theological freedom employed, and the third with the flaws in Greek culture recognized in that passage.

Not Judging from Today

I would almost say that the first *qualification* is sufficiently explicit in the passage. Certainly, the patristic period, or more specifically its theology, is being criticized *today* especially because of the Hellenism introduced into the categories that serve to acculturate Christianity in the world of that period. There may have been mistakes, but, the author tells us, we must keep in mind the freedom, life, and creativity with which these explorations are thought and expressed. It is obvious that when he says this he is arguing with those who criticize or regard this patristic theology as obsolete (or even harmful). It was in fact freer, more lively, and more challenging to the existing situation than the theology of our own time.

In other words, the implicit term of comparison in the assessment by González Faus is "today." The comparison would show something else if it were made with the "yesterday" of that same era — that is, with the previous period — and that is what we are seeking to do here. In other words, the (favorable) evaluation which can and must be made of the patristic period today should not mean, if I am not mistaken, that the crystalization, authoritarian centralization, or political utilization of dogma to which I referred was not real or had no influence on patristic theology.

I think I have done so with supporting evidence. Hence it means that the full effects which these changes would logically bring in *later* had not *yet* become so obvious. Such changes are now clear *in comparison with the previous period*. It is likewise clear that since they affected the way the Christian community was institutionalized and especially that of the authority charged with making certain that the community maintained genuine continuity in truth, in the future those changes were to prove decisive. The next period to be studied will be illustrative in this respect, and I now simply point that out. I believe there we will see and understand better how the church, which in the Middle Ages has to resolve the *pedagogical* problem of how to lead the new (barbarian) peoples occupying the Roman Empire to Christian truth, is lacking in this very freedom and creativity, which were *still* the patrimony of the patristic period.

Heresy Comes on the Scene

Nor does the second qualification constitute correction. It does not even try to insert any nuance absent from González Faus's assessment, but rather to call the reader's attention to what I think is the purpose of the author himself when he says that "theology was never more free than in the patristic age." It is not just that the author alludes unmistakably to the present. The point is (or so I think) that theology has (at least) two ways of being "free." One is when church authority furnishes it with ample freedom for moving around, investigating, expressing itself, and differing, and another is when theology as pursuit of knowledge fearlessly takes up its task as is its duty, along with the concomitant risks of being mistaken and erring.

The passage quoted shows very clearly, I believe, that it is in this latter way that the author understands the "daring" freedom that then existed. The nuances of the text in this regard are quite transparent. As synonyms of this freedom there are terms like "creativity," "life," attentiveness to the people and their issues (since the patristic writers were pastors, most of whom had been elected and they did theology for and with this same people), and even of a certain anarchy or lack of systematization, which was no hindrance to the necessary unity. Today we would call it pluralism.

Why am I so concerned to point out that this freedom is more internal than external? For the simple reason that even though all the foregoing remains true, it is precisely in this patristic age that there begins to exist something very much resembling a theological "censorship"—that is, a certain coercion, perhaps necessary, in the realm of thinking and of theological expression. Sometimes it is exercised by church authority and sometimes by what will later be called the "secular arm," or in other words political authority which utilizes the Christian religion for its own ends. That is especially true toward the end of the period when, as we have seen, Christianity is set up, directly or indirectly, as the state religion in the waning days of the Roman Empire.

Of course this is not an administrative sort of censorship. It is not institutionalized enough yet for that. It makes itself felt in a spontaneous, unorganized way. But it takes place, and violently so. We need only think, for example, of the ups and downs in the life of an Athanasius or in the monks armed with sticks led by Cyril of Alexandria who charge into the council hall and demand that one sort of dogma or another be adopted. There were denunciations, theological verdicts, condemnations, expulsions, exiles. In addition, conciliar anathemas, excommunications not limited to the domain of individual conscience, now come on the scene. We should not forget that the age of the first ecumenical councils begins toward the end of this period, and like the very first one in Nicea, they abound in "anathemas" hurled at opinions different from those of the majority of the assembled fathers. Not all theological opinions are heard, understood, or respected. Would it not have been possible to call these opinions "incomplete and temporary things" on the way toward truth? Perhaps not, but we should not lose sight of this element when patristic theology is called "free."

It takes time for causes to produce their effects. If in the Old Testament period "theological" disputes are as it were hushed up, we have already seen that it was because there was deep down a national identity, which out of something deeper and identifiable, prevented the community from splitting apart even while at the same time and in important matters there existed *forms of theological thought that were very different*. We have already said that identity or unity becomes more problematic and demanding with the shift from a national religion to one striving for universality. That is all the more the case when that unity is sought by an empire that is falling apart. *Orthodoxy* is increasingly felt to be a political imperative, to the same degree that variety in matters of dogma looks like rampant danger for both church and state.

It might be said that there is a great deal of vitality, creativity, and a bold willingness to risk falling into error *personally*—with the concomitant political risks—that follow from thinking for oneself and carrying out pastoral tasks. But it does not seem that the same risk is allowed (not even by the same people) when it is a matter of *the church as a whole*. During this period aggression against the heresiarch is as strong as the freedom and creativity González Faus justly points out. Nevertheless, it is clear that this fierce struggle for orthodoxy does not (yet) possess the institutionally unified means it possesses today for carrying out that function. That concern does not measure everything with the same gauge: it leaves doors open to initiative and to the personal quality of the contending groups, and therefore it is more compatible with that internal freedom of theological thinking which certainly existed.

As we have pointed out so many times, we should not fall into the anachronism of imagining that the theological questions which are so monitored today are of the same nature as those that aroused the theologians and pastors whose work is associated with the controversies of the early ecumenical councils. At that time there was a conviction not present today in the same measure, the conviction that beyond certain limits, the very process of learning through error went substantially off the track, either because what was already erroneous could become irreversible or because coming back to the truth would entail too high a cost. What is said of feelings may also be valid about truth: some kinds of love kill. Although perhaps any error can teach, some errors can kill before their crises produce life-giving fruits.

Of course when I claim that at that time this was a conviction (leaving aside the aggression involved) I am not saying that people consciously and clearly possessed the criterion for discerning those points beyond which the "anathema" actually meant being outside the "Christian way" (= *hodos*)[20] toward the truth. They knew that at a certain level of crystalization, certitude, and expansion, an erroneous theology might no longer be compatible with participation in the journey of the Christian community and in its faith.

I do not think that one can find in patristic theology any explicit treatment of this criterion, which is more intuitive than discursive and entails a good measure of implied futurology. Even today I believe that this is still the case inasmuch as the lack of such a criterion indicates that something is missing. This is a serious matter, since observing the church's past, it is not easy to know whether all the instances in which it excluded people were due to equally significant deviations—or to put it another way, if they have all been worth the trouble. The principle formulated at Vatican II on ecumenism—namely, that "there is an order or 'hierarchy' of truths, since they vary in their relationship to the foundation of Christian faith" (UR 11) — has not been explicitated, developed, and applied in the theology of the Catholic Church[21] — and perhaps has not even been fully accepted.

My aim here is simply to point out the developments I believe are significant. I think here we have one of these developments. Although there are some symptoms of it in Paul's condemnations of the Judaizers during the apostolic age, or in those of the Johannine theology against Docetists in the post-apostolic age of the New Testament, the problem of *heresy*, and of how to recognize, confront, and suppress it, seems to be first posed in practice and on a sociologically significant scale in the patristic age. At that point people feel sure that a halt must be put to a "pluralism" which seems to entail both admitting and denying the trinitarian idea of God or the full divinity and humanity of Jesus Christ. To claim to be following the same path without achieving a minimal agreement on such questions would be madness — or would it?

This very problem is possibly becoming just as serious and reaching a new level of relevance today. Arianism is dead of course, but the ecumenical current flowing out of Vatican II and supported by profound theological inquiry together with the reevangelization of peoples poorly brought into Christianity seem to be incapable of carrying out these tasks given what is already established dogmatically. Heresies are being rehabilitated and given new life. Within the church there are profound syncretisms joining the Christian religion to profoundly different ideas from other religions. There is no clear sense of what theology must do with regard to these approaches, which seem to be off track, but which yet seem to have contributed a great deal to human groups and may yet do so for the Christian pursuit of truth and for the enrichment of its dogma. On the other hand, how can it be denied that these ways continue to affirm what in a particular moment was regarded as a decisive and irreversible "error"?[22]

Alliance of Dogma with the Category of "Nature"

The third and last qualification has to do with what the passage quoted above has to say about the acculturation of Christianity within the categories of Greek thought. González Faus is right when he considers it a sign of vitality, creativity, and freedom on the part of patristic theology that it understood this task and carried it out more or less successfully. He is even more correct insofar as he has no illusions about the limitations of these Greek categories, which are "reifying, static, and Platonistic . . . lacking in the personal dimension and the historical dimension, and steeped in a dualism toward which we now feel somewhat allergic."

The aim here is not to revise that assessment of advantages and disadvantages which might seem to end in stalemate. Moreover, we all know that in matters of history there is no point in working with hypotheses of what "might have been." The fates of cultures, like those of human beings, are unforeseeable (given the almost infinite variables running all through them and conditioning them). For example, at their height Egypt and Mesopotamia possessed a learning that was more advanced, developed, and sophisticated than that of Israel, and a political power that seemed destined to last, and yet today nothing remains of them. On the other hand, Hebrew thought in its two forms—both of them "mounted" on Hellenism—continues to have a great deal of influence in a civilization which has reached planetary proportions.

What I would like to note here very briefly amounts to an evaluation on a different level of logic, in which the point is not so much to know whether or not Greek thought was deserving of having the Christian message acculturated within it. From a metadogmatic perspective the point is to delve into the conditioning that this inculturation created for *the very idea* of what a dogma is or should be.

Indeed, it is quite possible that Christian dogmatic thought came out preserved and even enriched on one point or another. A case in point is, I believe, the contribution of Nicea, Ephesus, and Chalcedon to the understanding of the full divinity and full humanity of Jesus. Albeit with shortcomings, the historic character of the God of the Bible was preserved. The God revealed in Jesus is not known through a philosophical deduction but through the "historic" predicates justified by the concrete life of Jesus.[23]

Furthermore, if we want an even more familiar example, we have the Johannine theology in the New Testament itself. We have already said that Paul, in his own fashion, and especially John were the first apologists, the pioneers in presenting the Christian message in categories elaborated or used by Hellenism in the Roman Empire. Thus the exegetical controversy in recent decades over whether the fourth Gospel is more Jewish than Greek or vice versa does not make much sense. It is trying to do both things at once. Hence it presents the life of Jesus as a paradigm of that world (more or less under the influence of a diffused Platonism) marked by a deep dualism: the imperishable world of eternal ideas up above and the apparent world of ephemeral copies down below. The Word or (only-begotten) Son of God enters into this world below and teaches human beings the way toward "knowing" the truth about the world above and also (and this is deeply Hebrew) "doing" that same truth. This way, however, is no longer that of contemplating the eternal return of the same things, but love for one's brother and sister. What is purest in Hebrew thought is maintained and prevails, albeit in new wineskins.

Such battles won, however, should not make us forget the war—which is on a different level of logic. Hellenism is a coherent and all-embracing worldview. This same love that emerges triumphant in the fourth Gospel must pay that worldview its tribute. It becomes a sign of the divine to the extent that it draws Jesus out of a conflictive and concrete history on the side of the poor. Why? Because Hellenism accustoms the mind to seek the truth in fixed essences— fixed as the *nature of things*, or what Platonism calls the world of "eternal ideas." History is not a category from which the truth emerges, despite all of John's efforts to show Jesus "pitching his tent among us" (Jn. 1:14). The conflict the fourth Gospel recognizes is that between Jesus and, let us say, the "machinery" of the world. This is now no longer the real world that makes most people poor and outcast.

It is true that the patristic period is still quite resistant to the unbalancing tendencies of Hellenism. That may be why it lacks a finished "synthesis." These will come later with a more complete victory of Plato and Aristotle in the great era of "synthesis," the Middle Ages, the era of the *perennial* philosophy (and theology). The seed is already planted, however.

What can I do to make the reader feel this point, which otherwise may seem to be an abstruse philosophical disquisition? The best way is perhaps to return to a fundamental question about the development of dogma *starting with Jesus Christ*. We have already noted that in accordance with John's own thought, St. Augustine translated the Gospel line "It is much better for you that I go" (Jn. 16:7), with the following line, which constitutes a dogma about dogma (meta-dogma): "The Lord himself, in deigning to become our way, did not want to hold us back but to move on." For Augustine the very absolute Truth which revealed itself to us is not awaiting us, all at once around the corner; it is not in the minds of any of those who saw it and touched it incarnate in our world, nor is it nearby, deposited in a book, even if that book is the Bible. In some way, the absolute Truth we possess does not hold us back but is ever putting us on the road — on the road *toward truth*.[24]

Thus far what Augustine says deserves our total agreement. However, as soon as we observe the immediate context of the sentence we will find a subtle but characteristic difference. The whole of Hellenism is present there, as is its (future) impact blocking the very idea of dogmatic development which it seemed to be setting in motion. Why keep seeking, or what is there to seek, when we already have the revelation of absolute truth? According to Augustine, Jesus himself must go on and not hold us back; but it is so that "we would not out of weakness remain attached to *temporal things*, even though he had received and operated those things for our salvation — but that we would rather run with enthusiasm so as to merit to be transported and led to him who *freed our nature from temporal things*."[25] Obviously, what is waiting for us in this "beyond" of Jesus is not a historic effort to build the complete truth (*on earth as it is in heaven*), but rather its opposite (existentially speaking): the contemplation of this eternal heaven now *free of temporal things* where Jesus is said to be awaiting us, seated "at God's right hand."

By contrast, when I spoke of the need for a process of learning to learn, of one day finding ourselves without the physical presence of parents, teachers, or books giving answers, I was referring to a step not toward the eternal but toward the fullness of history. This crucial moment is part of all genuine pedagogy. The process does not stop there, but it no longer "seems" to be "education" because the students have been left alone. Their *main* activity is no longer that of interpreting the guidelines offered by their educators for dealing with each case. It is in their *own history* that solutions are now being sought. What is left behind has become "spirit," and it is incorporated and acts in a way that is likewise "spiritual." Christian faith is to be translated into this fuller "truth" — namely, the "more human" solutions for which it was intended (GS 11).

This "spirit" (in lower or upper case) continues that "literal" presence of the educator even more effectively — even if it is the presence of incarnate truth itself. "Blessed are they who have not seen and have believed" are the strange words with which the Johannine Gospel closes (Jn. 20:29). The bold words of the poet León Felipe seem to echo them, "He [God] . . . knows that being alone, with no gods observing us, we work better."[26]

Between these two ways of conceiving the meaning of this "better" will be located the great hermeneutic gap either separating faith from human life in history, or not separating it. This chasm will become ever-wider to the extent that the balance shifts toward this "Greek present" of eternal ideas which is so difficult to avoid in undertaking the bold and necessary effort of translating Christian faith into the Greek world. Nonetheless, we must not think that the Spirit who continues the work of Jesus is a subtle and attenuated form of Jesus himself. It is a completely divine power, one continuing Jesus (Jn. 14:26; 16:13), active with all the power of grace that is in God, and acting in the world of human beings, both inside and outside the Christian community.

CHAPTER 9

New Peoples for the Faith

The point has already been made: this is not a book about history. It is not an attempt to trace the specific history of Christian "dogmas," even though the last two chapters might give that impression. In those chapters some observations based on historical scholarship had to be made in order to explain what happened with the "divine pedagogy" when, after the ten-century process in which the Old Testament was composed, it suddenly set the human being, in the New Testament, face-to-face with the Truth pure and simple, Absolute Truth.

Naturally I am aware that I am speaking in a language that readers will already have classified as mythical. They should keep in mind, however, that in both the Old and the New Testament this divine pedagogy takes advantage of human means which secular history could organize like any series of seemingly parallel historical events.

Inevitably the last two chapters had to look like chapters in a "history," because the aim was to apprise the reader of developments that decisively changed the direction of the idea of "dogma" and how it should be elaborated. Today that transformation cannot be fully understood without taking into account a number of developments during the five centuries examined in the two preceding chapters. It is not inconsequential that during that span of time the Christian community in which dogma is elaborated goes from being a few dozen witnesses of the life and message of Jesus of Nazareth to constituting a church operating legally during the final period of the Roman Empire preceding the cultural cataclysm entailed by its fall in the West.

It is practically impossible for a lay Christian today to conjure up an image of that church of the first five centuries. Few things in it have the same names as those today, and when they do, that very synonymy is usually misleading, as we have seen. One is aware, for example, that a church has dogmas and discusses them, but Christians today have little knowledge of what was discussed during those centuries. Moreover, the issues discussed in the early ecumenical councils say very little to them, for the problem that gave rise to Arianism is now confined to the shelves of history. The theology of the church fathers also says very little to them, for today this whole vast array of things related to faith in Christ is the property of a few specialists in that area. Augustine himself—not to speak of a Gregory Nazianzen, a Paul of Samosata, a Cyril of Alexandria—is more familiar as the saint who wrote the *Confessions* than as the one who reformulated Christian dogma for the Latin world.

Nor can lay people today readily imagine the life, activity, and self-governance of a church which was to acquire the visible structures so familiar today only at the end of the patristic period. Similarly, they would have to make an enormous effort at historical imagination to picture how a Christian church could have lived for at least a century using as scriptures consecrated by divine inspiration only what we today call the Old Testament. Yet unless they can imagine this situation, lay people today will not be able to imagine how this church for some time juggled the two opposite hypotheses: that the divine pedagogy which had been at work until that point in what was called the "Word of God" had come to a halt, or that it was still possible that the pursuit of truth could continue to expand and offer guidance, even though the incarnate Word was now departed from our earth.

Thus, without claiming in any way to be a historian, I have had to furnish readers with certain historical information in order to let them know what factors have been at work so that dogma has reached them today in one fashion and not in another.

That is going to change, however, from this point onward, and radically so. It is not simply that the new era we face (readers and myself) occupies a full ten centuries, and that the leap in historical material is immeasurably greater. Even more important is the fact that from the fall of the Roman Empire and the occupation of its territory by the so-called barbarian peoples, the landscape becomes more familiar to us. The events and documents of these Middle Ages, whether written down or chiseled in stone, while still remote, are more familiar, even if the meaning of many things still escapes us. We should not forget that through their particular histories, their literature, and their art, the peoples of Europe have familiarized us with this "Christian world" through which each of them lived, although in their own way and with their own characteristics.

Perhaps in no other realm of existence is this medieval past still present even today (in the Western world) as it is in the realm of Christian dogma, and particularly in that of the dogma of the Catholic Church.[1] In other words, within the bounds of the Catholic Church and perhaps only there, what was created for thinking and living the Christian faith in the Middle Ages survived almost untouched, right up to the eve of Vatican II, although always with variations in degree and intensity. Moreover, since the council has been slow to produce the changes that the popes who convoked and accompanied it were expecting, and since the church to some extent seems inclined to retreat from what was proposed there, certain features of dogma deriving from the Middle Ages are still exercising a significant or decisive pressure on Catholic theology even in the midst of the nuclear age. Only the need to separate the very abundant material at hand into three chapters, one on the Middle Ages and the other two on the modern age, will influence the (external) order with which I study these factors. In the way each is studied, however, the emphasis will be on continuity up to the present.

Of course this continuity, especially through the Renaissance and the so-called modern era, is that of a church *on the defensive* precisely against a modernity that is making inroads all over the church institution and its activity—and perhaps in dogma more than anywhere else. Even so, however, it would be artificial to divide this continuity into historical periods. That would require repeating too many things and in most cases over time we would note only a change of degree, not of direction. Hence this work herewith renounces even the minimum appearance of the sequential history present in the last two chapters. From this point onward, I will try to proceed by indicating in order of appearance the factors that may significantly condition the development of dogma up to the present. In dealing with each of these factors I will make use of data from different periods (even if I have to commute back and forth in time) insofar as I believe they are suitable for making more understandable the changes introduced into that development which, for well or ill, we experience today.

Nevertheless, one prior observation, both geographical and historical, is in order. The period in which I will enter at this point is quite clearly marked off, especially from the standpoint of dogma, due to the cultural event that begins it and ends it. At its beginning stands the fall—or rather the falls, since it was not a single fall—of what was called the Roman Empire of the West into the power of the barbarian peoples, around the fifth century C.E. At the end, and with the same degree of variation in accordance with the different European peoples affected, we find another cultural event that can easily be dated: the Renaissance. Following closely upon it is another event more closely related to the realm of dogma, the Reformation.

The problems involved in marking off this phenomenon—as well as much of its interest—begin when one tries to determine its geographical boundaries. Those boundaries are obviously those within which its cultural influence is most direct.

The Cultural "Organism" That Goes through Its "Middle" Age

That biology has had an impact on the interpretation of history (especially as influenced by evolutionary Darwinism, through Herbert Spencer) is very well known. Biology has indeed provided the mental categories for the way cultures are approached and studied. Like organisms in the animal world, and especially like human beings, cultures seem to go through birth, growth, and decline followed by death. Thus, the great cultures arise in history and then disappear, one after the other. In the past all—except one—extended their influence over particular geographical areas, and then died and were absorbed or destroyed by others (or survived for a time in small enclaves with none of their earlier splendor and influence). In the contemporary world Arnold Toynbee is perhaps the last of the great historians who use, albeit not always explicitly, the "organic" hypothesis, in order to establish a bridge and hence the possibility of comparing (insofar as they are regarded as organisms) phenomena that are extremely heterogenous.[2]

What kind of cultural "organism" are people talking about here? Where are

its spatial boundaries? The very term "middle ages" itself suggests a stage
between two cultures, the previous one and the one following. The organism
seems to remain *the same*, since only in that way can the expression "middle
ages" make sense. The previous stage can only be that which began to emerge
from prehistory and enter history with Greek culture. That approach downplays
how great a break is entailed in the shift in hegemony from Greece to Rome
(whose ancestors, the Etruscans, are lost in the mists of prehistory). Be that as
it may, such a "middle age" indicates a radically new stage, one that cannot be
confused with mere growth of the same thing. The newness begins with the
invasion and incorporation of the barbarian peoples as the dominant factor in
that part of the Roman Empire called the West—or with its falling into the
power of new peoples whose culture was so inferior as to suspend the cultural
process coming down from Greece. The medieval period is thus actually the
"middle age" of almost all of European culture. In these notions there is
unquestionably a degree of hermeneutic manipulation making it possible not
to admit the death of Greco-Roman culture (which is in fact to be resurrected
in the Renaissance) and to link it to the modern era of Western civilization.

Europe without Middle Ages—the Eastern Empire

As we know, when this fall occurs, the vast extension of the Roman Empire
and the difficulty of governing it from a single place has led to the establishment
of a state with two heads: the Western Roman Empire and the Eastern Roman
Empire, each with its own emperor and capital (Rome and Constantinople).
With regard to the issue we had begun to consider, the Eastern Roman Empire
actually has no Middle Ages, since its own (Greek) culture dies for practical
purposes, at the very moment that what amounts to the Middle Ages (in the
rest of the former Roman Empire) is ending. This empire encompasses Eastern
Europe, Asia Minor, and Egypt (in addition to all of North Africa) and includes
cultural (and religious) capitals like Antioch, Alexandria, and later, Constantinople. As a whole, this territory was never dominated by the barbarian peoples
as was its Western counterpart. The situation of Rome at the beginning of the
fifth century would continue in the East for almost ten centuries with no apparent break. There is no way to resolve the issue of continuity in culture, if one
ignores territorial extension. The Eastern Roman Empire will continue to be
the bearer of Greek culture, speaking that language and practicing Christianity
in the peoples that remain under its control until the fifteenth century.

It is only *on the periphery* of this empire (and somewhat later) that there will
occur something like the incorporation of some barbarian peoples into Christianity and into the remnants of Greco-Roman culture which takes place in the
rest of Europe. That, however, does not mean a break in history, because these
peoples will never occupy a central role during this period. The inculturation
of Christianity already discussed will continue its course. What brings about the
admittedly slow death of this culture is the fact that another people gradually
dominates the southern borders of the empire—namely, Islam. Gradually over
the centuries Islam pulls the African and Asian areas away from Christianity
and simultaneously away from the Eastern Roman Empire (and Greek culture)

until the fall of Constantinople in the middle of the fifteenth century (1453). For its part Islam possesses what the barbarian peoples of the West do not possess, a self-sufficient, albeit exotic, culture and religion. Its invasion of the empire does not create a power vacuum such as might lead to a belated repetition of the Christian Middle Ages.

Only a small part can be said, by extension, to have entered into the cultural framework known as the Middle Ages with its consequent backwardness. From the standpoint of the dominant culture in Constantinople that part is the least significant, that of the Slavic peoples of the north and one or other country in the Balkans. That process takes place late and with ups and downs, for indeed Islam is to reach the very gates of Vienna. These countries continue to practice Christianity and will later be culturally united to the rest of Europe.

Moreover, it is true that not all of what was the Western Roman Empire underwent a Middle Ages strictly speaking. With a good deal of truth it has been claimed that Spain had no Middle Ages and therefore bypassed the feudalism that imparted its social structure to medieval Europe. Indeed, all of North Africa, and for centuries Spain, were part of Islamic culture and from that time onward were to suffer its ups and downs. Spain, however, little by little returned to the Christian world and to the West in the only crusade that left lasting results. It completed this return at the end of the Middle Ages, and in a cultural reconquest that was so deep that a century later Spain was to play a leading role among the nations of the West in what was called its "golden age."

"Middle" Age(s) between Greek and Modern Culture

All these observations on human geography indicate how relative and complex is the phenomenon of history which serves as the *foundation* for the dogmatic development of Christianity in the period here to be studied. As I was writing a moment ago, the very concept of "Middle Ages" is something of a hermeneutic manipulation of a world forging its history as the history of a Europe on the rise, which in the next period is destined in its culture to become universal in scope. When kept within its proper limits, however, the term Middle Ages does not imply any evaluation. Indeed, when one visits the mosque of Córdoba today and looks at its oldest parts (contemporary with the high Middle Ages elsewhere in Europe) one is astonished at such perfection and beauty, and wonders whether non-Arabic civilization could offer any comparable work from the same period.

Furthermore, if it were necessary to attribute a Greek origin to the culture of Western Europe, one could assert that the true continuity goes much more by way of the Arab world which transmitted Greek knowledge to Europe, than by the barbarian peoples, who after a brief imitation of classicism, turned away from Greece to build another culture, that which is now called *modernity*.

Thus what really *emerges* from these "Middle Ages" toward the "modern age" in the fifteenth century is a mosaic of young peoples (young at least as permanently settled peoples) whose only common internal element, their "culture," is that they constitute or have constituted a "Christian world" — or at least a world that believes it is Christian. Indeed, it does not yet have any structure or identity that can both define and unify its geographical limits and the growing diversity of its nationalities.

These peoples and states differ among themselves and are often age-old enemies. As their common stock of memories, images, and norms they possess only that which has gradually been created well or badly for centuries within "Christendom"—even though the latter is already fatally wounded as a Christian *world*.

Thus the fact that they have undergone this period together and have made it their cultural tradition constitutes one end of the thread. The other is constituted by another point still located in the future of this world: that which will keep it united during the "modern era." It is likewise that which will regard the age being studied here as precisely the "middle term" between its origins in the Greco-Roman Empire and another kind of civilization which will eventually exercise its pressure and influence all over the planet. Thus it will become a civilization, if not a culture,[3] the first truly ecumenical human structure—that is, the first one which in its effects can unite in practical terms the whole planet.[4]

The Middle Ages and Christian Dogma—Methodology

What is important here is certainly not to come up with a "just" assessment of the Middle Ages, nor even of the kind of extended Middle Ages that the Tridentine church tries to represent—even if such an evaluation were possible. What we must do, however, is to note, as I have tried to do in the preceding, that a particular Christian conception of "truth"—that is, of *dogma*—due to unforeseeable historical circumstances went on to become a decisive element in the construction of this "Christian" world (whether it deserves to be called that or not). Not only did it guide and protect its unity (as in the previous period). One could almost say that it brought that world out of nothingness—not out of physical nothingness, but out of cultural nothingness. In some fashion it prepared that world—although it later regretted doing so—to take on a decisive role in the development of humankind (or its destruction, for that matter).

A historic "development" of this magnitude lasting many centuries—which we are dealing with in a single chapter—exempts the author from any sort of detailed historical research. The only thing that can and must be done here is to show whether (and how) the task to which the church was devoted during this long period of the Middle Ages (which was prolonged in a defensive stance far into the modern era) brought about significant changes in how human access to God's revelation—that is, to *dogma*—was understood.

The Barbarian Peoples

What Was Going on in the Sixth Century in Byzantium and Rome?

From a theological standpoint we find something striking at the outset of the Middle Ages in Europe, something that will pose a truly *new* problem for the formation of Christian dogma. It will not be easy, however, to demonstrate it to readers accustomed to think it is easy, for example, to move without blinking from Constantinian Christianity to the great dogmatic syntheses of the thirteenth century.

Hence I propose a kind of didactic compromise. In this first section of the chapter I am going to show—in contrast to what was happening in the Eastern (Roman?) Empire—a few events by way of example of what was going on in Rome (and in the rest of the Western Empire) toward the end of the sixth century and beginning of the seventh.[5] Although it is quite brief, this period is very characteristic because it provides a picture of Christianity and of its central institution, the papacy, confronted with something profoundly "new" and unexpected: the barbarian peoples who are occupying practically the whole of what was the Roman Empire of the West a century after its real fall. On paper Rome still belongs to the emperor in Constantinople and is not physically occupied by the barbarians.

To show how the task that the church is undertaking is new, I am going to be guilty of a small but innocent anachronism. I am going to try to describe this situation in Rome with a few brush strokes, assuming that it is almost contemporaneous with the situation of the church a century and a half previously in the other part of the empire, when the famous fourth ecumenical council was held in Chalcedon. At that council was debated one of the most sensitive and decisive points of Christian dogma, and also, we should note, one of the most complex and subtle. The issue was nothing less than the correct and meaningful use of the categories of the Greek language in order to speak of Jesus of Nazareth as true God and at the same time as true human being. This was certainly one of the most difficult points ever dealt with in the church: making a "concrete and contingent history," that of Jesus of Nazareth, the hermeneutical key for giving shape in the human mind to the image or idea of God. The language of a culture accustomed to thinking of eternal and universal ideas had to be bent so that it could think of the Absolute on the basis of the contingent par excellence: the free history of a human being.

In any case, what was going on in Rome *almost* during this same period? The East continued to buzz with intellectual activity. With its bouts of *monenergism* and of *monothelitism*, it continued to debate fiercely the subtleties of this profound unity of divine nature and human nature in Jesus. And what was going on in the other part of the ancient empire, the one practically occupied by the barbarian peoples, some of them now converted to Christianity? In particular, what was going on in Rome, the see by then recognized, as we have seen, as that of the vicar of Peter? How did the latter act in a city that was no longer the capital of any empire? Note that this was not just any pope. The one occupying the see was an extraordinary pontiff, St. Gregory the Great.

Rome is still inhabited by "Romans." The supreme pontiff is in fact a Roman from a patrician family. Although Rome has been occupied and devastated by barbarian hordes, formally it remains the possession of the Eastern Empire, whose capital is Byzantium. Nevertheless, the imperial power is now a long distance away, off in Constantinople, the name given to Byzantium in honor of the great emperor. By contrast, the Lombard barbarians have settled very close to Rome, and their generals practically have Rome at their mercy. It would seem, however, as though a certain ancient prestige, that of the old imperial city, prevents them from coming in and sacking it, or of setting themselves up there and pushing out its usual inhabitants. The hexarch, the representative of the imperial authority of Constantinople, does not live there but instead has chosen Ravenna as his see. Actually, like the empire itself, he is little more than a decorative figure in Italy, which he cannot even govern.

Rome has become impoverished in all senses, and very rapidly so in cultural matters. Even the pope cannot follow the theological debates in the East by himself, since he does not know Greek, the language of culture. Although the barbarians are not still in the city, since they are occupying territory in Gaul, Britain, Spain, North Africa, and a number of other former provinces of the Roman Empire, Rome is now a defeated city handed over to the new and overwhelming power of these young peoples. For Romans recalling the past, they are *barbarians* — that is, uncultured.

The unquestioned authority remaining in Rome who represents it to the barbarians as the center of a civilization which they have long coveted and which has attracted them from faraway lands, is the supreme pontiff. Through mass conversions, the sincerity and depth of which would provide material for considerable discussion, several of these peoples regard themselves as Christian and "practice" this religion — that is, its worship. Several of them have encountered and adopted Christianity under a heretical Arian form (for example, the Lombards who are near Rome and dominate a great deal of Italy). In the long run, however, more important to them than dogmas they do not understand is their respect for this religious authority centralized in Rome, which could almost be regarded as the heir of all that tangibly remains of the ancient empire that attracted and fascinated them for such a long time. Thus it is that all of them, some later than others, place themselves under the "orthodox" authority of the Roman pontiff:

> From the reconquest [of Rome] by Justinian, the Eastern emperor who retook Italy during the first half of the sixth century, the Roman see was an episcopal see on the outskirts of the Byzantine empire, kept under the close supervision of the *basileus*, while the overwhelming influence of the Eastern patriarchs within the Greek church questioned its spiritual primacy. On the other hand, the pope occupied a very favorable position in an Italy in ruins and disregarded by an overstretched empire. In Rome itself, due to the weakness of the civil authorities, he had become the true head of the city. The patrimony of Saint Peter, by far the greatest fortune in property in Italy, brought him abundant resources. Thus he had to take the lead in resisting the Lombard invasion and organizing recruitment of local militias. His authority, embodying Latin patriotism, gradually became identified with what still remained of the Roman *republica*. Alien as they were to the Greek world, the wandering barbarians were all the more inclined to regard him as the representative of Rome and of the imperial idea.[6]

Alien to the Greek world was a pope who, as we have said, was not too embarrassed to confess that he did not know Greek, the cultured language of the Roman Empire. This was a time when that Greek culture lent its most subtle concepts for the most arduous issues in Christian theology such as that of the "hypostatic union" of the two natures, divine and human, in the person of the Word of God, Jesus of Nazareth. The Council of Chalcedon had taken place and its ultimate consequences were still being discussed. Yet how little was left in Rome itself, in the center of (what was to be) "Christendom," of that culture into which Christianity was still struggling to penetrate and to acquire citizenship rights!

New Peoples or Barbarian Peoples?

It should not be forgotten that Greek culture had permitted itself to divide all humankind into two cultural categories, Greeks and barbarians, as though it were the most natural thing in the world. Even Paul testifies to it in his own way when he writes that Christ has abolished this division which he sees as running right through humankind (1 Cor. 1:24; 10:32; 12:13; Gal. 3:28; Col. 3:11). Of course he is thereby indicating that the "Roman" world is actually "Greek" with respect to higher culture, just as the slaves to whom the Roman paterfamilias tend to entrust the education of their children are Greek.

If the Romans themselves, strictly speaking, had been barbarians and with their spirit remained so, the Jews (descending from an alien culture, as high as it might seem to us) were so even more. Paul gives them a status apart because God's revelation made to them has raised this people to a rank similar to that of the Greeks (or even higher). Those on both sides, "Jews and Greeks," belong to the Christian community which is based on this same revelation made "first" to the Jewish people. Moreover, from the purely cultural standpoint, the Jews were no doubt likewise regarded as "barbarians," only a little less perhaps than the barbarians par excellence, such as the Scythians, who at that time were nomads on the edges of the empire (Col. 3:11). This Paul cannot allow.

Thus the peoples who in the period we are examining occupy the Roman Empire from its weakened borders are similar to the Scythians. What problem does that situation pose? At first glance it is very simple: the challenge is to pass the Christian message from the now converted "Greek" peoples to the "barbarian" pagans. A whole book would nevertheless be required to show in all its depth how our Christianity—or our Catholicism—today bears all the marks left by centuries of dealing with the extremely difficult resolution this problem required.

Again, however, wherein lies this huge problem? Is it not perhaps that the "barbarians" were easily and quickly converted to Christianity? While this conversion may have entailed a moment of pressure and violence on behalf of the gospel, the Christian faith soon became a kind of "tradition" inextricably rooted in these peoples. Almost the very same thing happened in Latin America with the pre-Columbian peoples inhabiting it before the Spanish and Portuguese conquest, and with the Africans brought to them as slaves.

This whole lengthy introduction in which I have been engaged in this chapter has been done with a purpose: to show that the peoples more or less fairly called "barbarians" are presenting in their culture and customs a picture very similar to that of the Jewish people under David. That is, the situation is similar to that under the first Yahwist king of all Israel at the moment when the biblical word of God begins to be composed and assembled.

Repeat Old Testament Pedagogy?

What should be done, then? Go back to square one in revelation and retrace the whole journey? Or bypass the route of experience and incorporate as quickly as possible the new peoples into the level of Christianity reached by the church in the Greek world? Or try something new, since neither extreme seems feasible?

In order to return to square one the church would have had to establish a watertight compartment between the two ways of being a "Christian" human being. But how high a price would have to be paid? Certainly that is how Old Testament "dogma" began to be created. Already alerted by what has been said earlier in part 2, readers will now ask the essential question which will remain present in the remaining chapters: *Why did the "divine pedagogy" not follow with the barbarian peoples the slow but sure path dogma took right up to threshold of the Christian message?* The answer I would like to propose at this moment, and which I will try to demonstrate thoroughly to readers is very simple. It is that the truth *is no longer being sought,* as it was in the past and as we have seen in the Old Testament. The right answers are already known; they simply have to be made comprehensible little by little, well or poorly, to those peoples who are asking for them. At least one part of the church knows those answers, and knows how to explain them. That is the *ecclesia docens,* the teaching church. This judgment is not meant pejoratively; it is, however, a very serious, critical, and problematic situation.

The Teaching Church: A Hasty Pedagogy

Necessary Simplification of the Christian Message

Readers will allow me to make some further references to obvious similarities which would make it possible, if history were to be repeated, to expect that in the Middle Ages there might begin a pedagogical process which, if not quite the same, would be very similar to that of Jewish people at the beginning of the monarchy, and therefore still at the beginning of the composition of what is today the deposit (of the first phase) of divine revelation—and of the "dogma" belonging to that phase.

First of all, the barbarian peoples' adoption of Christian faith does not produce anything like a rapid and widespread change in the violent customs existing among them up to that point. Murder and heroic virtue combine in the most startling fashion. The same mixture of barbarism and humanity that marks the story of David and his rise to the throne under Solomon, also marks the checkered and often violent succession of the first Frankish, Visigoth, and Lombard Christian kings.[7]

Secondly, the little that can be done to educate these peoples is to be concentrated in injecting the most basic civic morality in the minds of all members of the population. Given the level reached by the culture of these people, this morality, if it is to be internalized, assumes a kind of covenant with God similar to the one preached by the ancient prophets in Israel. Perhaps more importantly, it assumes an interpretation of the experience of history similar to what the Deuteronomist did with the ancient memories of the judges in Israel prior to the monarchy. There he used the familiar sequence: Israel forgets Yahweh; Yahweh sends powerful enemies who bring Israel to the point of crisis; in crisis Israel returns to Yahweh; Yahweh raises up a warrior leader (= judge), the liberator of the people. Such is the thrust of what is now called Providence (as it was formerly called the Covenant).

It is true of course that after the exile and the issues it raises, and after the theological crisis to which the book of Job attests, and after the effort to situate beyond death the moment when God's necessary justice is to be made manifest, and furthermore after Paul's creative effort to show the maturity and freedom to which one who has believed in Jesus' message ought to advance, it becomes difficult to conceive how the church could set out on this path again with the barbarian peoples and retrace with the people a journey already taken centuries ago.[8]

At the very moment I have chosen to make the comparison, we find something very suggestive in this regard in the figure of Pope Gregory. He is certainly not ignorant of the christological controversies perturbing the church in the East (and which come to a tiny informed minority in the West). It would seem, however, that he is conscious of the real issues facing the peoples he must lead and educate, using his authority for that purpose. Of the several works he writes, two will draw our attention here, since they reflect very well the popular and theological issues of that age.

One of them, now known as *Dialogues*, originally must have been called *The Miracles of the Fathers in Italy* (understood as fathers of the church in a broad sense). When his partner in the dialogues points out that the contemporary saints seem to work few miracles, the pope "begins to inform him of wonders that have not been told, and goes on to fill four books of stories that in themselves make up a 'golden legend.' "[9] As in the beginnings of the composition of the Pentateuch, "theophanies" accompany God's friends—judges in ancient times, monks and saints now—and with miracles God intervenes in history and is there made manifest.

In the realm of exegesis Gregory writes a book today called *Moralia*, whose earliest title was *Exposition of the Book of Saint Job*. It may seem strange that as a follow-up to his very popular previous book, which had a Deuteronomic slant, now with theological pretensions (as modest as they might have been at that time) he should write an exegesis of nothing less than the book of Job. This book itself is commonly regarded as almost a book of theology. It contains a refutation of the doctrine that God carries out *in this life* a retribution for the morality practiced by each human being. Perhaps a hymn to the divine transcendence whose creation and providence are beyond human comprehension,

Job was certainly not a work that could carry further the far simpler and less problematic teaching of the *Dialogues*. However, in it Gregory engages in the kind of exegesis proper to his own period which is very different from ours today. Employing an allegory[10] in which Job's false friends represent the heretics and Job the church, which is victorious in the end, he diverts attention from the deep problem of God's justice given the lack of a world beyond this one, toward the much simpler questions the church had to resolve in dealing with the conversion of some barbarian peoples (such as the Lombards) from paganism and the Arian heresy.

A reader may be a bit disoriented and think that these events are too pinpointed on a single moment and cannot be used here to analyze what happened to dogma during the ten centuries spanning the Middle Ages. That, however, is not my intention. As pinpointed as these events might be, they are sufficient to suggest the great problem the church had to resolve slowly and gradually, at least if it wanted to be guided by the divine pedagogy at work in the "learning to learn" of the people of Israel.

When the Answers Are Already Known

Indeed, if the barbarian peoples are to make *their own* way, dogma cannot drop down to them from heaven. As was the case with Israel, it must take root in the problems presented in their *experience*. Naturally it must produce things that are "incomplete and temporary" (DV 15)—or, rather, things that *are now known* to be incomplete and therefore temporary. For even "errors are explained by pedagogical necessity, since God was not going to fall into the error of the teacher in a hurry."[11]

While it may be true that God will not fall into such a thing, human beings certainly will. The "teacher in a hurry" will be the one who gives answers before the problem is clearly and deeply experienced and formulated—and even more in a hurry if he or she gives answers that do not belong to any question, anticipating merely potential questions. Thus the question of telling children the truth (in keeping with their advancing age, understanding, and responsibility) is often not so much a problem for the children, as it is an epistemological problem, a problem poorly posed by the adult.

The difficulty lurking at the dawn of the Middle Ages was unavoidable: like Israel and with it, the church had already traveled a long way, and had come to a series of solutions which it could quite rightly regard as (relatively) universal. Might it be necessary to keep silent about them when new peoples were coming to faith with a very elementary level of study? The temptation of the teacher in a hurry is to say everything one knows. The difficulty was real, nevertheless: Was it necessary or even opportune to keep silent? Should two churches be kept separate due to a difference in their cultures?

It would be unfair to think that the only thing to fear in this instance was a mistaken utilization of information. For that very reason the statement with which I ended the previous section was too brief. It was not *only* a matter of the church already knowing the answers. The *interlocutor's questions* must also play an important role. The barbarian peoples themselves, with their expectations, perhaps mistaken (as when children ask questions when they do not have the capacity to understand the components of the answer) or premature, also enter into the picture. Hence the difficulty is not simply a matter of the teaching church's ignoring the active role of those learning and thus abusing their passivity. These peoples were not passive in acquiring their Christian faith, but in their fascination over an empire they envied, their curiosity inevitably led them to ask for things that were regarded as ever-more wonderful the further they were from their comprehension.

What is clear is that the peoples engaging in dialogue with the church are using a language different from that of the Romans in the patristic era, let alone the set of issues guiding Pauline thought—namely, the changes the Christian message ought to bring into the mature existence of human beings, whom God has set as heirs in a world offered for their creative work. If words were not treacherous, some of the events I am to relate show how the church in the period in question knows that the new peoples are not inquiring so much about the maturity that Jesus' method may provide for their freedom, but rather about the enhanced effectiveness the Christian rites may provide to the magic they practice. Be that as it may, it is a fact that the answers reached in the works analyzed as well as in others unquestionably show that the anthropological problems of Pauline theology, vaguely intuited by the church fathers, vanish from the horizon of theology.

The new peoples occupying the former territory of the empire are not interested in such topics, but they are thrilled over what Christianity can offer them in the way of "theophanies." Hence the concern already noted in the question to which Gregory the Great's *Dialogues* provides an answer: Why are there fewer miracles? The work by Gregory of Tours in this same period responds to that same implicit question. Interest in, and fascination with, the miraculous is not merely concern that it be made more visibly abundant with mighty deeds. As occurred in the ancient Israel of the Yahwist, here also there emerged a fascinated pursuit of how to *manage* the sacred so that what it bears might be turned to the benefit of those employing it:

> One of the doctrinal points Gregory tries to anchor through the miracles [which he narrates] is the survival of souls after death, along with the punishments suffered in purgatory and the possibility that our prayers can liberate them from that punishment. During the middle ages and even to our own time the story of Justus, a monk and physician, killed in a quasi-excommunication for having hidden three gold coins, and permitted to enter heaven after Gregory, moved by compassion had the holy sacrifice [of the Mass] celebrated for his liberation thirty days in succession, became the support for a devotion which the church recognized as legitimate, the "Gregorian thirty days" for the repose of the souls of the dead.[12]

Again, *in itself* this single isolated item is of little consequence. It does suggest, however, several things about the formation of the "dogmatic" in this period. I believe it is worth pausing over some of these, since as the previous citation says expressly, the elements that we observe here, albeit by way of example, have continued to have influence down to our own time.

Example of Being in a Hurry: The World beyond the Grave

The first element is the one already indicated, and thus I am exempted from developing it at length. The problem of the extrinsic quality of something sacred that seems to regard not the uprightness of the human heart but rather certain sacral techniques leads to a crisis (of growth) in the Old Testament. That crisis, however, is experienced within reality: it raises an enormous and ever-more acute question within the historic experience of Israel vis-à-vis God. It is, for example, the sincere "annoyance" and the "fear" that a man like David comes to feel before Yahweh and which prompts his decision to remove the ark of God from his house. David has run up against the experience of the sacred, managed without the appropriate rites, which brings about Uzzah's instant death when he tries to keep the ark of Yahweh from falling as it is being transferred to David's new capital, Jerusalem (2 Sam. 6:7–12).

In the case here being examined, will there be a similar outcome to Gregory's "compassion" for a monk named Justus, who is about to be condemned for a "rite" — that is, for an action which violates the vow of poverty — independently of its real consequences? The answer must be no. Rather than a response that might draw the human away from the omnipotence of the rite to an experience with a richer interpretation, we find ourselves facing something that does away with the question: a more powerful rite is created. Why do I say that? Because the historian's account shows that the answer withdraws the event from the question that can be subjected to the test of experience. The problem is resolved through efficacy in the realm of the "immortality of the soul," where human experience is irrelevant. Such efficacy is not experienced but believed. Gregory's compassion confirms the fact that the church already has the answers, and silences critical experience rather than taking advantage of it. Even so, the answer may not be what his questioner deep down might want to hear. I repeat: we have here a pedagogy in a hurry, not because God's revelation has to be at the service of whatever human beings might desire, but because God is not revealed except in and for the humanization of human beings seeking to give meaning to their existence.[13]

Thus the first generation of some of the barbarian peoples who turned Christian immediately received theological information for which it took eight centuries to prepare in the process of the Old Testament. The price paid for this "rapidity" or haste turns out to be, as we have seen, a certain extrinsic quality which will leave its impact on dogma thus received. The "dogmatic" authority will not fail against "objective truth" and will no doubt be heeded, but the result will not be a richer experience, but a sacred technique for handling eschatological data. It is a technique that will later unfold even to the extreme of the "selling" of partial or plenary indulgences, which will in turn occasion the Reformation. However, to some degree the familiar "Gregorian Masses" already mean that the faithful become more withdrawn from historic time for the sake of a very primitive eschatology (although this is an individual rather than a collective eschatology).[14]

The "Learning" Church: Backward Questions

Dogma Draws on "Curiosity," not Problems

At this point, something new happens, as I have already hinted. What has just been said would seem to be based solely on the "teaching" (*docente*) church's possession of information which presumably should resolve (or dissolve) the problems of the learning (*discente*) church. Things are not quite that simple, even though this rush to teach is what is most plain to see. It is also true that the people, even these barbarian peoples who have just recently entered the church, play an active role in the construction of dogma. While they are by no means theologians, the peoples who make up the church largely condition the direction theology is going to take and the way dogma will be understood.

As much as theology (which is *dogma in fieri*) is somewhat separated from the people toward the end of the Middle Ages and is increasingly elaborated by specialists within the enclaves of the great universities then being founded in Europe and dealing with items of knowledge from the Bible and tradition quite removed from the basic knowledge of the people, the people nevertheless play an active, if less visible, role in that elaboration, and indeed they cannot but play such a role. On the one hand, their curious imagination gives rise to countless questions as well as some certitudes which eventually force open the very doors of theology, after it has taken refuge in the academies. Dogma is never so separate from the mass clientele of the church that it can ignore the "devotions" the people practice and regard as part of the identity of their faith. While dogma is sometimes critical of those practices, in most cases it supports them with its authority and often with reasoning and arguments well or poorly drawn from the Bible.

On the other hand, we need not think that this situation results from sinister intentions or demagogic indulgence. We only have to keep in mind here a negative but realistic limit. The very "pedagogical" (pastoral) concern to accompany the people by elaborating a theology "on their own level" explains both what we find and what is missing, from a dogmatic standpoint. With that context removed, these things now stand out in all their harshness. How does this theological element work? It does so both directly (catechesis, preaching, lives of saints, and so forth) and indirectly (respecting the intellectual limits of those peoples, using their inclinations in conceptual language and especially in art). For centuries all this continued to shape a good deal of the dogma with which the church sought to enter into the modern age, only to collide with the criteria of the Enlightenment.

The example chosen as the takeoff point for these reflections is that of purgatory. Naturally, we have here *one* case from among many others, but as the reader will see, it sheds light on these two ways (direct and indirect) by which the people make their presence felt in the elaboration of dogma, and not just as receivers of information but as an active element. Deep down, however, that does not mean that the need for a genuine "tradition" in the realm of religion and culture is being respected. We are going to look at both kinds of presence, direct and indirect, in the following pages.

The church found itself having to make an effort to "inculturate" the Christian message within the Greek mind-set. It is not my intention to compare values as though they were measurable quantities. I do not know whether Greek culture can be said to be superior to Hebrew culture. What is obvious is that its refinement and the (relative) universality of the way it conceived what is human demanded an arduous and slow labor on the part of Christian thinkers — starting with Paul himself. In this work I have tried to show how the overcoming of the Mosaic law (already present in Jesus' preaching although incipiently) required of Paul a deep reformulation of the moral questions escaping from the absolutization of a law justly regarded as given by God. That had to be done in order to put the whole universe at the serve of initiatives of love. This healthy relativization in turn implied a modification of the idea of God's judgment, shifting the emphasis from the *fate of individual persons* to the lasting worth of the overall historic endeavor of each human existence, even though that worth would become visible only in the universal palingenesis. This transformation of the universe in which human beings are associated in the divine plan not through their own merit, in turn entailed a disruption in the characteristically Yahwistic way of speaking enthusiastically of the divine creation, and its replacement by the idea that creation is condemned to futility unless human beings stamp their creative freedom upon it.[15]

Paul himself points out that *not all* — perhaps not even many — can immediately come to an understanding and put such maturity into practice in a balanced way. He says that he himself had to treat the new Christians as children until little by little they became capable of receiving as an enrichment this "gospel" of definitive human freedom. The Pauline theology on the anthropological transformation implied by the message, life, death, and resurrection of Jesus does not encounter in a Roman Empire in decline the appropriate context for being understood and practiced. The developments I have outlined in previous chapters, plus those in this chapter, outweigh what he says. Thus Christian morality, even purified of extreme literalism, continues to be a theology of the law. The most "Pauline" father of the church is no doubt Augustine, but even he, too much a prisoner of the legal spirit innate in the Roman temper, seems much more concerned about the power that gravitates toward breaking the law (= original sin and concupiscence) than about Christian freedom *above the law*.

The "inculturation" of Christianity in the mentality of the barbarian peoples who settle in the former western territories of the Roman Empire force a return to a plainly pre-Pauline and even, as we have seen, pre-Christian, conception of morality. After all, a Jew of David's time could not have been expected to understand and put into practice Paul's moral theology. All inculturations, if they are profound, pay a high price, as I have tried to show when dealing with Hellenism in the previous chapter. Some things are left out in any assimilation process, since those things can only be thoroughly thought, expressed, and developed in the culture in which the thought was created. Categories that freed the human being from fear of God's punishments and from the pursuit of security in the sacred as a way of dealing with these punishments mandated by law, did not square with the necessity—and duty—to channel solidly and sometimes violently the behavior and thinking of the people toward their basic civic and religious responsibilities. Christianity, let it be clearly noted, continually claims to be such, when in fact it has gone back to being a religion of law with its rewards and punishments.[16] As paradoxical as it might seem, the very people who suffer the consequences of a hasty pedagogy, force Christianity to go "backward."

Coming back to purgatory, many theologians would agree with Yves Congar's invitation to theology *today* to "purge purgatory," just as Rahner proposes doing with the concept of "hell."[17] Indeed with regard to purgatory, as we have already seen in the story Gregory the Great tells about the monk who hid three gold coins,

> Such a vast number of fantastic, odd and questionable pieces of information have been piling up, that it seems at least difficult to grasp the saving and liberating worth of this *truth*. Even when purgatory is not turned into a torture chamber, sometimes with unsavory details, *punishment continues to be the fundamental category for speaking of purgatory*, making it the place where God punishes and takes vengeance on human beings. It is the task of theology to show that *this vision is unacceptable*.[18]

—even if it is classified as dogma.

Unfortunately, however, the existing theology, like all the vestiges of the Western Roman Empire, became "barbarized"[19]—but not to the extent that it could offer these new peoples the experience of a deep construction of their existence *on the basis of the religion they already possessed*. As was to happen centuries later (to some extent the other way around) with the Spanish and Portuguese conquest of the pre-Columbian peoples and of the African slaves brought to the American continent, the "advanced" pedagogy imposed violently interrupts an indigenous process. The people continue to think, however, and since they are not given any other opportunity to put what they think into practice, it is their imagination that overflows uncontrollably, and does so without generating experience, except in an extremely slow process. That theology which wants to stand alongside the people then goes back, and indeed far back, without, however, managing to connect up with the life process of the people, which in this case became "barbarized."

Divine Apostolic Traditions and Human Traditions

Are All the "Dogmas" That Keep Mounting Up Really Dogmas?

Here we come to a central dogmatic problem in this era, one closely connected to preceding developments as well as those to come. Dogma makes space for a symbiosis between an "advanced" magisterium and a people with a good deal of curiosity. That symbiosis accordingly influences the way theology is done and, as in the case examined here, thereby legitimizes with the label of "dogmatic" a mass of "traditions" (rather than an overall coherent tradition). Converted into "dogmas" these traditions will render theology "backward" vis-à-vis the experiences that history will force it to undergo. In other words, they disconnect dogma from those experiences and are of no help for interpreting them and being enriched through them. "Gregorian Masses" support a popular devotion with papal dogmatic power, but bound up as they are with the conception of a God who punishes violations of law, they become "backward" when essential aspects of the Christian message, like those dealt with in Pauline theology, are rediscovered in the experience of history.

"Traditions" have been introduced but in the absence of an adequate education process it has not been possible to create an authentic "tradition"—that is, a wisdom not limited to transmitting things learned, but which might teach people to learn, and accordingly might challenge reality, proceed by trial and error, and accept new impulses following from richer and more adequate hypotheses. How then are we to carry out this necessary "purging" today in order to restore to this and many other "traditions" their vitality and flexibility? Here again the case of purgatory will serve as a good example.

In the last few sentences, readers will have noticed the ambiguous way the word "tradition" can be used. When I have spoken of *tradition* thus far, I have always referred to this kind of wisdom by means of which a human generation does not begin from zero its effort to find a meaning in the almost chaotic flow of events. In somewhat more technical language, the idea is that one generation transmits to another not so much a "what to do if—" but rather "epistemological premises"—that is, guidelines for understanding what happens that enable the new generation to gradually acquire its own experience. This is an extraordinary saving of energy, but not when it is taken to the point of a "reaction" mechanically learned and practiced. It saves energy *for the sake of experimentation*.

I think the reader will also have seen that in speaking of "tradition" we have been applying the idea to a process of "learning to learn." That is how "active" and creative agents are formed, whereas the "reactive" only know how to respond to similar stimuli with the same reaction. I am likewise keeping in mind that readers who have read the chapters devoted to the Old Testament will have seen that this is what happened during the successive crises in which the Israelites had to confront their notions of their God Yahweh with the complexity of the historic situation in which they had to live. In this fashion they shaped a "tradition," and to it they entrusted their faith, because they found that this process had been so rich that it could come only from God's pedagogy.

Now, however, with the unfolding of New Testament revelation fully underway in the church, we will have to enter into the thickets of a new sense to be acquired by the word "tradition." This new meaning is very attached to the Middle Ages we are studying and is indeed the source of most of the "dogmatic traditions" we have today. That is, they derive from the overflowing curiosity and religious imagination, backed up by apparitions, miracles, and particular revelations during those centuries of Christian life, of a people which was slowly developing its human possibilities. For example, the notion that thirty Masses celebrated *without interruption* for so many days should be especially effective for liberating souls held in purgatory is not only something "transmitted" and in that very sense a "tradition" (= transmission). Its character as a tradition observed universally over a long period of time in the end gives it a very special theological status which merges with the dogmatic. That is what happens during the Middle Ages, and even down to our own days. What seemed natural then, however, is beginning to look more problematic today, at least to thinking Christians.

How to Discern "Tradition" among the "Traditions"?

What is this "tradition" in comparison with the one discussed in the study of sacred scripture? What relationship is there with that tradition, beyond the use of the same term?

There is no better way, I believe, for understanding this theological tangle (vis-à-vis the situation we took as an example) than to pose the question as Karl Rahner has done in a more general terrain and with a much more technical language (for which I apologize to nonspecialized readers).

Rahner points to something very important for carrying out this "purge" of what is strictly "dogma": the need to distinguish between two components from within what is transmitted as "traditional." He offers the following explanation:

> Tradition, *historically* speaking, is simply the concrete sum of the theological propositions to be found in the Church, along with their transmission, in so far as the ordinary or extraordinary magisterium has not discounted such propositions as not permissible in the Church. This tradition contains, without precise, conscious and official distinction both the *traditio divina-apostolica* and the *traditio humana* (theological views and efforts and opinions, of profane, human origin), *which are propagated together*.[20]

The italics on the last phrase are mine because that is precisely where the problem lies. "Tradition" (Rahner calls it "divine-apostolic tradition") and "traditions" (Rahner calls them "human tradition") are propagated together and Christians today receive them that way. It should be noted that this does not happen in accessory and private matters. The church celebrates the appearance of the Virgin Mary at the grotto in Lourdes, thus bolstering such a belief with the authoritative seal of support that is a liturgical feast. Indeed to judge by my own country, many more Christians observe this feast than that of Pentecost or even Easter (although for this latter claim I may not have so much sociological corroboration available).

It could be said, and with some plausibility, that the fact that divine and human tradition go side by side is no problem (yet). Upon examination, the whole Old Testament tradition we discussed in part 1 is made up of this same mixture. The formation of the canon required a discernment in order to arrive at what, as part of the Bible, today appears as "divine tradition." Those elements had to be sifted out from other thinking and theological opinions which have been left out of the Bible as purely "human" traditions (the "apocryphal" gospels in the case of the New Testament, for example). We have also observed that this discernment was basically a matter of a coherent line in the process of learning to learn. What remains as "divine" tradition is what experience has indicated as valid and effective in the pursuit of an identity that stands up to the challenge of experience, is rich in meaning, and is therefore in the long run reasonably attributable to God.

As we have observed, the problem emerges after dogma becomes distinct through centuries of authentic human experience. In that process there is reason to fear that what is transmitted as "divine" and what is elaborated as "human" in the expression of faith will be mixed together, perhaps in an unbalanced and confusing way. That is what happens in the case of purgatory, to which I will return below, as well as in other instances, among which is the one Rahner examines and about which he recognizes this difficulty of discerning divine from human tradition today, the so-called Marian dogmas, and especially that of Mary's virginity *in partu*.[21]

Before coming to this dogma, however, Rahner offers as an example another instance in which the Bible understood literally (without taking into account the literary genres in which the truth is expressed), human curiosity, and dogmatic generalization have become inextricably intertwined: "One must be very careful with such arguments, as may be seen from the doctrine of the formation of Adam from the dust of the earth. Here too a tradition of two thousand years' duration expressed a permanent truth in a definite, concrete imagery, distinct from the truth implied and not a permanent form, which was not however distinguished by tradition from the truth implied."[22] Is there likewise a permanent truth transmitted under a(n) (unchangeable?) literary form: "he was born of the virgin Mary" (or as the Greek text says with more theological vigor in the first known creed, "he became incarnate by the Holy Spirit and Mary the Virgin"). Now is this *truth* a physical fact—as holy as it might be—about Mary, or a theological claim about Jesus? And if it is the latter, what is that claim?

The caution Rahner mentions tends to prevent falling into two opposite misunderstandings. "But it cannot be said that only such things are part of it, nor that *everything* [emphasis mine] is proved to be *traditio divina-apostolica* simply because it has been in fact unchallenged in the (whole) universal tradition and has generally held to be correct . . . If the magisterium does not note this difference at a given point, this does not mean that it does not exist."

What is Rahner trying to say here, if I may express myself more plainly? The *first* faulty understanding consists in thinking that things not taught for centuries which suddenly seem to be "discovered" in a correct but new reading of God's word cannot go on to become part of dogma, or if one prefers, of "divine" tradition. One example of such a "discovery" in the light of new contexts and crises would be the seriousness with which Paul speaks of a genuine universal salvation of all humankind in the context of the necessary maturity with which human beings ought to assume the burden of a mature freedom in faith.[23]

The *second* and opposite faulty understanding consists in thinking that things taught for a long time and unanimously, and seemingly without giving rise to any doubt, are part of dogma and of divine tradition. Indeed, given the mixture of imagination and genuine tradition that takes place and the theological support that custom and interest itself contribute to whatever stimulates the piety and religious practice of the masses, one finds, particularly in the Middle Ages, human things that have no basis in the Word of God. In the church, says Rahner, "there can be a *traditio mere humana* which is universal, of long standing, and universally held in the Church, and it need not be always expressly and consciously marked off and distinguished from the *traditio divina-apostolica*. ... Such conscious demarcations have a real history. To prove that they did not exist earlier is not a proof that such distinctions are not objectively justified."

An Example: What Is "Tradition" in the Virginity of Mary?

I think the most respected contemporary theologians, although few of them dare to take up Rahner's specific topic, agree with these observations on the prudence that should be at work when the credentials of statements which are too easily presented today as "dogmatic" — that is, as deriving from a "divine" tradition — are examined theologically. If Rahner expends so much effort around the virginity of Mary *in partu* (and logically also *after* birth) it is because this dogma has all the "apparent" features of a *divine-apostolic* tradition. I say "apparent" because, while it is not found in the New Testament, it was taught universally for centuries by the unanimous magisterium of the church and believed by the mass of the faithful. Rahner is right to be disturbed at the fact that when such features are present it is too easily "assumed" that this truth must have biblical support. (Later we will look at the problem of "tradition" as a second, and separate, source of revelation.)

Let us look at what the Jerusalem Bible says in its notes about the topic of Mary's virginity. To begin with, the only authors who deal with it are Matthew and Luke in the so-called infancy gospels. Although the magisterium urges us to bear in mind that these constitute a literary genre which must be determined and that they should not be automatically regarded without further study as a historical report on the facts, the intention of the authors could not be clearer. It comes down to excluding Joseph from the conception of Jesus, which is due to the Holy Spirit and to the Virgin Mary. Jesus is the son of God and of Mary. Hence, the only one who refers to Mary's condition when Jesus is born is Matthew, but he does so only with reference to Joseph: "He had no relations with her at any time before she bore a son, whom he named Jesus" (Mt. 1:25; see Lk. 1:31, 34–35). In a note on this verse the Jerusalem Bible says, "The text is not concerned with the period that followed, and taken by itself, does not assert Mary's perpetual virginity which, however, the *gospels elsewhere suppose* and which the Tradition of the Church affirms. On the 'brothers' of Jesus, cf. 12:46" [and note]. Why does it say "suppose"? Where is this supposed "elsewhere"? I have not encountered a single note commenting something like, "and this assumes Mary's perpetual virginity." Indeed this Bible could have said that not only is the text "not concerned with the period that followed" Jesus' conception, but that the authors had absolutely no interest in the issue. Indeed, when they speak about "Jesus' brothers and sisters" (Mt. 12:46; Mk. 6:3) the explanation usually given is that in the language used by Jesus the term "brother" could refer to cousins or other relatives. What is not said is that the primary usage is the most proper one and that by not explaining their own usage, far from assuming Mary's "perpetual virginity," the evangelists are allowing readers to think whatever they want about it, as long as they attribute the conception of Jesus to God and to Mary (= Virgin). In this note in the Jerusalem Bible we have a confusion that I would go so far as to say is produced intentionally in order to avoid the discernment demanded by Rahner.

Another Example: Purgatory

This discernment ought to be all the more necessary to the extent that one moves away from the central mystery of the life and message of Jesus. Such a case is that of "purgatory," already mentioned, even if it is useful only as an example of the creation of a human tradition within the divine-apostolic tradition.

As Colzani points out in his article previously cited, when it comes to seeking biblical support for the existence of purgatory, "current exegesis evidences a good deal of moderation; less concerned with combatting Protestant claims, it recognizes that the doctrine of the church is the result of a slow dogmatic process and therefore has no need to be sought literally in scripture."[24] I wonder what "literally" means here. Colzani is claiming in effect that "in the Bible there are some texts which point toward, and are legitimately open to the doctrine with which we are dealing." In other words, even if they do not "prove" the existence of purgatory by means of the Bible, they can give rise to this notion. Of course, given the precaution urged by Rahner, we may certainly ask Colzani whether such an "opening" is enough to serve as the basis for a dogma—which is just what happens during this period—that is, whether such an opening can become a "truth of faith." In any case, it is a good idea to pause over the two texts the author cites to support his case (and which are presumably the most "open").

The first is a passage from the (deuterocanonical) second book of Maccabees, where we read that among the clothing of Jewish soldiers fallen in battle were found idolatrous religious objects. Then "it became clear to everyone that this was why these men had lost their lives"—that is, what their sin had been. Judas Maccabaeus took up a collection "amounting to nearly two thousand drachmae, and sent it to Jerusalem to have a sacrifice *for sin* offered ... This was why he had this atonement sacrifice offered for the dead, *so that they might be released from their sin*" (2 Mac. 12:39–46). Like other passages in the same book, this text offers very important witness on the emerging belief in another life and in the final resurrection of the dead. Specifically about purgatory, however, nothing can be drawn from it. The fact that acts of worship or prayers for the dead might lead God to forgive their sins does not indicate that there is a place where those who die (and have not been sent to hell) must be purified for a certain period of time. If the idea is simply to show that this text "is open" to the doctrine of purgatory in the sense that it does not clash with it, we have already said that this is not enough to provide the basis for a dogma. It would have to be shown that it clashes with any other claim besides purgatory.

Without realizing it, Colzani draws on another text about the dead which shows that the need for a purgatory is not on the minds of the biblical authors — namely, the one in which Paul reminds the Corinthians (seemingly with some approval) of their practice of having themselves baptized on behalf of their unbaptized dead ones (1 Cor. 15:29). The only thing in common between these two texts is the (today strange) belief that even after death, the worship or prayers of the living can bring it about that God forgives sins and changes the fate of those already dead.

Rather than "opening" our mind to the possible existence of purgatory, the second text ought to close it. There Paul writes to the Corinthians that the work of human beings (or at least of Christians) is always a mixture in which the building materials have different qualities and resistance. He goes on to say that "the work of each will be made clear. *The Day* will disclose it. That day will make its appearance with fire, and fire will test the quality of each man's work" (1 Cor. 3:13), by measuring the varying resistance of each of the mixed materials which represent the total existence of each human being. The exegetically obvious consequence of this passage is that the day of judgment (= the Day) will find each human being as he or she left this life — that is, with a work which sums up his or her life and which is *still* mixed. During this final and decisive day fire does not purify: it "assays" — that is, it manifests the resistance and therefore the quality of a work that is difficult to judge as a whole in any other way.

Colzani finds himself forced to conclude that on this issue of purgatory "the caution of the biblical text is plain to see." That is putting it mildly, since the text is unaware of the topic rather than merely "cautious" about it. As in the example of the New Testament "supposing" Mary's perpetual virginity, here again one can make out the prudence with which a theologian ventures into the "purging" Congar mentioned.

Indeed, besides the existence of prayers and intercessions for the dead, the author finds nothing clear and certain on the existence of purgatory up to the end of the patristic era. He acknowledges rather that (perhaps under the influence of Hellenism) the dead are conceived as living in a kind of dozing state as they await the resurrection. "The idea of a final purification which is already *glimpsed* in Origen, mixed with other topics, will finally prevail in the fourth century fathers." We then see, however, that this is not actually the case: "The general context of eschatological doctrines makes it difficult to simply identify this *opinion* [of Origen] with the doctrine of purgatory." The author then seems to find this origin in St. Augustine (although we thereby arrive at the fifth century). In him "we can immediately observe that the doctrine of a purification beyond earth is solidly built up in its essential data. However, it is not hard to perceive certain inconsistencies on the topic in relation to how it is posed in the Bible: on the one side, there is an individualistic conception preoccupied with the eternal death of the individual ... In addition there is an expiatory-punitive idea emphasizing more the pains of fire ... than the purifying tension of the believer." Going further ahead, however, one finds something which from a dogmatic standpoint is even more important than these flaws. With or without these flaws, the author tells us, in Augustine we still find nothing more than a hesitant effort: "the post-Augustinian and *medieval* period simply confirms this Augustinian theology, expressing in terms of *certainty* what Augustine still left in a *hesitant* form."

Whatever one may think of Colzani's efforts in this matter, the important thing is that he correctly notes that the Middle Ages are actually the period in which things that were first taught quite late, and only partially and hesitantly, until they gradually gained widespread acceptance, were raised to the level of "dogma." It is only in 1245 that the Council of Lyons states that "these same Greeks truly and undoubtedly are said to believe and to affirm that souls ... can be cleansed after death ... since they say a place of purgation of this kind has not been indicated to them with a certain and proper name by their teachers, we indeed, [call] it purgatory" (D. 456). In 1336 Benedict XII "defines" the doctrine of purgatory as being *de fide* (D. 530). Thus in a letter to Eastern bishops Pius X was to call the doctrine of purgatory "sacred dogma" (D. 2147a) at the beginning of the present century.

There seems to be a logical line running through this growth and addition of new material. In Rahner's terms, however, can it be possible that something that has no assured biblical basis (and which would have to be classified as "human tradition") can become dogma because it has been taught everywhere and unanimously for a long time, as often is the case in this long medieval period marked by its stability and religious unanimity? Do we not have here something that goes out of bounds and is therefore counterproductive as a path toward truth?

A Dogma No Longer Going by Way of Experience

The Real Problem: Dogmas That Are Not?

Readers will be thinking that it is time (and it is, of course) to speed up this new aspect of dogma, which seems to become widespread during these thousand years of the Middle Ages and which in this book (which, I say for the umpteenth time, does not pretend to be historical scholarship, properly speaking) has been exemplified by means of the comparison between the period of Gregory the Great and the one prior to him. This procedure entails all the risks, if I may be excused for saying so, of holding up a few momentary items as *the characteristic* prevailing over a long period of time.

Yet what am I now going to do for such readers? I have to ask them for a little more patience, and I have to continue for a few more moments with the question that Rahner leaves somewhat in the air: Is it possible that matters which are dogmas today may belong to a tradition that is human, and not divine, and which have become "truths of faith" due to the difficulty of making discernment within history and under the pressure of curiosity and of popular devotions? If that has indeed happened, moreover, are we to trust in their infallibility, even if they are promulgated by councils or by supreme pontiffs? Have they not become "reformable" through the passage of time?

For my part, I feel that the very formulation of the problem on the basis of Rahner's illuminating distinctions may be ultimately leading very close to what I found liable to criticism in the way Hans Küng dealt with the irreformability of dogmas. This is something I would characterize as a kind of theological formalism or legalism. It is as though theology could examine dogmas in its own laboratory and determine which among them are really such because they come from God and which are pseudodogmas—and could do so without the aid of a praxis committed to building God's reign.

Hence, before moving ahead in time, I would like briefly to remind the reader that this chapter cannot ignore the changes studied in previous chapters, for the simple reason that even though they come from further back, they remain at work and continue to unfold during this period. Indeed, although it seems that it is fortuitous causes like the invasion of the barbarian peoples that are at work, the transformations that take place in the very idea of dogma are grafted, as it were, onto earlier factors.

Central Problem: Dogmas That Lay People Do Not Experience?

I am especially referring to the fact that all these changes analyzed in this chapter end up even further alienating lay people with their intimate knowledge of Christian truth from dogmatic clerical authority. However, upon close examination, this is the result of the uncertainty in which ordinary Christians are apparently left when they are told that during the Middle Ages much of what is human mistakenly made its way into the truths of faith as dogma.

As we saw in previous chapters, the internal structure is variable and this variation affects the development of dogmas. However, it is logical that it should have a greater impact during these long Middle Ages, insofar as the cultural abyss widens even further between the Christian people, still retaining a good deal of barbarism and paganism, and the magisterium (and subsequently the university), which preserves vestiges of a past in which Christianity rose to great intellectual heights through inculturation. The questions theology strives to resolve in these unexpected and marvelous works of medieval intellectual art constituted by the summae of theological knowledge, beginning with that of Thomas Aquinas, do not in the least resemble the hypotheses with which experience tries to fill the gaps between the expectations of faith and the complex reality of the world. What I mean is that—despite their inherent value as intellectual creation—they bear no resemblance to the crises which, through the work of prophets and writers, advanced the process of *second-level learning* within the people of Israel. The *videtur quod non* with which each problem is presented is no longer the voice of the people or of a real community questioning what it has held as true when it runs into the difficult and obstinate reality of history.

The uniformity of faith, demanded and imposed by an ever-more vertical dogmatic authority, does not allow space for questioning in a serious and realistic way things that many people at that time had to suspect were neither just nor humanizing. For example, one does not need a great deal of culture to realize that "punishment continues to be the fundamental category for speaking of purgatory,"[25] of hell, and of individual eschatology as a whole, and that punishment is not the best, most human, and just of reasons for doing or not doing something. During the modern era, more and more good-willed people will come to agree that it is "theology's task to show that this vision is unacceptable."[26] That was unthinkable, however, within the ecclesial structure of the Middle Ages, or at least unthinkable for the lay person. Hence we have the flights of imagination which.fill out this insufficient eschatology with the real history of human beings (compare Dante's *Divine Comedy*), or even the disguised challenge to this eschatology in an attitude that was both playful and irreverent which pops up here and there and goes unpunished (since it is not expressed dogmatically) in a semi-hidden aspect of the Middle Ages (compare the *Carmina Burana*, which Orf has set to music and popularized for our age).

This uniformity—not vital unity—of dogma increases in step with the ever-closer relations of the magisterium with the power of the secular arm. Never will the papacy come to feel as strong as it did with Boniface VIII toward the end of the thirteenth century, strong enough to claim the totality of this "temporal" power itself. It has already been pointed out that the well-known "investiture struggle" between popes and emperors of the Holy Roman-Germanic — Empire did not mean that the papacy was either losing or recovering its power. The issue was that of seeing who was using the power of whom. At one point in this struggle, on November 18, 1302, the pope writes the famous bull, *Unam Sanctam*, where among other things one may read:

And we are taught by evangelical words that in this power of his are two swords, namely spiritual and temporal . . . But the latter, indeed, must be exercised for the Church, the former by the Church. The former (by the hand) of the priest, the latter by the hand of kings and soldiers, but at the will and sufferance of the priest . . . For, as truth testifies, spiritual power has to establish earthly power, and to judge if it was not good . . . Therefore, if earthly power deviates, it will be judged by spiritual power . . . unless . . . he imagines that there are two principles, which we judge false and heretical. [D. 469]

Thereupon follows what in the mind of the pope cannot but be an *ex cathedra* definition: "Furthermore, we declare, say, define, and proclaim to every human creature that they by necessity for salvation are entirely subject to the Roman Pontiff"—in both spiritual and temporal matters, as the preceding passage makes clear.[27]

With regard to this definition, which theologians regard as mistaken, let it suffice to note that when Vatican Council I was hastening to define papal infallibility, the minority group of French bishops brought up this case from the bull *Unam Sanctam* (as well as the *Dictatus Papae* of Gregory VII) to show that in a solemn definition of a truth of faith, the Roman pontiff had been in error. If he was not formally a "heretic," it was only because in canon law this word is only used for one who maintains a heterodox opinion contumaciously—that is, *after* it has been condemned.[28]

Of course this is an extreme case. It is interesting because it shows to what extent the earthly power the magisterium acquires is translated into the practical elimination of the dogmatic function proper to the lay person, or better, to the whole people of God. In contrast to what Vatican II will demand in our own period, lay people lose their function in the creation of a faith capable of bringing "more human solutions" to problems in history (GS 11). Church teaching authority becomes accustomed to using dogma in order to provide ready-made solutions to problems arising in history, something which according to Vatican II is not its function. Indeed, *Gaudium et Spes* advises, "Let the layman not imagine that his pastors are always such experts, that to every problem which arises, however complicated, they can readily give him a concrete solution." In order to avoid creating the impression that this might change with regard to some issues, by waiting for answers that are less immediate or with better training of pastors, it warns that providing such answers is not their mission (GS 43).

From the more directly dogmatic standpoint, here I am not so concerned to do as several serious theologians have done, to take up any *particular* error by a supreme pontiff (or by two or three) in order to then examine how in the abstract this mistake might be compatible with papal infallibility as defined at Vatican I. What is very much the concern of this work, on a logically higher level, is how this unbalanced development of centralization and power in this agency, which also serves the dogmatic teaching authority, affects the pursuit of truth.

I believe that on the level of principle, readers will agree with me on a kind of proportional formula: to the extent that the development of dogmatic "power" moves away from the faith experiences of ordinary Christians vis-à-vis their future, it is all the more forced to justify this very development it has absorbed vis-à-vis its past. The summary of the main passage in *Unam Sanctam* proves it: it has to prove that this (practically absolute) spiritual and secular power of the papacy is based on "the words of the gospel." The church, which has this particular institutional form as the result of a historic process with its successes and mistakes, is in this fashion presented as though it constituted an eternal and unchangeable order, willed and determined to be just as it actually exists, or at least as it should exist if human beings were to obey the divine command.

Thus, as we end our examination of this period, we find a strange convergence between two tendencies, the ever-more vertical and pyramidal institutionalization of the church, and the need to support the curiosities and devotions of a people, which, unable to express its genuine problems, crises, and vital experiences, wishes to make the world of the divine its own. Both tendencies converge in having to *return to the sources*. Yet once more this tendency does not utterly prevail. The subsequent modern age is to reveal how little by little a tendency virtually imperceptible at one moment *really returns to the sources* restoring vitality and strength to the pursuit of truth.

CHAPTER 10

Dogma and Modern Culture

Since the point has been made so many times already, the reader knows that this is not a work of history, not even of the history of dogma. However, in trying to grasp a process—that of the very idea of what dogma is—history is necessary, insofar as the elements influencing the process can only be perceived properly when one knows the context. That context is more elusive when the events themselves are further back in time.

However, the reader is now approaching a period in which it may be enough merely to allude to developments that are quite well-known. With regard to our topic, that means what happens in the realm of dogma, and especially what happens to dogma in the Catholic Church since the beginning of this modern age.

Acceleration of History

Nevertheless, readers can certainly object that the ease with which the modern era can be studied is only apparent. We must take into account a feature of biological evolution which becomes much more visible in human history. The notion has been called the *acceleration of history*. Decisive events which once happened over vast stretches of time are taking place ever more rapidly as time goes on. Our own generation has gone from slow voyages by ship to supersonic airplanes; it has traveled through the atmosphere and space in vehicles that have enabled human beings to escape the earth's gravity and arrive on the moon, and to take pictures of other planets in the solar system with devices controlled from earth. From rudimentary radio communication it has gone on to television, initially local and then worldwide—not to speak of weapons which, if put to use, will destroy not only one's enemies but the whole planet.

That list is simply a clumsy attempt to appeal to the imagination. One could calculate much more precisely the geometrical expansion in the amount of available energy per capita from cave people up to nuclear devices. Our initial list has the pedagogical advantage of indicating the *decisive* thresholds, with new and unforeseen problems which a single generation has had to cross, whereas in previous periods human beings went for centuries without experiencing substantial changes in the variables affecting their individual and social lives.

Dogma on the Defensive in the Modern Age

The last hundred years have seen more decisive developments for humankind than the whole Middle Ages. One might assume that the proliferation of developments decisive for humankind must have been equally decisive for dogma. One might likewise assume that the very idea of what must be believed and the very pursuit of a more encompassing truth would have to take that into account.

But I do not believe that is the case. The only thing I can say at this point is that I am going to hold to a very different working hypothesis, one that is going to look preposterous. Nevertheless, I hope to make it plausible. My presumption is that the events that were decisive for humankind during this period *were not decisive for understanding dogma* — at least not in the Catholic Church, since it did not let them be decisive.

This working hypothesis is not so strange for anyone who has followed the previous chapters, especially the last one. For a myriad of reasons, added up and multiplied thus far in part 2, there was an effort in the pre-modern era to attain a kind of dogma that was perennial and unchangeable. People believed it had been attained and they went through practically the entire modern era defending and bolstering it. They ignored modernity. In other words, there was an effort to make dogma a remedy for withstanding the acceleration of history and the new human responsibilities that went along with it.

It is abundantly clear that such a hypothesis has its own considerable drawbacks. It would seem to minimize elements as original to, and distinctive of, the new era as the Reformation, to cite only the most noteworthy example, or the Enlightenment, which cannot be made a part of the Reformation nor identified with the enormous and rapid progress of the physical, chemical, or biological sciences. Nevertheless, I am going to show that although the Catholic Church takes certain steps, which can be identified historically on the basis of the different contexts through which it passes during this period, still, from the standpoint of the comprehension of dogma and of the pursuit of truth, the prevailing tone in each of these critical moments was entirely defensive. More importantly, this defense for well or ill was successful, although at a high cost.

What I mean is that the systematizations of dogma made in the Middle Ages predominated right up to the eve of Vatican II. This was not the only tendency in the church, of course. However, it was the primary tendency — and I would go so far as to say, it remains so even after Vatican II, with the qualification that I understand "primary" in a quantitative rather than a qualitative sense. Certainly matters have begun to change, and with some rapidity, starting with Vatican II, but the backlash and restoration which turn back to the past have also gained ground in important sectors since 1965, when the Council ended.

All this may explain the things that seem strangest and even craziest in the two chapters which follow.

The Renaissance and Dogma

Acceleration of History and Humanization

This acceleration of history is largely the result of the laws of thermodynamics which govern the availability of the energy of the planet and of all activity that takes place on it. Biological evolution proceeds unmistakably from a kind of giant computer for the earth and all its inhabitants, vegetable and animal, to the appearance of these minicomputers constituted by the individual minds which entail greater complexity and capacity of invention for the universe.

Thus we can understand that the *fact* of *humanization* in itself signifies a necessary element in the acceleration of the overall development of the biosphere. In their own domain, human beings are subject to the same acceleration and for the same reason. It is true that in this evolution it is difficult to decide exactly where what is properly human begins. Assessments of the age of humankind vary in accordance with the criterion used. On the basis of certain fossil remains, scientists can provide a basis for a time going from six million to one million years of human presence on the earth. However, even accepting this latter, shorter span, it may be difficult for human beings to "imagine" today how *recent*, for example, is agriculture — that is, the systematic cultivation of cereals and root crops. It goes back *only* eleven thousand years. In other words, humankind lived without it, in the most primitive and insecure way (collecting wild fruits, hunting, and fishing) with no notable changes, for ninety-nine percent of its existence! However, we must make a further effort to realize, for instance, that without agriculture there could only be tiny groups of human beings, settlements of a few hundred people. Such dispersion entailed a world *almost* without history.

Only in the hundredth portion of this very long period of time has agriculture made it possible for human groupings to begin to grow, to accentuate the division of labor and everything subsequently invented, to the point of making possible the arrival of human beings on the moon or the invention of instruments capable of destroying the planet earth several times over.

It is even difficult to imagine how much has changed for humankind — or at least for that part of it called "Western" — from the end of the Middle Ages to the present.

> Anyone observing the earth's surface from Sirius toward the end of the fifteenth century would have been astonished to observe how scattered and isolated human groups were. Entire civilizations were entirely ignorant of one another ... They were living by themselves with only superficial contacts at most, knowing each other poorly or not at all. It is Europe, armed with a truly universal spirit, methods and knowledge, that is going to unite the dispersed members of the great human family.[1]

Five centuries later as the twentieth century draws to a close, the interweaving of all the cultures of the planet has become so dense, complex, and interrelated that it is jeopardizing one of the deepest of human "rights" — that of "practicing" one's own culture and thus maintaining a group identity. Otto Klineber, a psychologist and social anthropologist, after explaining the immense wealth for humanity entailed by the development of the most varied cultures composing it today and the future prospects promised by its interaction, warns:

> The changes leading toward "modernization" will undoubtedly continue and they are necessary in the struggle against poverty, illness, infant mor-

tality, illiteracy, discrimination against women, and the political power-lessness of the popular masses. The *problem that remains unresolved* is that of knowing how these changes can be introduced while preserving at the same time the main aspects of the way of life of the people in question.[2]

No one is unfamiliar with this acceleration of history. Even if it is not called that, everyone is aware of its effects. Those who are disturbed today by the seemingly ever-greater difficulty parents have in communicating with their children, and call this *modern* phenomenon a "generation gap" (or "abyss"), may be unaware that they are referring to this accelerating of history which is more and more observable within the so-called modern age but which has always been at work in the evolution of the universe.

In other words, the acceleration of history was certainly at work throughout the Middle Ages and during all prehistory and the history of human groupings. It is not something that began with the Renaissance.

What is specific to the modern age to be sure is that if this acceleration once signified growth or progress, today people are beginning to think that it may soon become regression. Why this paradox? The reason is quite simple. Earlier in the development of humankind, there was a counterweight to the acceleration of history. Often this counterweight simply looked more like a brake on that acceleration, rather than a complement. The reason was the fact that development was not following a straight line (thank God!). To some extent each *generation* had to begin the journey anew.

Thus what happens with animal species also happened in human history: there was a barrier separating what genetic inheritance reproduced (with a tiny amount of chance) at a low energy cost from what each individual learned and could not pass on to the next generation except through the long, costly, and largely fortuitous process of an education. What is going on now? We have had to pay the price of knowing that "knowledge takes up space," and that civilization is moving so quickly and requires such rapid changes for survival in this rush that apparently we must give up passing on things that earlier generations regarded as very valuable for balanced and sound progress.

Thus, for example, what is called the modern age begins at the same time as the printing press and the subsequent spread of reading (very rapid in the West). For more or less five centuries it was reading that transmitted the most elaborate forms of culture and wisdom. These forms, it is important to note, were passed on not only through the content of what was read, but also through the refinement, analysis, and criticism involved in the very act of reading. Today, however, although a minimum of reading and writing is necessary, civilization uses other means besides reading (radio, television, and so forth) to instruct on how to use the instruments necessary for living usefully in society. Those instruments compete with reading, and indeed, they win right away, since with much less effort they provide an infinitely greater "quantity" of items of information adapted to uncriticized social ends.

However, I would like to offer an example closer to our set of issues.[3] What Freud said remains true: immediate satisfaction runs contrary to the building up of any culture and of any civilization. Any reader will have heard many jokes whose humor lies in how surprised adults are at the incredible information their tiny children have about sex. They will also have heard of the need to counteract in this regard all the sources of information which separate sex from what is regarded as the deeper source of moral satisfaction. In fact, however, the problem is not one of supplying a greater amount of information or not. The problem lies in the fact that the mass media "take up space in the mind" in such a way that long-range moral satisfactions (and all moral satisfactions are long-range) are checked by the lively information about satisfaction that civilization places immediately at the disposal of people who are ever-less mature and less accustomed to analyze critically what they receive through their senses.

In beginning this chapter, I do not want to go more deeply into a set of issues which would undoubtedly be no more than a commentary on things everyone knows, although they may not have always been well-assimilated. I do want to pause for a moment, however, on the shift from the Middle Ages to the modern age, for if the increasing acceleration of history has been present in all ages of humankind, it is worth asking why one age is separated so clearly from the next, or equivalently, what makes this phenomenon at the end of the Middle Ages so visible so that the following stage bears the name "modern."[4]

The Adventure of Modern Humanism: The Renaissance

It is time to take another step. The acceleration of history as such did not become perceptible until very recently, within our own modern era. As we have seen, however, it is inscribed in the very matter of biology, and perhaps in that of physics as well. Yet like the "cunning of reason" in Hegel's system, much before it is revealed as such—that is, as an ingredient in any endeavor in history—it takes possession of planned human endeavors and forces them to speed up their own *time*, without knowing or intending it. Moreover, just as the "cunning of reason" is not perceived by those who are "taken up" by it, if we may put it that way, and is only discovered by looking back at history, so also the very title "modern era" indicates that the "cunning of negentropy" (my term here for the acceleration of history) is, as it were, lying in wait for the end of that cultural universe built up over the centuries of the Middle Ages with such seemingly solid materials.

This chapter has already hinted that besides this omnipresent and continual acceleration of history as a consequence of the economy of energy prevailing in the universe, another factor, one more voluntary, conscious, and forward-looking, began to act or at least to become conspicuous at the beginning of the Renaissance.

Obviously, there are degrees in the acceleration of history. Moreover, as everyone knows, human endeavors can hinder or lessen for a time the increasing velocity of certain changes in history. While this is less clear today, I assume that the temptation to hold history back must have seemed feasible when the European world was still Christian toward the end of the Middle Ages.[5]

Why is that the case? What happens with this human being emerging from the Middle Ages, to which the last chapter was devoted? Upon completing the construction of a (feudal) world where everything is thought out, measured, and justified once and for all, this millennium has a certain right to think it has found a *perennial* order and that, furthermore, by wrapping it all up in dogma, it has provided it with the most precious foundation and safeguard, that of uniting this order to the certitude of a divine revelation—that is, of a truth valid once and for all. However, already at work there, opening fissures in the solid walls of this world that represents a sacred order and leading—cleverly, I would say—toward an unsuspected greater truth, is this maturing of the biosphere, which will later be translated into what I have here called the (conscious) acceleration of history.

Naturally, at this point we find the particular inclinations of historians to indicate what factor it was that led others to draw away from the medieval synthesis. It is almost a cliché, at least for theologians, that this factor was called *nominalism*.

I admit I would not like to get involved in that discussion. I prefer to stick with the realm in which the reflections in this work are unfolding, and thus to continue to sketch the overarching hypothesis of this chapter on the modern era and dogma. From this standpoint I prefer to follow the intuition of one of the books I have always admired as one of the broadest and most profound inquiries carried out by Protestant theology in the realm of anthropology, Reinhold Niebuhr's *The Nature and Destiny of Man*.

In his Gifford Lectures delivered in Edinburgh during World War II, he too is examining the panorama of humankind as it emerges from the Middle Ages in what is called the Renaissance and says the following: "It is not unfair to affirm that modern culture, that is, our culture since the Renaissance, is to be credited . . . with the greatest confusion in the understanding of man."[6]

Although a reader may attack me for making Niebuhr say the opposite of what he meant, I deduce from his statement that everything in the modern era can be summarized as a break with the *medieval concept of the human being*. It is the undertaking of a new phase of the human adventure that leads to this break and everything following therefrom. It is true that from the standpoint of value, my deduction puts a positive sign on what Niebuhr calls "confusion." Moreover, it is true that when he came to make his judgment in the middle of the twentieth century, the optimism with which that adventure recommenced in the Renaissance and continued in subsequent centuries had led to a vicious war, to be followed by nuclear holocaust. Confusion? So it appears from the standpoint of today, perhaps, but that is not how the modern era began, and Niebuhr himself recognizes that fact in a very cogent account of the Renaissance.

The Renaissance takes its name from the restoration of classic Greek and Latin culture, especially in Italy. That restoration, however, really goes only part of the way and is more notional than real. Looking back from a broader and more realistic perspective, one could say that Greek and Latin culture, supposedly reborn, was actually the only escape route allowed within that medieval Christian world. What people were really seeking was not Greek art or ideas; it was a humanism that would not clash with a (Christian) culture from which the medieval world had in some way emerged and which it therefore tolerated. One could almost say that the Renaissance thus used, cleverly, the only "paganism" then feasible for escaping from the confinement of established culture. The aim was to build a different kind of *humanism*, one that was free, at least from the ties of Catholic dogma.

A Rebirth That Isn't

What we have here, therefore, is a false rebirth, an adventure moving ahead, not backward. Niebuhr himself accepts that when he writes, "Thus an air of melancholy hangs over Greek life which stands in sharpest contrast to the all-pervasive *optimism* of the now dying bourgeois culture, despite the assumption of the latter that it had merely restored the classical world view and the Greek view of man."[7] The climate that initiates the task of creating a "new human being," different from the medieval human and more mature, and which, despite crises, persists through four centuries, proves that not all is confusion, at least up to a moment very close to our own. Even Bonhoeffer in the midst of the Nazi barbarism under which he is imprisoned and destined to be killed, assumes that contemporary (European) humanity is simply the human being "come of age."[8]

In accordance with the hypothesis I will use in these chapters, the Renaissance itself (with its great "humanists"), the Reformation, the (first and second) Enlightenment, the French revolution (and the rights of man), the industrial revolution, scholarly biblical exegesis, and so forth, are all different branches or expressions coming out of this single trunk of postmedieval *humanism*. Even though many of these "units" of history may be ambiguous or at odds with one another, all spring from this will to create a new human being, and all are nourished from the quickened hope of finding such a human being.

Humanism, Adventure of the Bourgeoisie

One last observation: before proceeding to see what relation some of these overall developments in modern history have with the conception of dogma in the Catholic Church, we must add a common element shaping many of the things within this European humanistic effort. This element was already mentioned in the passage in which Niebuhr speaks of "bourgeois culture."

Indeed one cannot escape from the structures of the medieval world simply by wanting to. Erich Fromm writes eloquently on the social ties binding medieval people:

What characterizes medieval in contrast to modern society is its lack of individual freedom. Everybody in the earlier period was chained to his role in the social order. A man had little chance to move socially from one class to another, he was hardly able to move even geographically from one town or from one country to another. With few exceptions he had to stay where he was born. He was often not even free to dress as he pleased or to eat what he liked. The artisan had to sell at a certain price and the peasant at a certain place, the market of the town. A guild member was forbidden to divulge any technical secrets of production to anybody who was not a member of his guild and was compelled to let his fellow guild members share in any advantageous buying of raw material. Personal, economic, and social life was dominated by rules and obligations from which practically no sphere of activity was exempted.[9]

From the twelfth century onward capital, individual economic initiative, and competition begin to increase in importance, while within the cities there emerges a powerful monied class which comes to take turns in power with the nobility. This is the bourgeoisie, which paradoxically has nothing in common with the conservatism with which it has become almost synonymous. The adventure of humanism is the adventure of the bourgeoisie. Niebuhr himself, returning to the key topic of the *optimism* of postmedieval humankind, writes, "The *middle-class* world begins with a tremendous sense of the power of the human mind over nature"[10] — and, it would be well to add, over this "second nature" that is society. Neither the aristocracy nor the incipient "proletariat" want, or are able, to be part of this adventure, except in very particular cases. The people remain oppressed not only by the aristocracy, but by the growing wealth and power of the bourgeoisie,[11] and the aristocracy correctly sees in the bourgeoisie the greatest threat to its hereditary privileges.

Keeping in mind these essential elements will make it possible to understand the fluctuations of Catholic dogma during the modern era.

The Renaissance and the Reformation:
Crisis of Dogma

Renaissance Humanism

Here I ought to begin to deal with the question of the Renaissance, the first breach that medieval people cross on their humanist adventure. First, however, I should alert the reader to a misunderstanding lurking in the preceding material.

Certainly the modern era in its various stages and ingredients is understood only as opposed to the world it has left behind. However, this opposition does not always mean head-on attack, especially at the beginning. People are not aware that they are destroying one world in order to build another, and even less is that their intention, even though any change or reform carries a critique of what previously existed or of one or another aspect of it. Particularly when time intervals are short, one is not likely to find a radical negation of the entire past.

Within this past there is a special respect for Christian dogma at the beginning of the modern era. What I mean is that even when certain important elements of Christendom are subjected to criticism, the revelation on which it is founded is still not unchallenged.

Even the "pagan" mood of the Renaissance, in contrast with the Enlightenment, does not struggle head-on with Christian dogma. Yet we must admit that some of the ridicule aimed at medieval attitudes does not shrink from taking on some aspects of religion. We have the examples of a Rabelais or a François Villon, although it may be difficult to know how extensive such attitudes may be.

Hence the Renaissance will not take up too much of our attention, and instead I am going to devote this section to the Protestant Reformation. One or other byproduct of Renaissance culture and its humanism will nonetheless be useful for understanding certain features that the Reformation is to develop more fully and which accordingly will be closely connected to dogma.

Although it is (apparently) a matter of turning back to a now dead culture, that of Greece and Rome, the shift entailed in Renaissance humanism will have a doubly relativizing effect on what is Christian. The first effect is external, as it were. The Renaissance shows that the medieval order is not eternal and therefore it does not belong to the very nature of things. Magnificent cultures that were not Christian have existed. Human beings and their power to create are greater than that which was regarded as "natural" and constant in the feudal, Christian world. The Renaissance thus moves away from a world previously regarded as rather like "nature" itself. Along with this "withdrawing" there begins to arise a certain coldness[12] toward what is connected with what is Christian, as though it were still largely barbarian. This is the case in the realm of art and intellectual life, and with a degree of prudence in the realm of dogma. We should not downplay the cliché portraying the Middle Ages as "dark ages," although the impact on dogma takes place over the long run.

The second effect is more direct, and, as it were, internal. Throughout medieval times, learned theology had been thought and written in Latin, and the written deposit of revelation was the Latin Bible, or the Vulgate.[13] Just because people were reading the New Testament in its original language and many humanists also learned Hebrew to read the Old Testament in its original language, theology was not necessarily going to be revolutionized. However, the very fact of reading the Bible in its original languages and connecting it with its real contexts demonstrated by contrast to what extent the Christianity lived and to some extent constructed in the Middle Ages constituted a world far removed from that of the Bible.

Speaking of the culture of the great Renaissance humanist Erasmus, E.G. Léonard writes:

> This remarkably complete education which was ahead of that of all thinkers at the end of the middle ages led in 1504 to the publication of an *Enchiridion Militis Christiani* (Manual of the Soldier of Christ) in which he "summarizes the methods of a new theology based only on scripture; defines his conception of the interior life, following Vitrier and Colet (his mentors at Oxford and Saint Omer); contrasts the Judaism of works with the spiritual law of the gospel; and even before Luther he draws from Saint Paul the doctrine of Christian freedom."[14]

Although it may be something of an exaggeration to recruit Erasmus into a reformed theology which he himself rejected, we do have here testimony to a certain "liberation" entailed in the approach to the Christian sources made possible by the Renaissance, together with a critical look at the claim that medieval Christianity stood in continuity with these sources. Léonard says:

> Erasmus is capable of surrendering himself to extremely daring thoughts which compensate for his conformity in practice. As was the case with all the Christian humanists, *his religion is focussed on the gospel*. Hence the need to establish the best texts of scripture, *interpret them without excessive allegory*, not seeking in them anything but Christ ... The church *must simplify and purify itself*, through the *distinction between the very small number of untouchable dogmas*, and the mass of "opinions," and by suppressing observances that have no basis in the scripture or the fathers.[15]

Erasmus probably does not represent what is most characteristic and widespread in the Renaissance. He is perhaps too original and too great for that. Nor is he a mere forerunner of Luther and the Reformation. The description of his thinking in the passages just quoted may be considerably exaggerated. The only thing of concern here is to continue to gather elements which indicate a movement forward, and which separate further the medieval world being left behind from the adventure of a humanism which will eventually question the "dogma" which has been "unanimous" thus far in the medieval Christian world.

The Reformation: Justification by Faith Alone?

Thus we come to a crucial point in this process, the *Protestant Reformation*.

Today a Catholic approaching this unquestionably decisive event in the history of Christian dogma encounters the following widespread notion: In terms of the Catholic Church's canon law, the (Lutheran) Reformation was a "heresy" — that is, a heterodoxy — and the destruction of Christian unity in the sixteenth century arose out of the problems of conscience of an Augustinian monk, Martin Luther, the "heresiarch," which means the founder or initiator of that heresy.

In our age of ecumenism, the terms I have just used are regarded as pejorative and are normally avoided. However, the fact that those who went in a particular direction in that period are still regarded today as "separated brethren," at least officially, shows that the terms I used are still valid and for better or worse they fit the juridical situation as the Roman Catholic Church views it, on the basis of its own dogma.

We have already said repeatedly that this is not a history of dogmas, but rather an effort to perch, as it were, on a higher level. This reflection, pursuing out the process of history, seeks to move from individual dogmas to what dogma itself is and how it is conceived. It is evident from history that the Reformation, or rather, Luther's (internal) problem, is about the pair of terms "sinner-justified." It is by reading and interpreting certain passages on this issue in the New Testament that Luther discovers in Paul's letters (Galatians and Romans) an inchoate dogma, which the church at that time (according to the conventional view) did not accept as orthodox and which, after many disputes and twists and turns, it condemned at the Council of Trent. Thus most Catholics, and many of the Protestants whom I know, think Christian unity was broken because Catholics were unable to accept the dogma of justification by faith alone without the works of the law—in other words, the solution to his own internal problem that Luther found through his exegesis of Paul.

Another Hypothesis on the Impact of the Reformation on Dogma

I do not propose to deny the "historicity" of these events. My hypothesis, nonetheless, is that from the standpoint of its conception of dogma, this is not the decisive origin of the Reformation. I do not think I am alone in this suspicion, although I cannot adduce proof that some of the important writers whom I am now going to cite would agree with my hypothesis.

More than four centuries after the Reformation and in an effort somehow to "renew" or "relaunch" its spirit (in view of the crisis of faith of the proletariat in both Europe and North America, for example), Paul Tillich writes profoundly about what he thinks "makes Protestantism 'Protestant' ":

> Protestantism has a *principle* that stands beyond all its realizations. It is the critical and dynamic source of all Protestant realizations, but it is not identical with any of them ... The *Protestant principle*, in name derived from the protest of the "protestants" against decisions of the Catholic majority, contains *the divine and human protest against any absolute claim made for a relative reality*, even if this claim is made by a Protestant church.[16]

Placing this "Protestant principle" thus defined in its true central place can give rise, I believe, to a number of surprises as well as rich hermeneutical consequences. That central place is that of the origins of the Reformation. For indeed if this is the Protestant principle, it must have been what impelled, if not Luther himself, certainly the movement that derives from him.

Now the *first* surprise that may strike a reader is that of discovering that this principle makes no mention of justification by faith. That there was a dogmatic break between Christians in the fifteenth century no one can doubt. Nor can anyone be surprised that those who were excluded by the Catholic "majority" protested that fact. This was certainly not the first time such a thing had happened in a dogmatic dispute. Nevertheless there must have been something new about this "protest" if that name has remained connected to one heterodoxy among others, one supposedly about justification.

This is not the end of the surprises, however, but only the beginning. The disputes, efforts at reconciliation, and elaboration of formulas to express what happens to human beings when God justifies them and the issue of how good works and acting uprightly and with love are related to justification are so intricate or ambiguous that on this precise issue it is very difficult to determine once and for all what features a Luther, a Melancthon,[17] a Bucer, and a Calvin have in common. On the Catholic side so many theories of justification are put forward, all of them presumably opposed to those of the Reformation, that it is difficult to know what the Council of Trent ultimately condemned.

In a recent journal, the outstanding and authoritative theologian, Yves Congar writes a long review of a work on ecumenical theology by the Protestant theologian Edmund Schlink. In that review one finds these words by Congar: "Schlink compares the statements of the Council of Trent to those of the Augsburg Confession. He *very correctly* notes that *the canons of Trent do not apply to Luther*."[18]

This observation has to do with the precise issue of justification by faith. On other issues, Trent is undoubtedly much more direct in condemning the teaching of the reformers. However, that very fact leads back to our original hypothesis, since we are no longer dealing with Luther's deep originating experience. Thus, if there was a break, as there undeniably was, at least today one has a sense that it was due not so much to the doctrine of justification by faith, but to something deeper.

Moreover, we also have history, especially when it takes a sociological approach, to show us that from its very beginnings the Reformation did not "represent" this same foundational experience. A rather eloquent "sign" is the fact that at least the "occasion" for the break was the campaign at Wittenberg by a preacher of indulgences. Readers will perhaps recall from the previous chapter how important they were from the start of the Middle Ages. The reaction against indulgences in some fashion signaled the end of that era, and provided Luther with the opportunity, says Léonard, "to reach *a much broader audience* when on October 31, 1517, he posted his famous ninety-five theses and sent them out of Wittenberg."[19] Significantly, Reformation Day commemorates that event and not, for example, the dates of some of the courses Luther had previously given on Galatians or Romans.

Furthermore, if the Reformation had indeed followed upon Luther's deep personal insight that it was impossible to emerge from sin by acting well, then it appears as almost a paradox of history that something as little "Lutheran" but as "Protestant" as Puritanism should soon arise, and indeed so rapidly as to be visible in the reformation Calvin conceived and put into effect in Geneva. Whether or not one agrees with Max Weber on the cause-and-effect relationship or at least the circularity between the "bourgeois" virtues (as sign of salvation) and the attitudes required by early capitalism, Puritanism does seem to be more Protestant than Catholic, even in our own day.

Anyone observing the Catholic attitude in the Latin countries of southern Europe would assume the well-known line *Pecca fortiter sed crede firmius* must have been coined there. Even reconstructing its true meaning (which is not an ad hominem defense of Catholic theology, but something like this counsel: "as much of a sinner as you might be, believe even more strongly" and you will be saved),[20] it is difficult to imagine this phrase operating as the basis and foundation for normal preaching in any ordinary Protestant church.

Finally, along the same lines, the problems of the Christian churches in Latin America confronted with injustice and the oppression of some human beings by others have made ecumenism easy, at least outside official circles. God knows whether the problem of Christian commitment, and the "works" thereby entailed, is central. Never in my experience have I had to raise the point with a Protestant who might be trying to avoid the issue by claiming to have faith. So what is it that still separates us? Note that I am not asking what "ought" to separate us. In many things we are not separated, but I suspect that if there is anything that prevents complete unity, it is the demand made on the church by what Tillich called the "Protestant principle."

The "Protestant Principle" and Its Impact

Here we find awaiting us the *second* surprise. If the *Protestant principle*, as expressed by Tillich, becomes a hermeneutic principle *for history as well*, the Reformation had to arise as a protest against undue "absolutizations" on the part of the Catholic Church. Contrary to what is generally believed, it is here, and not in the realm of justification by faith, that the events that lead to the breakup of Christian faith mount up. Here also contemporary ecumenism offers matter for reflection.

During the next to last session of Vatican II, the well-known Anglican bishop of Woolwich, the author of the theological best-seller, *Honest to God*, wrote another small book, *The New Reformation?* The contents of the book make it clear that the question mark after the title is superfluous. His main thesis is that the Reformation went only half-way, and that perhaps for that reason with Vatican II, the Catholic Church is catching up with it. Ecumenism for both Christian churches together, accordingly, is now a matter of going the rest of the way. Further on, I will say why I regard such optimism as premature, while still admiring its sincerity. What is of interest here is the vision of the past that emerges in that book and which to some extent manifests the "Protestant principle" Tillich talked about in action: "Indeed, the very issues which in the sixteenth century divided us—the Bible, the vernacular, the liturgy, the laity—are now bringing Catholics and Protestants together."[21]

As the reader will immediately appreciate, there is no mention in the list of items dividing the question what any of us might regard as the most serious and profound dogmatic obstacle to union, justification by faith alone. Moreover, when speaking about the unfinished side of the Reformation movement, Robinson calls it "Luther's involuntary contribution."[22] It is as if a certain "cunning of reason," without the knowledge or intention of the historical actor, had lifted the last barrier to a movement that had to overflow far beyond its own questions and answers.

Naturally, I am quite aware that it would be neither easy nor fair to assume that Tillich would agree that the "Protestant principle" that gave rise to the Reformation was at work in these very items and not in others. That is my own hypothesis, and I will try to demonstrate it with some facts from history that are not lacking in plausibility. However, even now I have to confess that there is something separating me from Robinson, to my own regret. In reading his book I have the impression that with the list of these divisive factors that are said to have (almost) disappeared with Vatican II, he is seeking *to shift the conflict from the terrain of dogma to that of practice*. I think Tillich quite rightly keeps the "Protestant principle" in a terrain I would like to call *theoretical/*

practical. The *abuse* of authority and institutionality that in the name of God and God's revelation divinizes what is human and absolutizes what is relative occurs both in the establishment of what is of faith and in the structures of the church community—or in principle it could occur, since we have not yet moved into the realm of historical events.

I want to cite just one of these events. Martin Bucer, the main reformer in Strasbourg in the mix of interests dividing (those who are to be) Catholics and Protestants into partisans of the emperor, Charles V, and of the king (Francis I of France), is advising against giving in to the anti-imperial feelings of the French court. "In agreement with Luther," if we are to believe Léonard, he writes, "to us his imperial majesty appears to be the instrument of God's goodness; when the Holy Spirit has revealed to him the 'abuses of the Roman church' 'he will congratulate us for having conformed to the pure and holy gospel throughout the Holy Empire.' "[23]

There is no need to insist that this is only an example. Even granting its particularity, however, we find here the beginning of an interpretation of a broader context and this interpretation very much agrees with the hypothesis I have proposed. The movement Bucer embodies, which was one of the first movements called "Protestant" (since it represents the city of Strasbourg in the *protest* presented to the emperor at the diet of Speyr in 1529 which gave rise to the term), in the name of the "pure and holy gospel" condemns the "abuse" entailed in calling traditions sacred and gospel-inspired when in fact they are not. Thus we have here, five centuries before Tillich, a clear forerunner to the formulation of the "Protestant principle" and of its critical application to the world of medieval Christian faith.

The Protestant Principle: Bible, Liturgy, and Laity

If this is the case, however—and all indications are that it is—we are now in for a *third* surprise. What is to constitute the great and lasting impact of the Reformation on *Catholic dogma* will be made up of matters that histories of dogma tend to downplay as simply resulting from the bitterness of the controversy and the incapability of those who stepped in to try to calm people down, prevent exaggeration, and avoid unnecessary conflicts. These matters that seem secondary prove primary on a *second level of logic*, that of the history of the very concept of dogma.

Entering into this surprise is the need to rehabilitate what Robinson, with his keen theological instinct, called "the very issues which in the sixteenth century divided us." The reader will recall that he pointed to four topics: the Bible, the vernacular, the liturgy, and the laity. In my opinion, and from the standpoint of dogma, these four elements can be reduced to two. What Robinson calls "the vernacular" is not a separate issue. It seems to touch each of the other three facets. The Bible in the vernacular language means the Bible read by lay people. Something similar is the case with the liturgy. In other words, "the vernacular" refers to the problem of the function of the "laity" in the church. Moreover, the liturgy, understood as "sacred efficacy," splits the faithful into clerics and lay people. Hence the four major problems the Reformation posed to the very conception of "dogma" in Catholicism are reduced to two: the Bible (as read by all, as well as its dogmatic authority) and the liturgy, with its sacramental origin (and its result: a laity passive in receiving and developing divine revelation).

Each of these two topics placed the Catholic Church as it emerged from the Middle Ages in a very difficult situation. It challenged its foundations and obliged it to "conceive dogma" in a way that could stand up to the doubts generated by such a critique.

Matters could not be otherwise. What Tillich called the "Protestant principle" is actually nothing but the Christian principle pure and simple. I would almost say it is nothing but a tautology of logic alerting any sincere person to the temptation to security involved in absolutizing what is relative. And obviously, where is this temptation more to be feared than in the realm of absolutization par excellence, that of organized religion? Logic alone would suffice to raise this issue had it not been explicitly raised by the historic Jesus as well as by Paul, in an exceedingly radical way.

Nevertheless, to say that the "Protestant principle" Tillich talked about is actually a central "Christian principle" does not mean taking the side of the sixteenth-century Reformation or assuming that today that protest is the exclusive possession of the churches issuing from it. Readers will recall that Tillich himself in formulating the principle is careful to state that it ought to direct its critique against elements in any church claiming to be Christian, including certainly the Protestant churches themselves. Moreover, Robinson believes that Vatican II makes it necessary to propose jointly a new reformation, not simply because Catholics have caught up with Protestantism on most points through Vatican II, but because Protestantism itself has only gone half-way in what it has done and it must undertake a "new reformation," one encompassing Protestants and Catholics alike.

Furthermore, we must realize that Protestantism, both past and present, has not been *simply* a "protest." It built, as it were, a church in which this "protest" became real. If in view of all the foregoing, I cannot deny the need for the Catholic Church to become sensitive to a protest challenging it out of the gospel itself, I cannot deny that the way some churches tried to give a concrete shape to their critique might have been worse than the disease. I am speaking in principle, but I thereby intend to indicate that agreeing with the critical principle does not in itself mean approving of all the historic embodiments actually emerging from it.

Nevertheless, this point is so central for the issue at stake and for what Catholic dogma is to be in the modern era, that I think it should be dealt with in a special section on the Catholic reaction (generally associated with the Council of Trent and the Counter-Reformation, although in some ways it extends much closer to our own time) if not to the "Protestant principle" as such, certainly to its consequences with regard to the Bible and the laity as elements of dogma. In the next section I am going to begin with the issue of how to take the Bible "alone" as dogmatic criterion. For reasons that will be better appreciated further on, I am going to leave the issue of the laity, which complements this one, to the next chapter.

The Bible: Only Source of Revealed Dogma?

Catholic Defense: Two Sources of Revelation

In this section I would like to put aside the concern for exact dating that a person committed to a scholarly historical procedure would follow, and leave the field more open to reflection. I have a very strong reason for this procedure, and referred to it at the close of the preceding section. From the time of the reformation – and its corresponding counter-reformation – up to Vatican II the two problems affecting dogma, that of the Bible as norm of truth and of the lay person as coauthor in the process of revelation, have grown ever-more acute. The defensive stance of the Catholic Church with regard to the world of medieval faith, far from softening in the face of criticism, becomes more accentuated. Contrary to Robinson's optimism, I would go so far as to say that although we have made great strides in coming together in the realm of Protestant and Catholic dogmas, the conception of *dogma* itself is increasingly different, and dialogue on this point is either nonexistent or is becoming increasingly difficult.

In claiming that only what is found in the *Bible* could be regarded as something revealed and requiring faith, the Reformation has put its finger on something essential in Catholic dogma: Does everything that the ordinary or extraordinary magisterium has declared "dogma" – that is, a truth of faith binding on every Christian – come from the Bible?

Readers will recall, and hence there will be no need to repeat it, what Karl Rahner said about the formation of dogma during the Middle Ages, and which we summarized in the previous chapter. Along with elements coming from *divine-apostolic* tradition, there are in the lists of Christian dogmas things that come from a *human* tradition, but which have been taught unanimously for centuries as truths of faith and after a certain period of such unanimous teaching have been declared dogmas and blended inextricably into divine Tradition.

Thus, the principle of *sola Scriptura* made necessary a distinction and a purification, something that would be very difficult to do without reversing directions already taken. It was not simply a matter of saying that the things people had previously believed were false, but rather, in accordance with the genuinely Christian "Protestant" principle, attempting to separate what was open to opinion from what was endowed with the assurances that it was absolute truth. What, according to Léonard, was Erasmus's position – namely, that "the church must simplify and purify itself, through the distinction between the very small number of untouchable dogmas, and the mass of 'opinions,' " now became imperative in the Protestant churches, as did "second-level dogma" – that is, dogma about dogmas.

Theologically speaking, on this point there is no doubt that the Catholic Church condemned this critical effort and refused to submit to it. While there may be room for doubt about whether Luther was or was not condemned for his ideas on justification, there can be no doubt that the church saw quite clearly the meaning of the hermeneutical principle of "scripture alone" as source of revelation and rejected it, at least until Vatican II.[24] In that rejection the unity of Christians was on the line.

Readers are already familiar with how the issue is raised and hence we are not going to repeat it here. What is important, because it was deliberately left hanging in the previous chapter, is the *solution* the Catholic Church provided at the beginning of the modern era at the Council of Trent.

Like everything dividing the churches, Catholic doctrine on the Bible is right, I believe, in one respect: the Bible does not become a human and rich norm except by becoming *tradition*. As we have seen, that is how the paradigm of divine pedagogy embodied in the Old Testament came about. Scripture become norm without tradition becomes a poison, just like the poison of tradition which generates dogmas not based on scripture (that is, which do not come from the "deposit" of the Word of God).

In order to defend itself against the "Protestant principle," if such a didactic anachronism is appropriate here, the Catholic Church spoke of a *second source* of revealed truths and called it (in church vocabulary almost always in opposition to scripture) "tradition" or "traditions," giving them the same foundational rank as the Old and New Testament scriptures. Thus the Council of Trent speaks of a truth which is without error and which, because it is God's revelation, is a norm for the thinking and activity of Christians. It says that "this truth and instruction are contained in the written books and in the unwritten traditions, which have been received by the apostles from the mouth of Christ Himself, or from the apostles themselves, at the dictation of the Holy Spirit, and have come down even to us, transmitted as it were from hand to hand." It goes on to say that the church "receives and holds in veneration with an equal affection of piety and reverence all the books ... and also the traditions themselves, those that appertain both to faith and to morals, as having been dictated either by Christ's own word of mouth, or by the Holy Spirit, and preserved by the Catholic Church by a continuous succession" (D. 783).

In other words, for the Council it is clear that the deposit of revelation ends with the apostles. It does not say it ends in Christ (with his death or his ascension?) because he did not leave anything in writing. His witnesses enter into the category of "revealers" in two ways. They either reproduce what they heard from the lips of the Lord, God incarnate and Absolute Truth, or the Holy Spirit was able to dictate truths to them as writers directly (that is, without going through Christ) just as he had dictated to the writers of the Old Testament.

These *two ways*, however, are not what is decisive for dogma at the *source*. What is decisive is that the transmission *starting with the apostles* of what is revealed by God apparently takes place through *two* distinct *ways* and we must learn to receive it through both in order to accept revelation properly. These things are either written down while the apostles are alive, or—and here is where there do not seem to be any perceptible boundaries—they can be transmitted from person to person, and turn up in writing centuries after an apostle received them from Jesus or from his Spirit.

Difficulty of "Tradition"—Back to Purgatory

From this point on, the church will insist that there are *two* completely distinct sources of revelation, as we have been able to appreciate. To make things worse, it calls the second one "tradition," thus losing sight of the kind of transmission—social, active, and creative—already implicit in scripture. As we could observe in part 1 of this book scripture is in itself "tradition" in the richest and most creative sense of the word.

By contrast a "tradition" which without hindrance can pop up in any century or in anyone's opinion can absolutize so many things that it unintentionally brings about the opposite of what it was striving to do: relativizing these things along with everything else. In the long run, many threads regarded as solid will be discovered to be extremely weak. One example already dealt with in the previous chapter will suffice to understand this fundamental aspect of the theory of the two sources of revelation.

We have already observed Rahner saying that to appeal to an oral transmission said to have been made in secret or in small groups until someone influential in possession of this message writes it down, in no way resolves the problem of how to recognize and purge divine revelation.[25] Let us take *purgatory* as an example. In passages already cited, Colzani says that its existence first appears implicitly and vaguely in Origen, whose career was in the middle of the third century. According to Colzani, we must wait until Augustine a century and a half later for this same opinion to become more precise, although still "hesitantly." Only in the Middle Ages will it be taught as certain. After so many centuries, how is it possible to arrive at the assurance, not that there is a purgatory, but that an apostle taught something of that sort as coming from Christ or from the Holy Spirit? How can something that appears simply as the implicit opinion of a writer two centuries after the apostolic period be transformed into divine-apostolic tradition?

In view of all this, is there any serious reason to believe that Origen is aware of the existence of purgatory because (even though he himself does not profess such an explicit belief) he heard it from someone, who in turn heard it . . . thus going back two centuries until coming to an apostle who passed on to a friend or disciple, as having been heard from Christ or inspired by the Holy Spirit, that there is a purgatory? If, moreover, it is necessary to invoke this method with regard to a large number of things that became "truths of faith" during the Middle Ages even though no one could find them in the Bible, What is the point of speaking of a second source of revelation that no one can make explicit or to which any doctrine subsequently taught could also likewise appeal with just as fragile a foundation?

In order to recover the explosive and creative power of the Christian message, will it not be necessary to go into reverse and reduce it to what was regarded as both biblical and true before being put into this crucible of the barbarian peoples where it became fused with their own ideas, apparitions, private revelations, or imagination?

All these problems that I am here presenting with theoretical questions actually come up one after another during the modern era. Indeed, it happens without them even being noticed as such at first. When do they become conscious questions? It resembles what happens at certain thresholds in biological evolution. It is not clear whether a particular kind of living one-celled being is animal or vegetable until we have more complex examples at hand. Something quite similar takes place in the topic here being studied. A passive laity (to be studied in the next chapter) does not question whether the church is teaching it truths of faith deriving from one or two sources of revelation. However, there are problems arising in this area which sooner or later will prompt repressed or timid questions to make themselves heard.

In other words, as a result of custom, routine, or passivity, it may be possible to hold onto medieval faith, no matter what questions one's contemporaries are raising about the meaning of human existence. However, a growing portion of the church, starting with theologians, will become aware that dialogue with these questions cannot be put off forever, even if that entails heightened pressures on faith. They also become aware that a church which holds as truths of faith what it learned as dogma in the Middle Ages is so loaded down with information that it cannot really dialogue with new problems.

The issue is no longer one of engaging in dialogue with those who are one's separated brothers and sisters as a result of the Reformation. The whole adventure of humanism starting with the Renaissance will assume ever-more varied forms and will change ever-more rapidly. The church's lack of dialogue will lead it to turn back with an obvious nostalgia for any ancien régime from which it can hope for a return to a world similar to that of the Middle Ages, and will accordingly create political and religious enemies with whom dialogue will be ever-more difficult.

The Case of Latin America and Its Christianization

The beginning of the modern era coincides with Europe's discovery of the New World and of its conquest by force of weapons—weapons that happen to be in the hands of Christians. In order to engage in "dialogue" with this world, the Christians bring their world of received Christian truths and no one raises the question of whether or not they come from the Bible. In any case "dialogue" between the world of pre-Columbian religions and the European Christianity which is arriving is *nonexistent*. Did that prompt explicit questions? I confess that personally I do not know.

However, one fact is enough to make me think. Significantly, the most creative project in this dialogue between two worlds with differing faiths entailed separating the native people from the (supposed) Christianity of the Europeans. That the behavior of the latter did not match the faith they professed was not the only reason for this separation. There are clear indications that the Franciscan and Jesuit missionaries were clearly aware that a church overloaded with dogmas could not dialogue with the very basic life of these people. The process had to follow its own rhythm, and this rhythm in turn required separation, such as was the case in the "reductions." Giving people space and opportunity for questions was far more important than piling up answers. "To ask men to believe in the doctrine or to accept the revelation before they see it for themselves as the definition of their experience and the depth of their relationship, is to ask what to this generation with its schooling in an empirical approach to everything, seems increasingly hollow," writes Robinson, in words very close to the previously quoted passage from Schillebeeckx.[26]

In Europe, Dialogue with Humanism Impossible

However, in Europe itself the acceleration of history and the corresponding crises and conquests of humanism likewise gradually force the church to confront a dialogue that is necessary but difficult. The more time is wasted in trying to avoid it, the more necessary and difficult it becomes.

Although we need not go into details, the reader will recall from European history that the development of the human sciences (paleography, ancient languages and literature) pose problems for those who think God dictated a Bible in which imprecision, contradictions, elements taken from other literatures, and so forth, are plain to see. Historic changes which are destined to create new societies in accordance with particular values, which are in themselves Christian, will leave behind a church which continues to read and explain ancient texts in which slavery and the inferiority of women are presented as deriving from nature and God's will. As a result of reason and its advances, one can no longer approach the Bible without "preconceptions" about what the human mind is and about its potential development. Developments in technology will bring on problems of life or death for humankind around the planet (overpopulation without the necessary social transformation within nations or internationally; nuclear weapons; nuclear energy; the contamination of earth, rivers, waters, and atmosphere) and they will render ever-more irrelevant a conception of life that deals with ideas and solutions valid for eras that we find it harder and harder even to imagine.

I cannot stop to deal with each of these and other similar points. What I would like the reader to take from this picture is the impression that a crisis has been dominating the theological scene in the Catholic Church, especially since the problem of modernism at the beginning of the twentieth century, and that this crisis affects the Protestant churches as well insofar as the Bible alone will not provide solutions for problems completely absent from it.

Theologians begin to think that a church cannot enter into a true dialogue when it is loaded down with dogmas, mixed together with revelation, and where what might have been an answer in another era is without qualification proclaimed as a truth of faith.

When Rahner, in very abstract terms to be sure, presents this picture (as observed in the last chapter), one has the impression that the main obstacle he sees is located in the fact that the theory of *the two sources of revelation* opened up a breach that allowed dogmas to come flooding in. In other words, an uncontrolled addition of truths of faith, far from aiding the pursuit of truth, paralyzes it. Ecumenism clearly proves the point. That is why he proposes that in ecumenical exchanges with separated Christian brothers and sisters there be a return to the "dogmas" held as such during the era when Christians were not yet discussing the problems that later gave rise to the division still existing today. That position will oblige us to take another step and move somewhat away from Rahner in the next chapter.[27] However, even to do that it will be absolutely necessary to return to the position that there is a single source of revelation. Although this problem had been discussed more or less tacitly for some time, it was discussed openly at Vatican II in connection with the constitution on divine revelation, *Dei Verbum*.

Discussion of the "Two Sources" at Vatican II

Discussion began when the Council fathers managed to change the title proposed for Chapter II, "On *the sources* of revelation," to the one it bears, which speaks only of "the transmission of divine revelation." Their avoidance of the plural meant that it could not simply be taken for granted that there were two sources.

Nevertheless, as is almost always the case with the teaching of the magisterium, the Council repeats previous conciliar formulas on the question, not only the previously cited words from Trent, but also the even more precise expression of Vatican I: "the word of God, whether written or handed on" (D. 1792; DV 10). At Vatican I both the overall historical context and the conjunction used (*or* = Latin *vel*) indicate that what is written and what is transmitted by tradition means two sources that are distinct and independent, at least to a great extent (even though they come from the same origin and author).

Does this repetition of the formula from the past represent Vatican II's entire feeling on this matter? To begin with, previous chapters have already noted the extremely important shift in exegesis that Pius XII's encyclical *Divino Afflante Spiritu* made mandatory for Catholic exegesis. By the time of Vatican II scholars had twenty years of working with a kind of exegesis in which they paid closer attention to what the human authors of the Bible had intended to say in their writings and thus had considerable experience in steering away from unrestrained transferred exegesis. Moreover, other aspects like the climate of ecumenism and a greater understanding of the values present in non-Catholic Christian traditions likewise were inclining them to think that on this point Vatican II could not simply repeat what had been said a century before.

It is true that the Council fathers did not see this repetition simply as a way of solving a problem that had arisen and been discussed after Vatican I. Rather they regarded it as a sign that Vatican II did not want to enter into controversy on this matter, which was open to discussion. They left things as they were.

Such is Hans Küng's opinion when he writes:

> The theological commission of the Council under pressure from the curial minority finally agreed to leave open the determination of the relationship: hence the text, "written *or* (*vel*) handed on." It was felt that progress had been made, although in fact it was scarcely progress, instead of separating Scripture and tradition, to bring them as close as possible together and let them flow into one—almost as in modern fittings hot and cold water flow together into one outlet.[28]

Küng's biting humor constitutes one more observation that the Council decided not to decide anything. At the end of that same paragraph 10, the document states that, "sacred tradition, sacred Scripture, and the teaching authority of the Church . . . are so linked and joined together that one cannot stand without the others." Küng comments, "Chapter II . . . covers up the problem with a leveling-out quasi-trinitarian formula and a praise of harmony which sounds very melodious in Latin."

Other serious theologians, who like Küng were involved in the debates swirling around the Council, agree with his assessment that compromise was the prevailing note on this important issue. In a commentary on the documents of Vatican II, R. A. F. MacKenzie also makes it clear that we have here a compromise, although he also is quite willing to accept the intention to interrelate these three elements as something positive. "The Constitution especially emphasizes . . . the coordination and interplay of Scripture, tradition, and the magisterium. In whatever way the question of the separate values of the first two may be answered in theory, in practice all three function together."[29] A. Grillmeier is more negative in his commentary on Chapter III of the Constitution:

> Because, for the sake of harmony, it had been agreed to avoid anything that would decide the question of the "material sufficiency of Scripture" [in order to communicate all of revelation] in a positive or negative sense, the formulation of the role of scripture in the transmission of revelation was made particularly difficult . . . Thus the difficulty was circumnavigated by silence and the avoidance of positive statements, which was certainly not to the benefit of the whole.[30]

A Marked Orientation toward the Future

Fully recognizing that these commentators have more authority, nevertheless I dare to express a different opinion. Naturally I am quite aware that the repetition of old dogmatic formulas, whether of councils or not, tends to silence or to lower the resistance of those who continue to defend the idea of two independent sources of divine revelation. That is what the compromise achieves. I have already indicated that advances in the process of learning to learn generally do not take place by counterpoising a yes and a no, but by showing how a better interpretation demands a different nuance—without making it necessary to declare the previous formula to be false.

Reading paragraphs 9 and 10 of *Dei Verbum* between the lines, one can perceive an intention that goes beyond the necessary compromise between two different tendencies. At the beginning of paragraph 9, on relations between tradition and scripture, we are told that "both of them, flowing from the same divine wellspring, in a certain way merge into a unity and tend toward the same end." The compromise, which is subtle and not lacking in humor, consists in the Council's use here of the term "wellspring" (=*scaturigo*) instead of its more usual synonym "source" (= *fons*)[31] to indicate that scripture and tradition are most closely united, but in such a way that the term "source" does not appear in the singular, which would do away with the possibility of holding theologically that there is a second source of divine revelation—namely, tradition.

It is precisely "tradition," however, that has enabled the church to maintain as "truths of faith" things not found in scripture and which the church believes it cannot do without (e.g., some Marian dogmas, some specific kinds of church authority, the existence of seven sacraments by Christ's explicit intention, certain ideas about eschatology, such as purgatory, and so forth). In other words for a church defending its truths and structures, what is required of "tradition" is that it be a *distinct and independent* source. By being such it can provide a basis for truths that lack a sufficient biblical basis.

This impression is heightened when we read in the line immediately preceding that "there exists a close connection and communication between sacred tradition and sacred Scripture." Unless this is understood in some magic sense, this connection and communication makes it quite implausible that what is not in one of them could be taken from the other. When one reads the statement between the lines, the whole possibility that there might be "two" sources of revelation rather than "one" falls to the ground.

The very next line reinforces the sense that it is impossible to read paragraph 9 as though it were dealing with two sources with different contents. Indeed it states that "sacred Scripture is the word of God inasmuch as it is consigned to writing." When speaking of tradition, however, the word "inasmuch" is not used again, although it would be grammatically appropriate to do so. However, the fact that the document continues to speak about another "aspect," about another "inasmuch" of *the same word of God*, comes out clearly in the "functionality" attributed to tradition: it helps the successors of the apostles "in their preaching preserve this word of God faithfully, explain it, and make it more widely known." Obviously, in this functionality there is no mention of what would be essential to the theory of the "two sources," that of *complementing* the information provided by scripture by means of what would also be passed down from hand to hand from the apostles (D. 783).

Anyone keeping all this in mind will, I think, read the crucial paragraph 10 in a different way. There after speaking of the "Word of God" the reader will find this incisive statement: the church "draws from this *one* deposit of faith *everything* which it presents for belief as divinely revealed."

Obviously the compromise which avoids any definitive exclusion of the theory of two sources, allows for the escape hatch of claiming that here the word "deposit" indicates both what went into the New Testament and what was passed on by word of mouth from an apostle until the moment it became the belief of the universal church.

Nevertheless, such a procedure grates on the theological ear, since the word "deposit" logically points toward what is placed or deposited in written form, while the word "tradition" — and even more the plural (nonwritten) "traditions" — suggests something that is not deposited but rather moving along and being transmitted.

Thus simply read as it stands and without excessive niceties, this Council statement seems to stand as a sign of the times: the Catholic Church is beginning to return to a dogmatic sobriety that can facilitate and humanize dialogue with its separated Christian brothers and sisters, and with other human brothers and sisters, whether believers or not. That this requires tact, long periods of time, and profound pastoral work is obvious. However, anyone reading *Dei Verbum* without deliberately understanding everything as a defense of the past, will note this statement as comprehending the unique place scripture exercises in giving shape to dogma and in purging it of spurious or secondary elements that have built up over the centuries.

At the end of paragraph 10 we find the threefold set of terms that provokes Küng's caustic humor. No doubt the mention of the teaching authority of the church alongside "sacred tradition and sacred scripture" offers an escape hatch for those still speaking of two sources of revelation. Such at least is the appearance, but a close reading reveals that this wavering, or compromise, or whatever one wants to call it, does not allow for such a conclusion. The same argument used with regard to paragraph 9 above, also applies here. The three elements converging in *any dogma* — and I think this is a lot more important than Küng does — are not on the same level. I do not think any sensible theologian would consider equating the ecclesiastical magisterium with sacred scripture!

However, what is important is the fact that by moving from two to three elements and in declaring that these three "are so linked and joined together that *one cannot stand without the others*," the statement dashes any claim tradition could present to provide any material of faith "independent" of scripture. It is just this "independence" that would enable things not contained in scripture but which had appeared at some point in the life of the church and were gradually accepted by everyone and finally taught as truths of faith to become dogmas. Purgatory has already served as an example of such a process.

The order in which the three items appear is interesting even for a theological instinct only moderately developed. For it cannot be by chance that tradition appears *before* sacred scripture. Even the two-source theory puts scripture first. It is my understanding that, whether deliberately or not, the Council is thus pointing to the historical origin in which the three elements emerge and function.

Certainly the New Testament, the Christian scriptures, gathers what is already the tradition transmitted by the apostles. Without believing in these witnesses (who are already church) it is impossible to believe in Jesus, for his (historic) life, his message, and his values — everything that will later be put into writing and canonized as sacred scripture in the New Testament — come to us only through the apostolic tradition. What is perhaps more important, however, is what comes after scripture, which in itself is not a sufficient norm for resolving the problems of the present.

In the commentary from which we have already quoted, Ratzinger points out that the close unity between scripture and tradition in Vatican II, one in which neither of the terms can stand without the other, should have silenced Protestant suspicions that dogmas without a sufficient biblical foundation could be established through "tradition." Perhaps Ratzinger is too optimistic when he asserts that both sides would accept that position "without any difficulty." Surprisingly, however, he adds that "the firm accent placed on the unity of scripture and tradition gives rise to the strongest opposition and showed that the Protestant idea of *sola scriptura* was of less concern with regard to the material origin of particular statements of faith (dogmas) than the problem of the scripture's function as judge over the church."[32]

Regardless of whether Ratzinger is accurate on this point, he is rightfully alarmed by another concern regarding the same issue. In paragraph 10, *Dei Verbum* states, "The task of authentically interpreting the word of God . . . has been entrusted exclusively to the living teaching office of the Church, whose authority is exercised in the name of Jesus Christ." At this point it should have been said that the church "goes forward together with humanity and experiences the same earthly lot as the world does" (GS 40), and that it stands itself under the norm of the word of God entrusted to it. While the church is certainly obligated to interpret that word, and has the Spirit of Jesus to guide it to all truth, it is also true that standing normatively under that same divine word, it should reform itself seriously and continually in order to carry out its task.

Hence the fact that the "teaching authority of the church" is put on the same level with apostolic tradition and with the New Testament scripture raises again, and with some reason, the alarm of the "Protestant principle"—that is, the need to protest against a pretension that seems to ignore the human and sinful side of the church.

Question Remaining: How Does the Bible Become the Norm?

There still remains, however, something to explain in this necessary task of the church. How does the Bible operate to become the specific norm of the church in situations that are completely different from those in which its being was established two thousand years ago? Naturally, part of this function is negative, as has been indicated in the preceding discussion—namely, to prevent dogmas from proliferating in the form of "divinized" human traditions. However, there remains a more positive function to carry out, one that assumes that the church is living in relationship to the problems posed to it with the unfolding of developments in history. What is the church to do or say, for example, about nuclear weapons and the pollution of the planet? Or how must it exist in an oppressed and poor continent like Latin America?

At the outset of the Reformation the Protestant churches defended a solution that might have been very good or seemed sufficient at that time: scripture alone (*sola Scriptura*) could be understood completely through the *free examination* by the reader with the help of the Holy Spirit. Expressed in this manner this would be the equivalent, I believe, of a true theological proposition to the extent that it remained up in the air, as it were. On the other hand, as a *social* structure generating a "wisdom" (as von Rad said) preventing each generation from starting from zero in the pursuit of a Christian meaning for problems not raised in scripture, it would either be some kind of continuous miracle, or it would have to fall into one of two possible, but equally defective, solutions: that of fundamentalism (taking the Bible literally and simply applying it to different contexts) or the solution followed by the more structured churches issuing from the Reformation—the creation of a kind of magisterium[33] with its own "clergy."

In Protestant churches these did not develop an explicit theology of this magisterial function, probably because it would not be quite consistent with one of the most central postulates of the Reformation, the priesthood of all believers. Nevertheless, in actuality such a teaching authority was exercised in the past and continues to this day.

Be that as it may, the normative role of the Bible *over* the church requires a *pedagogy* which, by scrutinizing the signs of the times with the Spirit mentality of Jesus, bridges the gap between the gospel and the present. In keeping with that norm thus made operative it judges the church and better prepares it for its mission. In other words, the triad Vatican II mentioned in *Dei Verbum* probably would have been better expressed as "tradition-scripture-tradition," understanding by the second "tradition," of course, not only the magisterium but the experience of the *ecclesia discens* (learning church).

I do not intend to go on at great length on this point about which a good deal more could be said, because from now on I think we must delve into another of those elements which the Reformation to its great credit at least raised, one that links the two terms already mentioned, liturgy and laity.

I would like to conclude this chapter by noting that European ecumenism, whose dialogue is primarily with the highly institutional Protestant churches (which have, as it were, their own clergy and their magisterium), rarely reaches beyond this point. I am referring to the fact that even Rahner, one of those who have gone furthest in unifying tradition and scripture in Catholic theology, seems to be concerned almost exclusively about the fact that a church more and more loaded down with dogmas, especially since the Middle Ages, cannot dialogue with the emerging forms of humanism.

What the next chapter will try to show is that this problem cannot remain at this point. Paradoxically at Vatican II the Catholic Church stated what was most crucial to restoring to the church an essential function in revelation— namely, *experience*. It did so, however, in the decree on ecumenism and not where in my opinion it deserved to be expressed in order that revelation might continue on its way in the present as it did in the past: the community of the faithful as an active participant in the construction of dogma.

CHAPTER 11

Liturgy and Laity

From the angle of dogma, which is our concern in this work, the question of the liturgy and that of the laity are very closely connected. In a way of worshiping God in which there are no sacrifices, either human or animal, the liturgy is centered on the "sacraments"—that is, on those gestures and words through which the gift (= grace) of God, which is God's very life, is signified and conferred. It happens, however, that the great divide between *clerics* on the one side and *lay people* on the other derives (at least in accordance with the theology prevailing since the end of the Middle Ages) from the fact that the former have been "ordained" in order to carry out this liturgy validly, officially, and normally—that is, to be its "ministers"—while the latter must restrict themselves to "receiving" their sacred effects.[1]

That being the case, readers will not be surprised to find that the ideas discussed during the Reformation period about the sacramental liturgy continue to have a decisive influence on the conception of the roles of the lay person and the cleric in all spheres.

The Laity and the Liturgy

Institution of the Sacraments by Christ

Were it necessary to provide a biblical basis for the sacraments in such a way that in a particular passage it would be demonstrated that Jesus himself had established a particular sign and granted it the function of conferring a specific grace, we could not really prove the divine institution of any sacrament. What I mean is that we would not find any passage in which all these elements are present at once: Jesus establishing a particular rite and indicating the specific grace that God would be communicating to human beings through it.[2]

That, however, would amount to excessive historical rigor. Seeking to return to *sola Scriptura* as a dogmatic criterion, the Reformation recognizes *two* sacraments (instead of the seven that Catholics recognized as all "instituted by Jesus Christ Our Lord"—D. 844). The two sacraments acknowledged by the Reformation are those about which a great deal is said throughout the New

Testament, although we cannot find all the elements mentioned above in any particular place. These two sacraments which the New Testament attributes to Jesus himself are baptism and the Lord's supper—that is, what Catholics call the eucharist.

Catholic theology's centuries-old claim that there are seven sacraments, each and every one of them instituted by Jesus Christ, is yet another typical case of a nonbiblical tradition. Hence for some time now competent theologians have tended to say that Jesus instituted them indirectly—that is, through a church, which, with his Spirit, went on its way, marking the existence of each human generation with the signs of a grace with which God accompanies human beings throughout their lives, following the course of the most important changes in their lives.

Efficacy of the Sacraments and the Status of the Lay Person

Remembering that we must be on guard against facile synonymies, it should be noted that the word "sacrament" does not mean the same thing in Catholic and Reformation theology. Although baptism, and especially infant baptism, gave rise to controversy within the Reformation and with the more "orthodox" line endowing it with a strange efficacy quite similar to the "supernatural" efficacy assigned to it by Tridentine theology, the overall tendency of Protestant theology with regard to the sacraments taken as a whole is notably different from that of Catholicism. At least that is how the Catholic Church understood matters and that understanding is what directly concerns us in this book. Trent thought that Protestant theologians did not see in the sacraments anything "granted" or "conferred," but rather saw the sacramental signs as prompting good thoughts and intentions, just like other acts of piety. Such efficacy was called *ex opere operantis*, an expression hard to translate into our modern languages. The point was that the result of sacramental practice is not substantially different from any other pious practice.

By contrast, Catholic theology held that a valid sacrament had an efficacy deriving from God, that it thus conferred through the minister ordained for the sacraments a grace that other pious practices did not possess (at least not infallibly) and hence these latter were called "sacramentals" rather than "sacraments" properly so-called. That is why the sacraments are said to confer grace *ex opere operato* (D. 850–51).

What does this have to do with our topic? A great deal, for the eternal salvation of the members of the church ordinarily depends on the grace the sacraments confer. If that is the case, the church is divided into those who possess sacramental power and those who receive its results. Clergy and laity do not even constitute different levels of authority or responsibility: they are two substantially different states, and one of them is entirely dependent on the other.

Example: The Sacrament of Orders

All of this, which may seem a bit abstract, will become more clear, I hope, through a reading of one of the canons of the Council of Trent: "If anyone says that there is not in the New Testament a visible and external priesthood, or that there is no power of consecrating and offering the true body and blood of the Lord, and of forgiving and retaining sins, but only the office and bare ministry of preaching the Gospel . . . : let him be anathema" (D. 961). A little further it says: "If anyone says that order or sacred ordination is not truly and properly a sacrament instituted by Christ the Lord, or that it is some human contrivance, devised by men unskilled in ecclesiastical matters, or that it is only a certain rite for selecting ministers of the word of God and of the sacraments: let him be anathema"(D. 963).

Of course what we can observe from the outset is that as the church emerges from the Middle Ages and finds its internal structure being questioned, it believes it is defending that structure by claiming that it comes directly from the Lord Jesus Christ. That is, in more technical terminology, that it is a structure "by divine right." Jesus himself is thus regarded as having wanted a church where everything really and decisively important would be in the hands of an estate "substantially" different from the rest of the faithful, that of the priesthood, or, if one prefers, the clergy. Recalling earlier chapters, readers will already be aware of how a church which in the beginning did not have differences set off by sacred structures, later gradually set up its own institutions and how these institutions became stronger and somewhat sacralized over time, as well as the historical factors that made such a development natural, if not inevitable.

In the modern age, however, this tendency becomes all the more sacralized the more it comes under attack. It is attacked for being unbiblical, and for hindering the church, with its passive laity, from engaging in dialogue with the problems human beings have to solve in the contemporary period even for their very survival. Perhaps February 1906 marks a turning point in history, a point from which things start moving back in the other direction. At that point an encyclical by Pius X presents what is said to be the definition of the laity and their function: "So distinct are these categories that with the pastoral body only rests the necessary right and authority for promoting the end of the society and directing all its members towards that end; the one duty of the multitude is to allow themselves to be led, and like a docile flock, to follow the Pastors."[3]

Nevertheless, I call the reader's attention to some observations arising out of the two canons from Trent quoted above. I believe they will add elements that are significant for beginning to understand better the impact of this passivity of the lay person in the area of dogma.

The *first* observation has to do with the origins of the sacrament of orders, or in other words, the very sacrament which divides the church into two categories of persons who are "essentially" unequal. This division is attributed to "institution by Christ"; the possibility that its origin might derive from a necessary functionality created by the whole church (following the Spirit of Christ) is rejected. According to the canon, the sacrament of holy orders, which separates these two categories, "is not a human contrivance."

What are we to think about this? Here the *second* observation comes into play. The modern age did not yet have all the resources of history now available for searching out the church's past. The reader will be aware of what has already been shown in this regard. It is only *after* many traditions have been introduced and accepted universally that an effort is made to find a biblical basis for what is already in practice everywhere. Such a biblical foundation to support the contention that Jesus Christ personally instituted the sacrament of orders is assumed to be present in the words making up part of the institution of the eucharist: "Do [who?] this as a remembrance of me" (Lk. 22:19; 1 Cor. 11:24).

When it is those exercising authority who search the gospel to find a basis for that authority, a fact that is very important for balanced exegesis is ignored: those who go around with Jesus and to whom Jesus gives many directions (even assuming that those referring to the future are not post-Easter) constitute both a group of Jesus' collaborators as well as his own community. If we wished to offer an anachronism to help understand this point, the exegetical principle at stake here is that Jesus' hearers would constitute both a group of bishops and a group of lay people (or better yet, the entire church undivided).

Now if it is assumed that Jesus said these words, "Do this as a remembrance[4] of me," to his disciples, are we thereby to understand that he addressed them as future hierarchical leaders of his community once he was gone? Or did he address his community, his whole "church" present there in the upper room?

Trent obviously has in mind the first alternative, which amounts to instituting the "priesthood" *which alone is capable* of "offering the true body and blood of the Lord." That has been the official understanding for centuries. As much devotion, sanctity, or concentration as a lay person might put into the words "this is my body," he or she cannot bring about the real presence of Christ in the commemoration of the Lord's supper.

The Priesthood of the Faithful

There are, however, many historical arguments that should incline readers today toward the second alternative. In designating the table companions present in the upper room, the text speaks of the "disciples." Interestingly, it does not use the word "apostle," which is generally more restricted and associated with an authority (apostle = envoy). After Jesus' death and resurrection, whenever there is talk of the disciples gathered in the upper room, we always note the presence of other disciples (besides the Twelve) and, more importantly, the presence of the women who followed and aided him in his ministry, and especially that of the mother of Jesus (see Lk. 24:33; Acts 1:14). Is it conceivable that in what is almost a farewell (since imprisonment, suffering, and even death seem to be imminent) Jesus would have excluded his mother from the particularly meaningful meal that took place on the eve of the passion, according to the evangelists?

Secondly, and passing rapidly over a long history,[5] in the early days of the church, the presence of an "authority" at the celebration of the Lord's supper does not seem to have any connection to the existence or nonexistence of a (magic) "power" to change bread and wine into the body and blood of the Lord. The presidency over the eucharistic meal is tied more closely to the aim of maintaining "order in the assemblies" and making certain that the "remembrance" of Jesus is correct (or apostolic). Hence all indications are that in the Pauline churches the heads of households whom Paul mentions (including women) presided over the eucharistic supper. Naturally, the tendency increasingly to structure the church's internal life leads to giving bishops and then to presbyters (their representatives) the function of exercising such a presiding role. Eventually only they are regarded as able to pronounce Jesus' words effectively enough to make him really present in the community which has gathered to celebrate his memory.

Without thereby being led to think, like the Reformation, that the institution of the "priesthood" was the work of "men unskilled in ecclesiastical matters," as Trent's first canon says (and assuming that it is interpreting the Reformation correctly), it is still conceivable that the Council did not take into account other aspects of the New Testament which are today being retrieved as healthy correctives to a tendency to construct this "unequal" church in which creativity — and as we will see below, dogmatic creativity — is shifted away from the laity and made an exclusively priestly function.

Even though it did not admit holy orders as a sacrament instituted by Christ, the Reformation of course did not fail to recognize the need for a degree of authority in the church. However, it did not attribute to that authority such an essential inequality above the faithful, and so its efforts to downplay lay creativity were thereby limited in principle. Indeed it emphasized what is a New Testament theme (which is likewise partly based on Old Testament prophecies): the universal priesthood of Christians, which is received in baptism itself.[6]

Coming back to the Catholic church, it is not surprising that Pius X's definition is repeated even today in theological circles. Naturally, the almost pejorative tone of the encyclical *Vehementer* is not used, but to the extent that lay people are defined by what they cannot do in the sacramental realm, and *ex opere operato* is understood as the kind of efficacy which belongs exclusively to the minister of the sacraments, lay people are being described in terms of what they lack.

It is true that this situation has changed remarkably with Vatican II. The best Catholic theologians now recognize the theological truth that the lay person holds central functions in the church. The implication is that, as an excellent article by Jon Sobrino summarizes, "there is nothing created that acts as an efficient cause to bring about God's saving approach, nor is anything of that nature needed."[7] This excellent article shows how, on the basis of the biblical tradition as uncovered by the best scholarship, the church's teaching authority has gradually come to understand that, far from defining lay people by what they lack in comparison with priests, the ministerial priesthood must be understood as a particular service to the common priesthood of all the faithful.

We Have Already Received All Grace in Jesus

While suggesting that readers consult this article in order to appreciate the sureness of this line of reasoning, which is supported by the magisterium, I would also like to add a reflection of my own which follows from previous reflections and moves in the same direction.

We have already seen that the work of Jesus Christ makes Old Testament worship obsolete; indeed, that is one of the central observations the New Testament makes about the significance of Christ. Again and again in the Old Testament there were attempts to obtain from God what was lacking in human beings. With Jesus everything that may be required for our liberation and salvation is given once and for all. In the middle of his letter to the Romans, Paul sums up this doctrine with a rhetorical question: "Is it possible that he who did not spare his own Son but handed him over for the sake of us all *will not grant us all things besides?*" (8:32). That was just what Sobrino was quoted as saying, albeit in a more digital and dogmatic language. Readers may test this by reading both statements together (for Paul's rhetorical question clearly amounts to an affirmation). In other words, henceforth Christian worship would no longer be a matter of obtaining day by day what human beings need from God, and which God would not grant unless a rite were performed or a sign placed by a sacred minister.

Moreover, this is the way the whole letter to the Hebrews deals with this question—that is, by showing how Old Testament worship has been abolished with Jesus Christ, who obtained everything we needed from God once and for all. What kind of worship opens up as a possibility or logical necessity for Christians? That of glorifying the humanizing and liberating God, worship that is "eucharistic" by definition (eucharist = thanksgiving) as appears in the Pauline letters (Philip. 4:6; Col. 3:16-17, etc.). However, this worship urged on all Christians, which does not have its own minister but belongs to all the faithful in the church and is focused on God's "glory," cannot mean anything but just what constitutes this glory itself. All theologians remind us (and Sobrino does so with a direct quote in his article) that Irenaeus defines this glory of God using the celebrated expression, "the living human being."

We should not be surprised, then, to find that in the New Testament the term "worship" (= liturgy) is not applied to the eucharist as such but to all services offered to people in need whether the persons providing them are set apart for that or not. This significant secular usage of the sacred word "liturgy" shows to what extent lay people are defined not only in positive terms but as central to the church.

I would add one more word on a topic that could be extended almost without limit. According to Matthew (18:20), when Jesus speaks about his "presence" he refers not to the eucharist but to this "worship" for which there are no ordained priests: "Where two or three are gathered in my name, there am I in their midst." Tons of books have been written on the possible modes of eucharistic presence that might follow upon the words pronounced by the priest, but practically nothing has been said about the very real presence Jesus promised to all Christians who come together for this liturgy around his name, something that happens every time a fragment of his reign is brought into the life of one's brother or sister. There is no theological reason at all for assuming that this presence is less real than the other. As the context indicates and theology confirms, these words of Jesus are not pronounced to priests but to all Christian believers.

It only remains to ask whether just as Christian worship demands the active and creative collaboration of the laity, the same is not true as well about revelation and the way the church grasps it.

Lay People and Dogma

Liturgical Passivity, Dogmatic Passivity

What happens with the laity's liturgical function is very closely paralleled by what happens in the realm of revelation and dogma. There is an extreme tendency to leave everything active and creative in worship and sacraments in the hands of one part of the church. During our own century this tendency has begun to reverse, and through a return to the sources, the creative responsibility of every baptized person is ever more appreciated and insisted upon.

Something similar takes place with regard to the magisterium and the understanding and development of revelation. The fact that I have to deal with these aspects one after the other, simply because the hierarchy speaks of the power of sanctification and the power of the magisterium as two powers possessed alike but distinct from each other, is in itself a pity and infidelity to the divine plan which does not conceive of God's self-revelation in this manner.

In *Theology of Revelation* Gabriel Moran writes:

> At the end of the Middle Ages, an unfortunate dichotomy in the picture of man, together with a superficial and allegorized understanding of sacraments, had clouded the inner relation of word and person. This led the reformers to deemphasize the sacrament ("a word for the unlettered") and concentrate on making intelligible the word of preaching. In this Reformation it was not the emphasis on holy Scripture and preaching that was regrettable, but the failure to carry the revelatory action beyond verbalization to a completion which Scripture itself indicates.[8]

Moran points to the consequences of his observations:

> Catholic writing, as well as Protestant writing, has been affected by these dichotomies even to the present day. Despite the constant assertion in recent writing that there is a close relation between liturgy of word and liturgy of sacrificial banquet, there still lurks the assumption that in the first part of the Mass man is "instructed in the revelation" and in the latter part he offers worship and is sanctified. What must be realized and thoroughly understood is that a liturgy of word is not only a speaking of revelation and a response of faith, but that it is at the same time an act of worship and sanctification. Conversely, the liturgy of the eucharistic banquet and the liturgy of every sacrament is not only worshipful-sanctifying, but also revelatory of God and an affirmation of faith.[9]

Infallibility of a Single Person: Vatican I

Now that the (wrong) reason for this parallelism characterizing lay passivity in the realms of both liturgy and dogma has been established, readers will recall that in chapter 6, just before part 2, this passivity was compared to the creative (and largely collective) activity of the whole people of God in the formation of dogma in the Old Testament.

There I took as the term of comparison with Old Testament dogma the culmination within the Catholic Church of a process that seems to place in the hands of a single person the possibility of infallibly defining what are to be believed as truths of faith. As was demonstrated in that introductory chapter, this culmination comes about during Vatican Council I. Gathered together there with their conciliar authority, the bishops declare that papal infallibility in matters of faith and morals is a dogma of Catholic faith when the supreme pontiff formulates an *ex cathedra* definition in those areas. The Council goes on to add something even more shocking for anyone who recalls the participation of the people of God, Israel, in grasping God's self-revelation: "and so such definitions of the Roman Pontiff from himself, *but not from the consensus of the Church*, are unalterable" (D. 1839).

Since such infallibility (which makes the formulas in which it is expressed irreformable) is a quality which only God, infinite truth, can communicate, it would seem that we have here a "third" source of revelation, since apparently the supreme pontiff could declare truths of faith where the church "believes" otherwise, or at least does not believe it stands before a truth of faith.

Hans Küng is too good a theologian to admit that this was the intention of the fathers at Vatican I when they defined papal infallibility. Thus he knows that when Bishop Gasser, who was responsible for explaining what was to be voted on in that session, spoke, he introduced important qualifications on the way in which the pope could make use of this dogmatic power. Theory by itself is one thing, however, and practice is something else. Küng is somewhat justified when he says about this practice, that for Gasser,

> and for the majority, thinking in Roman and pragmatic terms, such abstract-theoretical questions were not important. The main thing was the realistic-practical decision: that the pope, of himself, at any time, without necessarily bringing in the Church or the episcopate, can claim ecclesiastical infallibility and with finality decide alone any question of theory or practice that is important for the Church.[10]

Almost all historians of the church and particularly of its theology agree on one point which readers of this work will by now take for granted. The second half of the nineteenth century, and particularly the years preceding and following Vatican I (1870), mark the moment of greatest conflict between humanism and Catholic dogma since the Renaissance. The reason is obvious. The venturing and striving of humanism as it seeks to break the confining molds of the Middle Ages, continue until the end of the nineteenth century, pursuing a liberation and maturation of human beings through various routes. The sciences, the structure of society, the mode of production, the recognition of human rights (in theory), progress toward replacing an inherited wisdom with systems that are rational and seemingly scientific, all of this collides with the church's clear decision to uphold the medieval world at any cost. Naturally, the advances of humanism do not always have the humanizing effects expected of them. However, in addition to bearing Christian values—"Christian truths run amok" as Chesterton put it—they are plainly progressive in nature. Even if one should agree with Niebuhr that on the whole the result is a great deal of confusion about the meaning of human life, it would seem that only dangerously nostalgic people could think of turning back. That is just the way the church does think, however, and a measure of personal magnetism in Pius IX along with his predicament as one persecuted, has the effect of endowing this effort with prospects of possibility and even of probability.[11]

In 1864 Pius IX had published the famous *Syllabus* in which the reader will find an outright condemnation by the church of every single humanist effort of the age without the slightest inclination toward dialogue. It may be useful to recall one of the almost one hundred condemnations, the one I regard as the most significant, which from a human standpoint somehow explains all the rest: the pope condemns those who claim that "the Roman Pontiff can and should reconcile and adapt himself to progress, liberalism, and modern civilization" (D. 1780). One may ponder, how many harsh battles will theology have to fight and how many difficult and important victories will it have to win during the one hundred years separating the *Syllabus* from Vatican II, the council which, in the words of Pope Paul VI, "turns the church in the anthropocentric direction of modern culture."

Returning, however, to the climate prevailing at the moment when papal infallibility is proclaimed, it is in this context that we must understand what might seem to be excessive in the last sentence quoted from Hans Küng. He is aware that Vatican I did not grant the supreme pontiff a license enabling him to propose infallible truths about all matters that he might regard as relevant for the church. However, Küng is right in holding that the majority was to interpret the definition in that fashion, despite Bishop Gasser's efforts to limit the exercise of this *cathedra* whose infallibility was being proclaimed.

The Limited Scope of Papal Infallibility

In the debate that ensued over Küng's book, Harry McSorley criticizes Küng for giving the impression that papal infallibility could add innumerable items to a list of dogmas which are already unduly loaded down with human traditions and which have become divinized, as it were, along the way. However, McSorley is forced to admit, "True, it is only by studying the Vatican I *acta*, especially Bishop Gasser's exposition [on the scope of what was to be voted upon], that one can discern Vatican I's intention to limit infallibility to revelation or to matters necessary for explaining and preserving that revelation."[12]

In examining how far Vatican I conceives this limitation as necessary, McSorley employs two arguments. First, Bishop Gasser showed that "it was the intention of Vatican I that these 'matters' [vaguely defined as matters of faith and *mores*] be either revelation itself or truths intimately related to divine revelation." He demonstrated this with an example when he explained why the Council (Vatican I) rejected proposition number 45, which extended the scope of infallibility to encompass all moral principles. He said that it only went as far as those moral truths "which *pertain in every respect to the deposit of faith.*"[13]

It seems clear that from a theological standpoint we must take this restrictive qualification seriously. If we do so and then ask what it is seeking to avoid, the answer is clearly the declaration that something is a truth of faith, when, as true as it might be, it does not belong to the very substance of the Christian message. The upshot is that it is extremely important to highlight a serious and limited *core* of principles or of truths which "pertain in every respect to the deposit of faith" — that is, to something substantially identical with what the previously mentioned principle of ecumenism called "the foundation of the Christian faith" (Decree on Ecumenism, 11) — which is of course nothing but God's revelation — in matters of both morality and faith. In moral matters just as in those of faith, it must be recognized that there is an area of truths which are certainly connected to this foundation, but in a fashion that is lower *hierarchically* (to use the terminology of Vatican II).

The second argument McSorley brings up against the danger Küng perceives of a potentially ubiquitous infallibility is aimed more at dogmas touching on faith (and not particularly at moral principles, although I do not find this distinction very convincing). Vatican I's intention of *limiting* the scope of infallibility to revelation or to matters necessary for explaining and preserving this revelation, is evident in the way in which Vatican II (LG 25) draws upon and repeats (with minor variations) Vatican I's definition of papal infallibility. Now the statement runs: "This infallibility with which the divine Redeemer willed his Church to be endowed . . . extends *as far as* the deposit of divine revelation." Such a limitation which is expressed in "as far as" is important because it was stressed by the very *relatio* made before the vote in order to specify and clarify its meaning and scope: "The object of the infallibility of the church, thus expounded, has the same extension as the revealed deposit;[14] it therefore extends to all those things and only to those things (*et ad ea tantum*) which *either directly touch upon the revealed deposit or which are required for religiously guarding and faithfully explaining the revealed deposit.*"[15]

As is apparent, McSorley's argument is utterly clear and solid. Vatican II, in repeating the dogma of papal infallibility defined at Vatican I, does so by being even more careful to show that its scope only encompasses that of revelation and of that which, if not acknowledged, would prevent revelation from being understood correctly. If to that we add the "order or hierarchy of truths" of Catholic doctrine demanded by the decree on ecumenism, it all constitutes a reminder of how much the defensive context has changed, so much so, indeed, that understanding revelation — that is, elaboration of dogma — can no longer be concentrated in the authority of a single person "apart from the life of the rest of the church."

Central Issue: Ecumenism or the Laity?

Convergence toward a Central Issue

Nevertheless, the observations made about Rahner and Küng (although these two theologians differ on a number of points) lead one to think that it is the necessity of ecumenism that is driving toward this shift in direction rather than the church's own need to be wholly committed to experiencing the foundation of its faith in a living and critical way. One has less of a sense of the need to put the whole church, and especially lay Christians, "in a theological state," if one may put it that way. This is the point I will be dealing with in this final section.

In this section many important strands, perhaps the most important in this book, come together. For thus far they have been left stretching out toward other strands. When they are at last joined together it will be possible to pose the issue of revelation and dogma at this crucial moment in the modern age.

To begin with, as readers will recall, there is the strand followed since the beginning of this chapter. What is the source of this lack of creativity on the part of lay people in seizing divine revelation and moving forward with it? Can dogma move forward without a corresponding experience and reflection on the part of the laity?

Another important strand comes from further back. As some begin to note how dogma has become more and more unwieldy to the point of obstructing dialogue with our separated brothers and sisters, important theologians like Rahner and, as we have seen in this chapter, Küng, as well as those who take issue with him on papal infallibility, all seem to concur that theology must move toward greater sobriety in dogma. A church where everything turns into irreformable formulas is rather paralyzed vis-à-vis any dialogue.[16]

Connected to this strand is yet another which arises from the posing of an important question: By what principle was the "hierarchy of truths" of the Christian message put in the decree on ecumenism, and not in the constitution on divine revelation, as might have been more logical?

Experiencing Revelation in History

All these strands converge on a theological problem which thus far I have not wanted to state clearly, but which now I would like to lay out clearly so as to better orient readers. The point is nothing short of this question: In order for revelation to be just what it is, God's self-revelation, do Christians have to *experiment with it*—that is, put it to the test vis-à-vis the basic issues facing humankind?

Readers are already aware that when we consider the Old Testament the answer can only be a radical and resounding yes. In the words of Torres Queiruga:

> Precisely because revelation, which at each point in the "history of tradition" articulates the ultimate meaning of what is real, is expressed in a maieutic word, it continually inclines toward its own verification of this reality as interpreted. Moses, who illuminated the passage through the Sea of Reeds from the standpoint of God's saving action, or Hosea, who illuminated the believer's subjective awareness as always backed up by Yahweh's unconditional forgiveness, did not propose a blind faith: they urged their hearers to contrast it with their own experience; those who

accepted it, did so because they *recognized* that those words articulated the meaning of their lives.[17]

The crises in this "experience" were the very questions which were imposed by the situation and which served to thrust the pedagogical process forward—toward an expression of the truth which would grow along with the "empirical" (or experiential, if you will) maturity of the believer. Otherwise, how could "incomplete and temporary" things emerge under God's infallible guidance? The reader will recall that according to *Dei Verbum*, this did not occur *despite* the "*true* divine pedagogy"—as though it were stumbling up against human dullness—but rather those "incomplete and temporary" things themselves, which were present within this educational process, were a reliable sample, a "demonstration" of that pedagogy (DV 15).

In other words, the Old Testament formulas are not infallible by virtue of being irreformable, but rather the contrary. They are part of revelation which is based on God's infallibility, precisely to the extent that God gives humans the task, context, and guidance to "reform" as often as necessary, what is incomplete and temporary in previous formulations. To put it another way, and in an expression that may be shocking, the formulas are to be reformed (*reformanda*), because they are part of an *infallible* revelation of God to humankind. Of course I am aware that theology has gotten used to using "irreformability" as a synonym of "infallibility." Although I can understand this terminology, I do not favor its use, because that might lead to a dogmatic rigidity which the church's teaching authority itself seeks to avoid.

If that is how the divine pedagogy worked in the Old Testament, there is no reason to think that the presence of the Spirit of Jesus in the church in order to lead us to all truth takes another route. Truth is one, and humankind moving toward it is also one.

Why Dogmatic Formulas Are Reformed

The reformability of dogmatic formulas regarded as infallible has developed as a result of Vatican II even within the church's teaching authority. Nevertheless the fluctuating fortunes of the Council do not yet enable us to point to a unanimous understanding of its "wealth of doctrine," as Paul VI put it. In a June 1973 statement called *Mysterium Ecclesiae* the Sacred Congregation for the Doctrine of the Faith (under the signature of Cardinal Franjo Seper, then its head) mentioned five reasons why theological work had to provide dogmatic expressions from the past with a new form.[18]

The first reason is the expressive power of the language employed, which is not the same in one context as it is in another, or in one age as it is in the next. For example, who cannot see (no matter how little versed he or she may be in shifts in historic contexts) that in the formula "outside the church there is no salvation," the signifying power of the term "outside" is not the same in the time of Cyprian (or whoever it was among his contemporaries who coined the expression), as it is almost a thousand years later in the context of the Council of Florence (D. 714), or yet another five hundred years later at Vatican II?

The second reason is perhaps the one that goes most deeply into the issue. It indicates that no formulation expresses the truth with unlimited fullness and perfection. Thus it has to be complemented every time new experiences of faith or new human knowledge demand the solution of questions or the elimination of errors which the older formula could not foresee. Is there not a new experience of faith, as many contemporary theologians point out, in what biblical theology has discovered in Paul's writings about the salvation of humankind and the ultimate victory of grace over the abundance of sin in the universe? Is it not a "new" error that leads Christians to set themselves apart from other human beings by reason of their faith, to the point where their faith and life are separate from one another?

In accordance with the third reason, in simply reaching expression every dogmatic formula takes on types of thought which, although they are not confused with the truth they are intended to bear, have in fact been used for that purpose, even though subsequently they may have fallen into disuse or have been surpassed by other kinds of thinking that are richer, deeper, or more accurate. When the formula is repeated without being changed, it often happens that the accompanying thought, now surpassed, prevents understanding of what was originally meant by it. Thus for example, during the Middle Ages, in seeking to express moral judgments to the barbarian peoples, rewards and punishments constitute a way of communicating the fundamental idea of the importance and decisive nature of freedom. When, however, punishment no longer seems to be the best category for expressing the absolute seriousness of one's decisions, concepts such as purgatory and hell ought to be changed. In addition, there must be found in the life of each human being an act which situates his or her whole existence within a yes or a no to God. Where is the theologian to find such an act?

The fourth reason, very concisely expressed, is that which indicates most profoundly how any communication of a truth is conditioned by the way human beings understand. The point is that formulas have to be reformed so that the truth they bear truly be *alive* and remain so. Indeed, a correct interpretation can nonetheless present a truth as though it were dead—that is, as not rooted in life and its problems. To send correct information to a person who either has no problem, or does not see in that information something that is experientially a solution for a problem, amounts to giving up the effort to reveal a truth of the human condition. God, however, does not give up in that manner. In a secular world, any truth coming from the church will look dead, if it does not contribute to making more human the solution to problems history presents, along the lines urged by Vatican II (GS 11).

The fifth and last reason is that as much as a truth may have been understood through a formula, as time goes on, presenting both opportunities and crises, human growth and maturing demand greater *clarity and fullness*. I think this last word points quite unmistakably to the need for dogma to go by way of human experience. What other kind of fullness, for example, can one feel in belonging to the church, if it is not measured by the possibility of cooperating in this plan and glory of God, which is the humanizing of the human being: *gloria Dei vivens homo?*

From Information to Process of Education

As we can see, within these five reasons, or if you will, floating over them, we find the idea of a process of "education." The word does not appear, even though Vatican II had used it ("pedagogy") for things which had been inspired by God in the Old Testament and were to be reformed. However, all the lines stretched out here seem to converge toward this process that is maieutic by means of the experience of history, or of learning to learn by making use of that experience. What remains to be done is to make it explicit and connect these five reasons more logically to this notion of revelation, and likewise to establish within them the basic principle already in place for ecumenism, the "order or hierarchy of truths" in the Christian message.

Here, if I am not mistaken, we must take another step forward on the basis of what Rahner and most European theologians have proposed in this area. I think they have seen the need for a dogmatic sobriety that had been largely lost during the centuries when human and apostolic traditions became almost inextricably entangled. These theologians have seen that it is impossible to engage in dialogue with those who think otherwise, separated brothers and sisters or humanists of good will, without throwing some ballast overboard and thereby gaining some maneuverability and a disposition to dialogue. Something further is required, however, something extremely liberating for a Christian message: restoring dogma's *experiential* character.

That is why I propose one more question, and direct it to the text of the Roman congregation which I have summarized: Who is supposed to carry out this work of "reforming" (in the positive sense of that term) dogmatic expressions? The text does not raise this question, and that fact itself is suggestive. At one point it notes that if they carry out such a task, "theologians" will have provided a valuable service to the church. One could say that, although the passage is open to another interpretation, the prevailing note is that of caution, since there is more concern to control such things than to make them happen. Indeed, the image is that these things are "proposed or approved by the sacred magisterium."

For my part, I think this is a task of the whole church, just as infallibility is a gift God has made to all of it and not to one or other estate or authority. In order for this to take place, the experience of dogma must be returned to those who must experience it in their various contexts, sets of issues, and languages in history. I think the church is still not fully convinced that this is not quite the same as encouraging lay people to *study* theology: it is something deeper, and more difficult. As stated in *Gaudium et Spes*, the church as community of faith must reflect on what it believes so that:

> The faithful can be brought to live the faith in a more thorough and mature way ... Furthermore, it is to be hoped that many laymen will receive an appropriate formation in the sacred sciences, and that some will develop and deepen these studies by their own labors. In order that such persons may fulfill their proper function, let it be recognized that *all the faithful*, clerical and lay, possess a lawful freedom of inquiry and

thought, and the freedom to express their minds humbly and courageously about those matters in which they enjoy competence. [GS 62]

Here also the idea of a pedagogy is hovering over the practical demands being raised. Nevertheless, in the realm of ideas, revelation still seems to be conceived primarily as information.

In order that these observations, perhaps too speculative, take on life in readers' minds, I beg leave to present them with a case that is more concrete, although it is vast, like the continent from which this work has arisen and where for some time there has been an effort to return to lay people, and likewise to all human beings, the capability to reflect on what they believe and to experience it profoundly.

In 1992 there will be a celebration (to a greater or lesser extent depending upon how history is interpreted) of the five hundred year anniversary of a famous and decisive encounter: that which took place between Europe and the Americas as a result of the first journey of Columbus.

I call it an "encounter," fully aware that this event is usually called the "discovery of America." While it is true that the encounter of two different human worlds can be called a "discovery," my usage refers to the fact that only one of these worlds, Europe, took the initiative of moving toward the other. That movement itself, however, was not intended, since the aim was actually to find a different route to the Indies.

Nevertheless, by calling it an "encounter" and not a "discovery," I am referring to the undeniable, though almost always ignored, fact that this event brought two human worlds, or if you will, two different civilizations, face to face. Each thus discovered the other. It is true that the indigenous people Columbus found on his first journey to what was later to be called "America" did not bring him into contact with the most advanced part of the civilization present on this last continent. However, as "barbarian" as the inhabitants of the New World looked to the Europeans who ran into them on October 12, 1492, they were human beings who possessed a different culture.

Discovery, however, did not lead to dialogue. We cannot simply attribute this lack of an effort to delve deeply into the culture or cultures of this New World to a failing of Columbus, because what made his discovery possible was not a European desire to enter into contact with new cultures and be spiritually enriched by them, but interest in finding a new route to the Indies and their spices.

Since these new lands, which were not the Indies, were there, it was Europe's duty, political and religious, to conquer them. That conquest was rapid and violent. First Spain, and then all the major European nations brought to the Americas the whole Christian world emerging from the Middle Ages. The new continent was or had to be a branch of this Europe which was entering into the modern age, or as a recent world history already cited puts it, "the new European space."[19] Exactly five centuries after Columbus, English-speaking America is the greatest power in the (European) world, and "Latin" America is the only and last "Christian" continent.

What are we to think of this strange success? It is not the aim of this book to offer such overall value judgments. In a previous chapter we have pointed out that the encounter between the barbarian peoples and the Christianity of the declining Roman Empire to some degree had a (reverse) parallel in that which was to take place between the Christianity of Spain and Portugal and the "barbarian" peoples across the Atlantic. Both the beginning and the end of the Middle Ages thus presented Christian dogma with the problem of how to engage in a dialogue between a point of dogmatic and institutional development attained at a particular moment, and cultures which, whatever their worth, were in fact on a much lower level of development. The histories of civilization, which I have already cited, label the indigenous people the Europeans encounter as a result of the voyage of Columbus as people of the *neolithic* period. The same thing could probably also be said of the barbarian peoples who invaded Europe, back in their own territories—and also, since I have already made this comparison—of the different Israelite tribes at the beginning of the monarchy and the composition of the Bible.

Nor am I thereby making a value judgment comparing Spanish-Portuguese culture and that of the Aztecs or Incas in themselves. I am accepting the conquest as a fact. After the lightning blow of seizure through violence, what remains of what will thenceforth be called "pre-Columbian" cultures, if it is not primitive in itself, has become primitive by force. These are cultures subjected to a civilization that rides roughshod over everything, and sees in the Amerindian only potential labor for the mode of production which has been transferred from Europe whole and entire, and which functions first to serve Europe, and much later those Europeans who have emigrated to the new continent. Later on this labor force will be augmented, not replaced, by Africans uprooted from their culture and forced to work as slaves in the Americas.

The fact that what is pre-Columbian becomes in practice "prehistory" and only survives insofar as it accepts the economic, social, political, and religious structures of the conquering European countries, makes this situation notably different from what happens at the outset of the Middle Ages with christianization of the barbarian peoples. On that occasion, it is the barbarians who are the conquerors. The church is forced to make a minimum effort to adapt to their way of being and thinking. That is just what it does, although some of the features of that adaptation indicate that it is erring out of what I called, with a borrowed expression, "hasty pedagogy."

Here on the other hand, there is no such urgency—nor of course any such pedagogy. The division of labor in the New World makes it possible to avoid it, at least when it comes to religion. Some might say I am being unjust and that there are indications that the Catholic Church made efforts at adaptation and dialogue similar to those of the high Middle Ages, especially efforts to simplify and translate matters of dogma to simple and persuasive experiential criteria. In this respect the Amerindian missions and "reductions" of both Franciscans and Jesuits, for example, attempted to begin from the beginning. I would also say that they very sensitively connected the gospel message to a "good news" translated culturally and socially into Amerindian life (in their mission towns).

Merely as a symbol and no doubt an exception, I recall reading of an example of this some years ago in connection with the Franciscan missions in northern Mexico and the southern part of what is now the United States. When Amerindians outside the missions inquired what Christianity meant, the missionary is said to have answered by showing them a town of Christian Amerindians. That answer was marvelously to the point: that was indeed what being a Christian was all about.[20] One might say that this was an appeal to human greed and wonder how these "Christian" Amerindians were led to build and run their town along guidelines different from those of their own culture. However, even admitting that very human motivations were at work there—just as they were in God's choosing of Israel—these are still at most *peccata minuta* in comparison with the situation in which the Amerindians were assimilated in those towns and cities ruled by authorities from Europe.[21]

What calls this effort into question, and dooms it to eventual failure, is the fact that it must be carried out in a separate enclosure—that is, by shutting out the conquest and the (socially, politically, and economically) real world. That fact certainly sealed the fate of the reductions in Paraguay. The fact that the king of Spain had been able to isolate the Amerindians from the greed of the Spaniards in the Americas was later to become the major and real reason for the destruction of the reductions, which was the result of a political decision made between the courts of Spain and Portugal.

For the remaining *pre-Columbian* population (and subsequently for the mestizos) Christianity as it was lived in Europe, with its dogmas and morality (more theoretical than practical), its hierarchical structures and popular devotions, the same Christianity with which Europe was entering the modern age, was imposed as a norm. Those who might have a chance to thrive in the new world (Europeans and a small portion of the mestizos) must have been at home with the kind of Christianity built up over a thousand years by a culture that was quite foreign to the culture of the Americas and that suited other circumstances and requirements. The poorest sectors of the population, excluded from that culture and hence from elementary human rights (Amerindians and a portion of the mestizo and mulatto population) had to practice this Christianity, or a lesser version of it, at least in public. In general, however, with a degree of caution that became habitual, people found a way to continue to worship their own gods under Christian forms—right up to the present.[22]

An even clearer symbolization of this religious annexation by violence than that of the reduction is the tragic figure of St. Peter Claver, who evangelized slaves by taking advantage of a tiny fissure that the dominant Christian European society left to slaves arriving from Africa. The future slaves were not put into the power of their owners until they had been given a summary introduction to Christianity and had received the obligatory baptism that went along with it. The baptism that followed upon this "good news" of Christian freedom, meant—apart from all the compassionate love of a Claver—the beginning of real slavery. Was this evangelization or antievangelization?

In order to move along with readers to the issue they are no doubt expecting after such a long introduction, the question is as follows: What did divine revelation thereby lose? Even if it is agreed that there is a universal divine revelation beyond the boundaries of Christianity, we have already seen that this revelation evolves through experience. It is never information provided independently of context and challenges. However, where there is not enough freedom to process these necessary experiences, they remain on the level of the desperate need for cultural survival. Hasty pedagogy equals backward results.

An example may serve to shed some light here. I will take it from a recent effort at evangelization in Mexico, along the lines of Latin American liberation theology. This effort made use of the *Nican Mopohua* — that is, the ancient story of the appearances of the Virgin of Guadalupe to the Indian, Juan Diego. Base communities were encouraged to reflect on that story in the light of their own experience.

This effort was not based on naiveté. Behind it was an awareness that the appearances of the Virgin Mary to Juan Diego, which took place no more than forty years after the solemn date whose five hundredth anniversary will soon be celebrated, were not really between the Virgin Mary and a "Christian" Amerindian. I have in mind the fact that practically all pre-Columbian religious cultures that were even moderately advanced offered worship to the Pachamama (= Mother Earth). Within a supposedly orthodox Christianity imposed by force, the Virgin Mary represented the power of Pachamama. If we keep in mind that the narration read today for reflection in base communities is written very soon after the events it recounts, we may come to the same conclusion as Clodomiro L. Siller A. in his article, "The Method of Evangelization in the *Nican Mopohua*":

> The transmission and embodiment of the message of Guadalupe amounts to *assuming the former culture*: what already existed in the Nahuatl world is completed. Hence we find that the Virgin of Guadalupe presents herself to Juan Diego as the mother of the main gods in the Indian religion. "Know and understand, you the least of my children, that I am the ever Virgin Holy Mary, mother of the true God (*inhuelnelli Téotl*) through whom one lives (*inipalnemohuani*), mother of the Creator (*inteyocoyani*), alongside whom all exists (*in Tloque Nahuaque*), lord of heaven and earth (*in Ilhuicahua in Tlalticpaque*)."[23]

If we assume the angle of a pedagogy that follows the humanizing rhythm of the people's experience, such syncretism no longer has a pejorative meaning. It is like biblical monotheism which is built up slowly through crises and attempts to provide responses for dealing with the existing situation. Nevertheless, we cannot fail to recognize a danger, which is likewise pedagogical in nature. The quote above indicates the name given to the Virgin who appears to Juan Diego at Tepeyac. It is symptomatic that she presents herself as the mother of the gods of the pre-Columbian religion and yet indicates that she wants to be invoked under the title of a Spanish place and shrine. She is not to be called Virgin of Tepeyac, but Virgin of Guadalupe. Likewise the Amerindian Juan Diego is sent to the bishop who is to have a shrine built. That means that there is already a church hierarchy set up not for the Amerindians and in accordance with their needs, but following the pattern of European, and particularly Spanish, Christendom. That hierarchy will exercise its authority to organize worship at the shrine. Will it allow people to reflect critically on the relationship between the Virgin Mary and the existential experience of the Amerindians?

Today the influence of liberation theology is bringing to some base communities in Mexico this ancient story of the *Nican Mopohua* as something liberating, thus linking the ancient story with the process of God's revelation. How is the story being presented? Another of the articles in the little work here being considered brings together testimonies arising, if not from whole base communities, certainly from individuals of the popular sector who are to some extent leaders in these communities.

I do not know if I am being over-suspicious in doubting whether the interpretation of the old story in liberation terms is really spontaneous or comes from the suggestions of Christians who belong to other levels of culture (at another stage in God's revealing process) or belong to another social class. My suspicions, which may well be groundless, come from the fact that the story is interpreted as the "option for the poor" (Amerindians) that the Virgin is regarded to have made. Indeed, she appears not to the Spanish bishop but to the poor Indian, Juan Diego, and when she promises to protect the Amerindians, she orders him to take her message to the bishop who is to take on the building of the future shrine. It is not the poor who opt for the poor, however. The expression itself says so very clearly. The idea of the option for the poor arises in a middle-class church which is converted to the needs of the popular classes who are suffering oppression and extreme poverty.

Be that as it may, I think it is better to listen to some brief passages of these testimonies. One of the reflections says that the Virgin's message to Juan Diego demanded of the bishop "that he build a church, so that her children [poor Amerindians] could go there to be with her and [thus] relieve their suffering and pain." The statement goes on, "The most interesting thing is that the Virgin appears to a lowly person and asks him to tell the bishop [what he is to do], when it would have been much easier to appear to the bishop so that he might believe: but she chose a poor man, a lowly person, one on the bottom."[24]

This is certainly a beginning. Indeed this account suggests another similar evangelization: that of the God who chooses a poor and humble people to take them out of the oppression of Egypt and lead them to the promised land—or, if you will, the good news of Jesus that God, who is in effect king (= governing) in Israel, regards as the first priority of his reign that the poor cease being so, that they be filled and that they be able to smile as human beings. Nevertheless, these similarities to the exodus and the gospel proclamation (which the evangelization in these Mexican base communities seeks to utilize) do not stand up to a deeper comparison—even though they may be anticipations of such an evangelization.

Some points particularly deserve to be mentioned and considered. I admit that in thinking about them I feel as though I am very much lacking in all those things that could enable me to be familiar with the potentiality of the Mexican people, which is not my own. However, I do not think this should prevent me from offering, with the humility of one admittedly lacking in knowledge, elements for reflecting together on a problem in which all of us are involved, some of us more, others less.

The first thing that should be noted is the fact that the one opting for the Amerindian poor is not God, but the Virgin of Tepeyac. As we will see, in the modern and conscious reflection of community members who have received special preparation, one can observe efforts to identify the Virgin's option with that of God. Thus, for example, in one of these testimonies we read (and I highlight the strange order in which the two subjects appear in the testimony): "The Virgin *and God* have shown signs that it is we the poor who should struggle; that with his help we can change, as many have already managed to do [Nicaragua], and make progress."

Also pointing perhaps toward such a conclusion is the previously indicated fact that this Virgin of Tepeyac-Guadalupe, who possesses so many features that derive from the conception of the Pachamama, is the "mother of the creator." To what extent, however, is this Virgin *of Guadalupe* not overtaken by feminine images from Spanish religiosity, in which the "mother" consoles and "assuages the suffering and pain" to which the "father" (God as providence or fate) is more or less insensitive? Today in any case I think we cannot skip over the fact that the one making the option for the Amerindian poor is a typically feminine and maternal figure. Here we might have evidence (which centuries of oppression and religion have projected into the mind of the Amerindian) that *God* has not opted to change the structures of the unjust society in which they are suffering.

This point perhaps leads to a second item to think about—namely, that the Virgin by herself does not call for any deed in history.[25] In the name of the Virgin, Juan Diego is to ask the Spanish (religious) authority to build a *shrine*— of the Virgin for the Amerindians. Within these walls she will offer relief and consolation. It is true that here perhaps the secularized Western mind may mislead us by letting us forget that for many religious peoples a shrine is something like the navel of the world, the place where heaven and earth, the profane and the sacred, meet. The fact that this shrine is for the "Amerindian poor" may have a liberating force that I am here underestimating. In that case, however, we would have to admit that the reflection of the base communities has lost its roots, since the representatives of these communities also suspect that there is something shaky about the notion of the shrine as an expression of the option for the poor: "So *now* I don't know. Probably if she (the Virgin) appeared to someone, I think the first thing she would say is that *today there are already many churches.* I think the first thing she would ask is how we have used these churches."

Third, in a celebrated passage that provides a focus to the Medellín documents, we read:

As in former times, Israel the first people *experienced* [emphasis mine] God's saving presence when he was liberating them from oppression in

Egypt . . . and he led them to the land of promise, so also we, new people of God, *cannot but feel* his saving movement when there occurs true development, which is the movement from less human conditions to more human conditions for each one and for all.

What happens, however, with God's self-revelation to peoples who disappear without ever having had an exodus, as somehow one feels in some commentaries on the *Nican Mopohua*? Five centuries after the Virgin is said to have opted for the poor according to the story and its interpretation, they go on their way and this supposed option has not substantially changed their inhuman condition — unless it be in the more or less individual miracles that tradition attributes to the Virgin of Guadalupe and which are attested to in the votive offerings placed in her church. In the Old Testament, from the moment when Yahweh seems to have been defeated by the gods of Babylonia, there emerges as a living response the pure monotheistic conception of God. Here, unless we are to believe that some peoples are deaf or not very apt for journeying along this process of revelation, one would have to think that these people have had their ability to *experience* revelation taken away from them. Hence the ancient pre-Columbian religion remains in place as a defensive way of maintaining their identity, and not as a "tradition" developing and maturing.

Readers will be aware that this is merely an example — a heart-rending one to be sure, and one closely connected to liberation theology. How can this theology liberate human beings if it does not liberate theology and dogma from their conception of exact information given once and for all, from something that closes the path to thinking and searching rather than opening the way? If theology does not liberate itself, how is humankind to liberate itself by means of theology?

Certainly a first and decisive step has been taken when the community has been given confidence to reflect on its faith. I only fear that when people live in extremes of subjection and are just surviving on the edge, such reflection may not be capable of entering, even slowly, into this process of reflection or of maieutic that is needed in order that dogma may become the launching pad for the revealed glory of God, which is the humanization of human beings.

CHAPTER 12

Summary and Hopes

No reader will be surprised, I hope, to find the word "summary" in the title of the last chapter, but some may be startled to see the word "hopes" alongside it. That is understandable, since from the beginning of part 2 of this book, I have been showing how during Christianity's two-thousand-year journey thus far, an ever-increasing number of obstacles has been hindering dogma from being what it should be: the quasigenetic platform, one might say, from which the learning of new dimensions of meaning in human life ought to be launched in each generation.

Nevertheless, I also think readers will have noted that in our own century there have also emerged more visibly, clearly, and emphatically certain threads that are converging toward *another* synthesis of thought that promises to be richer than that represented by the mound of obstacles already described. In the previous chapter, I said that we Christians are in a situation like the one we faced on the eve of Vatican II. Then, we were somewhat overwhelmed by the weight of everything that had mounted up against a change we believed necessary, and we already held in our hands — admittedly a minority of us — the results of theological efforts on a number of crucial points. In other words, we were ready for a qualitative leap.

Looking back today, I believe that at that time we were sustained by the fuzzy hope that it would be enough that there occur what in fact happened: that the inspiration of the Spirit blow upon a pontiff like John XXIII and the things that were assumed to have the power of a number of centuries behind them would give way to other things that would be richer, more human, and more Christian.

If theology is good for anything it is perhaps to grasp such signs which may be minuscule in terms of quantity but which all point toward progress and change.

Some will no doubt say that there is no reason to expect much of the twenty-first century of the Christian era, since the heavy baggage (of routine and defensiveness) coming from the previous fifteen centuries seems irreversible. I do not agree, however. In a book meant to sound the alarm, *Feu la Chrétienté* [Christianity deceased], Emmanuel Mounier relativized the apparent power of these long lapses of time: "If we take a long-range view of Christian history, it may happen that a few dozen centuries from now, our christendom will look like a shapeless proto-history of the Christian era."

These words from a man who did not live to see Vatican II and could not imagine how soon it would come about, do not announce a utopia. We now know that. But I think his words are anchored in three solid bases in the overall situation we have been examining up to this point. I do not know if it is too much to ask readers to keep them in mind and perhaps assimilate them as an aid to reading this chapter.

The *first* such basis is a matter of rereading the centuries-long process from the high Middle Ages to our own day from the proper angle. During the patristic age, the Christian message seemed destined to go hand in hand with the deep reflection that Greek (or, if you will, Greco-Roman) culture had developed and would undoubtedly continue to develop. As it happened, however, the fall of the Roman Empire in the West introduced something rather unforeseeable into this picture, the prehistory of young peoples brought into the very heart of this devastated empire.

Since the guiding thread of Christianity is already present at this point, we cannot talk about prehistory with respect to the Christian message. It is true, however, that the long centuries in which the medieval world was created amount to a synthesis between this prehistory introduced by the barbarian peoples and the message of Christ which had been halted at the patristic age. In other words, we have a kind of slow, extended "protohistory" of Christianity.

I do not think I am going overboard in thinking that Christianity had to wait until the problematic explosion of the modern age made it possible for a minority from the medieval world to once more set the message of Christ before a mammoth venture in history, that of humanism, with all its achievements, crises, and fluctuations. The "history" of Christianity begins anew at that point—which is also when dogma as experience and search for meaning begins anew.

Here the *second* basis I mentioned comes into play. In order to fully enter into this adventure, God's revelation has to again take on its proper experiential basis. Only that basis, together with the spirit of Christ, can provide the impetus toward "the full truth." As it enters the modern era, however, the church is encumbered with too many things that did not exist in the beginning, but which it now believes it cannot do without. As long as it could exercise its religious power over the European world, it did not strive for a dialogue that would have led it back to the richness of history. It remained stuck on the defensive and making claims to perennial validity which prevented it from having enriching experiences.

Mounier here adds to the sentence quoted above something that I believe expresses this second basis I am talking about, "Kingdoms are being taken away from us one by one: and the reign of Christ begins with this marvelous increasing poverty." In these words, the church no longer feels that it must at any cost take a stand to defend its power or privileges. For better or worse, it no longer possesses them.

This poverty—optimistic, good-willed, and open to dialogue—is what emerges from those Vatican II documents that are most well-thought out and most outstanding, particularly *Gaudium et Spes*. Humanism is no longer the enemy against which God's banners must be raised. The day on which the Constitution on the Church in the Modern World was promulgated and the Council closed, Pope Paul VI made the following statements among others. After upholding the Council's "wealth of doctrine" placed at the service of human beings and their humanization (against those who might claim to see in Vatican II mere pastoral guidelines) he went on, "Has all this and whatever else we might say about the human value of the Council perhaps meant that the mind of the church in the Council has deviated in the *anthropocentric direction of modern culture?*" And when even the most optimistic expected this rhetorical question to be answered with a flat no, the response to this kind of poverty turning into service was, "deviated no, *turned yes*" (speech closing Vatican II, December 7, 1965, par. 13–14; emphasis mine).

This turn, this shift in direction, freely acknowledged, must necessarily recover all that was lost in the way of dialogue and the experience of new human possibilities in the process of defending the medieval world. The climate and context change, and the anthropocentrism of modern culture is no longer shocking, since no one is more anthropocentric than God and divine revelation. Dissent is understood (GS 19), studied, and appreciated (GS 21); searching takes place side by side with all human beings of good will, for they have aspects of truth that Christians need (GS 16); and that extends unabashedly and without resentment even to those who thought that humanization had to lead them to confront the church: "The Church herself knows how richly she has profited by the history and development of humanity ... Indeed, the Church admits that she has greatly profited and still profits from the antagonism of those who oppose or persecute her" (GS 44).

Perhaps it will be said that the church has not acted in this way during the years following the Council. Yet how can we not hope when in just five years the silent and suffering endeavor of theologians and faithful was able to assist this solemn and official shift toward these tendencies which seemed to be those of minorities?

There is yet a *third* basis for Mounier's intuitions of the future, although he does not indicate it in the lines quoted. What I have in mind is that through a kind of preestablished harmony, the threads I have been developing here now encounter human beings in a situation in which they can no longer continue to entrust their fate to the evolution of nature, but rather, to use an image dear to Teilhard, they must begin to take the helm of planet earth.

In this respect, it is indeed overwhelming to relate a particular message to a context. The message I have in mind is that of Paul at the beginning of Christianity. For him the gospel of Christ signified the moment of coming of age when the child and heir completely and entirely took possession of his or her parental inheritance. First to the Galatians, then to the Corinthians, and finally to the Romans, Paul shows that Jesus has made us children of the Father—that is, of the God who created the universe. He adds that if we are heirs we have to be ready to take into our hands our inheritance, which is the whole universe, and to carry forward a creation whose only direction is the building up of love. To that end, Paul notes that the suffering eating away at the created universe is not a fault in creation: it is the price God wants to pay so that our creative freedom be decisive. Our endeavors are necessary in order that the universe not function fruitlessly and in suffering. Paul points out that our resistance to taking on this responsibility is due primarily to fear. Hence, so that we may truly be sons and daughters, in the full faith that frees us from fear, he sets before us the assurance of God's plan leading all of humankind to salvation along with us, and he shows how we are inserted, with our freedom and vocation to creativity, into this plan for a new heaven and a new earth, where solidarity and justice reside.[1]

That is the moment when the message is delivered, Paul's message about Christ, two thousand years ago. However, even though humankind has been on this planet a million years or millions of years, our generation constitutes *the first* human context, the very first, to *feel* on its shoulders the weight of responsibility for the universe in which we live. We have learned that things that used to look inevitable, such as epidemics, the shortness of the average human life, widespread infant mortality, the common use of violence to bring about justice (or worse, so that the strong could vanquish the weak), were in fact *tasks* within reach of human endeavors (in the future). We have also realized that the fierce and enthusiastic concerted labor of human beings has been gradually becoming decisive in these and a thousand other matters. If the energy of the planet is not wasted on luxury for the rich and weapons for the powerful, soon cancer, or earthquakes, or the terrible gap between rich and poor countries will also fall within the domain of human responsibility. In any case, those who can destroy the world are the first capable of fully understanding Paul's message two thousand years ago. For *humankind is already*, whether it likes it or not, whether it accepts it or not, the heir of slow biological evolution—in other words, creator child of the creator God.

This is a bit like what Mounier was saying: there are twenty centuries between the Christian message and the emergence of the context in which this message is to take on its fullest meaning. The "protohistory" of Christianity is over; we are finally witnessing its history. Drawing together the threads we have been uncovering in the history of dogma, we sense vaguely how and why there is reason for hope. We also realize why this could not fully happen until certain elements central to Christian faith had come into existential contact with the context challenging humankind.

Are we to say then that Paul was guilty of a "hasty pedagogy"? I do not think so. Even in his time the message he draws from his deep reflection on the meaning of Jesus of Nazareth deals with real questions. He does not provide information on what is of no interest to anyone. Yet not everyone is ready for what he has to say. The liberation of Christians, his disciples, from the temptation of unloading the burden of their freedom on the law or on the church itself is not for all. As a result of subsequent developments in history his message was set aside, as though it were being held in reserve for a new context where it would acquire all its liberating power. For my part I can attest that Christians reading Paul in Latin America are astonished to see that a church that went through Vatican II does not yet seem to recognize these mature and humanizing horizons.

All that can explain why this summary is also a declaration of hope. The two sections to follow will try to gather together these theological threads, albeit somewhat speculatively (just because it is a summary), and then to offer a practical and pastoral perspective whose anticipations can already be discerned. Readers who want to save the trouble of going through the speculative part, or who do not think they need a summary after everything seen thus far, may skip directly to the second section.

Revelation and Faith: Signs of the Times*

The reader could think at first sight that the terms in the title of this section were three vaguely related items grouped together for an economical use of space. The very arrangement of the three items could suggest the arrangement of elements, in descending order, to be found in the customary theoretical treatment of the fundamental concepts of theology in any theological dictionary. Indeed, it would have been strange if "revelation" had not been one of these concepts. How could there be a theology that did not treat of what God has revealed? Or still more basically, of what is meant by God's "revealing" something? And one might likewise suppose that, if a particular theology has some specific characteristic, it will have to reflect on the manner in which divine revelation is approached, studied, and used; and therefore that, after having treated of "revelation," it should have to treat of the "faith" with which human beings must respond to this revelatory message when they discover that it actually comes from God, from infinite truth. Finally, a theology like liberation theology, which, as we know, is characterized by, among other things, an attachment (even in its initial moment) to the practice of faith, cannot, in its work of "understanding" that faith, prescind from the signs that the history of that practice and its crisis throw up to it as so many interrogations: "the signs of the times," as Jesus calls them in Matthew's Gospel (16:3).

This amounts to detecting an order—all but necessary, apparently—proceeding from the "word of God" to faith to the most significant concrete problems presented by history, that these problems may be "illuminated, guided . . . and interpreted in the light of the Gospel"[2]—that is, submitted to the criterion of the revealed word of God.

This order, while doubtless logical, is not, I should think, the order in which the three elements are presented in the human being's existence and concrete history. It surely represents a "theological" order. Nor does this mean that its use will be restricted to theological scholarship. Reflection on the most ordinary pastoral activity will show that Christians follow this path routinely. It is not, however, the only possible order. What would happen, for example, if the order of these three concepts were reversed? Unless I am mistaken, moving along

*This section, pp. 238-53, was translated by Robert R. Barr.

this road in the direction I have just proposed is crucial for a theology aiming at full human liberation.

Let it not be thought that this hypothesis—which we shall examine here—indicates the need for an option for either of the two orders as being the "correct" order. Each, in its own domain, has its explanation and raison d'être. They are not mutually exclusive, then, and it would be imprudent and naive to regard one of them as constituting the only correct way of relating the three terms in the list.

Nevertheless, I hold that the second orientation or sequence, in that it represents a more general process transpiring among human beings, has pedagogical advantages, as I trust will become clear in the first part of this section. I propose, then, to devote the three parts of this section to showing how each of the three items in the title conditions God's self-communication to human beings, and how, in this respect, the one last on the list is actually the first of these conditions.

From Faith to Revelation

When we proclaim that God has determined to "reveal" to human beings truths that they could by no means, or only with excessive difficulty, find by themselves (D. 1785–86), we correctly indicate the bountiful, gratuitous origin, in the divine plan, of that intervention of God in human history. God has determined to communicate certain truths concerning God and the human being. And always *both at once*.

Anyone claiming this "communication" to be possible is constrained to admit from the outset that the message communicated must fall into the category of what is understandable and important for the human being. It would be vain to pretend to conceive a "Word of God" addressed to human beings but not expressed in the language of human beings, or failing to call their attention to some value to be derived from knowing it.

Here, then, are two logical conditions, converging on the same activity: that of *communicating*. And in terms of the simplest definition, one who communicates conveys to the interlocutor "a difference that makes a difference."[3] If there is no understanding of the message, the (presumed) *difference* is not verified. Something whose identity is unknown is not added to what is already known. Likewise, if this transmitted difference does not *make a difference* in the existence of the one receiving the message, neither is anything communicated. And since knowledge, despite the old saw, really does "take up space" in the mind, psychology tells us that the mind rapidly strives (by forgetting) to reoccupy the space taken up by supposed differences, which, when transmitted, change the receiver in no way.

Of these two preconditions for God's being *able* to "reveal" something to us (since any revelation is either accommodated to our human manner of communication or it simply does not exist), theology has by and large accepted the first, although not without certain strings attached out of respect for the divine initiative and the divine object of that special communication.

Obviously the Infinite Being cannot speak to us in a language of its own, which would have the characteristics of that limitless being. For example, it cannot speak in an atemporal manner to a being whose (transcendent) imagination is structured by time. To put it another way, the human being cannot understand an "eternal" language, because the one destined to be and permitted to be the receiver of the transmitter's self-communication varies with time and circumstances.

Even before becoming personally incarnate in the Son, God, having willed to become revealer, had to speak to human beings by "enfleshing" the divine word in a human language, which uses signs limited in their being and their power of signifying. Hence in that act of communication, what is understood is only an infinitesimal particle, as it were, of a truth that always reaches us only "to the extent that we can understand it" (D. 1796; see Mk. 4:33).[4]

The greatest risk of deviation, however, lies in neglect of the second precondition. It is not a mere matter of perceiving something (for which it is necessary that our knowledge receive a "different" content from the one it had before). The "difference" must also *make* a difference." Otherwise the message, however well received and, so to speak, well "deposited" in the receiver, would not yet signify anything. And the mental mechanisms would soon take account of this "nonsignifying" difference and respond by forgetting it.

The difference transmitted begins to signify when the receiver perceives what it should affect or change in his or her actual existence or behavior—that is, when the perceived difference is related to another, correlative difference that ought to take place in the existence of the receiver.

Let us have an analogy from the material order. When the air temperature becomes "different" from the limits established on the thermostat, it does not yet strictly "communicate" anything until the thermostat "understands" that what has been transmitted regarding the different temperature ought to "differentiate" its current state, so that it will now turn on the furnace that will heat the area once more to the desired temperature. Only then is there a true "communication": when there is a difference that makes or produces a difference.

On this precise point, Vatican II complemented, and in a certain sense corrected, a potential misunderstanding of the texts of Vatican I that suggested and asserted that, in order to speak to human beings, God could only "enflesh" the divine word in the limited language of human beings. It must follow that, if God wished to speak to us of the divine mystery itself, this could be done only in a limited, obscure way that our finite capacity for understanding would, as it were, place at the divine disposal. Thus, that God is at once one and three remains "mysterious" even after being "revealed" or communicated by God (see D. 1796). Thus, it seems as if God had communicated something for the sole purpose of our knowing it, or better, had repeated it without its meaning any "difference" in our way of existing. Its relevance for us might seem to have proceeded not from our understanding our life more and living it better, but from a kind of power intrinsic to that message, which would be salvific before the judgment seat of God although having in no way modified the existence of the human being, like a magical safe-conduct, an "Open, Sesame!"

Vatican Council II, speaking of divine revelation, agrees with Vatican I that "God spoke by means of human beings *in a human manner*" (DV 12). But at Vatican II the accent was no longer on the limitation that this "human manner" imposed on divine revelation, and thus on the mystery that the revelation allows to subsist. At Vatican II the emphasis was on the fact that all of God's messages to us are authentic, integral "communication": a difference in the conception of God intended to become a difference in the way in which we understand and live our creative, communitarian destiny.

Indeed, the most complete, total, and personal revelation of God is, indivisibly, also a revelation of ourselves and our destiny: "The *same* revelation of the Father and of his love [in Christ] *fully* manifests the human being to the human being himself, and discovers to him the sublimity of his destiny" (GS 22). The Council, then, does not regard revelation as something that, without transforming our historical life constitutes a "truth": that is, something that can be possessed, be deposited, and have value in God's sight (see Matt. 25:24 and parallels) by performing its salvific activity in a magical manner (see GS 7, 43). Thus, according to the Council, the intent of God's revelation is not that we *know* (something that otherwise would be impossible or difficult for us to know), but that we *be* differently, and act better.

When this conception of divine revelation is analyzed more in depth, it becomes possible to understand the dogmatic reorientation that a Council that meant to be pastoral saw itself obliged to undertake in order that the "difference" entailed in its most novel orientations might be understood. Indeed, the Council is teaching that faith in God's self-revelation, far from turning the mind from the temporal and ephemeral toward the necessary and eternal, "directs the mind toward fully human solutions" of historical problems (GS 11). Thus, Christians do not possess, not even by understanding it, the truth that God communicates to them until they succeed in transforming it into a humanizing "difference" within history. Until orthopraxis[5] becomes reality, no matter how ephemeral and contingent that reality, Christians *do not yet know the truth*. On the contrary, in virtue of an imperative of their moral conscience, they must "join the rest of human beings [Christians and others] in the *quest* for the truth" (GS 16).

But this places us precisely before the problem of the priority of revelation to faith or vice versa. We had thought that faith came second, as a response to God's revelation of divine truth. Now we perceive that, in order for us to receive this truth, it must find us somehow engaged in a common quest of human liberation. This of itself implies a kind of "faith" — and what is more, a kind of "Abrahamic faith" — that is, a faith occurring antecedently to any religious classification. And indeed, this is how Paul presents Abraham (Rom. 4): as someone who, before being "religiously classifiable" in a particular category, already believes in a kind of promise that the history of human liberation and humanization seems to address to those who struggle for it. Abraham believed in "the God who gives life to the dead and calls to being what is not" (Rom. 4:17; see 4:21, 2:6–7).

What is this "faith" that precedes "revelation," and which, as we have seen, makes revelation possible as the necessary precondition for the revealed "difference" to effect the essential praxic "difference" without which there could be no authentic communication between God and ourselves?

One of our essential dimensions as human beings is what we might call the quest for the meaning of our existence. Absorbed as we may be in the urgencies of day-to-day survival, and little as we may perceive that we have a freedom that opens to us a certain spectrum of opportunities or routes to various values or satisfactions, all the same we realize that our free existence is a kind of wager. Why a "wager"? Because we have only one life and cannot "test out" in advance what we are going to choose. We are not granted to traverse a course to the end, observe whether it is has been a satisfactory one, and then, in all assurance and (empirical) cognizance of cause, return to our starting point—and then make our option knowing beforehand what awaits us at the end of the road. When you fall in love, you have no way of knowing what your beloved will be like fifty years from now. When you choose an ideal, and spend long years in preparation for it (for example, a professional career), you can as yet have no experience of what awaits you at the end of the road of your professional practice. When you start a revolution, you do not yet know what historical price it will demand of you, or what will remain of your project even after you have paid the price.

History is exciting. It is like an open promise. But there is no antecedent verification of anything as related to its overall worth. This does not mean that the wager of our entire freedom, and often our life (in one way or another) is blind and irrational. Human society provides each of its members with a kind of collective memory, within which the option under consideration becomes a reasonable one. But it is still a wager. The human species with its different cultures, the nation, the clan, the family, provide each individual with "witnesses" or "testimonials" of meaningful lives. The option of freedom is based on that memory, makes it its own, tests it, uses it, modifies it, and makes an option among the opportunities it offers. But at bottom, when all is said and done, it places its "faith" in one or more of the testimonials that the memory presents.

What does this have to do with our subject, which is God's "revelation"? A great deal. Why? Because the usual order in which the problem is presented is a theological order. And rightly so, in scholarly theology. But in the process of a human existence, the order is different—reversed, in fact. We are tempted to think: God reveals, and we, faced with this revelation (perceived and accepted as such), make an option to accept it or reject it (in unbelief or idolatry). But what we have just seen obliges us to modify this routine conceptualization. We are forced back on Augustine's radical question: If you do not make me better than I was, why are you talking to me at all? Augustine is not being impertinent. Human beings *understand only what affects them*, only what makes them better or worse. This means that, in God's revealing, faith does not come after something has been revealed. Faith is an *active*, indispensable part of revelation itself.

But there is more. True, the quest for the meaning needed to establish communication between God and human beings is not the same in everyone. But it is always "faith." God addresses the divine word to an (anthropological) faith that is always there, and that in each human being is the fruit of an option (antecedent to hearing).

To put it another way: the role of freedom is more active or decisive. It is part of the very process of "revelation." Orthopraxis is not an ultimate "application" of revelation to practice: it is a necessary condition of the sheer possibility that revelation actually reveal something.[6]

From People to Faith

But so far we have taken only the first step. We have shown that, in its very definition, there is no such thing as divine revelation (although there is such a thing as the "Word of God" in the Bible) unless there is a human quest that converges with this word, a quest for which the Word of God signifies a liberation of human potential and human values: the making of human beings "better than they were." This is the game God agrees to play in the divine self-communication to the human being.[7]

And yet, there is a great deal more. What God communicates to this human being is not a pure, simple, ready-made answer, valid once and for all, and for all questions, regardless of context or the problem before which we find ourselves. And this despite the fact that the church sometimes seems to utilize the Bible — the deposit of God's "revelation" — as a repertory of stock, universally valid answers.

In the first place, if we examine this "deposit" of revelation constituted, for us Christians, by the Old and New Testaments, it is possible, and even fitting, that we should be struck and overwhelmed by the multitude of images, words, testimonials, and episodes that we find there. God has supposedly made use of these to reveal something. Indeed, it is very possible that we should be equally surprised that such a process of communication between God and human beings is supposed to have terminated on a certain vaguely specified date, as if that revelation had exhausted its content, or as if we now needed no more of God's words in order to be delivered from all that prevents us from being collectively and individually human.

There are certain questions that Christians must ask themselves, regardless of their particular degree of perspicacity. One, perhaps the most obvious one, is the following. Now that God has revealed both God and the human being in the only-begotten Son, and now that, in that Son (and in the witnesses of his life and message), the deposit of revelation has been closed for good and all — why should we continue to regard the previous words, images, and personages as a revelation that continues to call for our faith (see D. 783, 1787)?

Another question, a related one, arises from the fact that, as we have said, very frequently in all this "deposit" of revealed truth, stock answers are sought to the questions of the human being of today. For example, What about marriage? To this question the church generally responds with the words that Jesus is regarded as having said about marriage (see Mt. 19:1–9), forbidding the separation of the spouses ("what God has joined together") — the repudiation of the female partner ("except in case of fornication," which no one is quite sure how to interpret) and the contracting of another marriage on the part of the husband (or the wife—see Mk. 10:12).

If faith obliges us to accept, on faith, this response for all cases today, then is that polygamy licit today that the patriarchs once practiced with God's approval, as well as the repudiation of the wife approved by the law of Moses (Deut. 24:1ff.)? If the answer to this question, which is only one in a thousand that we might ask, is yes, then it is in direct contradiction with what Jesus says. And if we answer no, then what meaning can there be in the claim that the entire Old Testament is the "Word of God," just as the New? Thus, there would not seem to be any logical response to this question the disciples put to Jesus, as long as we keep thinking of the "revelation" or "Word" of God as a repertory of questions and answers valid in some atemporal fashion, after the manner of "information," ever true, since it proceeds from Truth itself.

And the solution is not that this occurs only with regard to moral usages and questions. Almost to the end of Old Testament times, we find that the authors and personages of that collection of writings do not believe in a life after death. In what sense, then, can Christians say they believe in God's "revelation" in the Old Testament in the same fashion and for the same reason that they believe in it in the New?

In fact, even with regard to God there are important variations among the various Old Testament authors. The most eloquent case is that of the book of Job, where, on the basis of the misfortunes afflicting this legendary personage, the book presents a dispute between two theologies. According to the one, represented by Job's friends and by Elihu—as also by most of the books of the Old Testament—the evils that befall a person are in strict proportion to that person's sinful actions. Job, examining his own experience, and even taking his admitted sinfulness into consideration, denies such an equation, and thus opposes traditional theology. And God decides the question in favor of Job's position, despite Job's imprudence in demanding of God an account of his misfortunes. The "suffering just," who can even die without Yahweh's accommodating their fate to their moral behavior, thus become a theological crisis (see Ps. 73:44; Eccl. 3:16–22, etc.), to which Israel will give different solutions. After all, how indeed can the faithfulness of Yahweh—an essential divine quality—be reconciled with an entire human life in which justice does not have the last word?

Vatican Council II, precisely in its constitution *Dei Verbum*—that is, the document that treats of the "Word of God" and the divine "revelation"— indicates the most deep-reaching and complete solution to these comprehensive problems. There we read that, although the books of the Old Testament "contain certain imperfect and transitory things, they nevertheless demonstrate the *true divine pedagogy*."

This declaration is worthy of consideration on a number of counts. The *first* is that "imperfect and transitory things" are said to be part of "true" divine revelation. Obviously, in speaking of "transitory things," the allusion is to things that have ceased to be true (or at least completely and perfectly true), although they have been true in times past. It would appear that the concept of "truth" is relativized. Jesus indicated the same thing in referring to the validity or truth of his conception of marriage (see Mt. 19:8), or, to recall only one celebrated instance, in the matter of knowing what obligations God has imposed with regard to human activities on the sabbath day (see Mark 2:27). Once again, God seems concerned not that the divine "revelation" be true in itself—be eternal truth, unchangeable truth—but that it "become" true in the humanization of the human being. In other words, God speaks only to those who seek, and gives them no recipes, but rather guides them in their searching.

And this brings us to the *second* thing we must consider in the passage we have cited from *Dei Verbum*. "Divine revelation" is not a deposit of true information, but a *true pedagogy*. The divine revelation of God and the human being does not consist in amassing correct information in their regard. That revelation is a "process," and in that process we do not learn "things." We learn to learn—just as in any pedagogy, in which children are "guided" (the etymology of "pedagogue") to learn to seek after truth through trial and error. In any process of education, then—even in the most *true*, indeed, infallible, educational process of all—there are "imperfect and transitory" things. Thus, it is enormously important to know where the "truth" is located in these kinds of educational processes. It is not irrelevant that the Council uses the adjective "true" to characterize not the first level, but the second. Pedagogy is a process of *apprenticeship in the second degree*. And its truth lies not in some timeless truth on the first level, where information is accumulated, but on the second level, that of an apprenticeship, where the factors for seeking and finding truth are multiple.

Hence the necessity of conceiving "revelation" not as a mere providing of correct information about God and human beings, but as a "true pedagogy," a divine pedagogy. We must seriously modify our conception of the relationship between revelation and truth. However—and here we come to a *third* observation—*Dei Verbum* speaks of the imperfect and transitory only with regard to the Old Testament. It says nothing like this with regard to the New. This is food for thought. Will God have changed methods of "revealing" since the coming of Christ? Will God have begun to provide us with perfect and invariable, or perhaps merely explanatory, information? Indeed, in the presence of divine, eternal Truth itself, now revealed, will God perhaps have terminated this process of search, demonstrated in the Old Testament?

The Vatican II attribution of the imperfect and transitory specifically to the Old Testament, as well as certain explicit declarations of the ordinary church magisterium (e.g., D. 2012), might seem to suggest this. But there are serious reasons for thinking that, even after God's revelation in Jesus Christ, the only-begotten divine Son, the revelatory function of the Spirit of Jesus continues to accompany the process of the humanization of all human beings.

For one thing, the New Testament itself states this. According to the Johannine theology, the very physical disappearance of Jesus Christ, his transitus from this earth to his glorious invisibility, is "fitting." St. Augustine expressed it very simply, and with unmatched eloquence: "The Lord himself, as he deigned to be our Way, did not seek to detain us, but rather moved on."[8] Jesus himself says this, in different words, in his farewell discourse, according to the fourth Gospel (which, while not synonymous with historical fidelity, does belong to God's "revelation" or "Word"). And he explains the reason for this strange fittingness: "If I do not go away, the Paraclete will not come to you. I should be able to tell you many other things, as well, but you could not manage them now. When the Spirit of Truth comes, he will guide you to the whole truth" (Jn. 16:7,12–13).

At once we find the concern of every process of second-level learning—the concern in any process of teaching a person to think—with not "leaking" information on the pretext of its being true. The "truth" at issue in this process is situated on another level, and that level demands that one problem lead to others, and that information be framed within the problematic of the real. But furthermore we find, as in any "pedagogy," that the need for (mere) information diminishes with increasing maturity. At some point, learning to learn postulates the absence of a teacher—or better, the replacement of the physical teacher to whom one can go in case of doubt, by the "spirit" of the teacher, which, through what has already been learned, and new historical challenges, will continue to carry the process forward.

Paul makes this maturity the very core of the Christian message. The "pedagogue," or here, the Old Testament law but also church structures and even Jesus' very words, no longer stand over the heir, although they do not thereby cease to fulfill their original function.

With what we have said up to this point, we have taken a second step in our consideration of the relationship between revelation, faith, and the signs of the times. At first it had appeared to us that the divine revelation was already complete from God's side, and that all that remained, from our side, was to receive it in faith, hold it in reverence, and apply it in praxis. With this second step, we see, revelation presupposes not only a search and an antecedent faith, but also the constitution of a people that will *hand on* a wisdom from generation to generation.[9] Through things ever imperfect and transitory, handed down by the very existence of the community, that "people" becomes "tradition."[10] This means that memory and collective pedagogy have a decisive function in the very process of revelation: thanks to these, each new generation is exempt from starting its (second-degree) learning "from scratch." Through a process of remembering and readopting, in a vital fashion peculiar to its own identity, the past experiences of another process in which the search, solutions, and challenges of history converge, each generation is thrust toward a more perfect maturity, and toward a new, deeper, and richer truth.

In order to be part of this community-in-process-toward-the-truth, under the guidance of God, we must have "faith" in it. It is not in God directly that we place this "faith," because it is not God directly who speaks to us. God speaks through witnesses, and these divine witnesses are not isolated individuals: they constitute a community, a people, whom God, with a "true pedagogy," ever dispatches toward the liberative truth of all the creative potential of the human being.[11] The Israelite people, the Christian people, perform a function of interpretation and transmission without which we could not recognize where and how the "Word of God" sounds today. Without Israel, or the church, in the world we know, and in Christian tradition, there is no revelation of God.

Thus, this second step that we have taken, from "revelation" to "faith," shows us that the very fact of God's revealing something with meaning supposes not only an individual in search of truth, but a community, a people committed to this intent to "learn to learn," as it searches for the truth. Only then does God communicate something. Faith is not the mere consequence of a passive, individual acceptance in faith of a word addressed to us by God. Thus, the faith community does not follow the *fait accompli* of a revelation wrought by God. It is an integral part of it.

From Faith to Signs of the Times

But we must now take a further step, and discover to what extent, and in what way, the faith community is part of that revelation *in a creative manner*.

Indeed, from what has now been said, an important question still remains to be solved. How may we distinguish "God's" Word from other, "merely human," words? The language used is the same, and the options posed by that language are ranged along a spectrum of more or less equivalent possibilities. We have also seen that it is not required that divine revelation even deal with or explicitly cite the divinity. We must not forget that, even in Israel, not to mention other religions, two prophets—for example, Jeremiah and Hananiah—can appeal to the same God to justify contrary orientations on the part of the same "divine pedagogy" (see Jer. 28). What entitles us to include in the collection of "words of God" the prophecies of Jeremiah, and not those of Hananiah (especially since neither of the two prophetic messages was confirmed by subsequent events)? The Bible itself informs us that, for centuries, contradictory opinions—and biblical ones, espoused by different sacred authors—prevailed in Israel as to whether the institution of the monarchy represented the will of God, or Israel's sinful rejection of Yahweh as king (see 1 Sam. 8–10).

What is more, there is no radical change in this state of affairs when we come to the New Testament. It is not as easy to perceive this in the New Testament, since all the works it contains were redacted over the course of a period lasting surely no longer than half a century, while the redaction of the Old Testament extends over a millennium. But even in this reduced time span we notice serious unresolved divergencies between Paul and the author of the letter of James (see Rom. 3:21–30 and James 2:14–26), or again between Paul and James the "brother of the Lord" (or at least his followers—Gal. 2:12).

At the level of theoretical theology, the answer is simple, and almost tautological:

> When God reveals, we are obliged to offer him full obedience in faith . . .
> This faith . . . is a supernatural virtue by which . . . we believe to be true
> what has been revealed by Him not by the intrinsic truth of things . . .
> but on the authority of God himself revealing. [Vatican Council I – D.
> 1789]

The whole difficulty for the ordinary person is in distinguishing "when God reveals" from very similar occasions that might wrongly be taken as God's revelation. To be sure, the ordinary person identifies this special "when" that is deserving of our faith with the redaction of the Bible that we hold in our hands today. But then it will doubtless occur to us to ask: How did the church make this collection that separates what God has revealed from what God has not revealed? Here again, the theological solution is easy, and once more is furnished by Vatican I:

> The church holds [the books of the Bible] as sacred and canonical not because they were composed by human industry alone and then approved by her; nor only because [they] contain revelation without error; but because, written under the *inspiration* of the Holy Spirit, they have God as their author. [D. 1788]

As I have said, this answer is almost a redundancy. Obviously, if we claim that God has used something of human language to communicate to us, and if such writings nevertheless have a human author, then this author must be "inspired" by God in order for what is written to be regarded as "divine revelation." But we speak of redundancy because *historically speaking* the problem of a criterion is still unresolved. However, instead of claiming to know when God reveals (in order to be able to have faith in what is revealed), we must ask how we know when God "inspires" an author's writing.

The theology of liberation is especially sensitive to this question — a perfectly logical one, but one that is absent from the concerns of most current theology — because the recognition today of what would be, for "our" reality, the "word that God would speak," is a task that we must undertake a thousand and one times in the communities that form the base of the church and inquire into the enriching, liberative content of their faith. If God continues the work of divine revelation by the Spirit, how to recognize the divine "word" today becomes a crucial ecclesial criterion.

Actually, there are two answers to the question. One is Jesus' (paradigmatic and) absolute refusal to help his hearers identify the presence of God in God's deeds and messages by means of "signs from heaven." The other is constituted by the data furnished by the formation of the canon (or list of the books regarded as inspired by God) of the Old as well as of the New Testament. This history, while not completely known, is sufficiently well understood to support a judgment.

According to Luke, Jesus' refusal to call down signs from heaven as a criterion of whether or not his hearers are in the presence of God and a divine revelation, has a very precise context. Jesus has just restored the faculty of speech to a person who had somehow lost his faculty of speech. The bystanders now wonder whether they are in the presence of an event evincing the power and hence the presence of God, or whether there could be some other explanation — even, for example, the power of Satan (who was supposed to have deprived the victim of his speech in the first place) transferred to Jesus.

According to Mark, Jesus' refusal is absolute. This generation will be given no sign from heaven. But there is something else. As to the possibility that

Jesus has delivered the victim of Satan's affliction by the power of Satan, Mark now indicates the argument that all three synoptics will use: even hypothetically, the objection has no meaning. After all, whether it be God or Satan who humanizes a person, that humanization, in and of itself, is a sign that "Satan's reign has come to an end" (Mk. 3:26). Then the reign of God must be beginning, Luke explicitly concludes (Lk. 11:20).

God's self-communication to us is bestowed by way of actions or ideas. In both cases, this communication will be understood only by one who is attuned to the priorities of the heart of this God. And for such a one, the historical sign of the liberation of a person is the sign of the presence and revelation of God—just as one who reads a book does not understand what God wishes of the Sabbath, however divine the book, or however many thunderclaps or bolts of lightning may have accompanied its publication. Knowledge of God as "revealing" something to us occurs when we are discovered to have a historical sensitivity that converges with God's own intentions.

Hence, in Matthew and Luke (in dependence upon Q), Jesus gives two examples of persons who, without knowing "biblical revelation," have understood what God wishes to communicate to them, and have perceived God's revelatory presence in history: the inhabitants of Nineveh, and the "queen of the south" (see Mt. 12:38–42). According to Luke, these pagans "have themselves judged what is just" (Luke 12:57)—that is, they have recognized a sign that is in history, or as Matthew says, a "sign of the times" (Mt. 16:3).

In other words, the identification of God's presence or "revelation," first in the history of Israel, and then in the deeds and words of Jesus, does not fall from heaven packaged and labeled. God has entrusted us with the responsibility of searching them out, of verifying them in the best way possible, with the eyes and priorities of God (which are also those of the reign of God). Only from a point of departure in this commitment, which is the fruit of a certain sensitivity, has it been defined "when" God has revealed what today comprises the Bible. Thus, it is true today, as well, that, in the task of interpreting when we are in the presence of God, the documents of Medellín define the task of a liberative theology:

> Just as another Israel, the first people, experienced the salvific presence of God when God delivered them from the oppression of Egypt . . . so also we, the new people of God, cannot escape the experience of the divine passage that saves whenever there is . . . a passage, for each and all, from less humane conditions of life to more humane conditions. [Medellín Final Document, Introduction, no. 6]

These "signs" are already sufficiently clear and experiential for us to "believe" that "all growth in humanity moves us closer to reproducing the image of the Son, that he may be the firstborn of many siblings" (ibid., "Education," no. 9).

I have said that, besides the evangelical paradigm concerning the basic importance of the "signs of the times," I have sufficient historical data to construct what might be called a paradigm of the "theological fact" of the formation of the canon. With these data in mind, let us construct an example of how that paradigm functions. Let us take the case of Moses in the exodus. For simplicity's sake, let us say that in setting up this paradigm, we are not concerned to know who wrote the actual account. Tradition attributes it to Moses himself, but I think that its redaction is actually that of one or more chroniclers writing in the time of David or Solomon. As I have said, the fact is that the account was written. Neither, for the purposes of this study, are we interested in the "historiographical" status of the account at the moment of its redaction—whether it was taken as actual history or as a mythical event. In either case—and this is what interests me—it came to form part of the Yahwist "faith."

One of the theologians who, to my knowledge, has taken most seriously the *theology* implied in the construction of a canon, or list of writings containing "divine revelation," is A. Torres Queiruga, in his *La Revelación de Dios en la Realización del Hombre.*[12] Here is how this author summarizes the interaction of God and human beings in the creation of the word of God concerning the exodus—or, if you will, how "divine revelation" is recognized *in* the liberation of the Jewish people from their oppression in Egypt:

> From his religious experience, Moses *discovered* the living presence of God in the longing of the Jews to be delivered from their oppression. The "experience of contrast" between the actual situation of his people and what he felt to be the salvific will of God, who seeks the human being's liberation, gave him the intuition that the Lord was present in that longing, and supported the people. As he gradually succeeded in instilling this certitude of his in others, helping them, as well, to *discover* this presence, he awakened history, promoted religiousness, and ultimately *created Yahwism.*[13]

Starting with this text, I am going to make a series of observations on what it tells us, explicitly, and especially implicitly. Readers will bear in mind that I am using it for my own purposes, and not to determine the thinking of the author.

First, Torres speaks of a personage who has what he calls an "experience of contrast." It is unimportant for the moment what the name of this personage is. The biblical account calls him Moses, and presents him as the protagonist of the exodus narrative. But it is evident that, whatever the historical value of his account, the author *of the account,* at any rate, must have had this actual, historical experience, since this author judges it relevant to recount it and set it in relief as basic for Israel's faith in its God. It is this author who "discovers," in the facts of the past that others transmit, a revelatory presence of God, and separates these facts from the rest.

The first thing we observe about this author is that this "experience of contrast," as it is designated here, *presupposes* an already existing (anthropological) "faith"—that is, a determinate structure of values that sensitizes the author to this situation of oppression and instills the notion that God cannot wish it, when others think that this was the normal situation, or the lesser evil (see Ex.

4:1–9, 6:12; Num. 11:5, etc.). Here is the source of the author's interest, which makes of a mere event or situation a "sign" of something to be done. And it is this that converts the action of the author, the narrative, into a transforming "enthusiasm" that then infects others.

Second, Why do we say that this "faith" of "Moses" (whether of Moses, the Yahwist, or the author of Deuteronomy) was "anthropological" — that is, something seemingly contradistinguished from "religious" faith in Yahweh? By this we mean that this Moses has no Bible. He cannot have recourse, as we customarily do, to the "Word of God" in order to know what values to strive for, and in what order to strive for them. Nor, therefore, did he have access, among the manifold voices of historical reality, to an unequivocal "sign" that would enable him to make a divinely guaranteed "discovery" of the revelatory presence of God. To this purpose, he had to do what, according to the gospel, the Ninevites, or the queen of the south did, who worshiped gods who were not Yahweh.

True, in the account, narrated when Moses had already been accepted as Yahweh's witness, it is recounted that Yahweh give Moses "signs from heaven" — that is, magical signs that his mission, his duty, actually came from God. But let us notice, first of all, that other persons in the account claim, on the basis of similar magical arguments, that this is not the will of God (see Ex. 11:22, etc.). Furthermore, other books of what today is the Bible have been acknowledged as "the Word of God" without the mediation of any divine apparition to their author, indeed without so much as a single mention of God by that author (as the Song of Songs), in a work that could have been written, for example, by an atheist. "Moses," here, by definition, is — under pain of having to appeal to an infinite chain — the person without a Bible, without a deposited "Word of God." Moses must place a wager on what God "must" wish. And those who follow Moses must believe in the same way.[14]

Third, our text speaks of an "experience of contrast" — an experience of something that becomes a "sign" of what God does *not* wish, and therefore a sign of the divine will to "liberate" human beings from it, in this case the Israelites. However, there are other signs of the times that appeal to the same faith (to the same structure of value or of being), from other experiences than those of contrast: for example, the experience of the celebration of value attained (as in many of the Psalms), the experience of the covenant in the search for some of these same values (as in the preaching of various prophets), or the experience of the promise of a future or impending realization of such values (as in the Beatitudes).

Common to all these experiences is the presence in history of events or qualities in which the very meaning of existence is at stake. Whether or not these events or qualities will be noticed as signs — which is what happens in the case of Moses — rather than their being allowed to slip by as irrelevant, will depend on the strength with which this faith, which is antecedent to revelation (of which these peak moments are the vehicle), becomes sensitive to the vicissitudes of these values rather than others on our human earth.

Fourth, let us move from the *facts* of the book of Exodus to the *readers* of that book. And once more, we are not concerned with the difference between those who were with Moses in his deed and those who excitedly read of this same deed centuries later. In both, this accompaniment indicates the "contagion of an enthusiasm" and commitment. In consequence of the preceding, Moses' Israelite contemporaries regard him as "inspired by God"—exactly as those who read, with reverence, and as addressed to their lives, the book of Exodus hold the writer as "inspired." (We too, for simplicity's sake, shall call him "Moses" here, but he was the Yahwist, the Elohist, the Deuteronomist, and so on.)

Moses' contemporaries made an option between following him and following leaders who proposed other alternatives as the will of God. Later readers make an option among *books*, among various possible or real accounts of these events. There were works in which these same events either are not narrated, or are narrated in a different light, or finally, are not regarded as "signs" of the active presence of God. And all of this occurred also before a Bible existed. In fact, it is the Bible that arises from this selection among books (guided by the same witnesses and criteria as the events recounted there).

Fifth, the passage from Torres upon which we are commenting tells us that, by contagion of the enthusiasm aroused by the discovery of signs of a divine liberating presence, Moses—and hence the author or authors who recount his deed—"aroused history." This means that they gave rise to a historical process. And they did so by creating a community, a people, whose fundamental identity lay in the tradition (in the original sense of "transmission") that opted for the same values and for the same historical signs.

I say that it is a "process" that is created in this way, because that discovery of the presence of God is not static. For example, that discovery is different in Exodus (with its Yahwist or Elohist background) and in Deuteronomy. There are various "Moseses." But their plurality lies along a growth line, in the face of various historical challenges. Moses does not teach a package of "truth." He teaches how to learn to learn—how to "discover" more signs in the history of the same revelatory, liberative presence of God.

Sixth, Torres has the colossal audacity to say that this Moses—multiple and progressive—who awakened history, "created Yahwism." But was it not "divine revelation," which inspired Moses, that created it? Of course. But the data we have on the way what we today call the Old Testament was compiled in Israel—that is, the written deposit of revelation—tell of the crucial participation in this historical creation, beginning with the exile, of the people of Israel themselves.

The restriction of divine worship to the one temple of Jerusalem under Josiah, the impossibility of that divine worship during the captivity, and its later limitations, along with a swelling diaspora, had the result that the doubly "lay" institution of the *synagogue*, centered on "reading" and interpretation, gradually displaced worship—and thus became, "more than any other factor, responsible for the survival of Judaism [Yahwism] as a religion and of the Jews as a distinct people."[15] God speaks a human language, surely; but the divine revelatory word becomes such only when it is recognized, among so many other words, in the experience of the foundational liberation (in "Moses") and in the continuity of that liberation, which sustains Israel.

Seventh, finally, there is no reason to suppose that what is said here, with complete historical foundation, of the creation of "Yahwism" would not hold as well for that of "Christianity." And I am not speaking of some parallel that imitates a previous event. From the historical viewpoint, it is the continuation of the process of that "Moses" whose discovery founded a people, a tradition, a second-level learning. The initial "being attuned" that is required for one word out of a thousand to be recognized as a sign that God is speaking is later criticized by this same word in the face of new challenges. The hermeneutics is circular, or, as some would have it, a spiral.

Jesus and Paul have a new liberative experience: that of leaving the servitude of a situation of privilege and trying to be on the watch for signs of the times that come from where human beings suffer, are poor, oppressed, limited in their human opportunities. Thus, as Paul sees it, new branches are grafted onto the old tree. The old people learns, or better, keeps on learning to learn. It does not stop seeking the truth along one route in order to seek it along another. The same truth that was present in the beginning continues to guide the people toward the full truth.

The Gospel Once More

Why an "Evangelization"

I hope that the section just finished may have served to remind readers of the main lines of thought laid down in previous chapters, even though it did not follow a historical order similar to our procedure thus far. This time we were not looking back in order to explain the past, but rather toward the future, with the hope that it might issue in a church more mature and creative on all levels.

Nevertheless, given the weight of what is already done and established, what I have to say here, as well-grounded as it might be in revelation and even the church's teaching authority, may further the impression that thus far I have been talking about ideals which now run up against a situation that is already an irreversible situation.

The wager of this book is that such is not the situation, as I have already had occasion to make clear. The convocation and unfolding of Vatican II showed how in a very short time, a great deal of this barrier of what is routine and institutionalized could be opened to richer directions toward which the impulse of the Spirit seemed to be clearly pointing. That was the case even though subsequently the weight of the past and nostalgia for a world opposed to change which had its own safeguards and supports again made itself felt. Those changes gain acceptance in people's minds, because they were already present there, awaiting their moment. Many were put into effect, even though now the results may seem to go only part of the way.

One of these expectations that seems to be expanding and attaining greater clarity and consensus throughout the (thinking and hoping) Christian world, is the need for an *evangelization*. Of course not everything that is so labeled represents the same mind-set or attitude, or the same direction in practice. For example, in connection with the celebration of the anniversary of the encounter between the American and European worlds, there is talk of how necessary it is now to reevangelize the Latin American continent five centuries later. Obviously the assumption is that the historic process by which this part of the world came to be called a "Christian" continent is to be called "evangelization." Readers may have noted that thus far I have avoided applying the term "evangelization" to this process. I have spoken of "christianization" instead, for in some fashion, in sociological terms, one may speak of the imposition of the Christian religion. No one receives what is truly the "gospel" by force, however. You cannot have it both ways. By its etymology and by its direct relationship to the term Jesus himself used for his prophetic proclamation, the gospel means "good news"—and no one can be forced to receive "good news."

Even those who speak of a "new" evangelization of Latin America (without taking into account those who speak of an evangelization in "Christian" countries in Europe) cannot prevent this call for evangelization from unleashing a good measure of criticism of such Christianity as exists today, as well as the hope for a deep change. Indeed, why "evangelize" a continent that has been almost entirely Christian for four or five centuries and which continues to regard itself as such with censuses and sociological surveys to back it up?

To evangelize, even in the sense of *re*evangelization, means that the relationship of Christians to the gospel message has diminished significantly—that is, that there is lacking a serious, correct, living contact between what people think and their reasons for living on the one hand and the good news brought by Jesus Christ on the other. If one admits that something has gotten in the way, does that not amount to admitting that much of what we have seen in previous chapters has cut off that vital relationship?—unless of course one is ready to completely accept the hypothesis set forth here that such a close relationship never existed due to the way Christianity came to these shores. I have in mind not only the violence with which Western culture and the Christian religion were imposed, but also the inability to dialogue with the real life of the human world encountered on this side of the Atlantic when Columbus discovered the New World. That inability went hand in hand with a dogma that was extended boundlessly and was apportioned more as information than as experience.

Nevertheless, all of this makes it imperative that in order to finish stating my hope, I speak for a moment of the elements making up such an "evangelization" and of some consequences deriving from it.

How an "Evangelization" Should Be Carried Out

A year before the opening of Vatican II, André Seumois, an advisor to the Congregation for the Propagation of the Faith, wrote the following lines about the gospel *kerygma* (= proclamation), a synonym of what is today usually called "evangelization":

Aimed directly at making an *initial proclamation of Christianity*, the kerygma is preaching of a very particular kind. It is restricted to proclaiming the *deep core of Christianity*, the fundamental features of the Christian religion, and avoids overloading, as well as what is accidental, adventitious, or superfluous. This condition is absolutely necessary not only so that new people may assimilate the Christian message, but also for *introducing in them its elevating light*. The Christian message in its purity is so rich and revolutionary that it is necessary to carefully restrict ourselves to its content and even to be careful to present it in a *prudent step by step way*.[16]

Before examining more deeply what Seumois himself proposes, readers will allow me to make some observations which I think will be useful for understanding what is to follow.

First, I believe theologians and church authorities will be practically unanimous in accepting what the author says in that paragraph. However, as is so often the case, that agreement will be momentary and will probably end as soon as the implicit conclusions begin to emerge.

Secondly, such acceptance will be almost certain, or at least more likely, in some areas than in others. What makes it so easy to accept initially is that its author is an expert on the missions and belongs to the Roman congregation which deals with "mission" countries. Moreover, the text mentions this point when it alludes to "a *first* proclamation of Christianity." The difficulties begin when already existing Christianity comes on the scene, especially if this "first proclamation" calls into question things generally regarded as important, even if it does so only by setting them aside.

Third, the first area to become sensitive when the issue of "evangelization" is raised as it is in that passage will probably be that of catechesis. In principle, or in theory, if you will, evangelization and catechesis should take place in sequence and not work against each other. The initial proclamation of the gospel is followed by formation in this incipient faith on the basis of a different kind of activity called catechesis.

Reality, however, is more complex, and here it brings into play a misunderstanding that I would like to clear up. When there is talk of reevangelizing our continent, the aim is to present to Christian adults the genuine "foundation" of Christian faith. They may very well possess many aspects of "Christianity" in the form of information and even attitudes, without ever having truly received the "initial proclamation" of the gospel of Christ. Hence we can say that as things are in Latin America (and to a great extent in Europe and North America as well) the situation is inside out: catechesis comes first and only afterward does the issue of putting people in contact with the genuine substance of the Christian message arise. In other words, coming as it generally does in childhood and early adolescence, catechesis takes the place of evangelization. If, then, it is necessary to reevangelize, and to do so not with the child but with the adult, will what was presented to the child as Christianity not be called into question? This is the real problem that pastoral practice has to face, especially when it regards catechesis of adults as something extraordinary or ideal. I am not aware of any place on our continent where adult Christians are required to receive a catechesis appropriate to the issues which as young but mature people they must face and for which the "initial proclamation" constituted by Jesus' message was created.

The misunderstanding to which I referred above was that of assuming that the things that the passage says about what is required for evangelization can or should constitute the structure of childhood catechesis. Nor can they serve as an immediate criterion for checking whether catechesis of children is being carried out properly.[17] What we must keep in mind is that the existence of a catechesis for children in no way resolves the problem of offering adult believers a new and authentic contact with the primary and fundamental message of Christian faith.

Third, it is worth noting that although that passage was written before the Council and has to do with the issue of missions, it sounds remarkably close to the principle stated here about the "order or 'hierarchy' of truths, since they vary in their relationship to the *foundation of Christian truth*" (Decree on Ecumenism, 11). This principle requires that there be a "prudent step-by-step" process starting from the "deep core of Christianity." In other words, ecumenism makes it necessary to distinguish what is essential from what is "accidental, adventitious, or superfluous" so as to streamline Christian (or Catholic) faith and make it possible to dialogue with Christianity's other forms which have evolved along different paths starting from what is fundamental. The great resistance encountered to putting this principle in practice after the Council, to which I have referred in earlier chapters, shows that it is regarded as dangerous to lay down this difference, for it not only leads to limiting the field in which the infallible magisterium of the church may be exercised, as we have seen,[18] but it also relativizes things in which ordinary people believe, as remote as such things might be from the foundation of Christian faith. In response, ecumenism, if it is really characterized by dialogue, introduces this principle of relativization, all the more so to the extent that what is called tradition is made up of an inextricable mixture of divine-apostolic and human traditions, as Rahner has shown.

Fourth, and finally, it is worth noting that the Council relegated or exiled this principle on the order or hierarchy of the truths of Christian faith to the decree on ecumenism, when it should have occupied a central place in *Dei Verbum* — that is, in the constitution that deals with God's Word or revelation. My hypothesis, already set forth theoretically in the first section in this chapter, is that there is still no realization that this is much more important than streamlining the church's dogmatic burden for the sake of dialogue. We must restore to God's ongoing revelation its character as historic experience, since "revelation can take place only to the extent that free and conscious human subjectivity appropriates in history God's manifestation."[19]

Keeping in mind these observations, we can now probe the passage that prompted them for the elements that constitute a true *evangelization*. I find three:

Only the Substance of Christian Faith

The task we are speaking about here is only easy, or seems so, when it is stated in abstract terms. In reality, the aim is to present Christianity to each person in such a way that by its very content, by its inherent value, it may lead to a personal acceptance in that person, one that is sometimes heroic and always truly internalized, and intended to be put to the test in the challenges of history.

Why is this difficult? Because it represents a journey, one that first entails untying whatever binds. From what is routine and not thought about, from what is passively accepted and only minimally comprehended, we must journey to the heart of the Christian message, to its essence, its source. As startling as the answer might be, How many Christians today have made that journey? Previously this journey used to be unnecessary thanks to the social machinery which made one generation after another Christian in most countries that went through the Middle Ages. During that time generations were brought into Christianity, and so each person did not have to go to the source of the message and opt for it.

Today we no longer live in that kind of Christian world, and it is enough to engage in the least dialogue with a non-Christian to find that the other person understands neither the issues, nor the ideas, and often not even the words. In the past this happened to no less than Paul himself when he sought to evangelize the Athenians and used the expression "universal resurrection" in the formula with which he wanted to focus the substance of Christian faith for his hearers. Hence the great temptation that hangs over us today is that of returning to the "ghetto," to those who speak our language. Faced with the challenge of creating formulas that, as in former times, carry an intelligible and acceptable message, Christians go back to the tiny closed circle where everyone knows what a particular word, idea, or formula means — or they think they do.

There is, however, much more to the first aspect of evangelization here being examined. If the principle of the order or hierarchy of Christian truths, so frequently mentioned here and present in the Vatican II decree on ecumenism is to be taken seriously, how many Christians could line up the things they believe in different categories in accordance with that hierarchy?

Strange as it may seem, mature Christians who are creative in the fields in which they carry out their responsibilities would be hard pressed, even with the New Testament in hand, to indicate the formulas used by the synoptics, the letter to the Galatians, or the letter to the Hebrews to communicate the very core of Christian faith. I am not proposing this exercise in order to come up with ready-made formulas which were made for a context which was qualitatively light years removed from our own two thousand years later.

By contrast, these same Christians who do not know how Christian faith was expressed in the first century think they know (perhaps correctly, perhaps not) why Protestants and Catholics split apart sixteen centuries later. Indeed, those who instructed them in their faith did not think it was risky that they be ignorant of the substance of Christian faith, but they did think there was a danger that they might become Protestant if they were unaware of information that in fact could be supplied.

Generally, when Christians are required to observe the main feasts of the liturgical cycle each year, or are prepared to receive the various sacraments, or listen to the topics of preaching on Sunday, it is *assumed* that since they already possess what is essential, they are ready for things which in Seumois's words should be called (not false but) overloaded, accidental, or superfluous (perhaps not in themselves, but certainly when what is fundamental does not require them).

Indeed, speaking of dogma, should those who set out into the world bearing the gospel, quite unaware of the existence of purgatory, the blessed Trinity, the two natures and one person in Jesus Christ, original sin, the Immaculate Conception, Mary's perpetual virginity, or papal infallibility, be regarded as incomplete Christians or as not really Christian?

I am not saying, let me make it clear, that these dogmas are not really dogmas or are not true. I am trying to show that only a long, very long, educational process could prove to me why Jesus' proclamation in the synoptics "believe in the good news: the reign of God is at hand" leads to the conclusion, based on crises and much experience, that we cannot accept this proclamation without likewise believing in those other matters. I am also trying to show that while it can be shown, I believe, that such was the case for some of those dogmas, some of the others, far from helping people discover the meaning of human existence through a profound experience, are actually a hindrance to such discovery. That is true even if all of the dogmas are true. Hasty pedagogy and a retarded existential experience are not the product of errors, but of truths set at the wrong point in the development process of human minds.

As Humanizing Good News

As we move to this second element inherent in any genuine evangelization, we must avoid the kind of misunderstanding that might follow from assuming that these elements follow one after another. Logic itself and a careful reading of the passage on which we are commenting shows that at least in the case of the first two elements they are *simultaneously* constitutive of evangelization.

Indeed, if God's self-revelation takes place through the very nature of things, "in the fulfillment of the human being," the principle that the truths in which Christians believe stand at different distances from the core of their faith has very concrete consequences. The first is that the hierarchy of truths, which is in effect for God's manifestation, is likewise in effect for the liberation and humanizing of human beings. What God says of God's self must be at the same time a light, in the words of the passage being discussed, that elevates the meaning of human existence by rendering it more human.

On this point a sociologist or anthropologist may be more useful for our reflection than theology itself, since its conclusions are based on the way it has developed. I am referring to the way we must move beyond Rahner, as I have said before, when for the sake of ecumenism he proposes a return to the dogmas accepted by all Christians in the early ecumenical councils.

Even if Christians today were to come to such unanimous agreement, there would be no assurance that they had assimilated the issues of the early centuries of the church into their own deepest experience: how to live a meaningful human life. *In theology* no one can doubt that Paul's statement that "the good news of God about his Son ... [is] that Jesus Messiah [was] constituted *Son of*

God with power, by his resurrection from among the dead," is both the very substance of Christian faith and good news.

That is *in theology*, however. What happens, if instead of asking a theologian we consult a sociologist or anthropologist about the same matter? In that case, the question might be: For what kind of expectation, for what level of development of human experience, for what crisis of meaning, is Paul's statement a piece of "good news," as he himself claims?

If the question has to do with people today, the answer one would probably receive is that Paul's statement, in the way he put it into language, would hardly be humanizing good news for anyone at all. Why? To begin with, because very few people are familiar with the "story" of this Jesus, and lacking that, to know that the one bearing that name is or is not Son of God can only reflect a kind of information of an instrumental sort. Such information might state which divinity really has saving power, but that has no relation, at least directly, with any experience of meaning that enriches and sheds light on our existence.

Of course to the extent that these gaps are filled and more specific details on the life of Jesus are provided, the situation can change a great deal. As an example, let us take what sociological research tells us about what most ordinary Christians know about Jesus: Jesus died on the cross out of love for human beings and in order to gain their forgiveness or redemption. Here besides "instrumental" information, we find something referring to the meaning of existence: love and how important humans are to God, so important that God sacrifices him whom the resurrection has shown to be God's Son. However, one could just as logically draw a different conclusion: the monstrous character of human sin which requires nothing less than the (excruciating) death of the Son of God. This answer also has an existential "meaning," although it is far from being "good news" and tends in its experiential logic to make the human being someone who is terrified before the malevolent power of a freedom that arrives at such ruin (which the resurrection only half-way redeems). From our standpoint here, one would be facing an existential situation, but not one that by itself was good news. As in the case of the expression, "Christ died for our sins," evangelization can only be such when it has drawn the human being out of this crisis experience.

Thus we see that the same item can be interpreted differently in accordance with the level of experience one has reached. A God of love is not compatible with a being who can be offended to the point of having to sacrifice his Son in order to remain at peace with himself and be reconciled with the one offending, without slighting justice. Yet the church certainly does not seem to be concerned about the possibility of causing such a trauma, as long as people "believe" in the crucified Jesus Christ as Son of God.

I am going to try to go a little further in this vital logic, even though it is just an example. If what is missing in the story of Jesus, known only partially, is filled out a little more, in order to identify this Jesus who is constituted Son of God through the resurrection, the Christian believer may recall the proclamation around which the public life or ministry was focused: "The time is fulfilled. The kingdom (= reign, government) of God is at hand. Be converted and believe in (this) good news."

Now I pick up at random one of the missals produced as a result of the postconciliar liturgical reform. On the day when this reading appears (which in this missal is the first Monday of "ordinary time" when the Gospel of Mark [1:14–15] is being read), the first prayer, summing up the liturgy of the day, is addressed to (and to some extent defines) God with these words: "Almighty God, you who govern both heaven and earth." I do not know if I will annoy readers—and I beg their indulgence—by asking them a question: Could one really address God in this way if the prayer came right after the passage in Mark? And if another portion of the Gospel, this time from Matthew, were put forth, and one were to address God with the prayer Jesus himself taught his disciples: "May your kingdom come. (That is,) may your will be (finally!) done on earth as (it is already done) in heaven"?

What am I trying to say? Something very simple. If I were celebrating Mass in one of the small communities I accompany, my friends would stop me after that prayer, and would ask me, "Do you really believe that God governs both earth and heaven?" They would do so not just because we share a great deal of trust and friendship, but because it is very much an integral part of their living experience that the earth, as it is, does not reflect what God loves, but largely what God hates. If we translate Irenaeus's expression into the negative form, God's dishonor is the human being who dies, poor, oppressed, starving. The resurrection of Jesus is the answer I receive in the faith that God authorizes with "power," although not yet visibly, the proclamation that the reign of God is knocking at the door.

However, passive Christians, alone and anonymous in the crowd, can be told at the same time that God governs and does not govern the earth, and that what they see is God's will and what they see is what God spurns in horror. They accept both things because they do not experience them as the reason, the joy, and the very meaning of their life. They do not put up any resistance when they are told that "revelation is something 'outside' humankind and has to be put 'into' it"[20] through faith, since many people in the church understand things in that manner, as a result of the way Christians have been taught.

When on the other hand, human beings take on God's revelation in a creative way, its logic comes to permeate everything. That time-honored prayer is rejected not because it is false that God governs the entire universe, but rather because such a way of understanding seems childish to one who has seriously and enthusiastically lived the bold enterprise of Jesus and his commitment to God's plan.

Moreover, revelation continues to uncover for us the secrets of our existential experience. For although revelation (or better the deposit of revelation) ends with Christ, Christ has not ended.[21] He is completed and completes the reign of God, making use of us. That is why, thanks to a dogma that moves forward, Christians can understand that the humanizing good news of the resurrection of Jesus consists in the fact that if he was constituted Son of God in power, we his brothers and sisters are likewise made children in him. And if we are children, we are heirs of the universe, of an incomplete universe that we must draw out of futility thanks to the creative freedom that has been granted us freely (see Rom. 8). There is no longer room for the fear of the slave, but rather for the confident freedom of the son and daughter.

At a Pace in Which What Is Essential Remains Such

Nevertheless, returning to dogma, its experiential character cannot be simply a matter of watching over the number of truths in which one must believe. Streamlining dogma is undoubtedly necessary, but it is no more than a condition. The aim is that this whole Jesus, who does not stop growing with the revelation that accompanies new historical contexts succeeding one another, not be disconnected from the existential search for the meaning for living.

Earlier I indicated that the proposal to go back to a point where everyone was together at the same point on the road was not enough. In connection with the Old Testament I had already shown that going from one stage to another did not mean that all of Israel moved from one conception of God to another that was richer and more mature. Many remained with the previous conception or conceptions. Jesus' disciples, for example, on one occasion ask him (according to John), "Rabbi, who sinned, this man or his parents, that he should have been born blind?" On another occasion, when the Samaritans have refused to grant them lodging, they ask, "Lord, do you want us to call fire down on them to consume them?" (as Elijah did). From the tenor of these questions it would seem that the disciples had not undergone the experiences that led to the book of Job, or that of Ecclesiastes or of Wisdom.

Jesus clearly does not decide to wait centuries to admonish or correct these backward disciples. In earlier chapters when I spoke of the "pedagogues in a hurry" giving solutions to problems not yet raised, I had in mind those who systematically offer information without bearing in mind the vital issues their hearers are facing, therefore depriving them of any effort to assess what the situation itself is saying to them. That, however, does not mean that people cannot "prudently" be helped to get through stages more rapidly than they would just by letting time pass.

In this connection Paul provides indications that are very much on the mark, due to the special context in which his evangelizing labor unfolds. He acquired his title as the "apostle of the gentiles," as we know, for his effort, which the whole church sustained, to make converted pagans full-fledged Christians without having to go through the "law of Moses" — that is, through the whole educational process to which the Old Testament bears witness.

How does he bring it about that the proclamation of the good news of the gospel is introduced to his hearers as something vital, linked to experience, without which there is actually no revelation of God to the human being? We know that in one way or another he sought in pagan culture points of contact with biblical experiences, for even without going into the problem of whether there is any "universal revelation of God" outside biblical revelation, it was obvious that his pagan hearers did not begin from scratch their search for meaning in their lives.

It is not these correlations, however, that concern me here. Speaking of adult pagans (not of children, who, as I have already noted, are a separate issue) he addresses the Corinthians and reminds them of the beginning of the dialogue of evangelization: "Brothers, the trouble was that I could not talk to you as spiritual men but only as men of flesh [that is, as creatures who had not yet received the "spirit" of Jesus], as *infants* in Christ. I fed you with milk, and did not give you solid food because you were not ready for it" (1 Cor. 3:1). Through other passages of Paul from this same period in Galatians and Romans we know that this crucial and profound point was connected to the proclamation of Christian freedom—or, as I stated in the previous section, to the fact that with Christ we are made children of God, heirs in his creative task, masters of the universe, so as to be able to imprint upon it endeavors that may place it at the service of love and humanization.

In a long section of the letter to the Romans, Paul gives a glimpse of his experience of how in the Christian community believers who are still weak in the faith are living alongside others who have a full and mature faith. On the very question of freedom he teaches:

> Extend a kind welcome to those who are weak in faith. Do not enter into disputes with them [that is, do not discuss what *everyone* must do]. [For] man of sound faith knows he can eat anything, while one who is weak in faith eats only vegetables. The man who will eat anything must not ridicule him who abstains from certain foods; the man who abstains must not sit in judgment on him who eats ... Who are you to pass judgment on another's servant? His master alone can judge whether he stands or falls [in this process]. And stand he will, for the Lord is able to make him stand [in his crises]. [Rom. 14:1–4]

We might ask, however, whether what seems feasible to Paul in a small community is really possible in a church of vast numbers. Although Paul does not see how anyone can be a Christian without being on the way toward this maturity which assimilates and internalizes the experience of the liberating core of Christian faith, how can the journey of each person be accompanied without running the risk of being a scandal or stumbling block to the experience of other people who are at another stage? How can one avoid the extremes of returning to the law or disorienting chaos—and in both cases the loss of that revelation which becomes experience?

Only small communities where people know one another and share their experiences can bring back this character of God's ongoing revelation thanks to the Spirit of Christ who journeys with us and leads us to all truth. The base communities (especially in the generic sense Medellín uses to designate primary communities in which the entire church must be "based") can bring back to dogma its humanizing character, not by offering simple recipes but by undergoing the experience of crisis and the solutions that enrich and deepen experience.

I am not sure—and this I regard as something to be discussed—to what extent any community within a people which is regarded, and regards itself, as Christian, can covert its search for the substance of the Christian faith into experience-based reflection, or whether certain situations force communities to begin the search from pre-Christian contexts. In the previous section I offered the example of a community that goes into crisis when, after becoming deeply aware of the meaning of God's displeasure with what is happening on earth, it decides to assume the governance or reign it had previously relinquished to others, and now hears the (pre-Christian, Old Testament) "opinion" that God is already governing both heaven and earth.

It may be that a community living on the edge of survival may not yet have the capability for reflection so as to perceive the contradiction and turn it into a crisis, and then emerge with a deeper and richer revelation of the Christian message. It may even be the case that they think they are emerging from this crisis with an error. However, it would be even worse if by passively accepting scattered and contradictory bits of information, believers were to lose the experiential character (and hence the existential logic) of the message of Christ.

In other words, the danger of the Christian community going off track will always be less than is the case when divine revelation is suppressed and Christians are submerged in a multitude where under the guise of a superficial equality, everything is given free rein.

Hope at Last

These admittedly scanty and insufficient practical observations serve to repeat in a more immediate and practical language the elements that made up the theoretical summary in the first part of this final chapter.

In this book I have sought to show how all theology's tools and aids have been converging toward a kind of dogma that constitutes a platform for liberative human seeking and divine revelation. I also sought to show how a church that seriously intends to reevangelize its people and now possesses communities where without haste people are experiencing the journey of faith and where what is essential ever remains so — offers every reason for hope.

Vatican II opened the doors for us and left us on the threshold from which we are to journey without rushing, but also without becoming discouraged.

Notes

1. A Foreword That Isn't

1. I am not referring to the mental or epistemological structure in which these three operations follow logically in any theoretical and practical process, which is quite unobjectionable. Rather I have in mind a device which is unfortunately quite widespread in reflection—or nonreflection—groups. The device consists in going through these steps in every session in relation to a problem that has been observed and selected from practice as the "problem of the day" and made to serve for a group examination [revisión de vida].

2. Thus, for example, no one would try to discover in half an hour what reply the Christian message could offer to a question as crucial for commitment as the following: What perspectives can believers in Jesus Christ have for being able to devise politically a classless society in solidarity?

3. Within this search for meaning, when other kinds of questions ("Do you know Hebrew?" or "Doesn't this seem to be against the teaching authority of the church?") arise (too) quickly, experience shows that people are not really seeking a deeper scholarly treatment of the issue, but are expressing indirectly and courteously that they do not find interesting what the theologian has to say.

4. That is, when the creed speaks of the proceeding of the Holy Spirit, the so-called orthodox, unlike "Catholics," do not add "and from the Son" (= Filioque) after the words "who proceeds from the Father."

5. In this regard it is often said—with a good deal of exaggeration but not without some basis—that a moral theologian can justify any moral choice.

6. That is why today there is still discussion over whether Jesus had two self-awarenesses—two selves—one divine and the other human. Some theology manuals make a claim that is strange to our modern ears, although it is materially faithful to the christological councils: that Jesus had two *freedoms* (!). Readers whose centuries-old culture has accustomed them to regarding both terms as coextensive or synonymous will ask how one *person* can have *two* freedoms. The reason is that gradual spread of personalism has shifted the notion of freedom from being regarded as a part of rational nature (where the ancients placed it, since they saw freedom as a property of the will or the ability to desire) to the very center of the category of person. Hence, from the condemnation of the *monothelites* who said that Jesus had only one will, theologians drew the conclusion that he had to have two freedoms, one for his divine will and the other for his human will.

7. See Evelyn Waugh's great novel, *Brideshead Revisited*.

8. This is actually the same problem as dying without the last sacraments. Dying in the state of mortal sin and dying outside the church had the same eternal punishment (D. 693 and 714), because both cases fell under the same principle:

outside the church there is no salvation. A person in the "state of moral sin" was outside the *communion* of the church, since he or she was a member (through baptism) but dead (through sin). Strictly speaking, *ex*communion is nothing but a punishment that impedes (with unusually severe conditions) the reconciliation of the sinner with the church through the sacrament of penance.

9. The council adds the dogmatic reason for that conclusion: *"we ought to believe"* that the Holy Spirit in a manner known only to God offers to every man the possibility of being associated with this paschal mystery" (GS 22), i.e., being associated with the mystery of salvation. The emphasis is mine: it only highlights the fact that it is hard to get around the obvious dogmatic tenor of this statement, by mentioning the fact that the document on the church in the modern world is "pastoral." A statement that begins with the words "we ought to believe" cannot be "pastoral" as opposed to "dogmatic."

10. Both theologically and sociologically it is interesting to note that questions regarding the extent to which one must believe in the definitions of the magisterium generally arise in matters more directly related to faith than to morality—although those matters are related to the practical import of faith. One reason is that the lay Christian often feels competent to weigh the arguments the magisterium offers in documents for the moral positions it takes, but not those offered in the realm of systematic theology.

11. That does not mean that one should not recognize countless individual cases in which theologians (cleric and lay) have to undergo very painful problems of conscience when they begin to perceive that a formula is inadequate, without being able to attribute it to the specific limitations of a context that has not settled out yet, because it is too close. In such a case, a "reformulation" looks like relativization or negation pure and simple.

12. This affirmation can be understood only as arising from a crisis of meaning registered in books like Job and Ecclesiastes. Only after reaching this depth in seeking meaning did the two possibilities, affirmation or negation of belief in a life beyond death, begin to take shape as an alternative either/or. Even less can we say that the shift from one position to the other took place through a mere "explicitation" or development of the first (as was proposed by one now classic theological current to which this work will have to return).

13. It is just this contextual conception of a "Christian world" that gives impetus to the declaration by the council of the church that there is no salvation outside the church.

14. A residue of this distinction can be observed in the famous—and forgotten—paragraph 22 of *Gaudium et Spes*: "all men of good will in whose hearts grace works in an *unseen way*."

15. This attempt to make a distinction was met by Pius XII's encyclical *Mystici Corporis*, which insisted that the Mystical Body of Christ and the church as visible institution were the same thing, leaving no room for something broader. An example of the prudence with which theological work required to change inadequate dogmatic formulas was carried out at that time is the article Karl Rahner wrote on *Mystici Corporis*. After devoting about one hundred pages to indicating his overall agreement with the encyclical, in the last two or three pages he indicated that he disagreed with the narrowness of applying the concept of "Mystical Body" only to Christians who belong visibly to the ecclesiastical institution (see Karl Rahner, *Theological Investigations*, vol. II).

16. One of the theological currents present within Vatican II diverted the obvious broader meaning of "People of God" giving it a more restricted sense, and making it cover only the visible members of the Catholic Church. But that device no longer worked after a universalizing statement such as that in *Gaudium et Spes*, 22.

17. As an example of the attitude which at that time was opposed to all dialogue, see the entries under "communism" in the index of the Spanish translation of that encyclical: ignores eternal goods, truth, and justice, n. 2; principles, fruits, and doctrine of communism, n. 5; communism's false ideal, n. 5; does not admit difference between spirit and matter, n. 5; Marxist materialism founded, n. 5; openly atheist and materialistic, n. 5; spread of communism under the pretext of improving the lot of the working classes, n. 8; disgusting and crafty methods and principles of communism, n. 8; its diabolical propaganda has spread everywhere, n. 8; diabolical persecution against the church, n. 9; individual and communist society have no internal restraint, n. 10; horrors of communism, in Russia, Spain, and Mexico, n. 14; the group has no right to impose a despotic power over individuals, n. 15; communism's insidious campaigns, n. 25; it is intrinsically perverse and one cannot collaborate with it in any field, n. 25; the pope recommends prayer and penance as a means of defense against it, n. 26; all those who believe in God should unite to struggle against it, n. 33. *Colección Completa de Encíclicas Pontificias: 1830–1950* (Buenos Aires: Editorial Guadalupe, 1952), p. 1744.

18. Here in Latin America, which is regarded as the last continent still (almost completely) Christian, the list of those who have died for justice contains ten times as many names of non-Christians as of Christians (of course I am not referring to the scarcely relevant sociological fact of whether they were baptized nor not).

19. What I mean here is that in practice, I would never expose what I have tried to express about what is central to Christian faith to the potential ecclesiastical condemnation (which a lay person would see as a blanket condemnation) that might result from my giving my theological opinion that *Humanae Vitae* is wrong. What I am doing now, I am doing after coming to think that the most central and important things are sheltered under authoritarian excesses. However, I cannot thereby shrug off an issue that is real in persons with whom I deal.

2. Myths and History

1. Unless I am mistaken, the most important and renowned Catholic theologian who takes this position today is Hans Urs von Balthasar. He begins chapter 3 of his work *Puntos Centrales de la Fe* (Spanish translation, Madrid: BAC, 1985) as follows: "Vatican Council II has been a pastoral council. The renewed image with which the church has set out again is not so much for the sake of 'faith' and 'contemplation' (nothing new has been defined, but rather to enable us to act better." The remainder of the chapter is a summary of ecclesiology based on this assumption that Vatican II did not define anything new, since its intention was pastoral. It is puzzling how pastoral activity can be renewed without parallel dogmatic renewals. Paul VI, on the other hand, speaks of the "dogmatic wealth" of Vatican II, and it is hard to reconcile that with the assertion that nothing new was defined there (unless "definition" is understood strictly as a matter of "canons and anathemas," which is not what von Balthasar means when he talks about "faith and contemplation"). Even so, the habit of associating what is dogmatic with creeds and anathemas is so great that the same Paul VI who speaks of this "dogmatic

wealth," regards Vatican II as an expression of the church's "ordinary" magisterium, even though theologians traditionally regard all the ecumenical councils (in the restricted sense that this word has had since the Eastern schism) and the *ex cathedra* definitions of the Roman pontiffs as an expression of the "extraordinary" magisterium. Is the pope's shifting usage due only to the shift in literary genre?

2. In this and the remaining examples from the Bible, I will offer the reader only what seem to me to be the most well-established conclusions of contemporary exegesis. Given the very broad and uneven literature on this material and the nature of this book, there is no other way to proceed. Readers can certainly broaden their knowledge of this material (or check my own) in a variety of ways, such as reading recent reference works or critical notes in various editions of the Bible in modern languages.

3. A royal chronicler, probably of the court of Solomon (or David, according to other exegetes) who must have written between the 10th and 9th centuries B.C.E., although he passes on traditions that can be, and in fact often are, much older.

4. Priest (or priestly group) writing (what was also called the Priestly Code) during the Exile in Babylon or during the period immediately following the restoration of worship in Jerusalem. In this case as well, the traditions in question may be very ancient.

5. John L. McKenzie, *Dictionary of the Bible* (Milwaukee: Bruce, 1965), p. 189.

6. Gustave Lambert, "Il n'y aura plus jamais de déluge," *Nouvelle Revue Théologique*, t. 77, June 1955, pp. 581–601. Lambert held that this was the *main* (theological) intention of both biblical writers (Yahwist and Priestly) when they took on and changed the Mesopotamian mythical accounts of a worldwide flood. To be fair, I should add (Lambert does not deny this) that the biblical narratives had other important although secondary dogmatic elements. On some of these the two authors differ from one another. Although both are in agreement on the statement Lambert uses as a title, their very vocabulary is already a sign that they have different concerns and are writing in different periods.

7. An interesting version of the different myths of the deluge can be seen in the work of the great Latin American novelist Alejo Carpentier, in *Tierra del Tiempo* (Barcelona: Barral, 1970). In a novel written in his youth he also describes very forcefully the mythical—pre-Enlightenment—attitude of people who have not reached the secularizing and humanizing *dogma* that a new deluge is impossible.

8. Among other things, there is the fact that the manifestation of Yahweh on Sinai is not among the historical events the creed relates. It would have been logical to include it after the Yahwist and Elohist documents, which were in use in both the Southern and the Northern Kingdoms (see Gerhard von Rad, *Old Testament Theology* [New York: Harper & Row, 1962], vol. 1, pp. 121ff.).

9. As in the previous example, we find here as background one feature of what is "dogmatic" that we have already observed: that it is an identity. Whoever is not willing to be identified with this history as narrated, expels himself or herself—anathema—from the people of Yahweh.

10. Von Rad, *Old Testament Theology*, vol. 1, p. 122.

11. Ibid., p. 125.

12. The fact that there is no specific literary genre for "theology" in the ancient literature of Israel does not constitute an exception.

13. Speaking very generally the following items are commonly acknowledged to be historical: "Aramean" (or according to some due to a very natural anachronism,

Mesopotamian) origins of Israel's ancestors; early nomadism; captivity of (some) Israelites by Egypt; identification of "the God of our fathers" with Yahweh during the stay in Egypt (or a little later); an exodus or several of them; occupation of the land of Canaan (largely through peaceful means—that is, through infiltration, although in some cases through battle).

14. The wonders of the plagues which open the way for the Exodus (although some of them may be an exaggerated presentation of events that are relatively common in Egypt; defeat [likewise exaggerated] of Egyptians pursuing them in the "Sea of Reeds"; attribution of the "gift" of Canaan to Yahweh; description of Palestine [and even Judah] as a "country flowing with milk and honey").

15. On this problem of faith, of the punctuation of sequences of events which becomes "experience" with its corresponding "transcendent data," see my work *Jesus of Nazareth Yesterday and Today* (vol. I, *Faith and Ideologies* [Maryknoll, N.Y.: Orbis Books, 1984], Part 1), which deals with methodology. Here I want to say that a datum does not transcend its insignificant particularity unless in some way it falls under an ought-to-be, to which it is assumed that reality as a whole must be subject. For human beings whatever imposes an ought-to-be must be a *will*, a wanting, and our minds associate any will or wanting with a personal being. To speak of an impersonal will would be a contradiction in terms.

16. We have here a sequence that becomes so familiar to us that when something especially painful happens we ask ourselves "But what did I do?" "Why is God punishing me like this?"

17. In other words, if this sequence had to be reduced to an abstract formula, it would go: evil event + several seemingly chance events = good event. Period— because that is where the sequence *ends*. We will see it reappear when we find ourselves again facing the first item in the sentence: evil event. It should be noted that it is not by chance that I have used two common sayings as examples. The fact is that such sayings generally reflect "popular wisdom" in the sense that they are sequences that have been "verified" in the memory of the people and are then commonly used to interpret what happens.

18. Knowledge of the older traditions can help add another (and certainly significant) element to both sequences. Yahweh's protection seems to vanish to the extent that Israel is corrupted (crime of Joseph's brothers; greater attachment to what they had under slavery both before and after the exodus). A single individual who is faithful to Yahweh and an invocation of his power (in repentance) are enough to bring about God's saving intervention (Joseph, Moses, etc.).

19. Compare von Rad: "Jahweh was, however, to have further dealings with Israel; he did not intend to withdraw from her history because of this failure." A little further on, he states that the prophets "believed that salvation could only come if Jahweh arose to perform new acts upon Israel, an event which they looked on as certain—and they entreated those who were still able to hear not to put their trust in illusory safeguards (Mic. 3:11), but to 'look to' what was to come, and to take refuge in Jahweh's saving act, which was near at hand. The prophets were therefore the first men in Israel to proclaim over and over again and on an ever widening basis that salvation comes in the shadow of judgment. It is only this prediction of a near divine action, with its close relation to old election traditions and its bold new interpretation of them, which can properly be defined as eschatological . . . They were sure . . . that beyond the judgment, by means of fresh acts, Jahweh would establish salvation; and their paramount business was to declare

these acts beforehand, and not simply to speak about hope and confidence" (*Old Testament Theology*, vol. 2, pp. 182, 185–86). All exegetes acknowledge the prophetic influence on Deuteronomy. The "creed" in it identifies every Israelite with this emerging hope.

20. *Old Testament Theology*, vol. 1, p. 231.

3. Process and Truth

1. Despite the fact that what has been said about the writers shows that they brought to the account a way of punctuating events proper to the stage of their theological reflection, they are not regarded as true literary *authors* without reason. It is not a question of their having knowledge of facts more reliably than others.

2. It is interesting to point out how seriously early paleontologists in the infancy of their science sought fossil remains of a universal deluge, and indeed thought they had found them, when they found deposits from the ocean floor on what is now dry land.

3. This reflection actually leads the psalmist to imagine a sequence (in accordance with the "redundancy" with which God moves history) in which God is, as it were, asleep and allows events to go on for a while without intervening in them (to make them fit the morality of human beings). This goes on until God finally awakens from sleep and wipes out the wicked (Ps. 73:17ff.). Such an unsatisfactory solution could not last, at least on a certain level of thought. The (new) theology resulting from the book of Job (among others) dashes it to the ground and the theological problem of the just who suffer then takes on its true dimension. Nevertheless we should note that here as well as any place that there is question of stages of a dogmatic process in the Old Testament, we should not think that *all* Israel passes, as though impelled by a spring, from one notion to the other. Among ordinary people, the problem posed by suffering has still not been influenced by the theology of Job: if we are to believe John 9:2, the disciples ask Jesus about a man born blind. "Rabbi, was it his sin or that of his parents that caused him to be born blind?"

4. Correcting what is said in the text, it could be said that people have taken advantage the other way around—namely, as a convincing argument for the need to put Christian theology back into the literary form of story (although story is by no means the only literary genre in the Bible). The notion is to rescue literary procedures that are much more fit for bearing an incarnate faith, which otherwise tends to become as abstract as academic theology—that is, a sterilized and weak second act. See in this regard, J. B. Metz, *Faith in History and Society* (New York: Seabury Press, 1980, esp. chap. 12).

5. The very fact that one opts for punctuations applying only to one country (one's own) or to the whole continent will lead to different meanings and a different kind of historical consciousness.

6. Readers may already be aware of the effort to *rethink* on this second level of *the history of history* (or "metahistory") the series of events marking the presence of the Church in Latin America. Brought together in the group known as CEHILA, historians are engaging in this task, taking the viewpoint of the continent's most oppressed, Indians and slaves, as the unifying thread of this *metahistory*.

7. It is not easy to overcome such sloth and move up to a different level, for in most cases it is not really a matter of sloth but of ideological connivance. Certain

interpretations are connected to certain self-interested uses of history—not necessarily in the bad sense (although uncritical use will always be bad)—no matter how much such interests might be presented as sacred. Thus so-called salvation history in the Bible is nothing but one among numerous ways of organizing the mosaic of events (without daring to organize the mosaic of interpretations). It is just that *this* way, and only this way, is seen as sacred. This is the way which in principle leads to—and gets its full meaning from—Jesus, and hence it produces a *New* Testament, the meaning and (perhaps too easy) recapitulation of the *Old* Testament. In the epilogue to his beautiful book *A Theology of the Old Testament* (New York: Doubleday, 1974), John McKenzie has a sentence that may carry a good deal of *boutade*, but is also backed up by serious arguments: "In a review I agreed with Franz Hesse that it is time to say goodbye to *Heilsgeschichte*."

8. Later, with the aid of biblical examples, we will take up the escape mechanisms people have and use to maintain a previous punctuation of events, even when "reality" seems to render it invalid. Readers, however, will be aware that a pessimist sees a "half-empty" glass, where an optimist sees one "half-full." Furthermore, a pessimist receiving an apple as a reward after many experiences will figure it is rotten (or is meant to undermine his or her diet); if it turns out not to be rotten, it may still be blamed for the indigestion that comes a week later.

9. The Old Testament—and even the New—continually uses anthropomorphic expressions in reference to God. It is obvious that in earlier times some of these expressions were not regarded as metaphorical (for example, Gen. 4:14). The Greek idea of God as a purely spiritual being, in the sense of lacking material body (in later times since the Homeric gods and even those of the tragedies are corporeal) is not proper to the Hebrew Bible. The biblical authors sometimes use a certain corporeal language as a metaphor of Yahweh. When the Israelites in the desert build the statue of a bull and adore it, they are not adoring another god but Yahweh. They do so not because they think God really has a bull's body but because that is a metaphorical expression of power and fecundity: a symbol. The sin of the golden calf was not a matter of adoring another god, but of building and adoring an image of Yahweh; they did not sin against the first commandment of the decalogue but against the second. That did not prevent them from thinking of Yahweh as having a body like that of a human being. See McKenzie, *Dictionary*, p. 35: "the use of anthropomorphisms is the primary factor in the Hebrew conception of God as a living person."

10. See, for example, Ps. 6:5–6: "Return, O Lord, save my life: rescue me because of your kindness, For *among the dead no one remembers you; in the nether world who gives you thanks?*" One reason why the Catholic church kept its members from reading the Bible as long as it could in the past thus becomes clear. When the Reformation (and the printing press) opens Bible reading to all believers and at least in theory maintains that every Christian has a right to examine it freely in the light of the Spirit, two characteristic results of this shift are soon observable. On the one hand, the stable Protestant churches are very soon organized, or better reorganized around a less overt but still effective orthodox way of interpreting the Bible. On the other hand, wherever, due to the context, this structure does not work well—as in the conquest of the American West and among slaves in the South—private Bible reading leads to a dogmatic explosion, a point fascinatingly confirmed in American literature. The Old Testament in particular is found to provide religious justification for almost anything.

11. *Old Testament Theology*, vol. 1, p. 211. Even the careful Jerusalem Bible in a note on the passage cited by von Rad, writes that the "great anger" unleashed against the Israelites who were struggling against Moab was due to Chemosh, according to most exegetes. On polytheism in the religion of the patriarchs, cf. R. de Vaux, *Histoire ancienne d'Israël. Des origines à l'installation en Canaan* (Paris: Gabalda, 1971), p. 260.

12. The very term "idolatry" (adoration of images = idols) and especially the ironic way that Yahweh, previously jealous of worship of other gods, after the exile begins to speak of idols, evidences the beginning of strict monotheism in Israel. In passing it should be said that the *bene Elohim* (Gen. 6:2f. as well as the plural in 1:26, etc.) raise the issue of a kind of "heavenly court." That problem cannot be sidestepped simply by calling these divine beings "angels": "son" is a metaphor used for beings of the same or a similar nature, which in this case would be the divine nature.

13. One of these reasons was that, if there was no other life, it little mattered that the wicked man "would end up badly" or in ruin, if during the intervening period, the only one that had any substance to it, he had enjoyed all the advantages. Ending well or ill is not so important, if the ending itself is absolute. Here one could argue with the well-known tango line: Who can take away what I have danced?

14. The theory of the (intrinsic) development of dogma, associated with Newman and the Tübingen school, held that dogma developed through deduction, by making explicit what was already implicitly present in what had been previously defined or was in the Bible (see Hans Küng, *Infallible? An Inquiry* [New York: Doubleday, 1971], pp. 53f.).

15. Küng, *Infallible?*, pp. 57–58.

16. In other words in his book I find no middle ground or alternative path between the theory of the "development" of dogma (from implicit to explicit) and the timeless theory: true formula vs. erroneous formula. What has been said here thus far on the Bible was an effort to get away from this impoverishment of what in actuality amounts to journeying toward the truth, or in the particular case of the magisterium, guiding toward it. Gregory Baum offers a similar judgment, although it is perhaps shaded in a more highly conceptual form: "Here as well as other places in his book, Hans Küng is moving away from a highly conceptual understanding of truth, to a more realistic description of what vital truth is. Unfortunately, he never concentrates on this question" (in John Kirvan [ed.], *The Infallibility Debate* [New York: Paulist Press, 1971], p. 6).

17. In case the reader has not perceived it yet, it is important to note that despite the great degree of freedom the compiler of the psalms enjoyed, he did not think it was necessary or perhaps even permissible to correct those places where the residue of a now superseded theological past still remained. He simply left things as they were: "whatever the just man does prospers"; "never have I seen a just man forsaken, nor his descendants begging bread."

18. This practice or custom is difficult to trace but it must have existed from very early times in Israel. It seems to be based on "schools of *midrash*," or of searching, which used books regarded as sacred in order to read them in the present with benefit and edification. Thus exegetes regard the Priestly source of the Pentateuch or the author of Chronicles to be examples of *midrash*, and more particularly of *haggadah* — that is, of an "explanation of the narrative passages ... with an extremely wide scope of edifying lessons ... it is a meditation on the sacred text or

an imaginative reconstruction of the scene and episode narrated. Its goal is always the practical application to the present; thus a precept may be restated [*halakhah*] or an episode retold [*haggadah*], not in the terms of its own historical context, but in such a way that it gives light and direction to the generation which writes the *midrash*" (McKenzie, *Dictionary*, pp. 574–75).

19. The best exegetes are divided over whether the deluge should be attributed directly or indirectly to what is recounted in Gen. 6:1–5. Von Rad writes that "a still greater catastrophe had taken place. The Elohim-beings of the upper world of God had intercourse with human kind, and this brought about a fresh impairment of the orders of creation which Yahweh had imposed upon mankind. This catastrophe was more serious than any of the previous ones, since it was much more than something which concerned the world of man alone; now the boundary between man and the heavenly beings was thrown down. In face of this degeneration of his Creation, Yahweh resolved to annihilate mankind in the judgment of the Flood" (*Old Testament Theology*, vol. 1, pp. 155–56). E. Dhorme (in his French translation of the Bible) and the Jerusalem Bible make the sin of the "angels" more a prologue to the deluge than a cause of it: "example of the increasing human malice that is to provoke the Deluge" (Jerusalem Bible, note on the text). The reason for separating to a degree the sin of the angels from the motive for the flood is that the former already brings its own punishment for human beings—namely, that they must die at least by the age of one hundred twenty years.

20. As was indicated above in note 12 of this chapter with regard to polytheism, the "sons of Elohim" (which later monotheism neutralizes by treating them as "angels") were literally divine beings and as such were part of Yahweh's court (see the opening of the book of Job). That is probably the justification for the strange plural with which Yahweh decides to create the human being: "let us make . . ." When man sins in the garden of Eden, God ironically (?) comments on the result of this sin: "he has become one of *us*" (see G. Lambert, "Le drame du jardin d'Eden," in *Nouvelle Revue Théologique*, November 1954, pp. 1057–64).

21. Von Rad, *Old Testament Theology*, vol. 1, p. 156.

22. Even earlier we find something similar happening among the people when Saul tries to punish Jonathan with death for a similar "profanation" (see 1 Sam. 14:24–30, 36–45).

23. It cannot be validly argued that the first version had to be conserved because the kings really existed and were—some of them at least—faithful to Yahweh. That much could have been said without having to make Samuel responsible for a "divine election," as diminished as it might be in the antimonarchical version.

4. Inspiration and Inerrancy

1. On this basic and difficult issue of relations between the Old and New Testaments, see the profound observations made by John McKenzie in the closing epilogue of his work *A Theology of the Old Testament* already cited (pp. 318–25). If readers compare his observations with this chapter and the next, they will note that we are basically in agreement, although we may have certain differences over nuances. I think McKenzie goes too far on certain positions (or at least in his way of expressing them) as a reaction against the overwhelming way Christian exegesis has impoverished the Old Testament by its narrow way of using it. The effect has been to turn the Old Testament with its "prediction fulfillment, foreshadowing

revelation, allegory, typology, spiritual sense, fuller sense, or other similar techniques" (ibid., p. 324) into a kind of appendix (a prior one, if such can be said) to New Testament revelation.

2. This necessary summary like all summaries is somewhat unjust with Old Testament exegesis as practiced for centuries in the history of the church. It should be kept in mind that here we are talking about a "pastoral" usage—that is, the portion of this exegesis that reached ordinary believers. That did not prevent the practice of a much more sophisticated exegesis in certain church circles, allegorical exegesis as used by the church fathers and the New Testament writers themselves (see H. de Lubac, *Histoire et Esprit. L'intelligence de l'Ecriture chez Origène*, Paris 1950). Nevertheless, all the examples studied in the previous chapters and more generally the understanding of the Old Testament as a process of "theological" reflection which leads step by step almost to the point where Jesus and his message take up the process, is connected to comprehending the *literal sense* as understood in a way that will now be explained.

3. That order lasted a number of centuries until the liturgical reform that followed Vatican II. The reform made a significant effort to give the Old Testament reading which precedes the Gospel at Mass a more "theological" or at least more "spiritual" connection to it.

4. Emphasis mine. The reader will recall what was said about (and based on) the study of literary genres in previous chapters.

5. Of course Marcion is being quite consistent when he eliminates those works or passages in the New Testament that present Jesus as the end (in the twofold sense of terminus and culmination) of the law (for example, Mt. 5:21 previously cited, because of Mt. 5:17–20).

6. Including the book of Revelation, because of its obvious similarities with Jewish apocalyptic both in the Bible (e.g., Daniel) and in extrabiblical literature.

7. *Dictionary*, p. 120.

8. The aim in this work is not detailed scholarship but a reflection on the formation and functions of dogmas and specifically in this first part in connection with the Old Testament. Hence I do not think it worthwhile to provide detailed information here about the dates and variations of the drawing up of these lists (even to the limited extent that we know them with some assurance).

9. This "instrumentality" is regarded as all the more perfect insofar as it constrains the author and entails fewer limitations due to the "instrument."

10. Vatican II explains the fact as follows, without using the word "dictation": God "chose men and while employed by Him they made use of their powers and abilities, so that with Him acting in them and through them, they, as true authors, consigned to writing *everything and only those things which He wanted*" (DV 11, emphasis mine).

11. Observe the allusion to the "weakness" to which we must pay attention if we are to fully understand God's revelation. In biblical interpretation as in christology, "Docetism" is a radical theological deviation that is difficult to completely root out of the Christian mind.

12. The historical explanation of this seemingly strange observation by Léon-Dufour is that during the sessions of Vatican II there were heated discussions about chapter 2 of *Dei Verbum*. The Roman curia proposed a title that mentioned the "inspiration and inerrancy" of sacred scripture. Many, including X. Léon-Dufour, successfully struggled to prevent the use of the term "inerrancy" and to have it

replaced with "truth." Nevertheless, the observation made here that the result of that "victory" was more symbolic than real remains valid. On this point of the conciliar controversy, see Alois Grillmeier's contribution to H. Vorgrimmler (ed.), *Commentary on the Documents of Vatican II* (London: Burns and Oates, 1969), vol. 3.

13. I need not state how much I appreciate the intellectual honesty with which X. Léon-Dufour is struggling so that the presence of errors in the Old Testament and indeed in the whole Bible will not be ignored, and his efforts should lead to a revision of a simplistic idea of the "divine pedagogy." However, that will not help very much if it is not clear what should replace the term "inerrancy" so that I can continue to "have faith" in what the Bible says in its entirety. Hence my insistence further on in this chapter, when I comment on the principle expressed by Cardinal Lercaro that error and its correction are part of any process of deep and mature knowledge of truth. Léon-Dufour himself suffers, I think, from not having anything to replace the term "inerrancy" which he very understandably wants to abolish. When he rejects the idea that the death of Christ should be conceived as a "sacrifice" to please God, and meets the objection that such was the conception of the sacrificial death of victims in the Old Testament, he like many others feels obliged to excuse the Hebrew Bible for the many instances of sacrifices which imply that the death of animals is pleasing to God (1 Kgs. 8:62ff. and passim). He says the death of the victim did not have any meaning in Hebrew sacrifice (which is assumed to have purified this ritual idea present in all or almost all primitive peoples). What is said to be "pleasing to God" is pouring out the blood of the victims, since this blood was the life God put into humans and animals and which belonged exclusively to God. Why not say that the Old Testament moves slowly and with difficulty from primitive to more sophisticated conceptions? Indeed, if it were as he says, why not offer to God not drained animal blood, but that of living animals? I think we have here a kind of biblical "inerrancy" subconsciously internalized.

14. In his commentaries on the fourth Gospel, St. Augustine goes so far as to say the following about St. John the evangelist: "Brethren, perhaps not even John told things as they really are, but even he could only do his best; for being a man he spoke of God. *Inspired by God* certainly, but a man, nonetheless. As inspired he said something; had he not been inspired he would not have said anything. But since he was *a man* inspired, he did not say everything as it is, but rather he said what a man can say" (*In Iohannis Evangelium Tractatus*, I, 1. In *Obras de san Agustín* [Madrid: BAC, 1968], vol. 13, p. 71).

15. *Sacra Doctrina*, no. 10 (cf. *Documentation Catholique*, 1959, Col. 337ff.). Emphasis in both texts is mine. It is obvious that this conception of the intimate relationship between truth and error was neither understood nor put into practice in the church after this statement by Cardinal Lercaro or after Pius XII's address. The assumption, of course, is that the latter was really rightly understood by the former.

5. Recognizing Revelation

1. See *Jesus of Nazareth Yesterday and Today*, vol. II, *The Historical Jesus of the Synoptics* (Maryknoll, N.Y.: Orbis Books, 1985), chapter 3, pp. 28ff., and vol. 4, *The Christ of the Ignatian Exercises* (Maryknoll, N.Y.: Orbis Books, 1987), chapter 1, pp. 11–40.

2. Unfortunately the one-sidedness of a viewpoint often leads to mixing levels. That is what happens with the historic fact that Jesus was disturbed and anguished on the cross, which is attested by Mark and Matthew (Mk. 15:34 and par.) and suppressed by Luke (Lk. 23:46). Since those feelings are regarded as incompatible with the divine nature of his person, it is thought that that divine nature made present to Jesus' *human* consciousness the fact that this death (with its failure and uncertainty about the future, which are constitutive elements of an authentic human existence) would last only three days.

3. "The political activity of the prophets was of no use to the country. Nevertheless, where the monarchy had failed, they left something, living groups who gathered their oracles. The Bible was still being built and its witness was still incomplete, but the prophetic oracles *were going to constitute an important part of it.* Indeed, this prophetic action had made Israel's social structures move forward. Made state law under Josiah, it is probable that Deuteronomy, which was an important expression of the prophetic movement in laws, retained its authority among those who remained behind in the land of Palestine. Deuteronomy itself did not refer simply to morality and to 'social questions' but also dealt with purely political matters like the major institutions of the kingdom (kings, judges, levites-priests, prophets), recruitment for and conduct of war, and relationships with foreigners. Josiah's failure and the fall of the Jerusalem monarchy rendered its purely political aspect out of date. A strange thing about the prophets' political activity should be noticed: *it generally failed.* Despite this failure the disciples of the prophets were to collect their writings and *recognize their validity as 'divine Word'* " (Henri Cazelles, "Bible et politique," in *Recherches de Science Religieuse* [Oct.-Dec.] 1071, vol. 59, no. 4, pp. 518–19 and 512 [my emphasis]). It is enough to reflect that what is here called political "failure" refers to the nonfulfillment of predictions of the future made by the prophets, whether or not what they ordered was carried out, to see the problem with making such orders the direct expression of "the Word of God" dictating this to those prophets. Nevertheless—and here we have the issue with which this chapter deals—such writings were to become part of the Bible, and be "canonized" even though they contained failed predictions.

4. The formation of the "canon" was not thereby closed, since on this "Hellenic" list there were books whose canonicity was to be discussed and denied until the "Hebrew" canon was fixed vis-à-vis the Christian sacred books (which includes the Jewish books) probably around the end of the 1st century C.E.

5. Von Rad, 219ff.

6. Admittedly there is another problem—namely, that of determining to what extent this worship (especially in the North), was purely Yahwist, a syncretistic alliance of Yahwist and Baalism, or simply Baalism.

7. This is so to the extent that the (Christian) "sect" or "way" is gradually distinguished from the official Jewish religion. We know that the first Christians in Jerusalem continued to go to the temple (for a period of time that is difficult to determine, but it had to end with the destruction of the temple) and that the first preachers found it natural to go to Jewish synagogues in the diaspora until they were expelled from them as dissidents or heretics.

8. The letter to the Hebrews stands out in this respect. It is surprising, moreover, to note the "laicism" with which the first Christian communities avoid any worship terminology for their own functions and authorities, or divert it toward the exercise of mutual love. This is probably something deeper than most commentators

are ready to accept. See José María Castillo, *La Alternativa Cristiana* (Salamanca: Sígueme, 1979), pp. 239–43.

9. *Dictionary*, p. 856. For a general treatment of the internal organization of the synagogue, which is important for understanding origins of the church, see the whole article, pp. 855–56.

10. See von Rad, *Estudios sobre el Antiquo Testamento* (Salamanca: Sígueme, 1976).

11. Ibid., pp. 165–66.

12. See *Instruction on Certain Aspects of the "Theology of Liberation"* (Congregation for the Doctrine of the Faith (with the signature of Cardinal J. Ratzinger), Vatican, August 6, 1984, chap. IV.

13. In order to see to what extent, historically speaking, the assertion of canonicity does not depend on any visible criterion that would prove "inspiration" but rather the reverse, the Jerusalem Bible, after noting the wide variety of interpretations given to this book (precisely because it does not speak about God) adds that "doubts in Jewish circles of the 1st century A.D. were ... *settled by an appeal to tradition*" (my emphasis). Following the purely theological argument (examined in the previous chapter) doubts should have been dispelled by an appeal to *inspiration*.

14. For the following material on Ecclesiastes and Proverbs, see W. Zimmerli, "The Place and Limit of the Wisdom in the Framework of the Old Testament Theology," in *Studies in Ancient Israelite Wisdom*, James L. Crenshaw, ed. (New York: KTAV), pp. 314–26 and 175–207.

15. Although it is not made explicit, from all that has been said it is clear that for establishing canonicity and the criteria for it, there is no clearly defined line separating profane topics from "sacred" (or theological) topics. Zimmerli indicates this indirectly when he speaks of the way Proverbs deals with the issue of *death*. He shows how in Proverbs the problem of death is not its *what* but its *when*. In itself death is not a problem for the wise. The problem is how to avoid bringing about a premature death through foolish behavior (see "Concerning ...", pp. 190ff.). He goes on to show how the issue is deepened in Qoheleth. This deepening leads to the emergence of a deeper and more radical wisdom question. During the intertestamental period the book of Wisdom will try to respond to that question with the (explicitly theological and religious) idea of a life after death where God judges and fully exercises divine justice. It is only in this manner that the chasm separating the theology of Ecclesiastes and that of the Pharisees in the time of Jesus can be bridged.

16. Edward Schillebeeckx, *Christ: the Experience of Jesus as Lord* (New York: Crossroad, 1981), pp. 68–69. I think I can cite this passage as a perfect expression of the solution given here to the "theological" problem of whether "inspiration" precedes "canon" or vice versa.

6. Retrospective Summary and Evaluation

1. The reader may consult a brief schematic essay of what such a history of the theological process of the Old Testament might be in part 1 ("Etapas pre-cristianas de la fe") of my book *Qué es un cristiano* (Montevideo: Mosca, 1971), or in a slightly different version cut down to what is most essential in chapter 6 ("Lo cristiano dentro del proceso bíblico") of vol. 3 of the second edition of my work *Teología Abierta* (Madrid: Cristiandad, 1984).

2. The dogmatic definition approved by Vatican Council I says that "the Roman Pontiff, when he speaks *ex cathedra*, that is, when carrying out the duty of the pastor and teacher of all Christians in accord with his supreme apostolic authority he explains a doctrine of faith or morals to be held by the universal Church, through the divine assistance promised him in blessed Peter, operates with that infallibility with which the divine Redeemer wished that His church be instructed in defining doctrine on faith and morals; and so such definitions of the Roman Pontiff from himself, but not from the consensus of the Church, are unalterable. But if anyone presumes to contradict this definition of Ours, which may God forbid: let him be anathema" (D. 1839–40).

3. The clearest example I know of these efforts to remove from dogma its iconic elements and reduce it to the digital occurs in the case of hell. According to Timotheus Rast in Vorgrimler and Van der Gucht, (eds.) *La Teología en el Siglo XX* (Madrid: BAC, 1974), vol. 3, p. 259, the opinion that "final states in the beyond are connected to particular locations in space" was for a long time *sententia longe communior* [by far the most common], although "the location of the places human beings go after death cannot be determined with assurance." By contrast, says this writer, "the eschatology of the second half of the twentieth century moves away from such reflections. For the sake of a more personalistic vision it tends to reject the last things conceived in a physicistic manner, which sought to determine a more or less exact location in space." Likewise Karl Rahner in his *Foundations of Christian Faith* (New York: Crossroad, 1978), p. 443, writes, "We said that man is a being who in the course of his still ongoing history has to reckon absolutely and up to the very end with the possibility of reaching his end in an absolute rejection of God, and hence in the opposite of salvation . . . But he does not need to know anything more than this about hell. In any case he may interpret the eschatological statements in the New Testament in the light of our hermeneutical principle, and hence he may distinguish between the content of a statement and its mode of expression, between the nonperceptual content which is really meant and its conceptual model." According to these judgments or opinions, the one condemned would not have to be in any place outside heaven. Even there alongside the blessed such a person's no to God would be his or her hell. This kind of "imaginative purification" of dogma, which is obviously aimed at making it more acceptable, in the end is likely to have the opposite effect.

4. Of course theology, preaching, or catechesis can fill this gap or hole. Nevertheless, especially for the process of "recalling" what is dogmatic, the bare formula reduced to its most minimal expression, simplifies matters in such a way that when added to the prestige of infallibility, it can hardly be entirely replaced.

5. Such theocentrism, which strives and claims to be proper homage to God, often ends up not only dehumanizing the human being, but also attributing monstrous features to God. As an example, see the interesting book by James M. Gustafson, *Ethics from a Theocentric Perspective* (Chicago: University of Chicago Press, 1983), vol. 1. Consider the meaning of this statement by Victor Hugo as he confronted the death of his son: *Je conviens qu'il est bon, je conviens qu'il est juste/ que mon coeur aite saigné puisque Dieu l'a volu.* Pope Paul VI who presided over most of the sessions of Vatican II and signed its major and most characteristic documents, affirms the full orthodoxy of the anthropocentrism that some would be tempted to criticize in the conciliar documents: "Has all this and whatever else we could say about the human value of the Council perhaps led astray the mind of the

church in the council toward the human-centered direction of modern culture? *Led astray, no; turned, yes*" (Speech to the Council gathered for its close, December 7, 1965).

7. Encounter with Absolute Truth

1. Jean Daniélou, *The Lord of History: Reflections on the Inner Meaning of History* (London: Longman, 1958; translation of *Essai sur le mystère de l'histoire*), p. 7.

2. Daniélou in *Supplément du Dictionnaire Biblique*, art. "Eschatologie," 1356.

3. Daniélou's original expression, "L'histoire est en sursis" (*Essai*, p. 23) [translated by Segundo with Spanish idiom, "está 'en capilla' "].

4. The passage from Augustine, which certainly carries a heavy load of Neoplatonism, is as follows: "Behold how, even though Truth itself and the Word through whom everything was made, has become flesh and dwelt among us, the Apostle nevertheless says, 'Even if we did once know Christ in the flesh, that is not how we know him now' (2 Cor. 5:16). For he who not only wanted to be possession for those who come near, but also the way for those who come to the beginning of the ways, wanted to assume (our) flesh ... so that those who want to arrive could begin there ... For when one arrives at him, one also arrives at the Father ... Hence it is clear that nothing should hold us back when not even the Lord himself, insofar as he deigned to be our way (Jn. 14:6), wanted to hold us back but to move on; so that we would not out of weakness remain attached to temporal things, even though he had received and operated those things for our salvation, but that we might rather run with enthusiasm so as to merit to be transported and led to him who freed our nature from temporal things and set it at God's right hand" (*De Doctrina Christiana*, 1.1, chap. 34; *Obras de San Agustín*, bilingual edition, Madrid: BAC, 1957, vol. 15, p. 102). [Here following Segundo's translation, which he says he made striving to be more faithful to the Latin original.]

5. In this connection it is interesting that the Greek word "proselyte" which in practice indicates the closest a non-Jew can possibly come (through circumcision), in the Septuagint is simply the translation of the term the Hebrew language uses for *foreigner*. One remains a foreigner even after being incorporated into the religion of Yahweh.

6. Oscar Cullmann, *La Foi et le Culte de l'Eglise Primitive* (Neuchâtel: Delachaux & Niestlé, 1963), p. 57. Cullmann adds that this is "one of the oldest confessions of faith we know" (ibid.). With regard to other occasions when the church used such *short dogmatic formulas*, see p. 56. Milar material in Cullmann, *Early Christian Worship* (London: SCM Press, 1953), pp. 23 and 21, slightly different translations of *Urchristentum und Gottesdienst* (Zurich: Zwingli-Verlag, 1950).

7. In this connection, see my work *Jesus of Nazareth Yesterday and Today*, vol. 2 (*The Historical Jesus of the Synoptics* [Maryknoll, N.Y.: Orbis Books, 1985]), Appendix 2, pp. 185–88.

8. Rudolf Bultmann, *Theology of the New Testament* (New York: Scribner's Sons, 1951), vol. 1, p. 79; see also pp. 148–52.

9. Naturally, it is not easy to define the boundaries of these religions as differing from any other kind of religion. To some extent any religion has a soteriological and revelatory function, and to that extent can be called a mystery religion and salvation religion. What may be characteristic of the latter is a kind of exclusivity and immediacy: salvation is cut off from the ordinary world and is offered in an

initiation of rite and creed. In this sense I think it is very difficult to deny that the Christian religion with which the first New Testament document, Paul's two letters to the Thessalonians, is familiar, enters into that category. With Paul as he is in his greatest letters, we come to a much more complex and much richer vision of the religious as related to other areas of human existence.

10. Edward Schillebeeckx, *Ministry: Leadership in the Community of Jesus Christ* (New York: Crossroad, 1981), p. 8.

11. "For the New Testament, apostolicity is in the first instance a distinguishing title for the Christian community itself on the basis of the 'gospel of Jesus the Christ' which was proclaimed to it by the apostles, i.e., the gospel of reconciliation and the forgiveness of sins (see 2 Cor. 5:17–21; Mt. 18:15–18; Jn. 20:21ff.)." Ibid.

12. Ibid., p. 19. [In the Spanish version Segundo translates "Christianity" as *"Iglesia,"* i.e., "church," and explains:] Note that I translate *Christianity* as *church*. Neither "Christianity" nor (even less) "christendom" seemed to me to be a faithful translation (the latter because in Spanish it denotes the medieval Christian world, and the former because it denotes the Christian message or religion more than its concrete embodiment. It should be noted here that a reading of chapter 1 of Schillebeeckx offers numerous other valuable items of information enabling the reader to gradually see the factors influencing the conception gradually acquired by the apostolic and post-apostolic Christian community on how to approach dogmatic truth. The book does so, moreover, even though that is not its immediate and direct target.

13. The Council adds, "who [the Apostles] received them either from the lips of Christ himself, or through the inspiration of the Holy Spirit." Here, however, their logic breaks down, at least in its effort to express why a divine revelation *was completed* when it is still claimed that God could *continue to inspire* authors, such as Mark and Luke, who were not apostles and could not have been direct witnesses to the life and message of Jesus. It should be noted, moreover, as we have already had occasion to see, that inspiration is a theological concept which arises under the pressure of the need to account for the fact that there is a revelation from God and that it is not the result of purely human inquiry. Of course when that dogmatic definition is produced there has already been considerable reflection on the case of inspired evangelists like Mark or Luke, who are bearers of revelation, according to dogma, and are placed in the New Testament canon, even though they are beyond what is presumed to be the end of the revealed deposit. That is, they do not depend on any living apostle for their words. If they can be inspired, however, why cannot subsequent Christians enjoy the same divine "inspiration" and add their work to this list or canon? See note 24 of the next chapter.

14. *Dictionary*, p. 120.

15. José Ignacio González Faus, *La Humanidad Nueva: Ensayo de Cristología* (Santander: Sal Terrae, 1984), p. 359. González' observation about Justin is even more valid when transferred to John: "Justin is also the kind of Christian who is a discovery for Christians living under the yoke of the diaspora (today). If they can only get inside him, overcoming all the obstacles of his unsystematic approach and of a world and language so far from ours, it may happen that those who, for example, have wondered about the possibility of being both Christian and Marxist, may savor this faithful lay person . . . His effort to be both a Christian and a Platonist, in both his solutions and his errors, may have something to teach them." Ibid.

16. C. H. Dodd, *The Interpretation of the Fourth Gospel* (Cambridge: Cambridge University Press, 1963), p. 9.

17. Even people who have studied and thought about theology a good deal tend to contrast or add an argument taken from the synoptics to another taken from the Gospel of John, apparently without perceiving the step—or leap—between a (more or less historic) set of "memoirs" of Jesus and a theological claim by John. Naturally, the point here is by no means to minimize the latter, but simply not to confuse two different types of thinking or literary genres with regard to a single point of discussion.

8. Power and Truth in the Patristic Age

1. It has become a cliché to speak of the "Constantinian era" and to blame on it all the ills of the church's overdeveloped institutionalization in Western society up to the present. Like all clichés lining the shelves of history, it offers a handy way of making many oversimplifications and half-truths. Faced with such oversimplifications, scholarly history does not always attain equilibrium. Sometimes there is a movement to the opposite extreme. That can be explained by the disproportionate strength that these oversimplifications and commonplaces enjoy. Sometimes progress has had to be made by leaps. "Revisionisms" in history then propose what for well or ill are called "Copernican revolutions." Nevertheless, little by little we come to richer and more nuanced syntheses. Undoubtedly the path taken in this work will make it somewhat necessary both to use and demolish clichés like that of the "Constantinian era."

2. Especially in the realm of church institutions. Although they may argue over degrees, practically all serious theologians today accept that in fact there has been a tendency to point to the existing results of the church's institutional evolution over centuries as though they were *de jure divino* institutions—that is, established in their present form by God (or programed that way by Jesus). Such an operation requires establishing—and to a degree forcing—*synonymies* in order to make these institutions (which are the product of the exigencies of historical context) look like *the same ones* that emerge at the outset.

3. Cited by Schillebeeckx, *Ministry*, p. 38 and note 1. "Absolute" ordination meant that since he was a mere instrument, it was possible to ordain a presbyter and then wait for the time or place for him to be used. From a theological standpoint, the objections raised against Schillebeeckx that this was a frequent practice are of little importance. The important point is the very explicit reproach leveled by nothing less than an ecumenical council.

4. *Le Nouveau Peuple de Dieu* (Paris: Aubier, 1971), p. 3. Ratzinger says the following: "After the death of the apostles, the apostolic responsibility passes on to personages such as Titus and Timothy, thus reflecting a clearly defined crystalization of the episcopal function. By the beginning of the second century, the structure of this function has developed fully. In broad outlines it can be described more or less as follows: the duality of functions of bishops and deacons which came from the Christianity of the gentiles, was fused with the Judeo-Christian function of the presbyters thus forming a threefold ministry: bishops-presbyters-deacons. However, a certain amount of time had to pass in order to achieve the balance and differentiation between 'bishops' and 'presbyters,' which did not take place to the same extent in all circles of early Christianity."

5. Ibid., p. 45.

6. B. Botle, "Der Kollegialcharacter der Priester and Bischofsamtes," in (J. Guyot), *Das apostolische Amt* (Mainz, 1961), p. 82. Cited by Ratzinger, *Nouveau Peuple*, p. 47.

7. Cited by Schillebeeckx, *Ministry*, p. 40. Leo the Great offers another formulation of the same principle: "No one may consecrate a man bishop against the wish of the Christians and unless they have explicitly asked for this" (ibid., n. 7).

8. *Histoire Générale des Civilisations* by M. Crouzet, A. Aymard, and J. Auboyer (Paris: PUF, 1956), vol. 2, pp. 499–500.

9. Ibid.

10. Ibid. The author goes on, "These concessions were so excessive that a successor of Constantine reestablished the requirement that both parties give consent, and criminal jurisdiction over clerics was resisted until the middle of the 5th century" (ibid.).

11. See ibid., p. 501.

12. It is also the emperor who for similar reasons convokes the first five ecumenical councils, in addition to various provincial councils, such as the pre-Nicea council of Arles (314), which is directed against the Donatists.

13. Ratzinger, *Nouveau Peuple*, p. 49. He continues, "This idea, which does not appear until the beginning of the third century and takes on its distinctive shape in the fourth century, was still unfamiliar to Saint Augustine, for example (cf. *Retr.* I, 21)."

14. "This idea recurs continually from Ignatius of Antioch onward; it still appears in the *Decretum Gelasianum*, which certainly emphasizes Mt. 16:18s. but it goes on, 'There was also added the company of the most blessed apostle Paul, vessel of election, who not at some other time, as the heretics babble, but at the same time and on the same day, struggling together with Peter in the city of Rome, was crowned with death under the Caesar Nero. Together they consecrated to Christ the Lord that holy Roman church and placed it ahead of all the cities of the wide world with their presence and venerable triumph ... ' I have tried to develop the importance of the idea of the *Sedes Apostolica* (in K. Rahner, J. Ratzinger, *Episkopat und Primat*, Freiburg, 1961, pp. 52–57)." Ratzinger, *Nouveau Peuple*, p. 50, n. 18.

15. "Consequently, this primacy has a normative importance for the unity of faith of the church, but strictly speaking it does not have *any administrative character*" (Ratzinger, *Nouveau Peuple*, p. 54, emphasis mine). The arguments show that the primacy belongs to the see and by extension to the bishop who occupies it.

16. I must insist that the "centralization" around the Roman pontiff in the realm of dogma must not be confused with "centralization" in the administration of the whole Catholic Church out of a particular bureaucratic apparatus located in Rome. Although in this chapter we may note certain distant anticipations of this latter "temptation" (if it is true, as Ratzinger wrote in 1971 that the Roman primate "strictly speaking has no administrative character," see previous note) in the period being studied, administrative centralization is something much more recent. Bishops continued to be elected (or at least accepted) for centuries, largely by members of their communities. During the Middle Ages, the rise of the nationalities composing Christendom increasingly put the selection of bishops in the hands of civil authorities. The wars of religion after the Reformation only heightened this tendency. For example, the emphatic "Gallicanism" existing in France managed to survive even the persecution of the French Revolution. Only the establishment of republican

government, freedom of worship, and state neutrality has put this selection in the hands of the Roman see, which in this area operates mainly through papal nuncios. It is perhaps only in this most recent pontificate that such selection is seemingly subject to criteria intended to have a real impact in the domain of theology.

17. G. Ruggieri, "Revelación," in *Diccionario Teológico Interdisplinar*, L. Pacomio et al. (eds.) (Span. translation, Salamanca: Sígueme, 1983), vol. 4, pp. 195–96.

18. Ibid.

19. J.I. González Faus, *La Humanidad*, pp. 349–50.

20. "In Acts 24:14 it is plain that *he odos* (= the way) was what the Christian community called itself, while its adversaries spoke of it as a *hairesis* (= sect)," G. Ebel, "Camino" in the *Diccionario Teológico del N.T.*, vol. 1, p. 214.

21. What happens to ecumenism when in its dogma the Roman Catholic Church claims to be the "bearer of . . . fullness" and when it can only propose "to bring others to share fully in this fullness"? On the basis of Vatican II, K. Rahner and H. Fries proposed a common search which would somehow go back to the unity of the first five unquestionably ecumenical councils (*Unity of the Churches: An Actual Possibility*, Philadelphia/New York: Fortress/Paulist, 1985). This book or what it proposes was regarded as "irreconcilable with Catholic faith" in an article of D. Ols ("Atajos ecuménicos") published February 25, 1985. The article was apparently requested of the author by Cardinal Ratzinger; see Giancarlo Zizola, *La Restauración del Papa Wojtyla* (Madrid: Cristiandad, 1985), pp. 244–45 (translation of Italian original).

22. In this regard, see the interview of Cardinal Ratzinger by Vittorio Messori, *The Ratzinger Report: An Exclusive Interview on the State of the Church* (San Francisco: Ignatius Press, 1985, especially the section "Let us rediscover the true Vatican II," pp. 29ff., and chapter 11 on ecumenism). According to the interviewer, the cardinal stated that "in no way was it the intention of the pope who took the initiative for Vatican II, John XXIII, and of the pope who continued it faithfully, Paul VI, to bring up for discussion a *depositum fidei* which was viewed by them as undisputed and *already assured*" (p. 35). The "two extremes" described in that passage (one implicitly, the other explicitly) could, without doing them violence, represent the positions of the theologies of Hans Küng (who would subject the deposit of faith to discussion) and that of the one speaking, Cardinal Ratzinger. In view of everything seen so far in the present work, I believe *both* extremes constitute a threat to the faith: the first, because it does not manage to show clearly wherein lies the guarantee of truth in the formulas in which the church expresses its faith; the second, because it stands clearly in opposition not only to the spirit, but to the very letter of Vatican II, which acknowledges that unless there is a serious reform or "aggiornamento," serious threats hover over the faith *within* the church (see GS 19, last paragraph, for example).

23. See J.L. Segundo, *Jesus of Nazareth Yesterday and Today*, vol. 3, *The Humanist Christology of Paul*, chap. 1. The same topic is developed more fully in more theological terms in "Disquisición sobre el misterio absoluto," in *Revista Latinoamericana de Teología* (San Salvador), num. 6 (Sept.-Dec. 1985), pp. 209–27.

24. See above, chapter 7, n. 4.

25. In this continuation of the divine pedagogy after Jesus through a living community, there should be recognized a vague but persistent effort (which takes place at the end of the patristic period and the beginning of the next one) to *draw*, I would say, at least the overall teaching of the church fathers (despite or because

of its pluralism and lack of synthesis) closer to the New Testament canon—that is, to the "deposit" of revelation. The *Decretum Gelasianum* (495 C.E.) says that "the Roman Church does not forbid *these writings also* ... *to be received* after those of the Old or New Testament, which we *canonically* accept (D. 164–65). There follows a list of the first ecumenical councils and a selection of church fathers (such as Gregory Nazianzen, Basil, Athanasius, and so forth). When the patristic period ends there is a conviction, dogmatically taken up by the Fourth Council of Constantinople (869–870 C.E.) that "some fathers" (along with the "universal" and "orthodox" councils) enjoyed "divine inspiration" in their teachings (D. 333; see also a century previous the Second Council of Nicea: D. 302–3). Thus what the fathers have taught is part of our "faith" (D. 212), and strictly speaking faith can only be demanded vis-à-vis a word recognized as inspired by God and therefore as revelatory. Although, as we have already said, the haste with which the New Testament canon was fixed meant abandoning the idea of adding to it further works, the idea that God continued to reveal himself roamed about the church for centuries. There was an awareness that this happens not so much through someone writing, but as the result of an "interpretation" made in the Christian community of how Jesus' message continues to reveal *unsuspected* dimensions to human existence. We will return to this point later on.

26. León Felipe, *Antololgía Rota* (Buenos Aires: Losada, 1984), p. 32. The poem is called "La Ascensión," and significantly for the question we are dealing with, bears as an inscription the verse of Fray Luis de León, who does not seem to agree with the Johannine idea of what is "better": "And you leave, Holy Shepherd, your flock in this deep, dark valley . . . " León Felipe's verse is not that of an atheist or someone disrespectful. It is the measured expression of the faith of a Christian— although the daring goes so far as to put "God" (singular) in the place of "gods." In the same direction go Paul's frequent observations on acting as "children," heirs, and (real) owners of *everything*, not asking teachers, parents, or laws what is allowed, but rather judging for ourselves (in accord with the signs of the times) what is fitting and just (Mt. 16:2–3; Lk. 12:57).

9. New Peoples for the Faith

1. Certainly in principle the Reformation managed to knock down many "dogmatic" bridges built during the Middle Ages when it applied the principle of *sola Scriptura*, although it did so only slowly and sometimes timidly. I think that such will probably be the impression of a reformed theologian in reading this chapter. This elimination process, which means that in principle a Protestant is further removed than a Catholic from many practices, customs, and doctrines that arose in the Middle Ages, nonetheless has certain limits. Beyond those Protestant confessions that have been carrying out serious theological inquiry, one often encounters sharp traces of the Middle Ages, as for example in the eschatology of many evangelical sects, and even of more permanently structured churches. Still I believe that toward the end of this chapter the Protestant theologian will recognize a problem affecting virtually all Christians across the board: that of the proper relationship between divine dogma and human experience. Actually that was the very point of the discussion between Barth and Bultmann which took place in our own century.

2. A. J. Toynbee, *Guerre et Civilisation* (edited from his great work, *A Study of History*) (Paris: Gallimard, 1953). The author views the "death" of great civilizations

as associated with the complex phenomenon of *war*. With his work *The Decline of the West*, Oswald Spengler, who was to some extent Toynbee's teacher, has had perhaps an even wider cultural influence. However, it is just the "biological" hypothesis of the latter work which shows most clearly the insufficiency of these kinds of unities of historic meaning, especially when they are applied to this complex "universal" phenomenon of the "West." His main thesis reflects an unawareness of the shift from compartmentalized cultures to a civilization that is practically universal, thanks to progress in communications and consequently in increased economic interconnectedness.

3. There is no doubt that given the existence of a civilization spanning the planet, the familiar distinction between (more or less material) *civilization* and (more or less spiritual) *culture* is becoming more useful. The so-called developed countries on our planet unquestionably evidence very similar features in their mode of production. Nevertheless, there is something, indeed something quite deep, differentiating an English individual from someone who is American, Japanese, German, or French. The truly important question, especially in Latin America and in countries which must perforce live within this civilization, is the survival capability of cultures called "primitive" because they are linked to obsolete modes of production, vis-à-vis this quasiforced unification of the elements that compose and impose a civilization. To what extent will a culture almost totally foreign to the dominant civilization be able to maintain its individuality? If that is ever more problematic or improbable, what value or meaning does it have to hold that all cultures are "equal," or that all have the right to remain as they are and to cultivate their own values?

4. Darcy Ribeiro, the Brazilian anthropologist, perhaps due to professional deformation, denies the European and therefore Christian character of the civilization developing around the world, which he himself, for unexplained reasons, calls "Western": "Eurocentrism refers to the assumed differentiating quality of Western civilization, which is assumed to be a matter of its singular creativity. This vision of things presents as intrinsically European all the most recent material advances of civilization. Actually these are human cultural creations . . . Nevertheless, because they happen to emerge in Europe, they were imbued with 'Europeanness.' Hence we observe the error of regarding sources of energy, and mechanical or technical processes to be inherent in a civilization. This notion is as idiotic as assuming that gasoline is Christian or that electricity is English" ("Perfil de un continente," in *Correo de la Unesco*, Aug.-Sept. 1982, p. 11). In my opinion, the only thing valid in this claim is the warning not to lose one's critical sense, nor to simply regard whatever happens in Europe as "progress," or to defend any continuity with Europe as automatically "Christian."

5. Given the embarrassment of riches of a vast array of historical works that could provide a more or less trustworthy general image of this particular period of the Middle Ages, I am selecting volume 5 of *Histoire de l'Eglise*, Fliche-Martin (ed.), because of its availability to readers in Spanish and its acceptance in theological circles. This volume, *Grégoire le Grande, les Etats Barbares et la Conquête Arabe (590–757)*, was written by Emile Bréhier and René Aigrain (Paris: Bloud & Gay, 1938). Any other source used will be noted separately. Fliche-Martin will be cited only in the case of textual citations. Secular readers in these matters should note that this St. Gregory the Great (598–604) should not be confused with Gregory VII (1073–1085), who was responsible for the "Gregorian shift" mentioned below, and

who was another of the most influential (and powerful) popes of the Middle Ages
with respect to the topic under discussion. L. Pacomio (*Diccionario Interdisciplinar*,
vol. 4, pp. 195–96) lays down three key points in the history of the concept of
"revelation" in the age of Christianity. We have already looked at the first of these,
the inculturation of what is Christian into Hellenism, during the patristic age.
According to Pacomio, the second is that during the Middle Ages (although later
than the reference point I take here) of the so-called Gregorian reform or shift,
which refers to the moment when the magisterium entirely takes over what was
previously assumed to be the inspiration of the Spirit in the interpretation the
church fathers made of biblical revelation. The *Dictatus Papae* of Gregory VII
indicates this step. Pacomio cites Y.-M. Congar who says, in *La Tradición y las
Tradiciones: Un Ensayo Histórico*: "The Gregorian reform and its influence . . . indicates a decisive shift, the step from the viewpoint of God's vital presence to that
of juridical powers granted to the church, or rather in this case, to the hierarchy
for its free use, if not its possession." I do not claim that Gregory the Great was
more important in this regard. My choice of him is didactic, as I indicated. In other
words, he tends to make more visible or comprehensible a change that was slower
and perhaps deeper—namely, the situation of the church which, after confronting
the culture of the Roman Empire for five centuries, finds itself with the task of
accompanying a journey from a *starting point* that is much further back, that of the
barbarian peoples occupying the empire.

6. *Histoire Générale*, vol. 3, p. 26.

7. Fliche-Martin, vol. 5, p. 383. In more general terms, chap. 1, section 4, V;
chaps. 9 and 11.

8. The fact that the church here being studied is situated five centuries after
the New Testament does not—nor could it—mean that everything it teaches has
really passed through the threshold of the New Testament. I say it could not since
not even everything in the New Testament has passed over this threshold, despite
its acknowledged divine inspiration. Joseph Ratzinger, today a cardinal, says "Many
things of the church and in the church, place it not in the New Testament but in
the Old. The age of the New Testament and the reality of the New Testament are
not simply one and the same" ("Volk und Haus Gottes" in "Agustins Lehre von
der Kirche" in *Münchener theol. Studien*, systematic section, vol. 7, Munich, 1954,
p. 305. Quoted by Hans Urs von Balthasar, *Puntos Centrales de la Fe* (Madrid: BAC,
1985), p. 70.

9. Fliche-Martin, *Histoire*, vol. 5, p. 31. "While Gregory certainly does not want
to say anything not backed up by the authority of witnesses, he accepts all the
marvelous events he hears about without subjecting them to any very demanding
criticism, and from them he draws edifying lessons." The same "credulity" and
interest in the "miraculous" appear in the works of Pope Gregory's contemporary,
Gregory of Tours, who writes *De Gloria Martyrum, De Gloria Confessorum*, and
particularly, the well known *Historia Francorum* (ibid., pp. 380f.), as well as a sketch
of a theology of history that resembles, and is somewhat related to, the biblical
books of Samuel and Kings.

10. Fliche-Martin, *Histoire*, p. 29. Pope Gregory thought that his commentary on
Job was "too difficult to offer to all the faithful of his time" (p. 30).

11. A. Torres Queiruga, *La Revelación de Dios en la Realización del Hombre*
(Madrid: Ediciones Cristiandad, 1987), p. 149. This enormously fruitful book came
into my hands when the present work was already in its final stages. As indicated

by the title, it deals with almost the same topic as the present work (what is dogma if it is not the divine revelation in the "obedience of faith"—that is, insofar as it affects and supports human thinking and experience?), and it does so with ideas so close to those expressed here—unless of course Torres Queiruga judges otherwise—that I cannot be very objective in evaluating it. In any case readers looking for a more complete and scholarly bibliography on the topic being studied here will do well to consult this book. With regard to the exact point at issue, the author explains Lessing's idea of pedagogy and makes it his own although he incorporates it into a "maieutic" function (more historic than Socratic, cf. p. 134) which, unless I am mistaken, is in agreement with what I have here called second-order learning or the process of learning to learn. This maieutic, like second-order learning, stands in contrast to simply storing or adding up items of information. The latter would be "a revelation foreign to the human being, and heteronomous, like an 'asteroid' fallen from heaven. People today are justifiably opposed to such a revelation" (p. 129).

12. Fliche-Martin, *Histoire*, vol. 5, p. 32.

13. This is a reference to the title of Torres Queiruga's book: "the revelation of God *in* the fulfillment of the human being." I believe that in few cases does a book's title so encapsulate its whole content in a single theological expression as does this one. From another angle, which strictly speaking is not in a work on "revelation," Edward Schillebeeckx summarizes a thought which seems to me to be very close to Torres Queiruga's thought and to what I feel about this matter: "The divine revelation as accomplished in Jesus directs us to the mystery of man. Therefore, to ask people to accept the Christian revelation *before* they have learnt to experience it as a definition of their own life is an impossible and useless demand, which goes against the structure of revelation" (*Christ: The Experience of Jesus as Lord*, New York: Crossroad, 1981, p. 76). Torres Queiruga points out, "In Protestant theology Gerhard Ebeling sounded the warning with his work on the 'deficit of experience in theology.' In Catholic theology, it has become Edward Schillebeeckx's most intense concern and pursuit" (Torres Queiruga, *La Revelación de Dios*, p. 111).

14. In a way, medieval Christians will never experience deeply, down to its ultimate consequences, what is proper to the idea of historic covenant as it appears in the Old Testament. Despite the similarities that might seem to exist, this does not happen, for example, with regard to the Franks, as the *Historia Francorum* of Gregory of Tours presents it, or later during the crusades when we find the phrase *gesta Dei per francos*. It could not reach its ultimate consequences since the world where such battles were taking place was "a vale of tears," where the "exiled children of Eve" had to live, as the Salve Regina, sung in the eleventh century, reminded this very medieval Frank. The Jews who went seeking their land or yearned to recover it during their exile in Babylon, did not have such an easy answer, and therefore they had to create something deeper, more rooted, and more substantial.

15. See Segundo, *The Humanist Christology of Paul* (vol. 3 of *Jesus of Nazareth Yesterday and Today* (Maryknoll, N.Y.: Orbis Books, 1986), chapter 9. The demands of making a quick summary prevent me from indicating at this point other concomitant changes that are equally necessary. One such change is to halt the (incipiently Manichaean) notion that the fate of human beings is a matter of splitting humankind in half by drawing a clear line separating good from bad, offering heaven to some and to others the Gehenna of fire, the outer darkness, weeping and gnashing

of teeth—even though these expressions were probably part of Jesus' own vocabulary.

16. It should not be forgotten that at this point and throughout the Middle Ages, the church has much more "temporal" power than it won (or accepted) when it first became the official religion of the Roman Empire. The ups and downs of defeat and victory in the power struggle between papacy and empire during the Middle Ages should not make us think that "defeat" meant periods when the church was *without* power. Rather the question was which power, the civil or the religious, was able to use the power of the other for its own ends.

17. In this regard, consider another dogmatic "purging," that which Karl Rahner proposes to do with the *images* linked to hell in his *Foundations of Christian Faith* (New York: Crossroad, 1978, p. 103): "Nor do the scriptural descriptions of the end-times have to be regarded as conclusive eye-witness accounts of what is some day going to be. If we apply correctly an exact hermeneutic of eschatological statements, these scriptural descriptions of the end both of the individual person and of the whole human race can be understood as statements about the possibilities of human life, and as instructions about the absolute seriousness of human decision." He also notes that a Christian "may interpret the eschatological statements in the New Testament in the light of our hermeneutical principle, and hence he may distinguish between the content of a statement and its mode of expression, between the nonperceptual content which is really meant and its conceptual model" (p. 443).

18. G. Colzani, "Purgatorio" in *Diccionario Interdisciplinar*, vol 3. I would accept the noun "truth" for this notion if I could see this truth as arising from experience (which does not mean "removed from revelation") and being criticized by it in a process of second-order learning.

19. *Histoire Générale*, vol. 3, p. 21. Here it would be good to add by way of summary, "In this framework it could be observed that between the sixth and eighth centuries Roman traditions were gradually mixed with the customs brought by the invaders, and from this mixture was born an original civilization. Thus fusion took place particularly through a notable lowering of the cultural level . . . This regression which continued until the beginning of the eighth century affected political activity as well as the social structure, and economic activity along with intellectual and religious life" (ibid., p. 18). In the case of popular Catholicism in Latin America, we likewise have an instance of these peoples who so often after being defeated in history, were then able to triumph in their own manner, by bringing their own culture into that of their supposed conquerors through a subterranean route. In such a case popular religion ought to be called by its *own* original name (depending on which religion is predominant), whether that be Umbanda or one of the pre-Columbian religions, rather than Christianity. The point is not to take the latter away from these peoples, but to respect their cultural contribution.

20. Karl Rahner, *Theological Investigations*, vol. IV, *More Recent Writings* (Baltimore: Helicon Press, 1966), p. 141, n. 29. Subsequent quotes from Rahner (without references) are from this same essay, pp. 141ff.

21. Obviously Rahner disagrees with what Cardinal Ratzinger says in his interview with Messori: "the *four* Marian dogmas [perpetual virginity, divine motherhood, immaculate conception, assumption into heaven] have their clear foundation in sacred Scripture" (*The Ratzinger Report*, p. 107). Here Cardinal Ratzinger does not elaborate on his idea of what constitutes a "clear (biblical) foundation" for a

dogma of Catholic faith. For his part, Karl Rahner, speaking of Mary's Assumption says, "It is hard to conceive of any truth which is less directly and explicitly in Scripture than this" (p. 144, n. 37).

22. In addition I note that if one consults Denzinger (the classic handbook collection of the church's dogmatic declarations) one will find that the affirmation mixing this truth and its means (which is temporary and incomplete in understanding and expression) enters into dogma at the very beginning of the period here being studied. With regard to Adam and Eve, Pelagius I writes "For I confess that . . . the one [was created] from the earth, the other, however from the rib of the man (Gen. 2:7, 22)" (D. 228a). Fifteen hundred years later, well into the twentieth century, the Pontifical Biblical Commission in answer to the question, "whether in particular the *literal and historical* sense can be called into question, where it is a matter of facts related . . . to the special creation of man; the formation of the first woman from the first man" answers "In the negative" (D. 2123) (emphasis mine).

23. In *Foundations of Christian Faith*, Karl Rahner states that there are *two* distinct levels of certainty with regard to the possibility of eternal loss for each individual and the assurance of eternal salvation for all of humankind: "Eschatological statements about the meaning of 'heaven,' which is the final and definitive state of happiness and fulfillment for a person who enjoys God's self-communication in grace, and statements about 'hell' are not parallel statements. For since we are living in the eschaton of Jesus Christ, the God-Man who was crucified for us and who has risen for us and who remains forever, we know in our Christian faith and in our unshakable hope that, in spite of the drama and the ambiguity of the freedom of individual persons, the history of salvation as a whole will reach a positive conclusion for the human race through God's own powerful grace" (p. 435). "This open possibility is not necessarily the doctrine of two parallel ways which lie before a person who stands at the crossroads. Rather the existence of the possibility that freedom will end in eternal loss stands alongside the doctrine that the world and the history of the world as a whole will *in fact* enter into eternal life with God" (Rahner's emphasis). Dealing with this same issue, Timotheus Rast makes an important point concerning the impulse biblical theology has given dogmatic theology: "Eschatology is trying to reintegrate the problem of the fate of the individual into a genuine eschatology of all creation *biblically grounded* in the hope of salvation of the church of Christ and *of the whole cosmos*" (*La Teología en el Siglo XX*, Vorgrimler and Van der Gucht, eds., Madrid: BAC, 1974; Spanish translation). Rahner's solution, if it really is a solution, and even thanking him for the distinction, with all due respect, still leaves one wanting him to explain the contradiction.

24. "Purgatorio" (n. 19, above), pp. 997f. In order to summarize this dogmatic evolution—which is most vigorous during the Middle Ages—in terms accessible to any reader, I am going to follow this article step by step in this section.

25. Ibid., p. 995.

26. Ibid.

27. Should someone claim that the words *ex cathedra* do not appear in *Unam Sanctam*, one can answer that they are also missing in Pius IX's definition of the Immaculate Conception in 1854. That does not prevent theologians from speaking of dogma and infallibility in the latter case and of error in the former. Corresponding to the decisive words in this latter definition, "we declare, pronounce, and define," *Unam Sanctam* reads, "we declare, say, define, and proclaim to every human creature that they by necessity of salvation are entirely subject to the Roman

Pontiff." In addition, the contrary teaching is there declared to be heretical.

28. René Aubert, "Le Pontificat de Pie IX (1846–1878)," in Fliche-Martin, vol. 21, pp. 319–20. The French were more sensitive to the political implications of the papal errors brought forth, while the Germans were more interested in pointing out dogmatic errors, like those which led to the condemnation of Popes Honorius I or Liberius as heterodox (ibid.). According to Küng, the condemnation of Honorius "was indeed acknowledged by the infallibilists at Vatican I as an historical fact, but now—in virtue of what has become a customary anachronistic distinction and subterfuge—Honorius' decision was interpreted as not being an *ex cathedra* declaration" (*Infallible? An Inquiry*, p. 120).

10. Dogma and Modern Culture

1. *Histoire Générale*, vol. 4, p. 1.

2. "Cultura y culturas en un mundo cambiante," *Correo de la Unesco* (Spanish edition), July 1982, p. 16.

3. All ways of transmitting from one generation to another suffer from this speeding up, and Christianity is no exception to the rule. It is difficult to find the time and the way to make the Christian message pass truly and profoundly from one Christian generation to another. That is particularly true because of a "dogmatic" factor worthy of being examined, although we will not do so here, at least sufficiently. Christianity needs *more and more* time simply in order to be able to "translate" what was said in a context that is ever-more remote from that of the present. There is of course a general problem of being human, which varies relatively little in comparison with other aspects. However, it is not easy to situate these issues in relation to those values that *are visibly at stake* at the present moment. Schillebeeckx is very much on the mark when he says in *Christ*, "therefore, to ask people to accept the Christian revelation *before* they have learnt to experience it as a definition of their own life is an impossible and useless demand, which goes against the structure of revelation" (p. 76). That is true although the church has a hard time accepting it. Indeed it continues to attribute an almost magical value to books that are ever-more remote. People who are properly concerned about nuclear weapons, the balance between North and South, or the destruction of the planet's ecology, which are life or death problems for coming generations, if not for our own, do not find a single word about these matters in the Christian scriptures which are read and commented upon in the liturgy, for example. The Holy Spirit does not supply everything.

4. The fact that this work ends with the examination of dogma in the *modern age* may perhaps diminish this work in the eyes of European or North American readers, whom current fashion has told incessantly that they are *postmodern*. I nonetheless begin by noting that Latin Americans feel quite remote from this set of issues. Furthermore they are skeptical of a fashion that disconnects people in developed regions from the great human problems which have not been resolved yet for the vast poor majority of humankind. Hence I regard this fashion as no more than an evasion, at least for the present.

5. Even in the middle of the twentieth century the church still officially designated the medieval philosophy of St. Thomas Aquinas with the title "perennial philosophy," thus very much suggesting an attempt to hold back history.

6. Reinhold Niebuhr, *The Nature and Destiny of Man* (New York: Charles Scrib-

ner's Sons, 1961), vol. 1, pp. 4–5. Interestingly the author divides chapter 1 into three sections: the *classical* view of man (Renaissance), the *Christian* view of man (Reformation), and the *modern* view of man (Enlightenment). In other words, three "humanisms" all of which diverge from medieval anthropology.

7. The moment in which Niebuhr is speaking (in his 1941 lectures) is that of the period beginning in World War II and continuing with the increasing nuclear threat up to the present. The (supposed) death of *bourgeois* culture is a fact experienced and accepted in Europe (see supra, n. 4), but that news strikes the rest of the world as "greatly exaggerated."

8. "Come of age"—not only in the Pauline sense, but in the sense of the developed human being who no longer needs God in order to (gradually) dominate nature. Bonhoeffer in his prison letters begins to write to his friend about a "world now come of age," and "adult world" (June 8, 1944).

9. Erich Fromm, *The Flight From Freedom* (New York: Avon, 1965), pp. 57–58.

10. Niebuhr, *Nature of Man*, vol. 1, p. 20.

11. The popular uprisings are either crushed by the aristocracy (the peasant war during Luther's lifetime) or are manipulated by the bourgeoisie (the French Revolution).

12. Curiously both the Reformation and the Counter-Reformation speak of a "coldness" in Erasmus, although it would perhaps be exaggerated to transfer it to the whole Renaissance (and especially to that which is most properly so called, the Italian Renaissance). Two men as fiery as Luther and Ignatius Loyola expressed themselves in those terms. Luther seems to have said that Erasmus's words were "colder than ice." Loyola likewise said that Erasmus "gave him the chills." He was referring to Erasmus's ironic criticism of many things in the contemporary church. Perhaps Loyola had in mind the things mentioned together in the sixth of his rules "for feeling with the church" (or better, "in" the church): "To praise saints' relics, venerating them and praying to them: praising stations, pilgrimages, indulgences, pardonings, crusades, and candles lit in churches." His recent biographer, J. Ignacio Tellechea Idígoras (*Ignacio de Loyola: Solo y a Pie* [Madrid: Cristiandad, 1986]) writes (p. 230): "There has been a good deal of discussion over whether the Parisian section of the rules, the first thirteen, is aimed against Luther or Erasmus. This is a somewhat false alternative. What these rules champion or condemn often find their opposite pole in Luther and in Erasmus: in the former the opposition is utterly radical while in the latter it is ambiguous and nuanced. Confession, the Mass, the canonical office and hours, religious life, vows, celibacy, matrimony, devotion to the saints and to their relics, pilgrimages and indulgences, fasting and external penances, Lenten customs, vestments and sacred buildings . . . had all been rejected by Luther or blithely criticized by Erasmus."

13. We need only consider the fact that the notion of original sin, according to which all of us human beings sinned "in" Adam, derives from a mistake made possible by the Latin translation of the Bible (and therefore of Paul) which Augustine used. He understood Paul's statement in Rom. 5:12 "sin entered the world through one man, and through sin death, and thus death has spread through the whole human race *because* everyone has sinned," as though it read "*in whom* (Adam) everyone sinned."

14. The quote is from Emile G. Léonard, *Histoire Générale du Protestantisme*, in a deplorable Spanish translation (Madrid: Ed. Península, 1967), vol. 1, p. 34. In the

rest of this section I am using volume 1 of this work, "The Reformation," for factual material, an area in which the author, the dean of the Ecole Pratique de Hautes Etudes, is quite solid and learned. For the interpretation of these facts, on the other hand, I make use of Protestants, including theologians, who offer a deeper insight in this area, as well as my own reflections.

15. Ibid., p. 35.

16. Paul Tillich, *The Protestant Era* (Chicago: University of Chicago Press, 1957, abr. ed.), chap. 11, pp. 162–63 [emphasis Segundo's].

17. "In order to judge what was not simply agility and opportunism on Melancthon's part, it should not be forgotten that since Catholic theology had not yet been fixed by the Council of Trent, one could hold that he was always in line with the older church with regard to questions of faith but not on those related to the institutions and practices rejected in the second section [of a document approved by Luther and read in the presence of the emperor on June 25, 1530]" (Léonard, *Histoire Générale*, p. 167).

18. The review appeared in *Revue des Sciences Philosophiques et Théologiques.* The gaps in my bibliography prevent me from knowing whether in one of his major works Congar has previously expressed more clearly and at greater length this opinion, which, I confess, surprised me as a new development in ecumenism that deserves to be more widely known among Catholics. On the other side of the matter, it seems that Karl Barth, in defense of the thesis Henri Bouillard wrote on his work while at the Sorbonne, and later with regard to Hans Küng's presentation of the same issue, stated that he agreed with the interpretation which these theologians regarded as Catholic, but he also expressed his doubts that it was the same as the officially accepted Catholic view on the relationship between justification and faith.

19. Léonard, *Histoire Générale*, p. 56.

20. The immediate context of Luther's dictum is the letter he writes to Melancthon on August 1, 1521, where we read, "God does not save make-believe sinners. Be a sinner and sin vigorously, but have greater faith and greater joy in Christ, who is victor over, sin, death, and the world" (Léonard, *Histoire Générale*, p. 55). Protestants correctly complain that Catholic apologetics stresses the *pecca fortiter* as if it were an imperative standing by itself. To be a human being, says Luther, is to sin; it is a necessity. The accent is placed on what to do given this fact, and his answer is faith and joy in Christ.

21. John A. T. Robinson, *The New Reformation?* (Philadelphia: Westminster, 1965), p. 54. Lest it be thought that I am bringing in a set of issues foreign to Robinson's, he himself states, "The ninety-five theses nailed on the door at Wittenberg contained no mention of justification by faith" (ibid., p. 18).

22. Ibid.

23. Léonard, *Histoire Générale*, p. 214.

24. Commenting on A. Loisy's famous book *L'Evangile et l'Eglise*, the Abbé Allain wrote in *L'Univers* on February 22, 1903, "when the church is described to us only on the basis of the gospel, we are not offered the full truth. It does not merit our credit or our trust . . . Where in the gospel are the instructions that Our Lord, who was founding a new religion, at one moment or another, certainly had to provide the apostles on the sacraments, the liturgy, worship of the saints and of his most holy Mother, the sacred hierarchy, and conditions in the life to come? Nothing or almost nothing is found on all these things, which are so interesting and even essential, and about which Jesus Christ surely had to provide explanations." Note

how, in this list of what *is missing* in the Bible, the Abbé Allain puts topics whose theological formation I have examined rapidly in previous chapters (especially 8 and 9): papal authority, Marian dogmas, eschatology, and so forth.

25. "The theologian who (often even still today) has the impression that tradition must be called upon as a substitute for an apparent insufficiency of holy scripture, had (and has) in most cases also no conception of the number of matters contained in today's consciousness of faith which are also not immediately tangible in the earlier tradition of the Church. In other words, he usually has, in addition, no conception as to the fact that even under the presupposition of a material independence of oral tradition, the problem does not really become any easier, since even today's sharper historical consciousness finds it no easier in practice to retrace to an earlier tradition of the Church contents of today's consciousness of faith which cannot be easily traced back directly to holy scripture" (Rahner, *Theological Investigations*, vol. VI, pp. 105–6).

26. John A. T. Robinson, *The New Reformation?*, p. 40. For the Schillebeeckx quote, see above, chapter 9, note 14.

27. It is not easy to determine clearly Rahner's position on whether revelation comes through one or two sources. It should be kept in mind that he praises J. R. Geiselmann's position on the issue (see the latter's article "Tradition," in *Encyclopédie de la Foi* edited under the direction of H. Fries (French translation, Paris: Ed. du Cerf, 1967, pp. 344–46). Geiselmann writes, "The relations between sacred scripture and tradition cannot be interpreted univocally. With regard to *faith*, scripture and tradition overlap ... With regard to the church's *practices and customs*, not all are found in scripture, not even in principle or in outline form. That is what tradition also says from the beginning. Let us conclude: *faith* is found whole and entire in the scripture and whole and entire in tradition. *Practices and customs* are found partly in scripture and partly in tradition." If praising this position entails acceptance, an element of ambiguity would be introduced in other statements by Rahner to the effect that after Vatican II we can no longer speak of *two sources* of revelation. Thus in *Foundations of Christian Faith* he writes, "the Second Vatican Council refused to make tradition a second source for us which exists by itself alongside scripture, a course which testifies to individual, material contents of faith which have no foundation at all in scripture" (pp. 377–78). What are we to think of "practices and customs," then? For my part, I believe Hans Küng's position (which is also more common among theologians) is more on the mark when he regards as equally "dogmatic" what touches faith and what touches customs (and practices). Hence he takes as an example *Humanae Vitae*'s clearly "dogmatic" intention (something to be "believed") and applies to it the same criteria and exigencies that have been applied to other papal pronouncements such as those of Pope Honorius (which were condemned after his death) to the effect that Christ had a single will.

28. Hans Küng, *Infallible?*, p. 77.

29. R. A. F. MacKenzie, in *The Documents of Vatican II*, Walter Abbott, ed. (New York: America Press, 1966), p. 109.

30. A. Grillmeier commenting on Chapter III of *Dei Verbum* in H. Vorgrimler (ed.), *Commentary on the Documents of Vatican II* (London: Burns & Oates, 1969), p. 202.

31. Joseph Ratzinger in his contribution to the same commentary (cf. n. 30) attributes the use of a term different from "source" to the desire to avoid a "clash

between the singularist and pluralist understanding of the word *fons*." Hence "it is possible to continue to speak of the *duo fontes*" (p. 191). Naturally that possibility exists but I think it is theological minimalism to say that the Council regards it as just as valid an alternative as that of the singularist understanding.

32. Ibid., p. 192.

33. See John A. T. Robinson, *The New Reformation?*, chapter 3, especially p. 62. In my own poor knowledge and understanding, this is the problem implicitly involved in the controversy between Bultmann and Barth at the beginning of the century. But even Bultmann's "demythologization," which recognizes how a church in its interpretation of scripture cannot ignore the philosophical efforts of humankind, did not clearly pose the alternative options in the terms to which I refer.

11. Liturgy and Laity

1. Baptism when administered by a lay person in an emergency is of course valid. That is an ancient tradition in the church. However, this is an extraordinary case and sociologically it does nothing to disrupt the division between lay people and clerics. The notion that from a theological standpoint the parties themselves are the "ministers" of their matrimony is a recent formulation. What has *always been observed* in a religious wedding has been a priest in charge of the ceremony. Consequently, even more than in the case of baptism administered by a lay person, we can say that, sociologically speaking, matrimony does not disrupt the sensation that everything important at the heart of everyday life is in the hands of the ordained. That is true in both the realm of *sanctification* and in that of the *magisterium*.

2. The eucharist might seem to be an exception. Indeed in the words that we now call the "consecration," there seem to be found not only the institution of a meaningful gesture but also the mention of the grace that God wants to signify and confer in that gesture (on this point, see J. L. Segundo, *Teología Abierta* [Madrid: Cristiandad, 1983, 2nd ed.], vol. 2, "Los Sacramentos Hoy," especially chapter 2, pp. 256–86). Here I would only like to make two observations. The first is that the allusions made in the words over the bread and the chalice to the grace the sacrament is to confer ("new alliance," "forgiveness of sins") have post-Easter characteristics, and hence they do not derive from Jesus himself when he instituted the gesture. The second point is a reminder that the *real presence* is not the "grace" that is to be conferred by the sacrament. In order to know what that grace might be, one would have to go beyond the words of the supper to Paul's eucharistic theology (see 1 Cor. 11:23–27; 10:16–17) or to that of John (Jn. 6:51–57).

3. Pius X, *Vehementer*, no. 8. The encyclical also says, "It follows that the Church is essentially an *unequal* society, that is, a society comprising two categories of persons, the Pastors and the flock." According to the encyclical such is the teaching of the "Scripture ... and the tradition of the Fathers" (emphasis mine)—*Vehementer*, in Claudia Carlen, IHM (ed.), *The Papal Encyclicals 1903–1939* (New York: McGrath, 1981).

4. For a more thorough understanding of the term "remembrance," "memory" or "memorial" and its connection to the "real presence" of Jesus in the eucharist, see X. Léon-Dufour, *La Fracción del Pan: Culto y Existencia en el Nuevo Testamento* (Madrid: Editorial Cristiandad, 1983—translation from French), especially chapter 6, pp. 138–55. On the last page of this section, the author writes: "The remembrance

is carried out specifically through the 'narration' of what Jesus said and did. The purpose of this narration is to put me in the presence of the event of the salvific cross. Soon, however, things broke down. The narration focused attention on the letter of what had been said and done by Jesus. Gradually attention moved away from the overall sense of the words and deeds and became restricted to the literal pronouncement of the words, leading readers and hearers to focus on problems of the 'transubstantiation' of the 'species' of bread and wine."

5. In this connection, I have already cited Schillebeeckx's significant book *Ministry* when dealing with the creation of the church hierarchy (pp. 29ff.). That is the source of the data which I am presenting here in too summary a fashion, although I will try to make them a little less radical.

6. A balanced analysis of this point can be found in John A. T. Robinson's work already cited (pp. 54–77). Attributing the rediscovery of the lay priesthood to the Reformation, Robinson shows how in practice and without any dogmatic basis, the Reformation followed a course quite parallel to that of the Catholic Church. Reinhold Niebuhr also observes, "The fact is that the Protestant doctrine of the priesthood of all believers may result in an individual self-deification against which Catholic doctrine has more adequate checks" (*Nature and Destiny of Man*, vol. 1, p. 202).

7. Jon Sobrino, "Hacia una determinación de la realidad sacerdotal. El servicio al acercamiento salvífico de Dios a los hombres," in *Revista Latinoamericana de Teología* (San Salvador), no. 1, January-April 1984, p. 55. What this article by Sobrino demonstrates can in a way be formulated even more generally (and abstractly) in this principle which the German episcopate stated in its preparation for the synod on lay people (1987): "The gifts and tasks which have been entrusted to all as a body, come before any diversity, as significant as it might be" (Pastoral Letter of German Bishops, "The Lay Person in the Church and in the World").

8. Gabriel Moran, *Theology of Revelation* (New York: Herder & Herder, 1966), p. 124.

9. Ibid., p. 125. I would not insist so much that this happens at Mass. There we find, as I see it, an eloquent example of what extends to the Christian's entire life.

10. Küng, *Infallible?*, p. 101.

11. Along with many others, Küng highlights this historic context which is necessary for understanding the church's defensive reaction. It was "a time when people in Europe, after the confusion and excesses of the great revolution and of Napoleonic times, had an irresistible longing for peace and order, for the good old times—in fact, for the Christian middle ages—and when nobody better than the Pope could offer the religious foundation for the maintenance of the political-religious status quo or the restoration of the status quo ante . . . And would papal infallibility have been defined in 1870 if the whole work of the Restoration had not been threatened in its foundations during the second half of that century by liberalism?" (*Infallibility*, pp. 89–90).

12. Harry McSorley in John J. Kirvan (ed.), *The Infallibility Debate* (New York: Paulist Press, 1971), p. 85. In fact what has happened with infallibility substantiates such alarm. On the two occasions when it has been used in *ex cathedra* definitions— both of them Marian, the definition of the Immaculate Conception and of Mary's Assumption into heaven—what was added to the body of dogmas of faith were statements without a sufficient biblical foundation (see above, chapter 10, note 25)

at a time when there was no need to defend the faith against any serious danger
and when there was even a risk of making dialogue with our separated brothers
and sisters much more difficult. Furthermore, the Roman curia as it was preparing
the documents to be discussed at Vatican II, saw infallibility not as something to
be used in an emergency, but as a normal route for avoiding theological controversy
on issues still unresolved; that is, on matters which could not be regarded as articles
stantis aut cadentis Ecclesiae (in other words, on which the very subsistence of
Christian revelation would depend).

13. McSorley, *Infallibility Debate*, pp. 85 and 101, n. 56.

14. It is not within the scope of this book to show that by limiting the range of
papal infallibility to only those things which directly touch upon the *revealed deposit*,
or which are required for guarding it faithfully, a (qualified) majority of the fathers
at Vatican II already understand the "revealed deposit" to be sacred scripture. As
we know, a number of theologians have correctly pointed out, as I have had occasion
to indicate, that the constitution on revelation did not wish to decide the question
of whether there were one or two sources of divine revelation by clearly condemning
the contrary teaching. Nevertheless, it can be argued, as has been done in this work,
that at least as far as that constitution goes, the Council clearly inclines toward
acknowledging a single source, sacred scripture, while at the same time it recognizes
how important is the interpretation of scripture through "tradition" in the church
community. I believe that to present the Council as neutral on this question amounts
to minimizing its "wealth of doctrine," in the expression of Paul VI. The fact that
no oral "tradition" independent of scripture was recognized is obviously very important for limiting the "deposit of faith" to what is essential.

15. *Schema Constitutionis de Ecclesia* (Vatican City, 1964, p. 97, quoted by
McSorley, p. 86). A little further on McSorley asks how a theologian can show
"what these dogmas [the Marian dogmas declared by papal definitions including
that of the Assumption which is expressly made *ex cathedra*] have to do with salvation and with the mission of the church" — that is, if I understand him rightly,
with the "foundation of Christian faith." I do not see it myself either, and I do not
think that in this case we are dealing with dogmas that enjoy the infallibility God
granted to the church. I want it to be clear that I am not saying this out of doubts
over the infallibility of the supreme pontiff or particular arguments against Mary's
Immaculate Conception or Assumption, but because I understand that the clear
words both of the rapporteur at Vatican I on this matter (Gasser) and of Vatican
II (just quoted) do not allow for a ready application of the label *ex cathedra* to
anything whatsoever that might be related to Christian faith. Those two councils
seem to leave these two points outside the realm in which the supreme pontiff
enjoys the infallibility that God grants the church: that of articles that are *stantis
aut cadentis Ecclesiae* (or *christianae fidei*). In other words, the label *ex cathedra* is
misunderstood or misapplied.

16. Nevertheless, the Roman curia understood John XXIII's convocation of
Vatican II as the occasion to turn into truths of faith large areas of theology where
there existed a degree of freedom for inquiry and opinion. On a number of issues
the Council fathers therefore had to begin by rejecting discussion drafts prepared
by the Roman curia, so as to then discuss points that their pastoral experience was
indicating were relevant for further development and inquiry. Unfortunately, the
Council did not eliminate that tendency. It is still present today, at least in part, in
Rome's mistrust of theological research, which is regarded as negative and scan-

dalous for the faithful who might lose the respect due to the magisterium when future dogmatic definitions are made.

17. A. Torres Queiruga, *La Revelación de Dios en la Realización del Hombre* (Madrid: Ed. Cristiandad, 1987), p. 378 (see more generally, pp. 124ff.). As has already been pointed out, Torres Queiruga uses the term *maieutic* in a sense that is very similar, if not indeed identical, to what I suggest with the terms *deuterolearning* or *learning to learn*. As is observable here, given its Socratic origins, "maieutic" means that the new information added is not foreign or extrinsic to what is lived, but rather springs from it as a deepening or an explicitation that is not yet perceived but is already experienced. The effort to seek not existential structures but what I call *transcendent data* corresponds to the adjective "historic" with which Torres Queiruga qualifies "maieutic." The fact that we have here a historic maieutic is what separates this writer from a Rahner, with his transcendental and ahistoric analysis. "With this theory Rahner pays the price for the enormity of his discovery: portraying revelation as universal and intrinsic obscures its radical historicity" (p. 222).

18. In the text I have opted to summarize this document. Due to its importance, however, I am including it here in this note:

With regard to this historical condition, it must first be observed that the meaning of the pronouncements of faith depend partly upon the expressive power of the language used at a certain point in time and in particular circumstances. Moreover, it sometimes happens that some dogmatic truth is first expressed incompletely (but not falsely), and at a later date, when considered in a broader context of faith or human knowledge, it receives a fuller and more perfect expression. In addition, when the Church makes new pronouncements she intends to confirm or clarify what is in some way contained in Sacred Scripture or in previous expressions of Tradition; but at the same time she usually has the intention of solving certain questions or removing certain errors. All these things have to be taken into account in order that these pronouncements may be properly interpreted. Finally, even though the truths which the Church intends to teach through her dogmatic formulas are distinct from the changeable conceptions of a given epoch and can be expressed without them, nevertheless it can sometimes happen that these truths may be enunciated by the Sacred Magisterium in terms that bear traces of such conceptions.

In view of the above, it must be stated that the dogmatic formulas of the Church's Magisterium were from the very beginning suitable for communicating revealed truth, and that as they are they remain forever suitable for communicating this truth to those who interpret them correctly. It does not however follow that every one of the formulas has always been or will always be so to the same extent. For this reason theologians seek to define exactly the intention of teaching proper to the various formulas and in carrying out this work they are of considerable assistance to the living Magisterium of the Church, to which they remain subordinated. For this reason also it often happens that ancient dogmatic formulas and others closely connected with them remain living and fruitful in the habitual usage of the Church, but with suitable expository and explanatory additions that maintain and clarify their original meaning. In addition, it has sometimes happened that in this habitual usage of the Church certain of these formulas gave way to new expressions which, proposed and approved by the Sacred Magisterium, presented more clearly or more completely the same meaning. (*Mysterium Ecclesiae* in Austin Flannery, ed., *Vatican II: More Postconciliar Documents* [Grand Rapids, Mich.: Eerdmans, 1982], vol. II, pp. 433–34)

19. *Histoire Générale*, vol. 4, chap. 2 (Section 1: "Europeans in the Americas. The New European Space"), p. 421. Some particularly significant facts indicate that this was a matter of transferring Europe to its new space. We need only point out, for example, that only a half-century after Columbus's encounter with American Indians in the Caribbean there were three universities along European lines in enclaves conquered in the new world: in Santo Domingo, Mexico City, and Lima. Only a century after Columbus, Spanish America had five archdiocesan sees and twenty-seven dioceses with all their concomitant structures.

20. See Mauro Matthei, O.S.B., "Aspectos de la cristianización de Hispanoamérica," *Teología y Vida* (Santiago, Chile, second quarter of 1965), pp. 140–48.

21. Although this book has no intention of aligning itself with what has been called a "black legend" of the conquest of the center and south of the hemisphere by Spain, certain facts significant for our aim here cannot be denied. On the negative side we cannot fail to mention the obvious destruction of the entire religion of the indigenous population (with all its related monuments, documents, rituals, feasts, and so forth), whatever the reasons for that destruction might have been. On the positive side, we have the existence of many elements regarded as liberating in the Christianity of the subjugated peoples. There is also the selfless defense of the Amerindian carried out by (a few but eminent) individuals, and subsequent efforts to release them from the greed of the conquerors. (In this connection, one may consult Enrique Dussel, *El Episcopado Latinoamericano y la Liberación de los Pobres* [Mexico City: CTR, 1979] or the concise and well-done summary of that work done by J. I. González Faus in chapter 4 of his book, *Este es el Hombre* [Madrid: Ed. Cristiandad, 1986], pp. 107–44.)

22. With the ecumenical thrust of Vatican II, and thanks to sociological and anthropological research, there began to appear numerous studies of the survival of pre-Columbian religions (and their accompanying cultural elements) *under Christian forms*. One such example, among many, is the book by J. E. Monast, *On les Croyait Chrétiens* (Paris: Ed. du Cerf, 1969). This work was the product of pastoral practice over many years by a priest who was very close to his Aymara parishioners in Bolivia, and it reveals the process of discovery suggested negatively by its title. If I have understood what the author told me in conversation, the title was not of his choosing, and in fact he very much disagreed with what it seemed to imply — namely, that they were not Christians. I wonder, nonetheless, whether this book, which is the testimony of an entire life, might not be more respectful to these people of Aymara culture, if it called their religion, or what is most authentic in it, by its own name, rather than by simply hitching it up to a Christianity, which at least in its origins was imposed on them. Nevertheless, the situation is confused or ambiguous, since with the passage of time these Amerindians have lost their awareness of the origins of the religious syncretism they practice in order to preserve their own cultural worldview. In Brazil there are now many studies of the religion today practiced by the descendants of black slaves transported from Africa, who brought their own religion.

23. This article, like the one I will cite next by A. Zenteno, appears in a double issue (n. 83–94) of the review on pastoral work, *Servir* (Mexico; third and fourth

issues, 1981). The passage that gives rise to this note is found on p. 288.

24. This and the few other statements I quote here are found in the most suggestive of the articles in that double issue of the review *Servir*, "Experiencias. La voz de los pobres—un comentario del pueblo al relato guadalupeno" (pp. 297–324) by Arnaldo Zenteno. Given the way the testimonies are spread throughout the article, which follows the order of the story, the various testimonies I quote, and which point in the same direction, might come from the same person.

25. Here also some nuance is required since in some testimonies, including the one already quoted which takes the Nicaraguan revolution as an example, the interpretation of the story indeed calls for action in history. Nevertheless in many of the testimonies one senses discouragement over how little power the poor have in history. For example, "Only the bishop and a few others along with Juan Diego see the image. The others do not. But the bishop just had to say, 'We are going to do it,' and they went ahead and did it. But not because they believed Juan Diego. If he had said, 'Poor people come here, we are going to do this,' they wouldn't believe him because he is poor; it's the same thing that happens to all of us." Here is another: "The situation is sad, but if it had not been for the bishop to whom Juan Diego came bringing flowers, and telling him to build a church, it would not be done. It's simply a fact that a poor person always has to deal with someone who commands more respect to be believed; otherwise, no one knows what would have happened. Because that's what happens when there is a problem, when they throw people in jail, or whatever it is. There always has to be someone who commands respect so they'll believe him or they'll get them out of a problem, even though they do not believe him."

12. Summary and Hopes

1. See J. L. Segundo, *Jesus of Nazareth Yesterday and Today*, vol. 3, chap. 8, pp. 126–44.

2. Congregation for the Doctrine of the Faith, "Instruction on Certain Aspects of the Theology of Liberation" (Vatican City, August 1984) part 2, no. 4.

3. Gregory Bateson, *Pasos hacia una ecología de la mente* (Buenos Aires: Carlos Lohlé, 1972), pp. 487ff.

4. It cannot be said that this first condition for a "revelation"—a communication between God and the human being—has been generally understood. Accepted, yes. But a current originating outside Christianity and biblical thought (and introduced into them with Neoplatonism) has, throughout the centuries, placed its deepest hopes of approaching God in a certain "emptying" of the mind—as if it were by way of a denial or suspension of the limits of the linguistic, conceptual, and historical signs that one could arrive at a deeper, surer understanding of these signs. The mystics themselves, perhaps under the influence of this philosophy, in transmitting their experiences conceptually, have spoken of experiences of God bearing almost no resemblance to those of the Bible: alienation from or contempt of the created.

5. Correct praxis is the final *truth*. Hence, for the Johannine theology, truth is not "had," but "done" (see John 3:21, 1 John 1:6). Truth is not something that can be "put down" in a book or a formula, or in the perfection of some knowledge. Truth is *done*—put into operation.

6. Readers wishing to see an example of this, propounded by the magisterium of the church itself, although the term "anthropological faith" does not occur, can

find the equivalent of that term in the explanation proposed by *Gaudium et Spes* of the process leading the person of good will to atheism. Others, on the contrary, despite their repetition of the words of "divine revelation," may practice (and lead others to practice) a "faith" that is actually idolatry, since the values with which they confuse the "Word of God" do not correspond to the true God: "Atheism results not rarely from . . . the absolute character with which certain human values are unduly invested, and which thereby already accords them the stature of God . . . Believers can have more than a little to do with the birth of atheism . . . To the extent that they . . . are deficient in their religious, moral, or social life, they must be said to conceal rather than reveal the authentic face of God" (*GS* 19).

7. "Behold, I stand at the gate and knock" (Rev. 3:20). Of course, this does not mean that God recognizes any obligation to "say" precisely what we are ready to hear. Along with confirming our most authentic expectations, the "Word of God" also "judges" us. As we shall presently see more clearly, there is a circularity in this hermeneutic process. Hence the "Word" invites us to "conversion," or to the "betterment" of something existing. But even in this case, in order to be understood in its human element, the Word of God must be addressed at least to a kind of search or aspiration that we may have relegated to a second level, to a hypothesis that would be valid if reality were better, to something that "could be," and that therefore we favor even though it would mean the overturning and upsetting pre- cisely of values (or antivalues) that we are applying.

8. *PL* 34:33. Cited by Henri de Lubac, *Catolicismo* (Barcelona: Estela, 1963), p. 52.

9. What von Rad wrote of the "wisdom" whose most specific quest characterizes especially the last period of the Old Testament, is true here of the *entire* biblical process and "tradition": "One might almost say that knowledge of the good is acquired only in the common life, person to person and from situation to situation; however, an absolute beginning is not made each time, because there is always the base of an ancient knowledge, of a very rich experience" (von Rad, *Israel et la Sagesse* [Geneva: Labor et Fides, 1970], p. 98). And he explains how this "base" of collective wisdom is laid: "No one would live a single day had he or she not suc- ceeded in being guided by a vast empirical cognition. This knowledge, drawn from experience, teaches one to understand what is occurring round about one, to foresee the reactions of one's neighbor, to employ one's strength at the opportune moment, to distinguish the exceptional from the ordinary event, and a great deal else. We are not particularly conscious of being guided in this way, as neither of having ourselves developed more than a small part of this experiential knowledge. This knowledge is imposed on us, we are steeped in it from our most tender age, and [we are aware of it] only if we ourselves somehow modify it . . . This experimental knowledge acquires its importance and character of obligation only when it comes to represent the common good of an entire people, or a great part of the popula- tion" (ibid., pp. 9–10).

10. This is what was called, and should continue to be called today, "tradition"— not the dubious and unverifiable notion that Jesus personally "revealed" to one or more of his apostles or disciples things that were not consigned to the New Tes- tament, and thus remained lost until they reappeared years or centuries later. This is how the existence of a font of revelation "other" than the biblical is understood. While Vatican II did not wish to settle the question of the single or double font, everything in *Dei Verbum*, as well as the best post–Vatican II theology, tends to

understand by "tradition" not a separate, "other," font, but the fact that the process of transmission consists not in a book or a formula, but in a knowledge transmitted in the experience (institutional, to be sure) of a living community, the church.

11. While this faith is in continuity with what we have called "anthropological faith," it has special characteristics that make it "religious." Indeed, it is the adherence of a community that possesses a "truth" about God and about what this God means for all humanity.

12. The rigorously dogmatic problem posed by the formation of the canon (list) of the books containing "revelation"—the Bible—is conspicuously absent from works otherwise as perspicacious and profound as Karl Rahner's *Foundations of Christian Faith* (New York: Seabury, 1978). See A. Torres Queiruga, *La revelación de Dios en la realización del hombre* (Madrid: Cristiandad, 1987).

13. Torres Queiruga, *Revelación de Dios*, p. 63. I do not want to make this author responsible for the conclusions and extensions that I add to the passage cited. I do permit myself, in the spirit of friendship, to *use* this passage from his work for my intent. However, I understand that this excerpt has not been penned hastily, but is presented by way of conclusion of a lengthy discourse. The author repeats this summary, in the same or similar terms, in other places in the same book (see ibid., pp. 122, 125–26).

14. What I say of Moses here is paradigmatic, as I have indicated. Did Jesus not find himself in a similar situation? It will be said that Jesus did have the Bible, and thus could base his claims on the "Word of God"—and that he never hesitated to use it. But would this be strictly the case? Hans Küng is correct (although he draws a conclusion different from ours): "Jesus' whole preaching and behavior are nothing but an interpretation of *God* . . . Anyone accepting Jesus with firm trust necessarily observed at the same time an unexpected, liberative transformation of what he had thus far understood by 'God' " (Hans Küng, *On Being a Christian*, New York: Doubleday, 1974). Thus, Jesus could not rely on the Bible alone, without indicating an attitude that would cause a different hermeneutics of that Bible. Hence his allusions to the signs of the times, and to this antecedent, hazardous criterion: "Why do you not judge *for yourselves* what is just?" (Luke 12:57)—and this in the presence of God and of the "Word" of God present in the Bible.

15. John L. McKenzie, "Synagogue," in *Dictionary of the Bible* (New York: Bruce-Macmillan, 1965), p. 855. I call the synagogue "doubly" lay in the sense that not only was it an institution where the people (*laos*) assembled to feel themselves to be and maintain themselves as a people, with their own identity (among those who surrounded, governed, and oppressed them), but it was directed by laity (nonordained persons, elders). And the ordained, priests or scribes, when they visited the synagogue, were not essentially distinguished from the others, although they were treated with special courtesy (see ibid.).

16. André Seumois, O.M.I., *Apostolat. Structure Théologique* (Rome: Pontifical University Dc Propaganda Fide, 1961), pp. 86–87. The emphasis is mine, and I thereby wish to draw the reader's attention to the three components of "evangelization" to which I will refer throughout this section.

17. I believe that a good deal of present controversy over whether catechesis should inform (and await the moment in which this information given to the child can be profitably used by the adult) or whether it ought to "imitate" Old Testament pedagogy and be based on experiencing basic Christian values, cannot be resolved satisfactorily. Christianity is a message (prepared) for adults. What is true of psy-

choanalysis is also the case here. A child does not yet have the capacity for an analysis based on the means the psychoanalyst employs successfully with older people. By the same token, it is extremely unlikely that some day there might appear a psychoanalytic "catechism" for the use of children.

18. See chap. 11, section 4.
19. A. Torres Queiruga, *La Revelación de Dios, p. 330.*
20. Moran, *Revelation,* p. 16.
21. Ibid., p. 14.

Index

Also by Juan Luis Segundo

JESUS OF NAZARETH YESTERDAY & TODAY

This acclaimed christology by the Latin American Jesuit extricates the figure of Jesus from layer upon layer of intricate theological and exegetical hypotheses.

Volume 5
AN EVOLUTIONARY APPROACH TO JESUS OF NAZARETH
"Will transform christological discussion today."—**Roger Haight**
160pp. ISBN 0-88344-588-3 Paperback

Volume 4
THE CHRIST OF THE IGNATIAN EXERCISES
"Arguably the most profound work in the short history of liberation theology."—*Theological Studies*
160pp. ISBN 0-88344-569-7 Paperback

Volume 3
THE HUMANIST CHRISTOLOGY OF PAUL
"A constructive, hermeneutical study of Paul and a theological, anthropological groundwork for liberation theology."
—**Roger Haight**
256pp. ISBN 0-88344-221-3 Paperback

Volume 2
THE HISTORICAL JESUS OF THE SYNOPTICS
"Persuasive."—*The Ecumenist*
240pp. ISBN 0-88344-220-5 Paperback

Volume 1
FAITH AND IDEOLOGIES
"A must for those exploring the frontiers of contemporary theology." — **Alfred T. Hennelley**

368pp. ISBN 0-88344-127-6 Paperback

THE LIBERATION OF THEOLOGY
The classic analysis of liberation theology's method, integrally linked to the context of contemporary Latin America.
"Should not be missing from any theological library."
—Library Journal

240pp. ISBN 0-88344-286-8 Paperback